North Carolina Roster of Soldiers

in

War of 1812

1812–1814

❧ ⊙ ☙

James L. Douthat

Heritage Books
2024

HERITAGE BOOKS

AN IMPRINT OF HERITAGE BOOKS, INC.

Books, CDs, and more—Worldwide

For our listing of thousands of titles see our website
at
www.HeritageBooks.com

A Facsimile Reprint
Published 2024 by
HERITAGE BOOKS, INC.
Publishing Division
5810 Ruatan Street
Berwyn Heights, MD 20740

Originally published 2020

International Standard Book Number
Paperbound: 978-0-7884-9256-3

INTRODUCTION:

The original listing of the soldiers was produced from the records of the State of North Carolina and was under the direction of the Adjutant General, as a result of a resolution approved by the General Assemby on January 21, 1851. They were gathered and printed in 1851 by the Ch. C. Raboteau, at the Times Office.

This Resolution states: *"RESOLUTIONS directing the Adjutant General to publish copies of the Muster Rolls of the Soldiers of the war of 1812.*

Resolved, That the Adjutant General be and is hereby directed to have published a hundred copies, duly certified, of the Muster Rolls of the Soldiers of the war of 1812, which are on file in his Department; and that one copy be sent to the Clerk of the county court in each county of this State.

Resolved futher, That when it shall be made appear to the Treasurer, that the requirements of the above Resolution have been compiled with, he shall pay to the Adjutant General, as a compensation for his services, out of any money not otherwise appropriated, the sum of one hundred dollars.

Read three times and ratified in General Assembly, this 26ᵗʰ day of January A. D. 1851.

J. C. Dobbin, S. H. C.

W. N. Edwards, S. S."

This collection lists between 14,000 and 15,000 names of individuals that participated in the War of 1812 from every county in the State, except Greene County. A number of the counties actually had multiple units from that county and these are given as well. Many of these units served with a large number of Virginia units as they saw action in the war together.

Remember that these were militia units and not regular military groups. The organizations were quite loose and the records were not as well kept. Regardless, they were considered military fighting units by the standards of the day.

One of the major things you will notice, especially if you consult the Index of every soldier listed, is that spelling was very loose. This was a time in our history when not everyone could read and write and often the clerk spelled the name as they saw fit and may or may not reflect how the soldier would have spelled his names. Take a name like Hixson for example. This can be Hixson, Hixon, Hickson, Hickerson, etc. Many names are even more far off that this one. There might be brothers in the same unit, but their surname may be spelled totally different. The publisher of the original added a disclaimer at the end of the book with these words: ***Note by the Publisher - The names of the Soldiers are spelled just as we find them on the Muster Roll, which will account for the seeming inaccuracies in the list, according to the present orthography of proper names.*** When Mountain Press re-set the type for this publication, we did the very same thing. We spelled the names just as they were in the original and therefore, left the reader to determine which way it should be spelled.

One note in particular, there was one name that was clarified at the time of the original. It was just this "- - -, James, Jr. son of John". Normally we would have thought of James, Jr. and the son of James, Sr. but no he is the son of John. This is extremely helpful and we thank the original clerk for this note.

This set of records has been full name indexed for the first time to eliminate the necessity of searching the entire volume for one or two names. We have searched a number of various copies of the list and many of them vary in efforts to correct their listing. We opted to maintain the original all the way and therefore, rely on the reader's knowledge and interest to interpret the names as they see fit.

Just because the county you are researching does not appear on the list that was alphabetized in the end of the document does not mean your soldier is not there. It only means that your particular county was not formed at the time of this listing but the area must be in one or more of the older counties. Remember this is a listing for the entire state and not just one or two counties. Even the soldiers from Greene County can be in one or more of the other county units. It just means that Greene did not raise a unit for service.

We suggest that you consult the index frequently and study the spellings of the various names to determine where your soldier was listed. The index saves a world of time searching the entire listing, but when you find the spelling you are searching but the given name is not there, don't give up. Go to the unit[s] where the name is given and look carefully as your soldier might be there but with a variation of the spelling.

Good luck with your search!!

James L. Douthat
Signal Mountain, TN
2020

NORTH CAROLINA
ROSTER OF SOLDIERS
IN
WAR OF 1812

DIVISION

First Brigade - Detached from the 1st, 13th, 2nd, 3rd, 12th, 5th, 4th and 14th Brigades of the
Organized Militia of the State   **Thomas Davis - Brigadier General Commanding.**

FIRST REGIMENT: detached from the 1st and 13th Brigade of ditto.
    Josiah Flowers, Lieutenant Colonel - Commandant
    Caleb Etheridge, First Major
    John M. Cotter, Second Major

FIRST COMPANY OF THE
FIRST REGIMENT,
DETACHED FROM THE
CURRITUCK
REGIMENT

1. John Ship, Captain
2. Cornelius Jones, 1st Lieut.
3. Amburrus Walston, 2nd Lieut.
4. Gideon Bonney, Ensign

Privates

5. Joshua White
5. Samuel Beasley
7, Dennis Capts
8. John Smith
9. Jacob Wichel
10. John White, Jr.
11. Malachi Dudley
12. Levan Dudley
13, Jacob Williams
14. William Beasley
15. Caleb Wilson

16. Augustus Linton
17. James Northam
18. Merrit Ballance
19. Thomas Etheridge
20. Nicholas Elydon
21. William Garrett
22. Ivy Halstead
23. Joseph Sawyer
24. Charles Sawyer
25. William Bray, Jr.
26. Thomas Mitchel
27. William Bunnell
28. Joseph Poyner
29. Jonathan Wright
30. Richard Decker
31. Jesse Parr
32. Thomas Archland
33. Merese Jarvis
34. Henry Spence
35. Arthur Spence
36. John Boswell
37. James Fentus
38. Bartlett Burton

39. Charles Fulford
40. Joseph Fulford
41. John Gregory
42. Andrew Heath
43. James Whiteral, Jr.
44. James Nicholson
45. William Snider
46. William Perkins
47. Henry Doxey
48. Mitchel Gregory
49. John Baker
50. John Mayo
51. William Halstead
52. James Banks
53. James Gregory
54. John Gray
55. Josiah Taylor
56. Thomas McMooney
57. Hollowell Sawyer
58. Joel Poyner
59. Frederick White
60. George Fisher
61. Benjamin Taylor

62. Shadrack Kallum
63. William Thompson

Page 4
****
Second Company, detached
from the Currituck Regiment

1. Hillary Bell, Captain
2. Joshua Baxter, Lieutenant

Private

5. Michael Orneal
6, James Parker
7. William Spry
8. Thomas Gregory
9. Jesse Robeson
10. William Devout
11. Jeremiah Gorden
12. Thomas Whitehall
13. Thomas Writentt [sic]
14. Elijah Hunnings
15. John Griffin
16. Thomas Mercer
17. Caleb Harress
18. James Sawyer
19. Cornelius McCoy
20. Jasper Gibson
21. Thomas B. Jarvis
22. Ishum Hunt
23. Thomas Allen
24. John Demdtund
25. Josiah Beals
26. Noah Hobbs
27. Uriah Simpson
28. Mark Harris
29. Jonathan Chapter
30. Trininger Sandler
31. William Greves
32. Nathan Shannon
33 Peter M. Gray
34. Thomas Curis
35. Joseph Sanderson
36. Matthias Davis
37. Isaac Dowdy
38. William Leimpoon

39. Thomas Parker
40. Thomas Daniel
41. David Daniel
42. Baley Daniel
43. Avra Daniel
44. John Daniel
45. John Shannon
46. John Credworth
47. Joseph Baglen
48. John Barnett
49. Daniel Stow
50. Valentine Waite
51. Joseph Quidley
52. Thomas Scarborough
53. Wallis Stirran
54. Zachariah Burrus
55. William Gray
56. Benjamin Stow
57. John Quidley
58. Moses Auston
59. Cornelius Auston
60. Bartlett Quidley

****

Third Company,
detached from the
Camden Regiment

1. James S. Garling, Captain
2. Baley Barco, 1st Lieut.
3. Willis Wilson, 2nd Lieut.
4. Wilson Webster, Ensign
5. James Forbes, 1st Serg.
6. John W. Harrison, 2nd Serg.
7. James Godfrey, 3rd Serg.
8. Edward Pugh, 4th Serg.
9. William Godfrey, 1st Corp.
10. Simon Jones, 2nd Corp.
11. Jeremiah Jones, 3rd Corp.
12. Isaac Berry, 4th Corp.

Privates

13, Robert Boushel
14. John Gallup
15. Edward Curlin

16. Phillip Morissett
17. Timothy Berry
18. Nathan Gregory
19. Frederick Gregory
20. Etheridge Standley
21. William Berry
22. Joseph McCoy
23. Jesse Dowdy
24. Reding Mercer
25. Dempsey Wilson
26. John Shorter
27. James Willis
28. Caleb Jarvis
29. Elias McKoy
30. Henry Gregory
31. William Dowdy
32. Peter Seymore
33. Abner Sanderlin
34. Jonathan Gregory
35. Caleb Woodard
36. Wilson Sikes
37. Samuel Gregory
38. John Lewis
39. Isaac Avery
40. Jabez Garlington
41. Edmond Gregory, Sr.
42. Miles Berry
43. Shipperd Foster
44. Tully Morrissett
45. John Mitchell
46. David Dunken
47. James Garret
48. Jacob James
49. Abner Sikes

Page 5

50. Abner Cooper
51. Lemuel Gregory
52. James Huit
53. Cornelius Bryon
54. Nathaniel Hughes
55. Owen W. Harrison
56. Edmund Gregory, Jr.
57. Thomas Portlock
58. Joshua Gallup
59. Henry W. Harrison

60. Wilson W. Nash
61. Josiah Nash
62. Archibald Sawyer
63. Markum Stafford
64. Joshua Smisson
65. Joseph Bray
66. Thomas Gregory
67. William Procter
68. Wilson Duncan
69. Dempsey J. Burgess
70. Moses Brock
71. Bradley Smith
72. Zebulin Dunkin
73. Benjamin Carter

****

Fourth Company,
detached from the
Pasquotank Regiment

1. William Spence, Captain
2. Richard Muse, Lieutenant
3. Joseph Sutton, Ensign

Privates

4. John Graves
5. Jesse Bray
6. Edward Greves
7. Thaddeus Snowden
8. Peter William
9. David Griffin
10. John Low
11. Holowell Vardell
12. Thomas Denby
13. John Keel
14. Benjamin Lowry
15. Samuel Overman
16. Urias Turner
17. Samuel Spelman
18. Thomas Woodley
19. Joshua Benton
20. Charles Hunt
21. Jesse Jordan
22. William Hite
23. Elijah Munden

24. Isaac Gallop
25. Caleb Bundy
26. Nathan Bundy
27. Jonathan Garrett
28. William Turner
29. Nixon Low
30. Jesse Bundy
31. William Munden
32. Noah Perry
33. Benjamin Brothers
34. Josiah Mackey
35. Henry Cox
36. Enoch Pritchard
37. Joseph Harrell
38. Miles Turner
39. Arthur Gorden
40. Henry Raper
41. Daniel White
42. Samuel Cambell
43. Richard Clark
44. Christopher Cartwright
45. Samuel Dozier
46. Stephen Scott
47. Adam Deal
48. Jordan Gray
49. Thomas Humphis
50. Samuel Jones
51. Enoch Sawyer
52. Britton Temple
53. Isaac Williams
54. William Cartwright
55. Benjamin Gilbert
56. Lot Fentress
57. Richard Clayton
58. John F. Markum
59. John Lowry
60. William Nichilson
61. Cornelius Scott
62. Lemuel Barrington
63. Frederick Davis
64. Michel Phillips
65. Alexander Whitehouse
66. Thomas Cartwright
67. Joshua Cartwright
68. John Harris
69. James Davis
70. William Carter

71. James Jackson
72. Joshua Jackson
73. Robert Spence
74. David Nichols
75. Edward Scott
76. Julian D. Belinger
77. James Leonard
78. John Casa
79. Thomas Allen
80. Jacob Simpson
81. John Cartwright
82. Stephen Chaney
83. George White
84. Davis Spelman

****

Page 6

Fifth Company,
detached from
Perquimans Regiment

1. Thomas Myers, Captain
2. Matthew Jordan, Lieutenant
3. Willis Roberts, Ensign

Privates

4. Charles Clay
5. Exum Nuby
6. Reuben Overman
7. Lemuel Tucker
8. Benjamin Maudlin
9. Abel Rogerson
10. Elisha Harreld
11. Elisha Farles
12. Henry Garrett
13. William Standen
14. Joseph Bagley
15. Phillip Mason
16. William Tweddy
17. William Colleson
18. Harrison Turner
19. James Turner, Jr.
20. James Turner, Sr.
21. George P. Whidbee

22. Stephen Twiddy
23. Jonathan Bogus
24. Tully Williams
25. Myles Turner
26. Thomas Allen
27. William Hatfield
28. Joseph Arrenton
29. Joshua McCoy
30. Thomas Jones
31. Thomas Arrenton
32. Jonathan Smith
33. Joseph Jackson
34. Reuben Hobbs
35. Lemuel Bateman
36. John Jackson
37. Francis Wills
38. Hardy Bateman
39. Thomas Woodley
40. Obadiah Reddick
41. Reddick Hallswell
42. Lemuel Lain
43. Tully Moss
44. Joseph Pike
45. Samuel Maudlin
46. Isaac Twiddy
47. Thomas Allen
48. Sassel [sic] McCoy
49. Benjamin Bateman
50. Griffin Brinkly
51. Joshua Talton
52. Elisha Elliott
53. John Moss
54. Asa Lymons
55. Nathan Bagley
56. Moses Webb
57. Delight Nixon
58. William Burnham
59. Abraham Green
60. Aaron Green
61. Thomas Hudson
62. Tully Laden
63. Jesse Ward
64. Samuel Barelipt
65. James Stanton
66. Saphem [sic] Elliott
67. Benjamin Shinner
68. Samuel Weeks

69. Thomas Hendricks
70. William Baker
71. Isaac Wilson
72. Henry Hobbs
73. John Sylvester
74. Benjamin Munden
75. Edward Saunders
76. Joseph Arrenton
77. Edward Arrenton
78. Nathan Nichilson
79. Exum Newby
80. John Hardle.

****

Sixth Company,
detached from
Chowan Regiment

1. John Meguire, Captain
2. Thomas Tapping, Lieutenant
3. Welch Fullerton, Ensign
4. Thomas Tarlton, 1st Serg.
5. Abram Holloway, 2nd Serg.
6. Luke Holloway, 3rd Serg.
7. Green Meredith, 4th Serg.
8. Job Perkins, 1st Corp.
9. Julius Bunch, 2nd Corp.
10. Neil Sherwood, 3rd Corp.
11. Joseph Pain, 4th Corp.

Privates

12. David Welch
13. James Ward
14. Dachim Mansfield
15. Charles Miller
16. Reddick Wood
17. Elisha Hurdle
18. Archibald Leath
19. William Flury
20. Samuel Fitt
21. Thomas Webb
22. Abraham Pettiger
23. Charles Stewart
24. John Bond
25. Salter Bunch

26. John Standing
27. Nimrod West
28. Caleb Garnet

Page 7

29. Peter Markell
30. John McGlaughlin
31. Henry Morris
32. John Bysam
33. James Braughton
34. James Crery
36. William Wingate
36. Josiah Bogue
37. Felston Cotten
38. Nathaniel Bunch
39. James Robertson
40. Hana Jorden
41. Miles Halsey
42. Noah Smith
43. Demsey Tretman
44. Miles Elliot
45. John Ward
46. John Watson
47. William Walton
48. Micajah Ward
49. Daniel Harris
50. Jacob Perry
51. Abner Goodwin
52. George Webb
53. Levi Persons
54. James Swan
55. Elisha Parker
56. John Middleton
57. Daniel Liverman

****

Seventh Company,
detached from
Gates Regiment

1. Thomas Freeman, Captain
2. Robert Reddick, Lieutenant
3. Simon Stallings, Ensign
4. Edwin Ballard, 1st Serg.
5. Lemuel Goodman, 2nd Serg.

6. Lemuel Reddick, 3rd Serg.
7. Richard H. Lee, 4th Serg.
8. Henry Brnkley, 1st Corp.
9. Abbey Benton, 2nd Corp.
10. David Benton, 3rd Corp.
11. John Hare, 4th Corp.

Privates

12. William Lunding
13. Jacob Benton
14. John Blanchard
16. Ransom Phillips
16. Aaron Harrell
17. Abner Green
18. Elisha Robertson
19. Isaac Hiott
20. Kader Bereman
21. Dempsey Blanchard
22. William Green
23. Henry King
24. Timothy Robertson
25. William Spright
26. Moses Spivey
27. John Alphin
28. Luke Parker
29. Willis Figg
30. Kader Hurdle
31. Joseph Phillips
32. Moses Davis
33. John Saunders
34. James Jordan
35. John Spright
36. William Matthews
37. Elisha Matthias
38. Kader Reddick
39. Luke Freling
40. Harman Hays
41. Abram Parker
42. William Sumner
43. Benjamin Morgain [sic]
44. James Spright
45. Jethro Briggs
46. Thomas Brown
47. Jesse Carter
48. William Haffler
49. Arthur Boyett

50. Frederick Alphin
51. Jacob P. Jones
52. John Fanney
53. Elisha Peel
51. William Benton
55. Jesse Down
56. John Outlaw
57. Richard P. Curl
58. Miles Parker
59. Barnard Marsh
60. John Felton
61. Stephen Eure
62. Kinchin Phillips
63. Benjamin Cross
64. Cypron Eure
65. Vinson H. Jones
66. Robert Parker
67. Josiah Ellils
68. Reddick Peel
69. Jethro Benton
70. Henry H. Benton
71. John Arnold
72. Frederick Simpson

****

Eighth Company,
detached from the
Hertford Regiment

1. Irwin Jenkins, Captain
2. Everard Garrett, Lieutenant
3. Benjamin Hill, Ensign
4. Andrew Oliver, Cadet
5. James Spires, Cadet
6. William Walton, 1st Serg.

Page 8

7. Hardy Banks, 2nd Serg.
8, Josiah Battle, 3rd Serg.
9. John Scott, 4th Serg.
10. Arthar [sic] Booth, 1st Corp.
11. Elisha Horton, 2nd Corp.
12. Charles Jenkins, 3rd Corp.
13. James Witherington, 4th Corp
14. John Manning, Drummer

15. Wiley Brown, Fifer

Privates

16. James Early
17. Lemuel Holloman
18. James Hayes
19. Thoms Britton
20. Luke McGlaulum
21. Nathan Baker
22. Cornelius H. Goodwin
23. Anthony Brown
24. Anthony Williams
25. Noah Evans
26. Jacob Sewell
27. Jethro Sewell
29. Jacob Hare
29. John Baker
30. John Scull
31. Thomas Holland
32. Henry D. Jenkins
33. John Curl
34. John Denton
36. William Ballester
36. Thomas Clark
37. Josiah I. Askins
38. Lewis Carter
39. Jonas Atkins
40. Henry Brantly
41. William Williams
42. Henry Wiggins
43. Miles Hobbs
44. John Everitt
45. Alexander Booth
46. Levi Crecy
47. Thomas Thorne
48. Zachariah Brown
49. Edward Crump
60. Anthony B. Lee
51. John Benthall
52. Robert Brantley
53. Thomas Neale
54. Alexander Smith
55. William Brown
56. Isaac Pearce
57. George Asken
58. Edward Brantley

59. Henry Eure
60. Joseph G. Rea
61. William Wynns
62. Thomas Weston
63. Allen L. Ramsey
64. Elisha Minis
65. James Parker
66. Benjamin Ezell
67. Britton Sikes
68. William Andrews
69. Isaac Foster
70. John C. Montgomery
71. Reuben Clark
72. Lewis Boon
73. Josiah Robbins
74. Elijah Archer
75. Ephraim King
76. Samuel Boon
77. Mathuel [sic] Archer
78. James Raleigh
79. John Weaver
80. James B. Jones
81. Hardy Davis
82. Mills Walters
83. Abraham Boon
84. West Boon
85. John Bizzett
****

Ninth Company,
detached from
Washington Regiment

1. Henry Garret, Captain
2. Andrew Armstrong, Lieut.
3. John Rogers, Ensign

Privates

4. Zachariah Sutton
5. Joseph Snyder
6. Benjamin Cullipher
7. Eliakim Norman
8. Isaac Cullipher
9. Davis Biggs
10. Zebedee Tarkinton
11. Jehu Ambrose

12. Enos Tarkinton
13. Reuben Clifton
14. Levi Ambrose
15. Roger Snell
16. Nathan I. Swain
17. Edward Nar
18. Isaac Rawson
19. Samuel Jones
20. Isaac Skittlethrop
21. Edmund Skittlethrop
22. Joseph Spruill
23. William Forlan
24. Enoch Steely
25. John Simpson
26. John Airs
27. Jesse Collins
28. William Woodley
29. Miles Hopkins
30 Andrew Spruill
31. Arthur Skittlethrop
32. Isham Pearce

Page 9

33. Bethue Murray
34. William Allen
35. Ezekiel Blount
36. Thomas Smith
37. Hiram Snell
38. Frederick B. Jennings
39. Charles Morse
40. Edward Parish
41. Simeon Swain
42. James F. James
43. Joseph Sax
44. Starkey Tarkinton
45. Thomas Gilbert
46. Enoch Bundy

****

Tenth Company,
detached from the
Tyrrell Regiment

1. William Alexander, Captain
2. Richard Howell, Lieutenant

3. James Haysell, Ensign

Privates

4. Benjamin Brickhouse
5. James Davenport
6. Uriah Spruill
7. Emri Spruill
8. Uzzell Brickhouse
9. Benjamin Clayton
10. James McAlsten
11. William Brickhouse
12. Harman Alexander
13. Ricardo Rudd
14. William Steatman
15. Elisha Stirum
16. Solomon Creed
17. John West
18. William Swain
19. Isaac West
20. Benjamin Hassell
21. Spencer Midgitt
22. Isaac Liverman
23. James Sivels
24. Harry Charles
25. Stephen Powell
26. Joshua Swain
27. Ozias Roughton
28. Zadoch Hassell
29. James Whitbee
30. Maxy Davis
31. Shelby Patrick
32. Asa Barratt
33. William White
34. Thomas Sawyer
35. Peleg Simmons
36. Selby Armstrong
37. Bartlett Jones
38. Ebenezer Cohoon
39. William Russ
40 John Banks
41. Azariah Hutson
32. Thomas Clayton
43. William Ward
44. Mitchel Paine
45. Joseph Mason
46. Joseph Man

47. Hiram Hooker
48. John Mydgett
49. Robert Holmes
50. Michael Hadok
51. Hezekiah Mariner
52. John Wynn
53. Jeremiah Phillip
54. Noah Dowers
55. Enoch Davenport
56. Charles Philllips
57. Silby Powers

****

SECOND REGIMENT

Detached from the
2nd, 12th and 3rd
Brigades

Simon Bruton, Lieut. Colonel,
Commandant
Nathan Tisdale, 1st Major
John A. Lillington, 2nd Major

****

First Company,
detached from
Hyde Regiment

1. Beverly Rew, Captain
2. Joshua Bell, Lieutenant
3. James Cheves, Ensign

Privates

4. Moses Windley
5. Jasper Smith
6. Enoch Flinn, Jr.
7. Joshua Freeman
8. John Peartree
9. Christopher Matison
10. Maurice Jones
11. Benjamin Slade
12. James Daniels
13. Winfield Davis
14. Oden Wilkinson

15. Joshua Muse
16. John Winfield

Page 10

17. Benjamin Smith
18. Selden Henderson
19. William Banks
20. John Fortiscue
21. John Russell Fortiscue
22. Jeremiah Warner
23. Burrige Selby
24. Thomas Winfield
25. Jacob Caffee
26. Hugh Foddree
27. Ricyhard Migett
28. James Owens
29. Jordan Carrow
30. Thomas Simons
31. Edward Fuller
32. Levi O'Neale
33. William Berry
34. Thomas Daniels
36. Clement Daniels
36. William Bunn
37. Shadrick Daniels
38. Benjamin Bunn
39. Zephaniah Sawyer
40. William Cohoon
41. Jeremiah Hall
42. Joy Sanderson
43. Robert Hopkins
44. Robert Jennett
45. Selby Spencer
46. Solomon Thornton
47. William Casons

****

Second Company,
detached from
Beaufort Regiment

1. Frederick Brooks, Captain
2. Richard Barner, Lieutenant
3. John Vines, Ensign

Privates

4. Will Grist
5. John Bonner
6. Richard Bonner
7. John Langley
8. Thomas Heures
9. George C. Barbage
10. William Loveland
11. David C. Clark
12. Samuel Campbell
13. George Congleton
14. James Howard
16. Jonathan Wallace
16. Jonathan Waters
17. Fredrick Waters
18. Charles Waters
19. Eleazer Jackson
20. William Archibald
21. Absalom Price
22. James M. Mahow
23. James Boyd
24. James Eborn
25. Alfred Lanier
26. James Cowper
27. Abram Cox
28. Moses Evett
29. Jonathan Giddins
30. Thomas Morris
31. Jesse Evett
32. John Jones, Sr.
33. Samuel Vines
34. Gibbin Dickson
35. Thomas Vines
36. William M. Moreland
37. Meshart McReel
38. John Barrow
39. Arnett Latham
40. Henry Woodard
41. William Albird
42. Talbing Equals
43. John Barnett
44. Humphrey Cherry
45. Benjamin Cherry
46. James Brown
47. Zachariah Ferrell
48. Alfred Latham

49. Gideon Fannet
50. James Wood
51. William Rawts
52. Ephraim Dickson
53. Jesse Robeson
54. Samuel Philpot
55. Rowland Mayo
56. John Grist
57. Henry Harding
58. Cannon Smith
59 Bryan Archlin

****

**Third Company
detached from
Pitt Regiment**

1. Reading Shipp, Captain
2. Henry Smith, Lieutenant
3. John Smith, Ensign

Privates

4. William Browning
5. Eliphlet King
6. Sampson Wanley
7. David Smith
8. Elisha Holloman
9. Robert Thomas
10 Kinyan Downs
11. William H. Griffin
12. Henry Wright
13. Jepthah May
14. John Pumphrey

Page 11

15. Newman Dunn
16. Allen Chance
17. Edward Arnold
18. Major Boid
19. William Mumford
20. Joshua Robertson
21. Lewis Burney
22. Jesse Boyd
23. Joseph Sanders

24. Edward Browning
25. James Spivey
26. Absalam Cox
27. Abram Smith
28. Frederick Litchworth
29. Samuel Smith
30. John Cannon
31. William Mooring
32. John Hardee
33. Dennis Cannon
34. Freeman McDowell
35. William Chance
36. Henry Cannon
37. Grove Corbett
38. Frederick Mills
39. Allen Smith
40. Asa Starks
41. Samuel Corbett
42. Samuel Knight
43. Cannon Chance
44. Samuel Venters
45. Zachariah Cox
46. Kennedy Smith
47. Willie Smith
48. Palmer Cannon
49. Redding Peters
50. Obed Roundtree
51. Benjamin Bently
52. Isaac Robertson
53. Levi Stocks
54. John Roy
53. Nehemiah Dixon
56. Samuel Merrell
57. Stephen Right
58. Cannon Stocks
59. John Mattocks
60. Fred Mills, Jr.
61. John Vanpelt
62. Cullen Tripp
63. Warren Andrews
64. Witham Casson
65. Simon Barney
66. William Parkes
67. George Bland
68. Edward T. Salter
69. Richard F. Macklewain

****

**Fourth Company,
detached from
Craven Regiment**

1. Horatio Dade, Captain
2. David Murdock, Lieut.
3. Abner Neale, 2nd Lieut.
4. Daniel McBean, Ensign
5. William H. Ives
6. Thomas Leath, Corp.
7. James Delamar
8. William Caraway
9. Jeremiah Bateman
10. James Carney, Sr.
11. Vine Allen
12. George Washington
13. John Gettig
14. Thomas Skidmore
15. James Lewis, 1st Serg.
16. Jonathan Perkins
17. Darius Amyett
18. Ephraim Simpkins
19. Hardy L. Jones
20. Silas Miller
21. Jesse Vendrich
22. James Tingle
23. Major Tingle
24. Iredell Burnett
25. John Rice
26. Thomas Green
27. William Butler
28. Reuben Clark
29. Jeremiah Washington
30. Nathan Slade
31. John Dowdy
32. Smith Jones
33. William Shines, Corp.
34. Cornelius Bateman
35. Seldon Delamar
36. Jesse Broadway
37. Barney Wadsworth
38. William J. Loftin
39. Henry Carrow
40. Equilla Pollard
41. Hardy Willis

42. Radford Ernell
43. Allen Ernell
44. Alexander Prichard
45. Alderson Thomas
46. Lewis McKoy
47. Zadock Woods
48. James White
49. Daniel Humphrey
50. Lewis Humphrey
51. Fred Jones
53. Samuel Smith
53. Asa Purify
54. John Everington
55. John Forns
56. Charles Nelson

Page 12

57. Joseph Polyard
58. William Taylor, 2nd Serg.
59. William Ward
60. John Parks
61. John Parker
62. Joseph Fulshire
63. Paul Berbank
64. Jesse Barrington
65. Jedediah Dixon
66. James Sewell
67. Thomas Purify
68. William Stableford
69. Frederick Powers
70. Joseph Wiggins
71. Reuben Hubbs
72. Abner Cooper
73. Southey Weatherington
74. William Williams
75. James Atherly
76. Matthew Williams,
      Drummer
77. David Lewis
78. Moses Nichols, 3rd Serg.
79. David Russell
80. Tolson Ryal
81. Robert Carney, 4th Serg.
82. Abner Whitehead
83. John T. Baily
84. James Lovick

85. Sylvester Brown
86. William Edgar, Corporal

****

Fifth Company,
detached from
Lenoir Regiment

1. Francis Kilpatrick, Captain
2. Nathan Bird, 1st Lieut.
3. Benjamin Britton - 2nd Lieut.
4. Gabriel Parker, 1st Serg.
5. James Uzzell, 2nd Serg.
6. John Wooten, 3rd Serg.
7. Francis Bright, 4th Serg.
8. James Walford - 1st Corp.
9. William *Mullen, 2nd Corp.
        * Miller in one return
10. Spencer Phillips, 3rd Corp.
11. Robert Murray, 4th Corp.
12. Joshua Bird, drummer
13. Isaac Walters, fifer

Privates

14. Henry Parker
15. Peter Phillips
16. William Kittral
17. John Wiggins
18. Curtis Phillips
19. John Byrd
20. James Davis
21. James B. Miller
22. William Mosely
23. William Wayne
24. Samuel Abbot
25. Richard Jones
26. Zachariah Pate
27. Thomas Brown
28. Lewis Falkner
29. Francis Benton
30. John Goodman
31. John Whitfield
32. Henry Pickle
33. James Davis
34. Richard Pickle

35. Cornelius Harper
36. Alexander Thompson
37. William Carter
38. Ashael Herring
39. William Gray
40. Jacob Jackson
41. John Andrews
42. John Gray
43. William Miller
44. William Herring
45. Edwin Taylor
46. Francis Brown
47. William Gray
48. John Ritter
49. Francis Benton
50. Martin Hill
51. Richard Hill
52. Robert Mitchell
53. Nathaniel Walters
54. Joshua Mosely
55. George P. Lorrik
56. Kinnon Taylor
57. Selathiel Potts
58. John B. Hartsfield
59. Blount Coleman
60. Benjamin Hearing
61. Robert Wigggins
62. Nathaniel Hearing
63. Vinsten Andrews
64. Walter Allen
65. Rayman Surls
66. Joseph Henson
67. William Campbell
68. Shadrick Campbell

****

Sixth Company,
detached from
Wayne Regiment

1. David *Watson, Captain
   *Wasdon in one return
2. Needham Whitfield, 1st Lieut.
3. William Killegrew, 2nd Lieut.
4. Hatch Whitfield, Ensign
5. John Ammonds, Cadet

Page 13

6. Alexander Hines
7. Burwell Rowse
8. John Howell
9. David Jennigan
10. Bryan Barfield
11. Raphael Bird
12. Frinifold Manly
13. Amer McCullen
14. Henry Phillips
15. William Adam
16. David McDaniel
17. Need Pipkin
18. Joseph Pipkin
19. Morris Wyse
20. Thomas Fowler
21. Thomas Coor, Jr.
22. William Rose, Jr.
23. George Collins
24. Elias Harrell
25. Enos Teler
26. Charles Bendon
27. John Motton
28. Law Jackson
29. Joel Harrell
30. Needham Grantum
31. Daniel Bennett
32. John Musgrove
33. William Pipkin
34. William Bass
35. Aaron Lean
36. James Strilling
37. John Brogdon
38. Jesse Floid
39. Josiah Brown
40. John Casey
41. Samuel Flowers
42. Stephen Reeves
43. William Jones
44. Jesse Bass
45. Richard Falkim
46. Wiben Lewis
47. Ully Lewis
48. John Giddins
49. William Measles

50. Jehabud Herring
51. Abner Wiggs
52. Barna Cotten
53. James Johnston
54. William Wilson
53. Robert Jones
56. Levi Skipper
57. William Johnston
58. Edward Holmes
59. John Thompson
60. Phillip Hooks
61. Job Rooks
62. Mathew Daniel
63. George Mitchel
64. Thomas Pindar
65. Enos Holland
66. Joseph Fulghum
67. Joseph Taylor
68. Peter Rice
69. David Thompson
70. Jesse Harper
71. John Harrel
72. John Dean
73. William Hooks
74. Jacob Newson
75. Joseph Newson
76. John Britt
77. Wright Smith
78. Woodard Howell
79. Jason Macban
80. Dawson Smith
81. Curtis Daniel
82. John Sasser
83. Giles Ham
84. Oliver Donell

****

Seventh Company,
detached from
Green Regiment

1. Hymerisk Hooker, Captain
2. Thomas Hooker, Lieut.
3. William Hooper, 1st Serg.
4. John Harper, 2nd Serg.
5. William Doughty, 3rd Serg.

6. John H. Albritton, 4th Serg.
7. Joseph J. House, 1st Corp.
8. Lemuel Speight, 2nd Corp.
9. Patrick Dickson, 3rd Corp.
10. Absalom Tyler, 4th Corp.
11. Readin Jones
12. Joseph Harrell
13. Wiley Dale
14. Caleb Spivy
15. John Jackson
16. Calvin Mage
17. Right Canady
18. Riinehen Hollowday
19. Simeon Albritton
20. James Armond
21. Person Tutton
22. Benjamin Scarbrough
23. John Minshew
24. Peter Eppes
25. Jesse Pope
26. Thomas Edwards
27. Stephen Cooke
28. James Hooker
29. Bryant Kilpatrick
30. Michel Coward
31. John Brand
32. Alfred Hart

Page 14

33. James Butts
34. John Craft
35. George Belcher
36. Henry Barfield
37. Samuel Hay
38. Kinchen P. Epes
39. Jesse Coward
40. Stephen Johnston
41. John Buford
42. Alexander Williams
43. Stephen Chester
44. Abner Cox
45. Elijah Newson
46. John Mayton
47. Robert Hinson
48. Robert Hall
49. Winston Garland

50. Chewry Rogers
51. Hardy Dain
52. Kinchen Faircloth
53. Gideon Britt
54. Samuel Whitby
55. James Elmore
56. Gabriel Sherod
57. Giles Smith
58. Elijah Smith
59. William Hamm
60. Haywood Hamm
61. Noah Peacock
62. John Peacock
63. James Aycock
64. Silus Lamb
65. Jesse Peacock
66. Elisha Davis
67. Cullen Haywell
68. John Peacock
69. Nathan Turrell
70. Edwin Holswell
71. Hezekiah Smith
72. Joseph Hollowell
73. William Loveing
74. Harrison Love
75. Daniel Ellis
76. William King
77. James Woodard
78. Peter Wooten

****

Eighth Company,
detached from
Johnston Regiment

1. Thomas Folsome, Captain
2. Jarrat M. Jelks, 1st Lieut.
3. Henry Guy, 2nd Lieut.
4. John C. Guy, Ensign
5. Allen S. Ballenger, 1st Serg.
6. Willis Hinton, 2nd Serg.
7. Nicholas Lynch, 3rd Serg.
8. Newit Bridges, 4th Serg.
9. Mabry Richison, 1st Corp.
10. Jesse Wellons, 2nd Corp.
11. Stephen Hicks, 3rd Corp.

12. Reddick Hews, 4th Corp.
13. Thaddeus Duck, drummer
14. James Jordan, fifer
15. Braswell Bridges
16. Jacob Avera
17. Needham Lambert
18. Samuel Frost
19. Stephen Brown
20. Stephen Makins
21. Josiah Hinnant
22. Lewis Godwin
23. Amos Batten
24. Hardy Batten
25. William Batten
26. Micahah Wilkinson
27. Elam Smith
28. Jacob Walker
29. Etheldred Bagly
30. Reuben Pope
31. John Allen
32. Kedar Farmer
33. Joshua Damel
34. Joseph Farmer
35. Benjamin Sellers
36. Jones Davis
37. Benjamin Johnston
38. Bryan Adams, Jr.
39. Hardy Adams
40. Ridly Porter
41. Absalom Woodall
42. Reeves Joy
43. Myrick Joy
44. John Barber
45. Brittain Barber
46. Bright Bird
47. Jeremiah Blackman
48. Mathew Hinton
49. John Filgo
50. David Filgo
51. Nathaniel Johnston
52. John Killingworth, Jr.
53. Richard Rollins
54. Thomas Simpkins
55. Edward Lee, Sr.
56. John Brnat
57. Bold Robin Hood
58. Samuel Engram

59. Nathan Bryan
60. Noah Barefoot, Jr.
61. Benjamin Simpkins
62. Burnel Cole
63. Francis Harrell
64. John Kean
65. John Sellers
66. Henry Lee

Page 15

67. Fredrick Biggoner
68. Oliver Raines, Jr.
69. William Holt
70. Hervey Raines, Sr.
71. Amos Peden
72. John Peden
73. Willis Woodard
74. Benjamin Bridges
75. Thomas Hollowell
76. Malichi Humphrey
77. Reuben Perry
78. John Lee
79. Nathan Stancel
80. David Bailey
81. Jonathan Fuller
82. Frederick Oneal
83. John Pender
84. Martin Hall
85. Drury Baley
86. Bud Price
87. William Green
88. Jacob Adams
89. Micajah Woodard
90. William Richardson
91. Thomas Gerald
92. Thomas Taylor
93. Jonathan Hinnant
94. Hardy Hinnant
95. Loverd Pearce
96. Bannister Grissel
97. Tobias Goodwin
98. Levi Richardson
99. William Pender
100. John Richardson
101. Lewis Hayly
102. Reddin Green

103. Nathan Stansill
104. Benjamin Martin
105. James Stevenson
106. Richard Whittington
107. George Mainard
108. Silas Goodwin
109. Brittain Honecut
110. Brittain Johnston
111. Bartley Stevens
112. Reuben Gower
113. James Johnston
114. Kiah Copeland

****

Ninth Company,
detached from
Duplin Regiment

1. Bryan Glissen, Captain
2. Stephen Williams, Lieut.
3. Samuel Cherry, Ensign
4. James Grimes
5. James Sullivan
6. Joseph Osburn
7. Jonathan Jones
8. Richard Bradley
9. William Frederick
10. Thomas Bennett
11. Charles Gibbs
12. John Denmark
13. Buk [sic] Jernigan
14. John Blanchard
15. David Rouse
16. Abram Connegay
17. David Carr
18. John Greer
19. Moses Manchy
20. James M. Cam
21. Elijah Mallard
22. George Bray
23. Feliz Candy
24. Robert Sand
25. Owen Lanier
26. David Brooks
27. John Hankin
28. Elijah Tucker

29. William Best
30. Lewis Bowen
31. John Bowen
32. Nathan South
33. Andrew Wallace
34. James Evans
35. Richard Sellers
36. Thomas Lee
37. John Lanier
38. Henry Matthews
39. Richard Rusley
40. James Matthews
41. Samuel Sumner
42. Isaac Weston
43. Stephen Grimes
44. John Peale
45. Isaac Phips
46. Robert Williams
47. John Grimes
48. Joseph Dickson
49. James Gaylor
50. Stephen Duncan
51. Warren Blount
52. Reuben Blanchard
53. Jacob Harrell
54. David Allen
55. Amos Walder
56. Daniel Jernigan
57. Jacob Gillmore
58. Jesse Outlaw
59. James Carter
60. Zachariah Carter
61. Lott Batts
62. Owen Hale
63. Stephen Herring
64. John Glisson

Page 16

65. Harget Kornegay
66. James Flannigan
67. Stephen Carmon
68. James Brown
69. William West
70. Isaac Powell
71. Jacob Powell
72. John Manor

73. Fountain Brown
74. Daniel Kethly
75. David Collins
76. William Sellers
77. Joshua Murett
78. William Smith
79. David Noles

****

Tenth Company,
detached from
Jones Regiment

1. Anthony Hatch, Captain
2. James Huston, Lieutenant
3. Donald C. Burkly, Ensign
4. Zadock Cox
5. Hall Bags
6. James Rhodes, Jr.
7. John Jones
8. John Saunders, Jr.
9. Urban Williamson
10. James Williamson
11. Thomas Hay
12. George Hay
13. Joseph Hay
14. William Wise
15. Simeon Simons
16. Barge Gooding
17. Asa Fasene
18. John Stanly
19. Benjamin Miller
20. Peter Elliot
21. David Jones
22. Joshua Davis
23. James McDaniel
24. David Ketchum
25. James Frazier
26. James Masburn
27. William Hop
28. Hardy Saunders
29. John McKenny
30. William Giles
31. John Pitman
32. Stephen Conaway
33. David Berry

34. James Perry
35. Jesse Lee
36. Westly Davis
37. Edmund Howard
38. William Simmons
39. George Koonce
40. John Morris
41. Edward Bryan
42. Samuel Hatch
43. James Wood
44. Rigden Hewit
45. Edmund Jones
46. George Smith
48. William Hubbard Houston
49. Theophilus Best
50. Masburn Raimer
51. David King
52. Theophilus Williams
53. William Richerson
54. Abraham Spencer
55. David Jones
56. Asa Sumner
57. Bryan Smith
58. Lewis Smith
59. Benjamin Brittain
60. Felix Jones
61. Andrew Adams
62. James Sandline
63. Lewis Mariner
64. James Daffin
65. Jordan Moore
66. William Lewis
67. Joshua Shepperd
68. Isaac Coverton
69. Benjamin Wooten
70. William Mason
71. William Anderson
72. Isaac James Jones
73. John Rue
74. Sherwood Faulk
75. Benjamin Gause

****

Eleventh Company,
detached from
Onslow Regiment

1. Jacob Galden, Captain
2. William Mitchel, Lieut.
3. Hardy Pitts, Ensign
4. Benjamin Scott
5. Isaac Scott
6. David Scott
7. James Wade
8. Aron Fox
9. Washington Hamnor
10. Jacob Hufman
11. Nathan Thompson
12. Robert Wallace
13. James White
14. Hardy Wood
15. Jess Gregory
16. Bryant Williams

Page 17

17. Ebrey Sanding
18. Henry Shepherd
19. James Saunders
20. Elijah Hardeson
21. Neal Grisson
22. Burney Humphrey
23. Samuel Jones
24. Bray Harrell
25. Lewis Stenkman
26. Ephraim King
27. Thomas Alphin
28. Micajah King
29. Thomas Garnto
30. James McCullok
31. Benjamin Barrow
32. William Phillips
33. Abner Anders
34. Isaac Henderson
35. Beverly Simmons
36. Isaac Haggins
37. Henry Henderson
38. Hillory Henderson
39. Joseph Simmons
40. Hardy Newton
41. Elijah Russel
42. Alexander Nelson
43. Thomas Ennett
44. Joshua McDonald

45. William Williams
46. Francis Venters
47. Whitehurst Ennett
48. Edward Pearson
49. Stephen Hawkins
50. Benjamin Ward
51. Aldridge Hicks
52. Humphrey Marshall
53. Seth Hadnok
54. William Howard
55. John Milson
56. Ezekiel Askins
57. Edward Fonville
58. Densy Wilson
59. Calvin Howard
60. John Wills
61. John Grant
62. William Grant
63. John Stephenson
64. Isaac Gilbert
65. Bazzel Grant
66. Isaac Riggs
67. John Crane
68. Aquila R. Hill
69. Walter Hellen
70. Hill Williams
71. William Humphrey
72. Lewis Oliver
73. Moses Cox
74. Samuel Davis
75. William Ennett
76. John Hawkins
77. Malachi Wilder
78. Niehodemus Gargamy
79. Daniel Mitchell
80. Abram Burnett

****

Twelfth Company,
detached from
New Hanover Regiment

1. John Mitchel, Captain
2. John Watson, Lieut.
3. D. W. Griffith, Ensign
4. Collin Blue

5. Levi Chace
6. Henry Farrand
7. John Holmes
8. Jacob Levy
9. Ezekiel Trussel
10. James Marshall
11. Ezra Peck
12. Niel Robson
13. Peleg Pierce
14. Jesse Wingate
15. John M. Wright
16. John McFarland
17. William Branch
18. Jesse Saunders
19. Fredrick George
20. William Larkins
21. James Stanly
22. Josiah Piner
23. Joseph Glifford
24. John Howard
25. John Hulett
26. Hardy Micks
27. Jacob Caston
28. Frederick Quinby
29. Henry Quinby
30. Oliver Caston
31. William Smith
32. Joseph Quinby
33. William Parmer
34. Alexander McAlister
35. Walter Simpson
36. Samuel Moore, Jr.
37. Joseph Simpson
38. William Berring
39. William Moore
40. Thomas Sharpless
41. James Goff
42. James Pinner
43. William Hand
44. Ambrose Smith
45. Luke Pawnly
46. Jeremiah Sutherland
47. Henry Williams
48. John Filyaw

Page 18

49. Abram Hall
50. Lewis Hall
51. William Pegford
52. Nathaniel Wheeler
53. Angus Kurr
54. George Corbett
55. William Jones
56. James Fennell
57. Bennet Fellows
58. Arthur Evans
59. William Hawsley
60. William New
61. Zachariah F. Burfield
62. Joseph Picket
63. Israel C. Burdeaux
67. Hiram Brocket
65. James Price
66. John St. George
67. Kinchen Nichols
68. John Messick
69. Lean Messick
70. Owen Hansley
71. Woodman Shepherd
72. William Jones Larkins
73. James Walker
74. Swinson Gurgarmus
75. Moses Moore
76. Cornelius Murphy
77. James I. White
78. Abijah Hanson

****

THIRD REGIMENT

Detached from the
5th Brigade

Jeremiah Slade, Lieut. Colonel
Commandant
James J. Hill, 1st Major
Andrew Joyner, 2nd Major

****

First Company,
detached from

1st Halifax Regiment

1. James Overstreet, Captain
2. Wilson C. Whitaker, Lieut.
3. William Brickle, 2nd Lieut.
4. John Vaughan
5. William Crowell
6. John Riks
7. James Whitaker
8. Thomas Applewhite
9. Moses Grimmer, fifer
10. Wallis Nicholson
11. Timothy Connell
12. Samuel Simmons
13. John Parker
14. John Scott
15. James Gaskins
16. Henry Bradford
17. Thomas Bradford
18. William Willey
19. John Bradford
20. George Goodwin
21. Willie Watson
22. Thomas B. Parker
23. David Douglass
24. Wilson Brantly
25. John Glover
26. Hall Hudson
27. John W. Branch
28. John Knight
29. James Merrit
30. Washington Turner
31. Samuel Bickle
32. John Shields
33. James Youngs
34. John Bryant
35. James Brantly
36 James Lawrence
37. Benjamin Pearce
38. John Matthews
39. Hansel Horne
40. Cullen Grimner
41. Jethro Barker
42. Miles Cross
43. Willis Shelton
44. Robert Saunders
45. Patrick McDaniel

****

46. Wilson W. Carter
47. John Scott
48. John Clark
49. Edward King
50. Hiram King
51. Jesse A. Brooks
52. Blake Baker
53. Lewis Lewis
54. Joseph Pully
55. Rinchen Harris
56. Jacob Bartholomew
57. James Abington

****

Page 19

Second Company,
detached from
2nd Halifax Regiment

1. Isham Matthews, Captain
2. Thomas Nichilson, Lieut.
3. John Alston, Ensign
4. Zachariah Sullivan
5. Francis Anderson
6. Halvin Ash
7. William Brown
8. James Ash
9. William H. Ballance
10. Robert Brinkley
11. Jesse Blackburn
12. Asa Blackburn
13. William J. Bradie
14. John Cooley
15. John Curling
16. Jesse Christie
17. Samuel Carter
18. Gideon Dameron
19. William R. Daniel
20. Rhoderick Easley
21. Allen Easley
22. Eaton F. Allen
23. Allen Flood
24. Wilson Green
25. Thomas Green
26. William Gurly

27. Thomas Y. Grimsted
28. Benjamin Green
29. Jesse Hamblet
30. Miley Harbin
31. David Harriss
32. Jesse Harlow
33. Gabriel Hawkins
34. John Hawes
35. Hansel Hathcock
36. Edmund Jackson
37. Beverly Jackson
38. Robert Jones
39. John Jordan
40. John King
41. Solomon Locklear
42. Exum Low
43. Samuel Locklear
44. John Lee, Jr.
45. John A. Losset
46. Jesse Moore
47. Alfred Moore
48. John Moore, Jr.
49. William Montford
50. William Moore
51. John Mann
52. James Mason
53. Arthur Manly
54. Guilford Nicholson
55. Thomas H. Green
56. William Onions
57. Eaton Powell
58. Rica Pullin
59. John Pugh
60. Ransom Powell
61. Frederick Pully
62. John Porter
63. Allen Powell
64. Michael Rand
65. Joseph Studivant
66. Abner Spear
67. Thomas Sammons
68. Benjamin Saunders
69. Peter Ship
70. Whiles Studivant
71. Arthur Spear
72. John Thrower
73. Lemuel Wilkins

74. John Wright, Sr.
75. Caleb Woodard
76. Thomas Ward

****

Third Company,
detached from
Northampton Regiment

1. James C. Harrison, Captain
2. [blank]
3. Sterling Milton, Lieut.
4. Whitmel Rulland, Ensign*
   * 2 Captains and 2 Ensigns on
   the returns.
5. [blank]
6. William Erwin
7. Willis Jasey
8. Samuel Bryan
9. John M. Williams
10. James Slightfoot
11. John Bryan
12. Obadiah Bowing
13. Elisha Boon
14. David Boon
15. James Vaughan
16. Willis Edge
17. Kinchen Murrell
18. John Sandefur, Jr.
19. Cullen Mitchell
20. Byrum Harriss
21. John Woodruff
22. John Jones
23. Charles Love
24. Zachariah Allen
25. Solomon Holmes
26. John Norworthy
27. John Warwick
28. Randolph Newsum
29. John Simons

Page 20

30. John Umphreys
31. Williby Hastey
32. George Garris

33. Henry Smith
34. Barnaba Bunn
35. John Benion
36. Jiles Jewter
37. Abel Gay
38. Nathan Pope
39. Newit Morgan
40. Richard Pilano
41. Lewis Short
42. Alexander McGridor
43. William Friear
44. Thomas Norworthy
45. Reuben Scott
46. Elisha Ryno
47. Cullen Artis
48. Robert Burnett
49. Thomas Williams
50. Calson Futtrell
51. Robert Warren
52. Morris Parker
53. James W. Davis
54. Nehemiah Vinson
55. Rhodes Gary
56. Drury Britt
57. Francis Parker
58. Drew Walden
59. Hardy Hale
60. Henry Gilliam
61. Riggan Newsom
62. James Valentine
63. Willie Wilkinson
64. Edmund Thompson
65. Benjamin Newsom
66. Barnes Bridges
67. James Warwik
68. Benjamin Griffin
69. John James
70. Dennis O'Conner
71. Thomas Norman
72. Hermon Rowell
73. William Boon
74. James Griffin
75. Gilbert Griffin
76. Shadrack Grant
77. Lewis Boon
78. Stephen Wimborne
79. Henry Evans

80. Joiner Boon
81. Austin Kindrik
82. Henry E. Simons
83. Joel Price
84. Stott Watson
85. Jep Boon
86. Cordal Newson
87. John Newson
88. Seamore Newsom
89. Kinchen Artis
90. Herbert Scott
91. Whitfield Cross
92. Aaron Fly
93. Warren Bridges
94. Brittain Lassiter
95. Daniel Futrell
96. Samuel Parker
97. Micajah Futtrell
98. Moab Underwood
99. Benjamin Vaughan
100. Isham Curl
101. Sterling Dupree
102. Arthur Tyner
103. Robert Thompson
104. James Love
105. James Smith
106. Richard Harrison
107. Lemuel Vaughan
108. James Morriss
109. Jones Glover
110. John Richards
111. Benjamin Edwards
112. William Collier
113. Littleton Tocke

****

Fourth Company,
detached from
Edgecombe Regiment

1. David Barnes, Captain
2. John B. Watlen, Lieut.
3. Josiah Wood, 2nd Lieut.
4. James Knight, Ensign
5. Paul Randolph, 1st Serg.
6. Alexander Cotten, 2nd Serg.

7. John L. Southerlin, 3rd Serg.
8, Littleberry Burfield, 4th Serg.
9. Pelasky Dudley, 1st Corp.
10. Jonathan Bailey, 2nd Corp.
11. Etheldred Gray, 3rd Corp.
12. Joshua Warren, 4th Corp.
13. Jonathan Thigpen, drummer
14. Pitman Worsley, fifer
15. Bythel Staton
16. John Garrett
17. Thomas Edmondson
18. James Knight
19. William Savage
20. Thomas Baten
21. Noah Cushing
22. Lawrence Mayo
23. John Rhodes
24. Whitmell Hardy
25. James Alsobrook
26. Spear Bradley
27. Kader Hales
28. Bartholomew Bryan

Page 21

29. Theophilus Parker
30. John Parker
31. Samuel Parker
32. Stephen Harper
33. Benjamin Portis
34. Samuel Portis
35. Joseph Portis
36. Charles Cobb
37. Abner Eason
38. David Rayner
39. Raging Sugg
40. Bartholomew Bowers
41. Andrew Clark
42. Wilie Cotton
43. David Dancy
44. Gideon Jolley
45. James Bilberry
46. Samuel Wood
47. Gray Thigpen
48. James Thigpen, Jr.
49. Howell Thigpen
50. John Nowell

****

51. James Cobb
52. John Blackburn
53. David Tennison
54. Benjamin Barfield
55. Michel Parker
56. David Morris
57. Brittain Pitman
58. Reuben Pitman
59. James Teat
60. Kalib Warren
61. Isaac Horne
62. Jacob Brake
63. Henry Horne
64. Theophilus Thomas
65. David Brake
66. Elisha Thomas
67. Thomas Price
68. Thomas Haughton
69. Lott Stalling
70. Josiah Crocker
71. Noah Davis
72. William Morgan
73. Eli Vann
74. John Hines

****

Fifth Company,
detached from
Martin Regiment

1. Durham Davis, Captain
2. James Reddick, Lieut.
3. James Howell, Ensign
4. John C. Williams, 1st Serg.
5. George Harrison, 2nd Serg.
6. Luke Bennett, 3rd Serg.
7. Jesse Lolly, 4th Serg.
8. Hosea Lanier, 1st Corp.
9. James Hardeson, 2nd Corp.
10. Selathiel Sherod, 3rd Corp.
11. Jehu Pearce, 4th Corp.
12. Jesse Hardeson, drummer
13. Samuel Robeson, fifer
14. James Garrott
15. William Bultry
16. Thomas Lassiter

17. John Amis
18. William Applin
19. Harmon Girkin
20. Jo0hn Smithwick
21. Joshua Hardeson
22. Silas Wollard
23. Nathaniel Wollard
24. James Cottran
25. Timothy Brogden
26. Westley Floid
27. Edmond Rogers
28. Seth Meazel
29. Aaron Meazel
30. Jesse Meazel
31. John Rogerson
32. James Ward
33. Benjamin Futrell
34. John Rowbuck
35. William Everitt
36. David Robeson
37. Nathan Morris
38. Darling Cherry
39. William Beach
40. James Caraway
41. Whitel Pierce
42. Richard Airs
43. Henry Best
44. William Rogers
45. Raleigh Rowbuck
46. Newton Coburn
47. Arden Taylor
48. Perry Brewer
49. Solomon Kelly
50. John Hawkins
51. James Stalls
52. Balentine Page
53. William Smith
54. Henry Smith
55. Willis Hoard
56. Thomas Ross
57. Chancey Davenport
58. William Correl
59. William James
60. William Whorton
61. Jonathan Calloway
62. John Weathley
63. William Hines

64. Moses Weaver
65. Lawrence Hyman
66. Thomas Bryan

Page 22

67. Elias Bryan
68. Nicholas Lord
69. Augustus Wood
70. Benjamin Amis
71. David Baston
72. Jesse Peal
73. David Cooper
74. David Rogerson
75. Micajah Perry
76. Thomas Cary
77. John Manning
78. Robert Daniel
79. Noah Robeson
80. James Hynes
81. Daniel Medford
82. Reuben Griffin
83. John Beach
84. Henry Robeson

****

Sixth Company,
detached from
Nash Regiment

1. Francis Drake, Captain
2. Isaac Watkins, 1st Lieut.
3. David Daniel, 2nd Lieut.
4. Willoughby Manning, Ensign
5. Samuel Sorsby, 1st Serg.
6. William Lepford, 2nd Serg.
7. Samuel Williams, 3rd Serg.
8. Alfred Bunn, 4th Serg.
9. Henry Bridgers, 1st Corp.
10. Archibald Wheless, 2nd Corp.
11. Joseph Whitehead, 3rd Corp.
12. Thomas Beckwith, 4th Corp.
13. Guilford Whitfield, drummer
14. Green Henry, fifer
15. Thomas Davis
16. Levi C. Arrington

17. Richard Carlisle
18. Jinnes Hackney
19. Joseph Green
20. William Griffin
21. Nathan Evans
22. Edward White
23. John Evans
24. Henry Hunt
25. Bennett Jones
26. George Evans
27. Wilson Hammons
28. Nathan Sikes
29. Thomas Bryant
30. Woody Tucker
31. David Wall
32. Cader Bass
33. Loody Ferrell
34. Thomas Lloyd
35. Hutchins Ferrell
36. Burton Ferrell
37. Henry Morgan
38. James Ferrell
39. Gillum Cone
40. Archivald Lemon
41. Clalon Mann
42. Samuel Davis
43. Edward Crowell
44. Benjamin Gloveyer
43. James B. Crowell
46. Thomas Brown
47. Eli Tisdale
48. Jacob Atkius
49. Richard Triggler
50. John Poulan
51. Daniel Bachelor
52. Joseph Tucker
53. John Williams
54. Jacob Row
55. Elijah Wiggins
56. Elen McCome
57. Edwin Brantly
58. Harrell Horn
59. Richard Stallings
60. Alston Gandy
61. Sampson Sikes
62. John Gandy
63. Thomas Valentine

64. Griffin Ganday
65. Soloman Thomas
66. Peter Gray
67. Amor Backwith
68. Newit Edwards
69. John Hawks
70. William Richards
71 Jorden Barrow

****

Seventh Company,
detached from
Warren Regiment

1. Charles Allen, Captain
2. Thomas Starkhouse, Lieut.
3. John Motholand
4. Micajah T. Hawkins
5. Nathan Turner
6. Amos P. Sledge
7. Doc't M. Robertson
8. Samuel Dowlin
9. Wilmot E. Egerton
10. Owen F. Myrick
11. Richard Ward
12. Thomas David
13. Icy Allen
14. William Breadlove
15. Phlemon Perdue
16. William Oliver

Page 23
17. William Turner
18. Arthur Tussell
19. Ransom Stroud
20. Lemuel Mitchel
21. Thomas Harton
22. Joseph Wren
23. William Powell
24. Allen Wren
25. Wiles Person
26. James C. Bennet
27. Joshua Harper
28. Ransom Acock
29. Cudburth Neal
30. Henry Pearson
31. Richard Davis

32. James Powell
33. Peter Randolph
34. John Robertson
35. William Sherrin
36. Charles Stoddard
37. Lewis Sherrin
38. Kinchen Williamson
39. George Hazlewood
40. Jasper Capps
41. Thomas Walker
42. Elisha Sherod
43. Buck Robertson
44. Jiles Carter
45. Joshua Davis
46. Benjamin Davis
47. Thomas Newman
48. Pleasant Ellington
49. John Allen
50. Daniel A. Perdue
51. Charles Bennet
52. Joel Ellington
53. James Thompson
54. D. G. Williams
55. Anderson Peebles
56. James Alston
57. Solomon Jenkins
58. Hardeway Davis
59. William Pertilla
60. Edward Pertilla
61. Richard Beach
62. Joel Tally
63. Miles Ellis
64. James Tally
65. Thomas Tally
66. Simes Ellils
67. Claton Lambert
68. John Hawks
69. Henry James
70. Daniel White
71. Obadiah Ellis
72. James Smith
73. Leonard King

****

Eighth Company,
detached from

****

Franklin Regiment

1. Marmaduke N. Jeffreys, Captain
2. Benjamin Stewart, Lieut.
3. Nathaniel Hunt, 2nd Lieut.
4. James Harrison, Ensign
5. Richard Wright
6. Winson Cook
7. [blank]
8. Newsome Bridges
9. Stephen Davis
10. Nathaniel Hayes
11. Thomas Tharington
12. William D. Jones
13. Dabney M. Duke
14. William T. Dent
15. Izekiah Stephens
16. Benjamin G. Richards
17. William Baker
18. Martin Murphray
19. James Bridges
20. John G. Perry
21. Benjamin Lanier
22. Duncan McLean
23. William Bird
24. Reddick Neilsmall, 1st Serg
25. Kinchen Boon
26. Thomas B. Arendel
27. Elijah Izzard
28. Julius Hill
29. Robert Thomes
30. John Baker
31. James Murphy
32. Willie Hight
33. Green D. Honse
34. John Prince
36. Breedlove Pippen
37. Reddick Haswell
38. Thomas Haswell
39. Ignatius Goldsberry
40. Albert Perry
41. John M. Sherod
42. Willie O. Davis
43. Thomas Davis
44. Jesse Collins
45. David Collins
46. John Hill
47. Guilford Lewis
48. James Nelms
49. Willis Cool
60. Joseph Stevens
51. James Barrow
52. Henry Thomas
53. Joseph C. Harris
54. Alexander Carson

Page 24

55. James Vincent
56. Guilford Bass
57. Bennett Perry
58. Miles Cary
59. Joseph B. Flemming
60. John Wichidht
61. Green Wood
62. Simson Jenkins
63. Eaton Freeman
64. Mathew Walker
65. Alsey Young
66. John Young
67. William Simmons
68. Macomb Alfred
69. William C. Perry
70. Julius Alford
71. James Hunt
72. Hugh Hayes
73. John J. Lancater
74. Drury Denton
75. John Jones
76. William Alford
77. William Debnam
78. Dilworth Sledge

****

FOURTH REGIMENT

Detached from
4th and 14th
Brigades

Alfred Rowland, Lieut. Colonel
Commandant

John A. Cameron, 1st Major
David Gillespie, 2nd Major

****

First Company,
detached from
Bladen Regiment

1. John Nicholson, Captain
2. James C. Cumming, 1st Lieut.
3. Robert McKee, 2nd Lieut.
4. James Campbell, Ensign
5. Alexander McIver, 1st Serg.
6. Thomas Smith, 2nd Serg.
7. Neil McMillan
8. Thomas Clardy
9. Turpin Cheshire
10. Colin Shaw
11. Anguish McMillan
12. Evan Rice
13. David Davis
14. Julias High
15. Mercer Grimes
16. William C. Singletary
17. David Singletary
18. Jasper Hester
19. Daniel Gooden
20. Thomas Averit
21. Abel Burney
22. Willie Adkison
23. Edward Pemberton
24. James Kelley
25. John Campbell
26. David White
27. James McLelland
28. Sampson Davis
29. Arthur Baiter
30. Patrick Murphy
31. William Davis, Jr.
32. William Davis, Sr.
33. William McKay
34. Thomas Brown
35. John B. Cowan
36. George B. Thomas
37. Archibald Pattison
38. Samuel Plumber

39. Dennis Kellerham
40. John Kelleham
41. Pierce Kellerham
42. John Taylor
43. James Stredy
44. John McFallen
45. Dugald McKitchen
46. John Savage
47. James Salter
48. Alexander Lamer
49. Barnabas Brown
50. Joseph Hester

****

Second Company,
detached from
First Cumberland Regiment

1. Arch'd McCrapie, Captain
2. Daniel Shaw, 1st Lieut.
3. John Shaw, 2nd Lieut.
4. John Hodges, Ensign
5. Robert Shaw
6. John Steele
7. Jesse Betha
8. Owen Boon
9. James Sorrel
10. William Hodges
11. Neil McNeil
12. William McKinsie

Page 25
13. John Gordon
14. John McLelland
15. Ebenezer Folsome
16. Murdoc McRae
17. Hector McAuthnr [sic]
18. Benjamin Morrison
19. Samuel Searsey
20. Rowland Fauckner
21. Aron Searcy
22. Peter Munro
22. Angus Ray
24. John McKellar
25. Neel Munro
26. Theophillus Denny

27. Cornelins Cofield
28. John McDougal
29. John Wilkinson
30. Hector McNeil
31. Richard Cade
32. Richard Wilkinson
33. Absalom Hammonds
34. James Norris
35. David Bone
36. Richard Bone
37. John Jackson
38. Thomas Gill
39. Joshua Jesop
40. Samuel Reeves
41. John Taylor
42. Robert Harwell
43. Francis Hobby
44. Thomas Paine
45. Drury Massey
46. Frederick Yarborough
47. Wilson Ray
48. Darius Cox
49. Murdock Campbell
50. Elisha Brown
51. Jesse Northington
52. Alexander Mekellan
53. Sion Tedder
54. Allen Campbell
55. Neil Bowie
56. Malcom Pattison
57. William Lathem
58. Needham Moore
59. Horatio Griffin
60. Lewis Moore
61. Benjamin Moore
62. James Stephens
63. Allen Northington
64. Neil McNeil
65. Bogle Ferrand
66. Thomas H. Massey
67. Joshua Carman
68. Aurthur [sic] Core
69. Shadrack Johnson
70. William Daniel
71. John Lewis
72. John Johnston
73. John Moore

****

Third Company,
detached from
Cumberland Regiment

1. David Evans, Captain
2. George Jones, 1st Lieut.
3. John Leonard
4. John Evans
5. James Rush
6. Phillip Horton
7. Samuel Salmon
8. Etheldred Syke
9. Thomas McMurray
10. Phillip McRae
11. Council McCullin
12. Pitkin McCullin
13. John Carver
14. Sion Horne
15. Waddel Cade
16. Mathew Hayes
17. Gilbert McCull
18. William Taylor
19. William Nunnery
20. John Bryan
21. Robert Olery
22. William Anderson
23. John Thagard
24. Samuel Reeves
25. James McDaniel
26. Zachariah Butler
27. Norman McNeil
28. John McKinzie
29. Samuel Butler
30. John Langdon
31. John Shaw
32. Douglass McLaughlan
33. James Denton
34. Hugh McGuire
33. Thomas Bowen
36. Jonathan Evans
37. John Ray
38. James Kirkpatrick
39. Murdock Orchillred
40. William Tilllingast
41. Jesse Anson

42. Thomas Evans
43. Murwin Carrington
44. James Stevens
45. John B. Smith
46. Murcock McLeod
47. German Seawell
48. George Holmes
49. William Horn
50. Thomas Cole

Page 26

51. Jacob Seawell
52. John Burgess
53. Jonathan Hare
54. Dugald McIntyre
55. John Johnston
56. Duncan Pharis
57. Jacob Faircloth
58. Daniel Everitt
59. Joshua Edward
60. Mathew Freeman
61. Richard Everitt
62. Thomas Richardson
63. John Everitt
64. Malcomb Patterson
65. Allen Dudley
66. John Law
67. Isaac T. Cushing
68. Samuel Smith
69. John B. Troy
70. William Atkinson
71. Thomas Wilkinson

****

Fourth Company,
detached from
Sampson Regiment

1. George Lassiter, Captain
2. Robert Lassiter, 1st Leiut.
3. Josias Lee, 2nd Lieut.
4. Abram Nailor, Ensign
5. Pharo Lee, 1st Serg.
6. Sion Danfont, 2nd Serg.
7. Starling Otary

8. Jacob Mannels
9. George Warwick
10. Joseph Two
11. Granbury Goodwin
12. John Warwick
13. James Jones
14. Gardner Keen
15. Isaac Manner
16. Bryant Flowers
17. Jesse Manner
18. Hugh Burke
19. Whiting Ryolds
20. Lewis Johnston
24. Jesse Ezzel
22. John Bird
23. Herrin Gregory
24. Landen Two
25. Daniel Hall
26. Samuel Gavin
27. Owen Shorton
28. Samuel Standly
29. John White
30. Nathan Young
31. William Lee
32. Joab Whiley
33. John House
34. Robin Pope
35. James Harden
36. Jonathan Edge
37. David Ryold
38. Elias Two
39. Jacob Stanly
40. Thomas Jacobs
41. Edmond Goodwin
42. Reddick Jones
43. Owen Ryold
44. Daniel Two
45. Laban Williams
46. Stephen Maner
47. Hardy Stephens
48. William Turner
49. Joshua Bell
50. Samuel Robeson
51. Arthur Hare
52. Joseph Herrin
53. Stephen Herrin
54. Phelix Chesnut

55. Samuel Gavin
56. Edmund Manuel
57. Nathaniel Boyet
58. Elias Whilly
59. Jonas Quinby
60. Warren Jackson
61. James Hobbs
62. Raiford Faireloth
63. Henry Lee
64. Joel M. Lamb

****

Fifth Company,
detached from
Sampson Regiment

1. Thomas Boykin, Captain
2. James Williamson, Lieut.
3. Timothy Williamson, 2nd
Lieut.
4. Lavis Spell, Ensign
5. Reyney McIlwines
6. Laban Morgan, 2nd Serg.
7. Hartwell Porter, 3rd Serg.
8. Peter Ryan, drummer
9. John Boykin
10. Daniel Cooper
11. Simon Reynolds
12. John Porter
13. Michel Porter
14. Core Cooper
15. Thomas Stephens
16. William Ryon
17. Henry Pope
18. Solomon Boykin
19. Edward Broy
20. Allen Parker

Page 27

21. John Ammonds
22. David Underwood
23. Zachariah Williams
24. Rayford Cooper
25. Willis Royal
26. Angus Johnston

27. Lewis Pope
28. Israel Tarlington
29. Henry Hart
30 Joshua Herring
31. John Pope
32. Hardy Royall
33. James Porter
34. Owen Crumpler
35. Jesse Strickland
36.   [blank]
37. John Blackwell
38. William Turner
39. William Pope
40. Neil Campbell
41. James Frazier
42. John Simonds
43. Rayford Grist
44. Noah Faircloth
45. Aaron Cummings
46. William Miller
47. Thomas Frazier
48. Sander Fisher
49. Sutton Grist
50. John Manor
51. John Orion
52. Blackman Tews
53. Samuel Revells
54. John Carter
55. Aron Peterson
56. Abram Sellers
57. Thomas Green
58. Luke Parker
69. David Whitney
60 Mathew Hall
61. Isaac Carter
62. Charles Butler
63. Henry Hall
64. John Blount

****

Sixth Company,
detached from the
Moore Regiment

1. Nathaniel Tucker, Captain
2. Neil Morrison, 1st Lieut.

3. Hugh McDaniel, 2nd Lieut.
4. John Garner, Ensign
5. Dougald Mathew
6. Robert Kennedy
7. Erwin Stephens
8. John Tyson
9. Alexander Black
10. William Goings
11. William Jackson
12. Stephen Berryman
13. Edward Goings
14. Neil Thompson
15. David Jones
16. George Anderson
17. John Myrick
18. Andrew Anderson
19. Malcolm McGilvery
20. William Wilson
21. Charles Smith
22. John Phillips
23. Drury Richardson
24. Ralford Phillips
25. Joab Cheek
26. John McLeod
27. Benjamin Pope
28. William Page
29. George Carlbin
30. John Laughon
31. Elisha Rogers
32. Sampson Muse
33. Malcolm McDuffy
34. John Medlin
35. John White
36. William Gillmore
37. Alexander Medlin
38. John McDonald
39. John Spicer
40 Isom Sowell
41. Everitt Sheffield
42. Daniel Holllin
43. Simon Lewis
44. James Morgan
45. Jacob Gargle
46. Frederick Autry
47. James Owen
48. Aben Brown
49. James Garner

50. Edward Moore
51. Bailey Garner
52. Augus McAuley
53. John Bird
54. John Martin
55. John Graham
56. John Patterson
57. Donald Mclean
58. Argus Morrison
59. John Richardson
60. John McLeod
61. William Williamson
62. Lauchlan McKinnon
63. Daniel Love
64. Duncan Blue
65. John Bluc
66. Malcolm McNeil

Page 28

67. Duncan McLean
68. Hugh Cameron
69. Edward Patterson
70. Archibald Blue
71. Neil McLeon
72. Nathan Maples
73. Thomas Maples
74. John Maples
75. James Maples
76. John Cole
77 John Johnston
78. William Sterling
79. William Koy
80. Thomas Rhodes
81. Joseph Stephens
82. Duncan Smith
83. Benjamin Morris
84. Robert Tapley
85. Benjamin Bushup
86. Malcolm Folsum
87. Mathew Wicker
88. Charles Crawford
89. Benjamin Huckaby
90. John Bushup
91. Josiah Hogwood
92. William Oliver
93. John Underwood

94. John Baker
95. John Bledsoe
96. William Dairymple
97. Benjamin C. Bennett
98. William Murchinson
99. Archibald Bue
100. Benjamin Wicker

****

Seventh Company,
detached from
Columbus Regiment

1. Caleb Stephens, Captain
2. John White, 1st Lieut.
3. Alexander Taylor, Ensign
4. James Smith, 1st Serg.
5. Thomas B. Wooten, 2nd Serg.
6. Michel High
7. David Baldwin
8. Prosper forma Duval
9. Thomas Hobbs
10. Amos Allen
11. James Baldwin, Jr.
12. Elijah Reynols
13. John Reynols
14. William Hooks
15. Daniel Fowler
16. Richard Reynols
17. Anthony Cribb
18. Elijah Warley
19. Richard Folk
20. John Carteret
21. Frederick Door
22. Archibald Bogleman
23. Aron Floid
24. Robert Carlisle
25. John Gore
26. Richard Fowler
27. Isaiah Smith
28. Thomas Cribb
29. Hardy Duncan
30. Moses Duncan
31. Isaiah Sessions
32. Willis Lamberton
33. John Folks

34. Frederick Sasser
35. Josiah Powell
36. Archibald Taylor
37. Allen Barfield
38. Eli Nichols
39. Isaac Nichols
40. Amos Tyson

****

Eight Company,
detached from
Anson Regiment

1. Frederick Staton, Captain
2. Solomon Trull, 1st Lieut.
3. Henry James, 2nd Lieut.
4. James White, Ensign
5. James King
6. Thomas Ward
7. William Anderson
8. John Walden
9. Benjamin Williams
10. Francis Mullis
11. Isaac Watson
12. William James
13. Newbern Williams
14. Richard Manes
15. Mathew Rumage
16. David James
17. Elisha Griffin
18. Hosea James
19. Balis Carr
20. John Hagler
21. Asa Baggett
22. Robert Preston
23. John Fornberton
24. Moses Thomas
25. Reuben Vinson
26. William Gurley
27. Jesse Leay
28. Needham Gurley
29. Jesse Barnett
30. Alsey Hyatt
31. [blank]
32. John Winctuster
[Winchester ?]

Page 29

33. Abram Wimberly
34. James Perkins
35. James Morris
36. Lewis Collins
37. John Brown
38. Asa Rushing
39. David Hendrick
40. [blank]
41 Arris Roser
42. Micajah Taylor
43. Absalom Stegall
44. Moses Pearce
45. Ason Pearce
46. William Sikes
47. William Pearce
48. William Mulder
49. George Mulder
50. William Oniel

****

Ninth Company,
detached from
Anson Regiment

1. James Tindall, Captain
2. Boggan Cash, 1st Lieut.
3. Malach Goulde, 2nd Lieut.
4. Hezekiah Billingsby, Ensign
5. William Jasper
6. John Goodwin
7. Thomas C. Threadgill
8. Austin Fort
9. William German
10. John German
11. Lemuel Ingram
12. John Ingram
13. John Rushing
14. John Jones
15. Charles Strother
16. James Copeland
17. John Webb
18. Benjamin Sinclair
19. Orrin Sinclair
20. Jacob Phillips

21. Jesse Turner
22. William West
23. Stephen Nash
24. Westly Wortrind
25. Booky Dickson
26. Isham Ingram
27. William Worhine
28. Howell Threadgill
29. Nathaniel Davis
30. William Dabbs
31. Mathew Bushnell
32. Jeremiah Gullidge
33. Mills Ballie
34. John Moore
35. Mathew Hubbard
36. William Fielding
37. Jesse Cox
38. Christopher McRae
39. John Julding
40. James Brooks
41. Benjamin Teal
42. Harman Adams
43. Jurguhard McRae
44. Isaac Little
45. John Chewning
46. John Ross
47. Thomas Tyson
48. Bennet Williams
49. William Lewis
50. William Julke
51. Thomas Slay
52. Jesse Ratiff
53. Francis Downer
54. James Capel
55. William Wood
56. Handy May
57. James Miller
58. James Martin
59. Thomas Handcock
60. John Barber
61. John Williams
62. James Briley
63. Henry Adcock
64. William Scott
65. Thomas Jones
66. Neel McBride
67. Samuel Ratliff

68. Daniel McLeran
69. John Russon
70. John Short
71. James Morsham
72. Neil McLeran
73. Benjamin Hanley
74. Hezekiah Ingram

****

Tenth Company,
detached from
Richmond Regiment

1. John Blue, Captain
2. John McAlston
3. Daniel McAuley
4. Alexander Brown
5. James Terry
6. James Watkins
7. Fenly McSween
8. William Wakins [Watkins ?]
9. John James
10. Alexander McLeod, Sr.
11. Amos Corbett
12. Luke Barnett
13. Elisha Crowson
14. Lorick Stephen

Page 30

15. Alexander McRae
16. Dempsey Pitman
17. James Williams
18. John Bostwick
19. William Harris
20. Stephen Jones
21. Angus McLoud
22. John McSween
23. Charles Hawley
24. Donald McSween
25. Kenneth McInnis
26. David Britt
27. James Dawson
28. Cannor Weaver
29. Edward Gantlia
30. Martin James

31. Luke Woodle
32. James Smith
33. Berry Norten
34. Elias Pate
35. Hanly Snead
35. Henry Covington
37. William Robeson
38. Isaac Vaughan
39. James Brown
40. Alexander McDonald
41. Daniel McNair
42. Daniel Carmichel
43. John McRae
44. John McMillian
45. John McEwen
46. Peter Patterson
47. William Bringman
48. Alexander Shaw
49. Duncan Buie [sic ?]
50. James McDonald
51. Daniel Watson
52. Archibald McLeod
53. Josiah Bozeman
54. Gilbert McEachin
55. Roderick Campbell
56. Alexander McPherson
57. Malcom Shaw
58. Mathew Rainwater
59. John Chase
60. James Molton
61. John Migginson
62. Daniel Williams
63. James Mask
64. Sammuel [sic] McHock
65. John Black
66. Wader Shepperd
67. Josiah Shepherd
68. John McDonald
69. Archibald McDonald
70. Donald McDonald
71. Lechlin McLennan
72. Jess Williams
73. Benjamin Thomas
74. Kenneth McKinsie
75. Moody Ingram
76. John McLeod
77. Isaac Mason

78. Calloway Stephens
79. Eli Northam
80. John Stogner

****

Eleventh Company,
detached from
Robeson Regiment

1. Isaac Sullivan, Captain
2. William Brown, 1st Lieut.
3. Benjamin Blount, 2nd Lieut.
4. Elias Thomas, Ensign
5. James Stewart
6. John McMillan
7. Archibald Stewart
8. Charles Campbell
9. Jesse Musslewhite
10. Spencer Porter
11. William Council
12. John Wilkerson
13. Allen Buie
14. Stephen Banley
15. Charles Oxendine
16. Thomas Locklier
17. Silas Strickland
18. John McNeil
19. Daniel Chrisholm
20. Alexander Chrisholm
21. William Edward
22. Ralph Revell
23. Isaac Streaker
24. Hugh Locklier
25. Joseph Walters
26. James Ivey
27. William Davis
28. William Bodiford
29. Harman Cox
30. William Britt
31. Charles Storm
32. John Cox
33. Hardy Cox
34. Nathaniel Hawthorn
35. Daniel Pate
36. Duncan Baker
37, Isham Ivey

38. John Wilkins
39. John McKellar
40. Martin Lewis
41. Lemuel Thompson
42. John Drake
43. Peter McCormick
44. Daniel Stewart
45. Smith Dease
46. Amos Taylor

Page 31

47. James McKay
48. Hardy Pope
49. Josiah Ratley
50. John Walters
51. John Drinkwater
52. Thomas Pope
53. Thomas Lowe
54. Jacob Pitman
55. William Walters
56. Dawson Walters
57. Moses Bass
57. Daniel McPhallair
59. Radford S. Witherell
60. Francis F. Varnum
61. William Parvis
62. John Thompson
63. William Ballard
64. Reading Blount
65. Solomon Thomas
66. James Reeves
67. Charles Ivey, Sr.
68. Elijah Hammons
69. Joseph Blount
70. Duncan McMillan
71. Roderick Sutherland
72. Augus McCulland, Sr.
73. Angus McQueen
74. Alexander McKay
75. Hector McLeon
76. John McKay
77. Angus McCullum
78. Archibald Morrison
79. Daniel Niehilson
80. Daniel McRae

****

SECOND BRIGADE
detached from the 6th and
7th and 11th, 8th, 9th 10th
and 15th Brigades of the
Organized Militia of the
State

Ephraim Davidson,
Brigadier General

FIFTH REGIMENT
detached from the
6th and 16th Brigades

Richard Atkinson, Lieut. Col.
Commandant
Simpson Shaw, 1st Major
Benjamin Elliott, 2nd Major

FIRST COMPANY
of the Fifth Regiment,
detached from the
1st Orange Regiment

1. Hugh Munbollen, Captain
2. James Latta, Lieut.
3. James Smith, Ensign
4. John Munhollon, 1st Serg.
5. George Mebane, 2nd Serg.
6. Thomas Bradford, 3rd Serg.
7. George Tate, 4th Serg.
8. Joseph Bardford
9. James Bird
10. Joseph Bird
11. William Reddin
12. John Wilson
13. Robert Barnhill
14. Nathaniel Beane
15. Joseph Hodge
16. James Wilson
17. John Warren
18. Lewis Simpson
19. William Smith
20. William Gilan

****

21. William Cherehall
22. James Browning
23. Royal Willis
24. Elisha Glenn
25. James Wood
26. Samuel Willis
27. Lewis Durning
28. John Sikes
29. Joel Parish
30. Bird Lean
31. Miles Jones
32. Richard Howard
33. Francis Crocker
31. John O'Neal
35. Moses Atwater
36. Gardner Ballard
37. Benjamin Bridges
38. James Chambers
39. George Smith
40. Charles Canley

Page 32

41. William Bishop
42. John Curthington
43. Benjamin Price
44. Abner Jackson
45. Bradley Collins
46. William Jacobs
47. William Clemons
48. Scearly Docherty
49. James Lindsey
50. Theophilas Thompson
51. John Crabtree
52. Uriah Crabtree
53. William Mebane
54. John Jones
55. Thomas Thomas
56. Richard Wilson
57. Joseph Wilkinson
58. Martin Liggett
69. James White
60. Richard Jones, Sr.
61. William R. Tate
62. John Wood
63. Alexander Patten
64. Elijah Hart

65. William Price
66. Gabriel Finn

****

Second Company,
detached from
1st Orange Regiment

1. Robert Thompson, Captain
2. Samuel Strahorn, Lieut.
3. William Bradshaw, Ensign
4. William Kirkland
5. Davis Davis
6. Asa Couch
7. William Herndon
8. Isaac D. Dollar
9. John Horn
10. Robert Allen
11. John Turner
12. William Allen
13. James Dollar
14. John Ivy
15. William Harris
16. John Hurt
17. William Lingo
18. Thomas Patterson
19. Thornton McFarlin
20. Francis Roberts
21. Levin Ellis
22. Harrison Parker
23. Henry Newton
24. Andrew Gay
25. Amos Nichols
26. John Horner
27. John Nichols
28. George Riggs
29. Wilson Ball
30. Isaac Morris
31. Mathew Durham
32. Edward Howington
33. Thomas F. Cardwell
34. Henry Shepherd
35. Pleasant Herndon
36. Nathan Malcomb
37. James Ashley
38. Henry Trill

39. William Lyhu [sic ?]
40. John Hart
41. William Kirland
42. William McDavid
43. Alfred Hill
44. William Woods
45. Fisher Clendenning
46. Archibald Pugh
47. John Thompson
48. Jacob Green
49. James Ray, Jr.
50. Samuel Stuart
51. Thomas Lynch
52. Robert Jeffries
53. Hugh Wood
54. John D. Covington
55. Thomas Cate
56. Adam Douglass
57. James Lindsey
58. [blank]
59. William Ragans

****

Third Company,
detached from
Second Orange, or
Haw River Regiment

1. John Stockard, Captain
2. John Albright, Lieut.
3. Jacob Efland, Ensign
4. John Proxter
5. Jacob Jackson
6. Henry Loy
7. Thomas Steel
8. Matthew Baswell
9. Edward Baswell
10. Hugh Haglas
11. Thomas Moore, 2nd Serg.
12. Joseph Cable
13. Drewry Ballard
14. John Ireland
15. William Moore
16. David Barber
178. Peaton Wilson
18. Ziah Horniday

****

19. John Foust
20. James Upsom

Page 33

21. Thomas Bevers
22. Joseph Murray
23. Ned Heathcock
24. Alexander Filmor
25. Palmer Freeman
26. William Hughs
27. Abraham Hawey
28. Henry Hardle [Hurdle ?]
29. John Wallis
30. Joel Tate
31. John Lewis
32. James Burrage
32. Lemuel Thompson
34. James Grimes
35. Osborn James
36. Daniel Criscow
37. Elisha Willis
38. Phillip Hodge
39. Charles Shanks
40. John Wilson
41. John Cable
42. Nehemiah Thomas
43. John Cook
44. Adam Long
45. Boston Graves
46. Daniel Thomas
47. David Spoon
48. John Hornaday
49. Nathaniel Robeson
50. William Holt
51. James Turner
52. Joel Albright
53. Alexander Taddis
54. John Long
55. Isaac McAdams
56. Michel Ryke

****

Fourth Company,
detached from
Randolph Regiment

1. Joshua Craven, Captain
2. Adam Winningham, Lieut.
3. Jacob Worthington, Ensign
4. Raley Spinks, 1st Serg.
5. Peter Kivet, 2nd Serg.
6. Marmaduke Swean, 3rd Serg.
7. Fredrick Brown, 4th Serg.
8. Absalom Harper, 1st Corp.
9. William Patterson, 2nd Corp.
10. Daniel Jackson, 3rd Corp.
11. Henry Johnston, 4th Corp.
12. James McMasters, drummer
13. James Cude, fifer

Privates

14. Lewis Martin
15. Robert Haskin
16. Abel Winningham
17. Silas Davison
18. Isaac Vinson
19. Solomon Luther
20. Asa Peacock
21. Jacob Lassiter
22. Isham Harris
23. William Jackson
24. Thomas Shaw
25. Hezekiah Andrew
26. Lewis Scarlet
27. Henry Boss
28. James Wade
29. Martin Chandler
30. Archibald Dubar
31. Thomas Nelson
32. Seth Wade
33. Duncan Harvey
34. William Brown
35. Cambell Powell
36. John Ferguson
37. William Cole
38. Isaac Miller
39. Frederick Fentress
40. Alexander Robins
41. Alexander Cunnigan
42. Frederick Steed
43. John Steed
44. Elijah Williams
45. John Malone

46. Stephen Hervey
47. John Smitherman
48. Alexander Dockery
49. Isham Steed
50. John Reid
51. John Pierce
52. Garrat Spinks
53. Joseph Argee
54. James Harris
55. Lewis Garner
56. Thomas Bray
57. Ezekiel Mills
58. William Conner
59. West Hicks
60. Jacob Briles
61. Rhudolph Weymire
62. Ezra Bukerdite
63. Will Acborn
64. Abram Elliott
54. James Sweany
66. Henry Lamm
67. Samuel Beson
68. Dum Lamm
69. Henry Burton
70. James Barker
71. Michel Jackson
72. Jeremiah Barker
73. George Wilson
74. John Chaplain
75. Enoch Williams
76. John Wood

Page 74

77. William Maples
78. Henry Underwood
79. Henry Kivett
80. Miles Stephens
81. James Savage
82. John Burgess
83. William Nelson
84. Anderson Roach
85. Nathan York
86. William Howe
87. Thomas Alexander
88. Larkin Curtis
83. Henry Curtis

90. William Gay
91. George Black
82. John Brown
93. Abijah Moore
94. John Johnston
95. George Lean
96. John Bryan

****

Fifth Company,
detached from
Chatham Regiment

1. Carney Cotton, Captain
2. Daniel Smith, 1st Lieut.
3. John M. Gee, 2nd Lieut.
4. Riddick Burns, Ensign
5. Jonathan Rickets
6. William Sloan
7. George McDaniel
8. John Coley
9. James Burns, Jr.
10. Aron Bryan, Jr.
11. Benjamin Dowdy, Sr.
12. Frederick Phillips
13. Elisha Jackson
14. Michel Welch
15. Robert Barker
16. Lemuel Underwood
17. John Bray
18. John Lawler
19. Thomas Mullins
20. Edom Edwards
21. John Purvis
22. Josh Brooks
23. Benjamin Emmerson
24. George Smith
25. James Eastis
26. Ezekiel Mazey
27. William Mathews
28. William Jordan
29. Guilford Gardner
30. Elisha Kurhy
31. Isaiah Cole
32. George Merrett
33. Samuel Harris

34. Larkin Straughn
35. James Edwards
36. Josiah Kurhy
37. Cornelius Myrick
38. Wm. F. Richardson
39. Joseph Elliot
40. Joseph Hart
41. James Myrick
42. Azel Myrick
43. James Dixon
44. James Wamble
45. Johnston Barber
46. Daniel Nevin
47. Stephen Upchurch
48. Matt Jinks
49. Jesse Patridge
50. Alexander Moore
51. William Spivey
52. Moses Archer
53. James Perry
54. John Noblet
55. John Eastbridge
56. John Whitehead
57. Leonard Johnston
58. Duty Durset
59. John Craton
60. Henry Harris
61. John Evans
62. Joseph Alston
63. Joseph Tomison
64. Milliner Burk
65. Reuben May
66. David Blacklock
67. Isaac Field
68. William Stedman
69. James McMath, Jr.
70. Edward Buckner
71. John Taylor
72. John Gear
73. Isaac Richison
74. Benjamin Curl
75. Jesse Davis
76. John Carton
77. Matthew Hogan
78. John Boon
79. Banston Chaves
80. Benjamin Pytent

81. Armstead Heynes
82. James Tidder
83. Richard Evans
84. Charles Evans
85. John Collerson
86. David Fox, Jr.
87. Aron Spont [Spout ?]
88. David Vestal
89. Barnell Fox
90. John Davis

Page 35

****

Sixth Company,
detached from the
Wake Regiment

1. William McCaller, Captain
2. John Walton, Lieut.
3. Britton Sanders, Ensign
4. Littleton Hutson
5. Burtess Upchurch
6. Nathaniel Ward
7. John Scott
8. John Pride
9. William Harwood
10. Little John Utley
11. Whitmill Hunter
12. Alvin Utley
13. Jyre [sic] Parish
14. Wiley Womak
15. John Watson
16. John Rand
17. Darling Jones
18. Giles B. Bledsoe
19. Miller Sexton
20. Anthony Pilkinton
21. Isma Kellum
22. Noel Norris
23. William Holland
24. Peter Angel
25. Arthur Reves

****

Seventh Company,
detached from
Wake Regiment

1. John T. C. Wiatt, Captain
2. Lewis S. Muse, 1st Lieut.
3. Nicholas Sheffield, Ensign
4. Samuel Combs, 1st Serg.
5. Thomas Rice, 2nd Serg.
6. Samuel Pearson, 3rd Serg.
7. Dawson Atkinson, 4th Serg.
8. David A. Knott, 1st Corp.
9. John R. Kart, 2nd Corp.
10. John Carney, 3rd Corp.
11. Abraham H. Boylan, 4th Corp.
12. Preston Pearson
13. Hie [sic] Nunn
14. William W. Seaton
15. Mark Cook
16. Robert Harrison
17. Alfred Jones
18. Jonathan Busbee
19. Willis Parker
20. Martin Adams
21. James B. Ruth
22. John Rice
23. Thomas Powers
24. Edmond R. Pitt
25. William Brown
26. Robert Calum
27. James G. Mitchel
28. William Harrison
29. Littleberry Williams
30. Nelson Andrews
31. William Davis
32. Allen Parks
33. John Olive
34. James Olive
35. Elias Gay
36. Allen Griffin
37. Thomas Bowden
38. Jesse Gibbs
39. John Dodd
40. Oran Vincent
41. Samuel Bake
42. William W. Bell
43. William Brantley
44. Christopher Woodard
45. Joseph Woodard
46. William Bell
47. Shadrack Haywood
48. Jeremiah Bell
49. Willis Nelms
50. Josiah Davis
51. Cader Nutt
52. Robert Rutherford
53. James Morris
54. Wiley Roberts
55. John George
56. Wylie Carpenter
57. John Burges
58. Daniel George
59. John Lynn
60. James Thorn
61. Brittain Stephenson
62. Willis Holderfield
63. James Head
64. Little John Utley
65. William Harwood
66. John Pride
67. John Scott
68. Nathaniel Ward
69. Beatess Upchurch
70. Littleton Hutson

****

Eight Company,
detached from
Granville Regiment

1. Willis Johnston, Captain
2. William G. Brown, Lieut.
3. William Dolby, Ensign
4. Willie M. Spears
5. Green B. Walker
6. Tandy Walker

Page 36

7. James G. Tate
8. John Bass
9. Richard Weed
1-. Francis Clark
11. Wiat Johnson
12. John Barnett, Jr.
13. John Barnett
14. Solmon [sic] Hayes
15. Kinchen Higgs
16. Kinchen Bynum
17. Thomas Cole
18. James Mayson
19. William W. Ananias
20. Valentine Mayfield
21. John Davis
22. Kade Kittrell
23. William Parks
24. John Roberts
25. Abram Lawrence
26. George Lieuter
27. John Lyod
28. John Paskill
29. James Allen
30. James Gill
31. Moses Winston
32. Wiat Kennedy
23. Newmon Robertson
34. Jehu Spear
35. Benjamin Huffman
36. Arthur Fuller
37. Lain Moore
38. Thomas Lile
39. Henry Morris
40. Flecher Taylor
41. John Sherril
42. Asa Green
43. James Sewit
44. David Byers
45. William Book
46. Henry Avery
47. Lazarus Minor
48. George Byers
49. William White
50. Wiat Cazart
51. Samuel Clemons
52. James Medders
53. Michael Christon
54. John Stephenson
55. Jesse Acock
56. Benjamin H. Wartham
57. Henry Chambles

58. Samuel Persyth
69. Henry Jones
60. Mertin Freeman
61. Payten Madison
62. Merkle Tom Kithrell
63. Egreppy [sic ?] Nance
64. Edward Weathers
65. Henry Hendley
66. William Adcock
67. Arthur Fuller
68. Asa Green
69. Nicholas Green
70. John Mitchell

****

Ninth Company,
detached from
Granville Regiment

1. Lestly Gilliam, Captain
2. William Gilliam, Lieut.
3. Thomas Hunt, Ensign
4. Thomas Howard, 1st Serg.
5. John Downey, 2nd Serg.
6. Thomas Downey, 3rd Serg.
7. Moses Pettiford, 4th Serg.
8. Horatio Bass, 1st Corp.
9. Charles Pratt, 2nd Corp.
10. Benjamin Ward, 3rd Corp.
11. William Oakley, 4th Corp.

Privates

12. Peyton Hayes,
13. William Terry
14. Charles Duncan
15. Scarlet Anderson
16. Ransom Hester
17. Solomon Satterswhite
18. William Daniel
19. Overton Haines
20. Thomas Daniel
21. Phillip P. Pool
22. Charles Smith
23. Meredith Lampkin
24. William Blanks

26. Elkshel [sic ?] Ellis
26. Robert Wilson
27. Robert Jenkins
25. William Hargrove
29. William Collins
30. John Norwood
31. Reuben Hawkins
32. William Barnes
33. Pleasant Mangam
34. Rowland Perdue
35. John Daniels
36. John Montague
37. Robert Stamper
38. John Chavis
39. Thomas Evans
40. William Evans
41. Jeremiah Anderson
42. Lemuel Tyler
43. Meredith Lampkins
44. William Griffin
45. Thomas Lewis
46. William Seares
47. Benjamin Grissom
48. Reuben Parish

Page 37

49. Zachariah Mitchel
50. William Johnston
51. Robert Elliston
52. Robert Gordon
53. Robert Longmire
54. David Jones
55. Thompson Hedgepith
56. Bewdie Howard
57. William Gordon
58. James G. Tate
59. Lervey Pettiford
60. John T. Peace
61. Thomas House
62. Ransom Harris
63. Willie Grissom
64. Barnett Higgs
65. Edward Setton
66. Payton Madison
67. Samuel Persithe
68. Miston Freeman

69. Henry Jones
70. Henry Chambers
71. Benjamin H. Wortham
72. Jese [sic] Adcock
73. John Stephenson
74. Michael Christian
75. James Meddows
76. Samuel Clement
77. Wyat Cazart
78. William White

****

Tenth Company,
detached from
Person Regiment
No. 2 Returns

1. Sampson Glenn, Captain
2. John Glenn, Lieut.
3. Robert Williams, 2nd Lieut.
4. Solomon Pain, Ensign
5. Gabriel Davey, 1st Serg.
6. Edmond Dixson, 2nd Serg.
7 Hosea Fuller, 3rd Serg.
8. Lewis Ramsay
9. Phillip Singleton
10. Alexander Elixor
11. Asa Hudgins
12. William Nelums
13. Samuel Nipper
14. Phillip Day
15. John Cooper
16. Joseph Rogers
17. Isaac Vanhook
18. William W. Chambers
19. John Mann
20-. Robert Cochran
21. Hutchens Burton
22. John Rainey
23. Charles Ward
24. John R. Eskrige
25. William Gill
26 Giles Rogers
27. Jeremiah Stanfield
28. John W. Graves
29. Solomon Walker

****

30. William Jones
31. Jesse Bull
32. Thomas Lawson
33. Robert Mann
34. John Ingram
35. John Pullum
36. John Atkinson
37. James Branch, 4th Serg.
38. John Stanfield
39. Duncan Rose
40. Bird Walker
41. Thomas Gonlan
42. Thomas Dancey
43. Edmond Mitchel
44. David Nellum
45. Aron Chrisenburg
46. William Pope
47. William Singleton
48. Jeremiah Blanchard
49. Thomas Halley Burton
50. John Carton
51. James Mann
52. Jeremiah Rimer
53. John Filnlond
51. James Jacobs
55. William Buchannon
56. Leonard Morris
57. Vinson Tapp
58. John Ehnore
59. John Moore
60. David Lareson
61. John Fuller
tw. Walter Fuller
63. Reuben Conner
64. James Waddy
65. John Toler
66. Walter Buchannon

****

Eleventh Company,
detached from
Caswell Regiment

1. Joseph Benton, Captain
2. John Mitchell, Lieut.
3. John Lea, 2nd Lieut.

4. William B. Graves, Ensign
5. Allen Gunn
6. Joshua Hightower
7. Samuel Wood
8. Richard Jones
9. Armstead Watington
10. Carter Malone

Page 38

11. Goodwin Evans
12. Moses Simpson
13. Alexander Watson
14. Oliver Brintle
15. Hiram Parks
16. John Nighton
17. Tilmore Stone
18. William Night
19. William Martin
20. Lemuel Chilton
21. Isham Normand
22. Turner Nighton
23. Isaac Patterson
24. Robert Ware
25. Josiah Stanfield
26. Isaac West
27. Westly Normand
28. Richard Swift
29. Lewis Billard
30. Bartholomew Ellis
31. Thomas Fielder
32. Benjamin Cantrall
33. Henry Collier
34. John Brown
35. John Shackleford
36. Robert Bruce
37. Spencer Jackson
38. William Johnston
39. James Bruce
40. James Somers
41. John Badget
42. Eli Sharp
43. Hiram Wetherford
44. Daniel Morgan
45. Baldy Ramson
46. Edward Jones
47. Walter Brayfield

48. Hugh Howard
49. Francis Wattington
50. Henry Booker Hailey
51. Jepthah Parks
52. George Brooks
53. Jonathan B. Wattington
54. William H. Wattington
55. John Williams
56. James Scott
57. Parabo Brazwell
58. William Terrell
59. John H. Humphries
60. John Stadler
61. Haroway Swift
62. Joseph Burrough
63. Stewart Farley
64. George Randolph
65. Matthew Hubbard
66. William Kersey
67. Robert Stadler
68. Lewis Hall
69. Younger Hardwick
70 William Nipper
71. Edward Glare
72. Sandy Smith
73. Robert Wilson
74. William Fullington
75. James Johnston
76. William Harwell
77. Virgil M. Rainey
78. John B. Farley
79. Stephen Burton
80. William Gordon
81. Noel Burton
82. Benjamin Crider
83. James Atkins
84. Zenas Martin
85.   [blank]
86. Daniel Smith
87. Joshua Butler
88. Laban Hunt
89. William Singleton
90. Pleasant Rudd
91. Benjamin Loafmand

****

****

SIXTH REGIMENT

Detached from the
Eighth Brigade

John Martin, Lieut. Colonel
Commandant
George Lemmond, 1st Major
James Johnston, 2nd Major

****

First Company
detached from the
2nd Guilford Regiment

1. William Meats, Captain
2. William Dinkey, Lieut.
3. Grovenor Marsh, Ensign
4. Elias Prickhard
5. John Chance
6. Arthur Forbes, Sr.
7. Elijah Lingold
8. John Clark
9. Frederick Sheaver
10. David Story

Page 39

11. Andrew Law
12. Stephen Griffin
13. Reuben Anderson
14. Maxwell Wilson
15. Aron Sprouts
16. Jacob Wilker
17. John Barnhart
18. John J. Matthews
19. William Forster
20. Alanson Forster
21. Daniel Cobb
22. Ludwith Seabold
23. William Smith
24. Henry Swing
25. Henry Greason
26. David Glass
27. Henry Bowman
28. Henry Shaw

29. John Charles
30. John Shepperd
31. Lewis May
32. Christian Cline
33. Daniel Mitchel
34. William Tade
35. Shadrach White
36. Christian Isley
37. Peter Wamick
38. Bartin Garringer
39. Richard Fentress
40. John Wilson
41. Robert Elkins
42. Thomas Jackson
43. Joash Reynolds
44. Levin Sullivan
45. Obediah Leonard
46. Samon Wilson
47. Robert Parsons
48. Thomas Elkins
49. Solomon Ward
50. George Montgomery
51. William Jackson
52. Dempsey Whitney
53. James Leonard
54. John Howell
55. John Strickland
56. James Williams
57. John Thomas
58. Andrew Thomas
59. John Spoon, Jr.
60. Ebenezer Whitney
61. Thomas Lane
62. William Spoon
63. Samuel Herney
64. Isaac Leonard
65. Samuel Montgomery
66. Stewart Hardin
67. Benjamin Field
68. Daniel Kirkman
69. James Witherly
70. Thomas Lincheum
71. Johnston Alexander
72. Daniel Gladson
73. Robert Fields
74. Fisher B. Taylor
75. William Hacket

76. William Meed
77. Elias Bowen
78. Francis Wrightet
79. Gradathan Harper
80. Isaac Rolan
81. William Dunning
82. William Watson
83. Thomas Ross
84. Elijah Ward
85. John Buchannor
86. Charles Clemer
87. James Walker
83. Peter Wetherby
89. Wilkins Lucaus
90. John Starks, Jr.
91. Israel Brown

****

Second Company,
detached from the
1st Guilford Regiment

1. Samuel Hunter, Captain
2. Abraham Riples, 1st Lieut.
3. John Moore, 2nd Lieut.
4. Thomas Bevill, Ensign
5. Nicholas Ogborn, Cadet
6. Levy Ross, 1st Serg.
7. Thomas L. Moody, 2nd Serg.
8. Miat Carter, 3rd Serg.
9. Alexander Bevill, 4th Serg.
10. Phillip Bevill, 1st Corp.
11. James Cole, 2nd Corp.
12. Noel Parish, 3rd Corp.
13. Alfred Branner, 4th Corp.

Privates

14. Charles B. Harris
15. Henry Maga
16. Wilson Patterson
17. Kinchen Vaughan
18. John Osburn
19. Nathan Barham
20. Aron Walker
21. Parrum Ray

22. Payton Ray
23. Felix M. Bince
24. Elijah Beasel
25. Silion Turner
26. William Billingsby
27. Jonas Case
28. William Walker

Page 40

29. David Fairbanks
30. John Walker
31. Walker Dowet
32. Levin Canik
33. James Gaugh
34. Reuben Parish
35. Harbert Tatum
36. John Willy
37. George W. Bell
38. John Flemming
39. Enoch Tomlinson
40. James Nelson
41. Valentine Garoll
42. Caleb Lawrence
43. Edward Wilson
44. John Dork
45. David Lanin
46. Isaac Howlet
47. William Winchester
48. William Parmer
49. Thomas Maga
50. Charles Case
51. Reubin Garlick
52. Archibald Whitworth
53. Bryant Pearcy
54. Lodwick B. Wilson
55. Thomas Jackson
56. Robert H. Brinkle
57. William A. Stephens
58. David Archer
59. James Archer
60. Zenas Bunker
61. Peter Brown
62. Henry Reed
63. Thomas Dunning
64. John Pegg
65. David Beason

66. Jacob Lovell
67. William Shelly
68. George Middleton
69,. Jesse Pegg
70. Joab Pegg
71. Martin Pegg
72. Danut North
73. Absalom Williams
74. Jacob Riggins
75. Joseph Edoll
76. Hezekiah Lock
77. Robert Bevill
78. Moton Riggins
79. William Riggins
80. Thomas Hunt
81. Danil [sic] Barnell
82. Jacob Waggoner
83. Argis Suthard
84. John Kindle
85. Nathan Underwood
86. William Dunning
87. Valentine Waggoner
88. Isaac Lee
86. Malcomb Morrison
90. Andrew Cain
91. Wiat Lare
92. Silion Turner

****

Third Company,
detached from
Rockingham Regiment

1. William Lenmon, Captain
2. Reubin Lindsay, Lieut.
3. Thomas Galoway, Ensign
4. Jesse Vermillon, 1st Serg.
5. Elijah Thomas, 2nd Serg.

Privates

6. Enock Hinston
7. William Berwick
8. Robert Walker
9. Elvard Massey
10. Thomas Botts

11. William Husford
12.   [blank]
13. William W. Brown
14. James Hudson
15. Valentine Morgan
16. Robert Barnes
17. Pleasant Barnes
18. John Bondrant
19. Reece Watkins
20. William Griffith
21. Samuel Jelton
22. Zera Summers
23. Joseph Maye
24. Archills Wynn
25. William Henderson
26. James King
27. Matthew Covey
26. Peter Wall
29. Abram Jerald
30. James Young
31. Chesley Wooders
32. David Heron
33. Stewart Dramond
34. Joshua Jarralls
35. Reason Waters
36. James Sparks
37. Baldy Rice
38. Durham Pearce
39. William Sharp
40. Ambrose Joice
41. Pleasant Joice
42. Thomas Barfield
43. Thomas Elenor
41. Peter Horn
45. William Haynes
46. James Lemon
47. William Alexander
48. Bartlet Gregan

Page 41

49. Thomas Godsey
50. William Smothers
51. David Chadwell
52. Robert Hall
53. David Buchannon
54. William W. Burk

****

Fourth Company,
[Grenadiers]
detached from
Rockingham Regiment

1. James Campbell, Captain
2. William J. Mongus, Lieut.
3. David Barry, 2nd Lieut.
4. George Adkins, Ensign
5. William Wardlow, 1st Serg.
6. John Shivers, 2nd Serg.
7. George Cantrill, 3rd Serg.
8. Eli Coram, 4th Serg.
9. John H. Taylor, 1st Corp.
10. Morgan Lillard, 2nd Corp.
11. James H. Seales, 3rd Corp.
12. [blank]
13. Martin Jones, drummer
14. Richard Coram, fifer
15. John Serkin
16. Jeremiah Nichols
17. James W. Olington
18. William Grogan
19. William Mobly, Jr.
20. William Brown, Jr.
21. John Molesby
22. John Hancock
23. William Miller
24. John Wall, Jr.
25. Joseph Berry
26. Elijah Cantrill
27. Daniel Ellington, Jr.
28. Fedding Wright
29. Grieff Ellilngton
30. John Barry
31. Skipwith Wray
32. William Williams
33. Joseph Woldrige
34. Daniel Carter
35. Henry Miller
36. John Mount, Jr.
37. William Coram, Jr.
38. George Coffer
39. Davis Heron
40. James Wardlow

41. James Barry
42. John Sinclar, Jr.
43. Robert Cantrill
44. Lewis Dodson
45. John Cantrall
46. Daniel Forster
47. James Walker
48. Lelin Molenby
49. Frederick Miller
50. Edward Godsey
51. James Mackey
52. John Wellington
53. James Taylor
54. Jesse Thomas
55. Isaac Pitle
56. Pleasant Mount
57. Allen Caldwell
58. Thomas Wammot
59. John Jones
60. Lemiah King
61. John King
62. Edward Nunon
63. Joseph Asbrige, Jr.
64. John Powell
56. Matthias Mount, Jr.
66. William King
67. William S. Haney
68. James B. Rice
69. Robert S. Stewart
70. John Sims, Jr.
71. Zacha Lewis
72. Eli Young
73. Daniel Tucker
74. John Griffin
75. Reuben Grady, Jr.
76. Thomas Jarold
77. George Stewart
78. William Lewis
79. Robert Grady

****

Fifth Company,
detached from the
2nd Stokes Regiment

1. Alexander Moody, Captain

2. Thomas Yarrell, Lieut.
3. William G. Haynes, Ensign
4. Henry Fry
5. Thomas Westmoreland
6. James Cooper
7. William Cox
8. William Hubbart
9. James Hargrove
10. John Cox
11. William Dalton
12. Jesse Stewart
13. Henry Donbe
14. Henry Briggs
15. John Stofel
16. Jacob Teats
17. Peter Moses
18. Robert Hill
19. Samuel Aldrige
20. John Binkley
21. Henry Stipe
22. Leonard Conrad
23. Simon Croon
24. Jacob Miller, Sr.
25. Jacob Hixt
26. Elijah Purdon
27. Charles Anderson
28. Austin Smith
29. Charles Chitty
30. Christopher Zimmerman
31. Archibald Davis
32. William Boly Jack
33. Henry Hitner
34. John Hyer
35. Elisha Stator
36. Andrew Krowse
37. Abram Beck
38. Edward Tatom
39. Stephen Riddle
40. John Barr
41. John Rick
42. Joseph Holbrook
43. David Linvill
44. William Holbrook, Jr.
45. William Holbrook, Sr.
46. Willis Cooper
47. Daniel N. Repton
48. James Ham

49. James Reid
50. George Hubbard
51. John Wright
52. John Smith
53. George Kennemon
54. Jesse Swim
55. Kelan Pittcord
56. Campbell Sutton
57. Francis Jackson
58. John S. Leight
59. Asbury Arnett
60. James Crews
61. John Harald
62. William Beason
63. Daniel Huff
64. John McPherson
65. Solomon Fulp
66. Elijah Gerrell

****

Sixth Company,
detached from the
1st Stokes Regiment

1. William Goode, Captain
2. David Dalton, 1st Lieut.
3. Samuel Martin, Ensign
4. Robert Young
5. Berryman Knight
6. James Fountain
7. Joshua Southam
8. William Ward
9. Elijah Night
10. Richard Flynt
11. Bradford Vanter
12. James Marshal
13. William Smith
14. Michael Smith
15. William Riggs
16. Joel Smith
17. William Welch
18. Thomas Reddick
19. Benjamin Morgan
20. William Daggins
21. Richard Vernon
22. Samuel Heath

23. William Eads
24. William Sisk
25. Aurelua Woodrige
26. Thomas Westbrook
27. William Harris
28. Benjamin Haynes
30. Hezekiah Tore
30. William Oliver
31. Lambert Dodson
32. Henry Baker
33. William Cannon
34. Samuel Neil
35. Pillis [sic] Priddy
36. Lewis Tilly
37. James Young
38. Benjamin Hutchison
39. Thomas Wilkins
40. John Priddy
41. Elisha Vernon
42. Thomas Jinkins
43. James Griffin
44. Clifford Yates
45. George Wilkins
46. James Beasley
47. Joel Kitchum
48. Elisha Nelson
49. Lewis Bower
50. William Nelson
51. Benjamin Fry
52. Henry Bolling
53. Larkin Burge
51. Pleasant Bridgmore
55. Moses Hiett
56. William Gregory
57. Daniel Scotte
58. James Bavick
59. Isaac Jackson
60. Samuel Jackson
61. Christopher Sponse
62. James Eaton
63. Raleigh Darnold
64. Thomas Franklin
65. Solomon Spanehour
66. Joseph Zimmerman

Page 43

67. John Pratler
68. William Stone
69. Henry Alberly
70. Jesse Brown
71. Clisby Robertson
72. John Crammer
73. Jesse Childress
74. John Cook
75. John Segimore
76. James Walker
77. Mereday Bennet
78. Nicholas Frost

****

SEVENTH REGIMENT

Detached from the
7th and 11th Brigades

Jesse A Pearson, Lieut. Colonel
Commandant
David Kerr, 1st Major
John Still, 2nd Major
****

First Company,
detached from the
1st Rowan Regiment

1. Jacob Krider, Captain
2. Hugh McKnight, Lieut.
3. James Gelispee, Ensign
4. Fredrick Cauble
5. Henry Lippart
6. George Fisher
7. John Tinkle
8. Conrad Smitteds
9. Henry Casey
10. Jacob Lane
11. Daniel Brown
12. Pleasant Tapley
13. Sion Keeth
14. James Ross
15. Phillip Hoofman
16. John Kastor
17. William Snow

18. Solomon Miller
19. Charles Ryer
20. George Hodge
21. John Ross, Sr.
22. Mertin Miller
23. Mertin Happner
24. Andrew Holshouse, Jr.
25. Henry Caulans
26. Adam Cauble
27. John Lingle
28. John Lane
29. John Clutz
30. Jacob Lingle
31. Meihall Delow
32. Phillips Carter
33. Jacob Skussing
34. Peter Deal
35. Peter Albright
36. Henry Sudler
37. Leonard Craigh
38. John Hauston
39. Hiram Davidson
40. Edward Heulin
41. John Rudisil
42. John Smith
43. Morris Pinkston
44. Peter M. Smith
45. William H. Horoh
46. John Utzman
47. George Utzman
48. Jacob Utzman
49. Jesse James
50. William Dickson
51. Robert Wood
52. John Wood
53. Ralph Kasier
54. David Ewell
55. Eps Robertson
56. Skiles Foster
57. Daniel Cress
58. John B. Lonona
59. Daniel Shuford
60. John Holshouser
61. George Withellens
62. Moses Lamb
53. John Lance
64. Phillip Lytiker

65. Samuel Felker
66. Peter Upright
67. Jacob Rary
68. Malikiah Bowers
69. Henry Singenwinder
70. Andrew Kindcade
71. James Gleen
72. Samuel Rice
73. Samuel Kincade
74. Thomas Huston
75. William Bar
76. William Cowin
77. John Patterson
78. Isaac Cowie

Page 44

****

Second Company,
detached from the
2nd Rowan Regiment

1. Henry Katts, Captain
2. John Beard, Lieut.
3. James Lowe, Ensign
4. Julius Strange, 1st Serg.
5. Barnabas Bowers, 2nd Serg.
6. John Brinkhart, 3rd Serg.
7. Wilson Wiseman, 4th Serg.
8. Jacob Stoner, 1st Corp.
9. Thomas Ceicel, 2nd Corp.
10. Elijah Northern, 3rd Corp.
11. Even Thomas, 4th Corp.
12. James Wiseman, drummer
13. Jacob Bringle, fifer

Privates

14. James Silvers
15. Benjamin Sineanger
16. Josiah Cuningam
17. Adam Hendrick
18. George Birkhart
19. Christian Sink
20. Alfred Owens
21. Shadrick Hill

22. Christian Lucanbill
23. George Bowers
24. George Myers
25. Henry Hepler
26. John Myers, Sr.
27. James Jones
28. James Moss
29. Bryant Fry
30. Abram Shular
31. Abraham Hunt
32. Oliver Hunt
33. Jonathan Davis
34. Michel Myers
35. Samuel Williams
36. John Sims
37. Edmond McCarn
38. Jesse Lane
39. Joseph Warford
40. Barnard Living
41. Thomas Workman
42. William Workman
43. Peter Livenger
44. Phillip Headrick
45. Micajah Hill
46. Smith Hill
47. Abram Johnston
48. Isaiah Hicks
49. James Lacey
50. Zachariah Coggins
51. Thomas Davis
52. Lewis Beard
53. James Ziveley
54. John Stoutenberg
55. Barzilla McBride
56. John Delow
57. John B. Crump
58. James Owen
59. Walter Northern
60. Isaac Grist
61. Moses Holmes
62. John Williams
63. James Gallimore
64. James Green
65. Charles Savage
66. Henry Cline
67. Phillip Cline
68. Cornelius Smith

****

69. Jonathan Walk
70. David Bierly
71. Phillip Willis
72. Reuben Nunby

****

Third Company,
detached from the
3rd Rowan Regiment

1. John Frost, Captain
2. William Duffy, Lieut.
3. Charles Anderson, Ensign
4. James Wilson, 1st Serg.
5. John Ford, 2nd Serg.
6. James Gamble, 34rd Serg.
7. Samuel Dial, 4th Serg.
8. William Wiatt, 1st Corp.
9. Samuel Frost, 2nd Corp.
10. John Hodgers, 3rd Corp.
11. William Hutson, 4th Corp.
12. James Warren, drummer
13. Samuel McGire, fifer

Privates

14. William Bissent
15. Daniel Lark
16. George Claybrook
17. Thomas Horn
18. Howell Horn
19. William Chapman
20 Conel James
21. Isaac James
22. Juley Smith
23. Caleb Brock
24. Edward Williams
25. Richard Haxwood
26. Robert Clark
27. Thomas Smith
28. Oliver Griffin
29. Richard Jarvis
30. John Speak
31. Dennis Jarvis
32. Clare Maxlin
33. Thomas Gears

34. Baker Johnston

Page 45

35. Elwin Howard
36. James Orton
37. Richard Luckey
38. Henry Luckey
39. Gustavous Boswell
40. Francis Kinshaw
41. Teneson Cheshen
42. Georg Taylor
43. Thomas Taylor
44. Thomas Leach
45. Richard Jones
46. Joseph Lewis
47. Brice W. Isam
48. William Brogdon
49. Alfred Brogdon
50. Jonathan West
51. John Becketh
52. Daniel Cane
53. Virtue Sweat
54. Richbell Mott
55. Samuel Beaman
56. Jacob Newton
57, William K. Aire
58. Jacob Gawood
59. Isaac Gawood
60. Edward Buckner, Jr.
61. Zachariah Booth
62. James Owens
63. Aron Tucker
64. Enoch Chamberlain
65. David Hampton
66.   [blank]
67. James Park
68. John Douthet
69. Thomas Gentle
70. Freeman Bate
71. George Smith
72. John James
73. Zachariah Tenneyhill
74. Christopher Erwin
75. John Graham
76. John Buck
77. Andrew Morrison

78. Arthur Smith

****

Fourth Company,
detached from the
4th Rowan Regiment

1. Thomas M. Times, Captain
2. Jones Enoch, Lieut.
3. George Lowry, Ensign
4. John Wilborn, 1st Serg.
5. Micajah Eagle, 2nd Serg.
5. William Cecill, 3rd Serg.
7. Benjamin Pain, 4th Serg.
8. George Snider, Jr., 1st Corp.
9. Brummel Sap, 2nd Corp.
10. George Kelly, 3rd Corp.
11. Edmond Cawil, 4th Corp.
12. John Farrington, drummer
13. Micajah Haworth, fifer

Privates

14. George Saner
15. Jacob Douthit
16. Abraham Brindle
17. Ransom Ellis
18. David Marklan
19. Abner Brown
20. William Swim
21. James Kelly
22. Phillip Smith
23. Daniel Chriswell
21. Jaret Wood
25. Jeremiah Haworth
26. William Welborn
27. John Cecill
28. Obadiah Twidwell
29. William Twonay
30.. Samuel Cecil
31. Daniel Waworth
32. Meredith Pearce
33. Barnabas Idol
31. Hugh Robertson
35. Matthias Idol
36. John Donaway

37. Jacob Miller
38. Francis Barncastle
39. Henry Hill
40. Christian Fash
41. Henry James
42. Larkin Scott
43. John Oaks
44. Joseph Farabee
45. Andrew Clinard
46. Abraham Everitt
47. William Pain
48. Samuel Weer
49. Samuel Spurgia
50. William Weer
51. Jacob Williams
52. John Merick
53. Adam Frits
54. David Darr
55. Henry Long
56. John Grub
57. Jacob Averhart
58. Jacob Sowens
59. Jacob Grub
60. James Skider
61. George Myers
62. Jacob Kesler
63. Richard Graham
61. Macoy Gallispie
65. Daniel Lynch
66. Moses Thompson
67. Jonathan Burns
68. James McLaughlen

Page 46

69. Richard Foster
70. Andrew Morrison
71. Caleb Webb
72. William Dickey
73. John Hugey
74. Andrew Renshaw
75. William Summers

****

Fifth Company,
detached from

Iredell Regiment

1. John Moody, Captain
2. William Carson, Lieut.
3. William Moody, Ensign
4. Thomas Prather, 1st Serg.
5. Caleb Conbey, 2nd Serg.
6. Joseph Duporster, 3rd Serg.
7. Samuel Hayes, 4th Serg.
8. Heary Marshall, 1st Corp.
9. Milus Privitt, 2nd Corp.
10, David Fox, 3rd Corp.
11. Richard Privitt, 4th Corp.
12. Richard Cook, drummer
13. Harris Swivit, fifer

Privates

14. William Millsaps
15. William Martin
16. William Gordon
17. James Martin
18. Samuel McKoy
19. George W. Robertson
20. Erwin Privitt
21. George Lackey
22. Richard Sparks
23. William Blackenship
24. Seke [?] Harris
25. John Teague
26. James Lack
27. Walter Beill
28. John Cash
29. Henzy Giddens
30. Thomas Green
31. James Templeton
32. Samuel Templeton
33. Hugh B. King
34. Joseph Edson
35. John McConnel
36. Solomon Claywell
37. Samuel Mitchel
38. Hugh Currant
39. Greenbury Haire
40. John Hath
41. Reuben Barnrd
42. Turner Welch

43. Ashiey Johnston
44. John Rector
45. Bleasant [sic] Owen
46. Benjamin Moody
47. Bresom Hez'ah
48. Benjamin Bently
49. Henry Carson
50. John M. Clerland
51. Nathan Baker
52. Michael Tague
53. Lovet Phelps
54. Abram Cook
55. Samuel Henderson
56. William Looper
57. Allison Gapp
58. Richard Mears
59. Hiram Flecher
60. Thomas Lovelus
61. Reasoon Beill
62. Elias Lazenbury
63. Thomas Galloway
64. Alexander Read
65. Andrew Well
66. Joseph Moon
67. John Young
68. Phillip Phillips
69. Randolph Roads
70. Benjamin Brown
71. Richard Booker
72. Henry Buck
73. Joseph Donaldson
74. George Masters
75. Samuel Hart

****

Sixth Company,
detached from
Iredell Regiment

1. Neil McCoy, Captain
2. Abram Nelson, Lieut.
3. Alexander McCoy, Ensign
4. Thomas Davidson, 1st Serg.
5. James Jones, 2nd Serg.
6. William Freeland, 3rd Serg.
7.   [blank]

8. Andrew Kilpatrick, 4th Serg.
9. Benjamin Sterns, 1st Corp.
10. John Fenster, 2nd Corp.
    Elijah Tucker, 3rd Corp.
11. Thomas Campbell, 4th Corp.
12. Daniel Rector, drummer
13. William Arthur, fifer
14. George L. Davidson
15. Thomas Crawford
16. Robert Allison
17. Theophilus Simonton
18. Theophilus Falls
19. John Cleton
20. John Parker
21. John Beil
22. John Murdock
23. Ephraim Ewin
24. James Parker
25. William Preil

Page 47

26. James Templeton
27. Henry Conner
28. Robert Westmoreland
29. David McCrery
30. Andrew Caldwell
31. Joseph Rogers
32. Joseph Templeton
33. Robert Rankin
34. Edmond Taylor
35. Robert M. Hughs
36. William Horsliam
37. John Scott
38. Neil Brawlie, Jr.
39. Robert West
40. David Mulholland
41. David Currell
42. John Bector
43. Michel White
44. Hezekiah Grey
45. Neil McCastle
46. William Wintosh
47. Thomas Morrison
48. David Moore
49. Archibald Essleman
50. Samuel McMillan

51. John Wintosh
52. Alexander Wintosh
53. Joseph Alexander
54. Mosey Stephenson
55. John Houp
56. James Hill
57. Samuel Freeland
58. James Freeland
59. Thomas Morrison
60. Andrew Watts
61. Andrew Morrison
62. Samuel Wah
63. John Morrison
64. Alexander Kilpatrick
65. George Braddy
66. And'w McAdams
67. Joel Bruce
68. Hugh Copland
69. David Pottts
70. Levi Moore
71. Laban Bracker
72. Ninian Steel, Sr.
73. Thomas Archibald
74. John Gay
75. Reason Bell
76. John Hait
77. Samuel Chambers

****

Seventh Company,
detached from the
1st Mecklenburg Regiment

1. Joseph Douglass, Captain
2. William M. Kary, Lieut.
3. William Walker, Ensign
4. Hamden Brevard, 1st Serg.
5. David Gibony, 2nd Serg.
6. Samuel Brown, 3rd Serg.
7. William M. Barrett, 4th Serg.
8. Thomas Allen, 1st Corp.'
9. John Solon, 2nd Corp.
10. Isaac V. Pitt, 3rd Corp.
11. Robert Duchworth, 4th Corp.
12. Adam Harrison
13. Hugh Wiley

14. James Moore
15. John Caldwell
16. Junius Hood
17. David Alexander
18. James Parker
19. Matthew Wallace
20. Thomas McRae
21. John Phillips
22. Henry Farr
23. Hugh Todd
24. Hugh Elliott
25. Arthur Jimison
26. Nicholas Parish
27. Andrew Walker
28. Upton Roden
29. David B. Wilson
30. Joseph Lore
31. Isaac Beaty
32. Joseph Bingham
33. William Sharply
34. Hugh Greggs
35. Francis Erwin
36. Richard Mason
37. John B. Elliott
38. John L. Darnell
39. William Camerson
40. Samuel J. Hutchison
41. Joshua Clark
42. James Hutchison
43. John McLure
44. John Darnell
45. Benjamin Thompson
46. Alexander Moore
47. Alexander Smith
48. William Darnel
49. David Darnel
50. Jacob I. Cunnigham [sic]
51. Hugh Harris
52. Eli Alexander
53. Mitchel Johnston
54. Allen Lucas
55. William Downy
56. Samuel Graham
57. Will Bushbey
58. Thomas Shepherd
59. Allen Sloan
60. John Fat

Page 48

61. Andrew M. Lane
62. Alexander Washam
63. Howard Weir
64. William Sullivan
65. John Ferret, Sr.
66. David Henderson
67. Arthur Garretson
68. Will Robertson
69. James Simmimer
70. Drury Solomon
71. Hugh Holmes
72. Thomas McIlie
73. Hugh Stevenson
74. William Munteeth
75. Will Scott
76. Palau Alexander

****

Eight Company,
detached from the
2nd Mecklenburg Regiment

1. Robert Wood, Captain
2. Jacob Shaver, 1st Lieut.
3. Peter Mape, 2nd Lieut.
4. John Wilson, Ensign
5. William Flenigan, 1st Serg.
6. John Hooker, 2nd Serg.
7 John Barnes, 3rd Serg.
8. James Watson, 4th Serg.
9. John Hammuns, 1st Corp.
10. Obed Dafter, 2nd Corp.
11. Will John, 3rd Corp.
12. Charles Hart, 4th Corp.
13. Allen Stewart, drummer
14. John Rice, fifer

Privates

15. James Walker
16. John Brown
17. Robert Flenigan
18. William Sharp
19. Elias Flenigan

20. Randolph Cheek
21. Samuel E. Flanigan [sic]
22. Elias McCallok
23. Andrew Stewart
24. Samuel Wiley
25. Ash John
26. Cunninghan [sic] Sharp
27. John Wiat
28. John Black
29. Paten Bambow
30. Joseph Bryan
31. Antheris Purvius
32. Henry Clontz
33. Charles Crowell
31. John Cathberton
35. Wm. L. Lemmond
36. John Flow
37. Jacob Starns
38. Robert Boid
39. Daniel McLoyd
40. Roderick McReley
41. Moses Stanford
42. Allen Broom
43. Charles Lancey
44. John None
45. Brelon Belk
46. Samuel Holden
47. Valentine Prifly
48. Michael Flenigan
49. Henry Moser
50. Eli Coughran
51. James Robertson
52. William Redford
53. Jesse Yandles
54. Will Rea
55. Thomas Henley
56. Samuel Ormand
57. John Fobes
58. Adam Ormand
59. Lewis Howard
60. John McCorkle
61. Will U. Irvey
62. James Thompson
63. John Long
64. Thomas Miller
65. Samuel Givens
66. William Martin

67. Robert Shannon
68. William Barns
69. Solomon Morris
70. William Pirant
71. William Pool

****

Ninth Company,
detached from the
2nd Mecklenburg Regiment

1. John Garretson, Captain
2. Isaac Wiley, Lieut.
3. Natheil Sims, Ensign
4. Archibald Sawyer, 1st Serg.
5. Ire B. Dixon, 2nd Serg.
6. William Smith, 3rd Serg.
7. Joro Kimmons, 4th Serg.
8. William Mays, 1st Corp.
9. John Holbrooks, 2nd Corp.
10. Frederick Kiser, 3rd Corp.
11. Andrew M. Grady, 4th Corp.
12. George Kemy, drummer
13. John Jaccour, fifer

Privates

14. John Irwin
15. Sam'l H. Harris
16. James Ross
17. Houston Harris
18. John Alexander

Page 49

19. Isaac Harris
20. Laid Alexander
21. Cyrus Campbell
22. Robert M. Cochran
23. Jno. Morrison
24. Robert C. Morrison
25. Hugh McCain
26. Daniel Bost
27. Jacob House
28. Henry Miller
29. Jacob Rinehart

****

30. Henry Rowe
31. Matthias Bost
32. Michel Owrey
33. John Light
34. Robert Carrigan, Sr.
35. Robert Carrigan, Jr.
36. Theophilus Gayler
37. John Carrell
38. Joseph Hamilton
39. David Houston
40. Andrew Neele
41. James Neele
42. George Flemming
43. Martin, Icehour
44. George Dove
45. William Smith
46. George Linker
47. Daniel Smith
48. John Barnhard
49. Son Fink
50. Andrew Carriher
51. Phillip Fink
52. John S. Taylous
53. John Johnston
54. Rufus Johnston
55. David H. Black
56. John Black
57. Johnston N. Biggers
58. William Newit
59. George Right
60. Josiah Gilmore
61. Edward Martin
62. William Kelly
63. William Wines
64. Ebaneser Keelough
65. James Hall
66. Jacob Gangus
67. John Goodnight
68. Adam Freeze
69. John Fereland
70. John Clisk
71. Jesse Chaple
72. Reuben Sneed
73. John Goodman
74. James McGraw
75. Charles Walter
76. Martin Shank

77. Daniel Luther
78. Jacob Simmon

****

Tenth Company,
detached from
Montgomery Regiment

1. Elijah Hartam, Captain
2. William Moor, Lieut.
3. Hardy Morgan, 2nd Lieut.
4. Wyett Scott
5. Hamlin Freeman
6. Stephen Morton
7. William Folks
8. Sion Pearce
9. William Gillan
10. Jacob Cockram
11. Allen McKackie
12. James Hellen
13. Hector McKinsie
14. Mathew Ingram
15. Joseph Killis
16. Nimrod Bradley
17. Robert B. Wood
18. Richard Urry
19. William Thompson
20. William Trusty
21. William Eights
22. Daniel Hurley
23. Robert Berton
24. James Wiot [?]
25. James Stephens
26. Zachariah Collins
27. William Johnston
28. [blank]
29. Etheldred Blake
30. Micajah Rogers
31. Abraham Cochran
32. Daugle McDuffy
33. Colin Pall
34. Joseph Blake
35. Benjamin Johnston
36. Hennith McKinsey
37. Myerdoh Loyd
38. Abel Rolan

39. John McRae
40. Aulas McCalar
41. Patrick Thompson
42. Joseph Haltom
43. Marrel Suggs
44. James Bennett
45. David Blallock
46. William Morgan
47. Nathaniel Mekins
48. John Still
49. William Morton
50. William Holton
51. George Heair
52. Rolen Crump

Page 50

53. Wiley Harris
54. John Crump, Jr.
55. West Harris, Jr.
56. Allen Harris
57. Ezekiel Hearn
58. Daniel Redwine
59. William Hurley
60. Banister Porter
61. Frederick Randle
62. John Smith
63. John Durgan
64. Jeptha Milton
65. John Merrett
66. Abram Trusty
67. Robert G. Steele
68. James Balton
69. Joseph Morgan
70. Ephraim Coker
71. Major Russell
72. Francis Jordan
73. Brantly H. Gallihan
74. Terrel Blalock
75. Drury Bennett
76. [blank]
77. Reuben Hicks
78. George Martin
79. John Braves
80. Green Harris
81. Thomas Morris, Jr.
82. Eli Harris, son of J [?]

83. William Hansen
84. Deray [?] Jones
85. John Hancock
86. Jesse Bell
87. Elijah Grisham
88. Elias Morris
80. John Cotton
90. William Harris, son of K [?]
91. David Tillman
92. Nelson Smith
93. John Poplin

****

EIGHTH REGIMENT

detached from the
9th, 10th and 15th Brigades

Nathan Horton, Lieut. Colonel
Commandant
Merritt Burgin, 1st Major
Samuel Davidson, 2nd Major

First Company,
detached from the
1st Surry Regiment

1. William McCraw, Captain
2. John Shipp, 1st Lieut.
3. Bernard Franklin, 2nd Lieut.
4. William Potter, Ensign
5. Eleon G. Moore, Cadet

Privates

6. Bailey Johnston
7. Micajah Reaves
8. Watson Holifield
9. Richard Reaves
10. Ezekiel Desern
11. William Holder
12. Charles Combs
13. John Parish
14. Charles Bryant
15. David Gerwin
16. Ralph Holifield

17. Joseph Cartwright
18. Joseph Muncas
19. Seward McCraw
20. Elijah Muncas
21. Jesse Howard
22. Solomon Griffith
23. Benjamin Baker
24. Isaac Pucket
25. Martin Forkner
26. Joshua Garrett
27. Samuel Laurence
28. William Smallwood
29. John Griffith
30. Samuel McCraw
31. Calvin Robertson
32. Henry Sparger
33. Isaac Holtrooks
34. Daniel Reece
35. Lewis Raper
36. Gentry Hodges
37. William Hodges
38. John Ryan
39. Thomas Ketchum
40. William Vest
41. Thomas Bray
42. Benjamin Cummin
43. Dudley Reynolds
44. Daniel Barker
45. Thomas A. Ward
46. Ephraim Stone
47. Jonathan Reynols [sic]
48. John Watson
49. James Graves
60. Moses Smith
51. Peter Graves
52. Richard White
53. Robert Baber
54. Conway Stone

****
Page 51

Second Company,
detached from the
2nd Surry Regiment

1. Samuel Speer, Captain

2. Thomas D. Kelley, 1st Lieut.
3. Bowen Whitlock, Ensign
4. John Kelly, Jr. Cadet

Privates

5. William D. Kelley
6. Benjamin Howard
7. Edmond Swenny
8. William Frady
9. William Spelman
10. Allen Willard
11. Asa Dinkins
12. Isaac Jones
13. Francis Moreland
14. Samuel Goff
15. Thomas Oliver
16. Strangerman Johnston
17. Abraham Wooten
18. Joshua Angel
19. David Anthony
20. Jesse Felbet
21. John Parks
22. Thomas Osbourn
23. Stephen Wood
24. Solomon Johnston
25. Joseph Phinney
26. William Masters
27. James Harris
28. William Sparks
29. Joel Patterson
30. Daniel Teasly
31. George Speer
32. Robert Martin
33. Robert Lyon
34. Thomas Dyal
35. James Lakey
36. Archer Poindexter
37. Joseph Lovill
38. Edward Lovill
39. John Logan
40. Joshua Pumm
41. William Pigg
42. Jacob Shouse
43. Joseph Hickman
44. Ephraim Williams
45. Jonathan Pendry

46. John Martin
47. Jesse Chinn
48. Garret Mahaly
49. James Pilcher
50. William Brown.
51. Johnston Lindsay
52. Wilie Dickinson
53. John McDonald
54. Thomas Kell
55. Richard Cook
56. Jonathan Rosea
57. William Holloman
58. John Sutliff

****

Third Company,
detached from
Wilkes Regiment

1. Walter R. Lanoir, Captain
2. Michel Swain, 1st Lieut.
3. Lewis Carlton, Ensign
4. William Ferguson
5. James Davis
6. Thomas Lands
7. Aron Fox
8. Jesse Cronch
9. Thomas Carlton
10. William Brookshire
11. Smith Ferguson
12. Joseph Howard
13. Isaac Vanderpool
14. David Robertson
15. Clifton Keeton
16. Charles Ragen
17. Elijah Dyer
18. Alexander Brown
19. John Vannoy
20. William Gullet
21. William Goforth
22. Francis Fox
23. David Hickerson
24. Ebenezer Castle
25. John Japs [? Hays]
26. David Laird
27. Adam Kilby

28. Joel Foster
29. John N. Broyhill
30. William Morgan
31. John Hall
32. Charles Main
33. Joshua Morgan
34. William Broyhill
35. Joel Dyer
36. William Kilby
37. Abner Trebble
38. Lewis Cash
39. Martin Baker
40. John Eversale
41. William Bingham
42. Laban Adams
43. Aron Wiatt
44. Enoch Chapman
45. Edmond Dorson
46. Thomas Craton
47. James Brown
48. Stephen Roberts
49. Joseph Teague
50. John Carnest

Page 52

51. Thomas Crumpton
52. Achillis Stipp
53. William Alloway
54. Jeremiah Hendrikson
55. Richard Hawkins

****

Fourth Company,
detached from
Wilkes Regiment

1. James Martin, Captain
2. Moses East, Lieut.
3. James Benge, Ensign
4. Benjamin Rose
5. John Martin
6. Sterling Rose
7. Henry Welton
8. William Curby
9. William Denny

10. Thomas Ellis
11. Edmund Bryan
12. Isaac Martin
13. John Green
14. William Green
15. Joseph Johnson
16. Abel Nichilson
17. William McBride
18. James McBride
19. Joseph Longbottom
20. Ephraim Nichilson
21. John Sale
22. Hyram Ryan
23. Barney Carter
24. David Caperham
25. John Cockerham
26. Stephen Gentle
27. Richmond Gordon
28. John Shoemaker
29. John Hawkins
30. Isaac Adams
31. Thomas Keelin
32. Henry Trusty
33. John Brooks
34. Gorden Chavers
35. Joseph James
36. James Matthews
37. Eli Brown
38. William Underwood
39. George Combs
40. Benjamin Gamble
41. George Laurence
42. Henry Gamble
43. Benjamin Adams
44. John Adams
45. James Tolby
46. Thomas Roberts
47. Willis Alexander
48. John Brown
49. John Blackburn
50. Aron McDaniel
51. John Chustley
52. Jeremiah Abshire
53. John Abshire
54. William Donally
55. Colin Edwards
56. George Brown

****

Fifth Company,
detached from
Ashe Regiment

1. William Horton, Captain
2. Squire Wilcoxen, Lieut.
3. Phillip Baker, Ensign
4. William Johnston
5. John Kerby
6. William Tolliver
7. Stephen Crow
8. Moses McBride
9. David Maxfield
10. James McMillan
11. James Hart
12. Jacob Stamper
13. Alexander Cox
14. John Price
15. Elijah Smith
16. William Ellison
17. Edward Hart
18. Thomas Collins
19. Matthias Williams
20. Archibald Blankinship
21. William Baker
22. George Crider
23. Samuel Wilcoxen
24. David Horton
25. Joseph Green
26. Lewis Tarckler
27. James Fatam
28. John Bear
29. Henry Holoclaw
30. Henry Holsclaw
31. Benjamin Chambers, fifter

****

Sixth Company,
detached from
1st Lincoln Regiment

1. Edward Boyd, Captain
2. Edwin S. Gingles, Lieut
3. John Hill, Ensign

4. Mason Harwell, 1st Serg.
5. Joshua Abernathy, 2nd Serg.
6. David Linebarge, Corp.

Page 53

7. John Club, Corp.
8. Samuel Harwell
9. Gardner Merys
10. Levi Perkins
11. Frederick Abernasty [sic]
12. Thomas Long
13. Michel Sides
14. Henry Eddlemon
15. Moses Abernathy
16. [no listing]
17. Jacob Eddman
18. Joseph Burk
19. Peter Evans
20. George Club, Jr.
21. Ezekiel Abernathy
22. James McGinnis
23. Robert Ramsey
24. Martin Gruson
25. Robert McCullock
26. Henry Holland
27. Matthew Holland, Jr.
28. William Robinson, Jr.
29. Robert Huggins, Jr.
30. James Rhodes
31. David Rine, Jr.
32. John Ryne
33. Joseph Senter
34. Frederick Hovis
35. Jacob Dutcherow
36. Jonathan Nardike
37. Nicholas Dillin
38. John Friday
39. Samuel Armstrong
40. Matthew Armstrong
41. John Neagle
42. Alexander Irwin
43. George Oliver
44. William Oliver
45. John Henderson
46. William Hawkins
47. John Linebarger

48. Archibald Cathy
49. Daniel Morrison
50. Alexander Moore
51. Adam Clominger, Jr.
52. Jonathan West
53. George Hager
54. William Stephenson
55. Thomas Henry
56. Andrew Forguson
57. William Falls
58. Samuel Carson
59. John Hager
60. Daniel Tucker
61. Robert Beale
62. Levi Sides
53. William Hinkle
64. William Hunt
65. John Blalock
66. John Little
67. George Ferguson, Serg.
68. Miles Farrer, Serg.
69. Sherod Little, Corp.
70. John Ganny, Corp.

****

Seventh Company,
detached from the
1st Lincoln Regiment

1. Henry Rudasil, Captain
2. Robert Oats, Lieut.
3. Phillip Hain, Ensign
4. Moses Herring, 1st Serg.
5. Peter Crites, 2nd Serg.
6. Christopher Lewis, 3rd Serg.
7. William Fullbright, 4th Serg.
8. Abraham Wiatt, Corp.
9. Linas Sanford, 2nd Corp.
10. David Cline, 3rd Corp.
11. Samuel Edgin, 4th Corp.

Privates

12. John Master
13. John Tucker
14. Jepeth Shaw

15. James Clark
16. Henry Barclay
17. Jesse Wheeler
18. John Ballard
19. George Sifford
20. Menucan Shelton
21. George Freet
22. William Sifford
23. Isaac Flemming
24. John Sifford
25. Gatlip Sifford
26. Adam Hopppis
27. Martin Delinger
28. Robert Williams
29. William Lowe
30. Iasiah [sic] Abernathy
31. Drury Baggett
32. Abram Baggett
33. Absalom Bungarder
34. George Moore
35. William Walker
36. Nicholas Laurence
37. Thomas Ash
38. Moses Bungarner
39. Colbert Sherrell
40. Isaac Roberson
41. Jacob Burns
42. John Caldwell
43. Frederick Summey
44. Jacob Fingo
45. Elias Plot
46. Henry Chipperd
47. Christopher Hoffman
48. Jacob Isaac
49. Jacob Dunsill
50. Solomon Cline

Page 54

51. Elijah Call
52. John Wilson
53. Alfred Moore
51. Aron Moore
55. William Johnston
56. Francis Asbury
57. John Kistler
58. James Martin

59. Samuel Turner
60. John Brim
61. Thomas Hannon
62. Edward Sneed
63. William Bennett
64. Jacob Miller
65. Robert Wilson
66. John Crage
67. John Murphy
68. James Lindsay
69. Adam Speight
70. Christy Speight

****

Eighth Company,
detached from the
2nd Lincoln Regiment

1. George Hoffman, Captain
2. David Bailey, Lieut.
3. Daniel Cline, Ensign
4. John Jarrall, 1st Seerg.
5. Jacob Conner, 2nd Serg.
6. Thomas Bandy, 3rd Serg.
7. Robert H. Simpson, 4th Serg.
8. Phillip Fry, 1st Corp.
9. Thomas Simpson, 2nd Corp.
10. John Norman, 3rd Corp.
11. Christopher Acer, 4th Corp.
12. Daniel Shuford, Jr.
13. Daniel Whitenet, Jr.
14. Adolph Fodz
15. Michel Prolst
16. David Bost
17. John German
18. Andrew Sieter
19. Abram Kilyon
20. Jacob Kink
21. Daniel Peterson
22. Abraham Sieter
23. George Fisher
24. Payton Vaughan
25. Conrad Yoder
26. George Mosteller
27. Silas Wilson
28. Jacob Therue

29. George McEntosh
30. Thomas Huskey
31. Reuben Copelin
32. William Harlson
33. Peter Harman
34. Epraim [sic] Davis
35. James Patterson
36. Samuel Gladdon
37. Benjamin Waterson
38. William Scoggin
39. Solomon Harmon
40. Abner Camp
41. David Wier
42. Perry G. Reynols
43. Uell Reynolds
44. John Rudaice
45. John Turner
46. Cyrus Peed
47. Isaac Williams
48. Benjamin Edwards
49. Jacob Raugh
50. Michael Hepner
51. John Miller
52. John Taylor
53. William Caldwell
54. William Hull
55. William Bird
56. William Carrol
57. John Trout
58. Peter Howzer
59. Jacob Spengler
60. James Center
61. John Eders
62. Wiley Harris
63. John Harvener
64. Robert Watts
65. Joseph Kyson
66. Thomas Laming
67. Adam Husslatter
68. Peter Beem
69. John Vickers
780. Joseph Carpenter
71. Peter Kiser

****

Ninth Company,

****

detached from the
1st Rutherford Regiment

1. John Goodbread, Captain
2. Robert Baker, Lieut.
3. John H. Crow, Ensign
4. Michael Hudlow, 1st Serg.
5. Jesse Milton, 2nd Serg.
6. Robert Porter, 3rd Serg.
7. Edward Elms, 4th Serg.
8. William McCurry, 1st Corp.
9. James Griffy, 2nd Corp.
10. Littleton Parram, 3rd Corp.
11. Charles Chitwood, 4th Corp.

Privates

12. Samuel Campbell
13. Joseph Harmon
14. Benjamin M. Gakey

Page 55

15. Leonard Painter
16. Coleby Sutton
17. William Wood
18. Jeremiah Bennik
19. Thomas Davis
20. William Early
21. Richard Fortune
22. William Fortune
23. Abner Green
24. Henry Norbet
25. Archibald Weeks
26. Queen Hicks
27. Daniel Hicks
28. Christy Mooney
29. Samuel Miltoe
30. John Jones
31. William Milton
32. James Sargent
33. James Thompson
34. John Guffy
35. John Walker
36. Julias Logan
37. William Carson
38. James Dalton

39. Joseph Hunter
40. William Watson
41. George Fluman
42. William Freeman
43. William Vickers
44. William Adain
45. Jonathan Hill
46. Edward F. Fennington
47. Peter Coon
48. John Ownley
49. William Fluman
50. Thomas Williams
51. Summons Bradley
52. Terry Bradley
53. Isaiah Wadkins
54. Hiram Dunkin

****

Tenth Company,
detached from the
2nd Rutherford Regiment

1. Abram Irvine, Captain
2. John Craw, Lieut.
3. John Alexander, Ensign
4. Isom Weather, 1st Serg.
5. William Harder, 2nd Serg.
6. Abner Wessen, 3rd Serg.
7. John Williams, 4th Serg.
8. James Lemons, 1st Corp.
9. Mark Harder, 2nd Corp.
10. James Lefever, 3rd Corp.
11. Archibald Moore, 4th Corp.

Privates

12. Henry Johnston
13. Jacob Smith
14. John Levan
15. Hillery Scott
16. Larkin Lea
17. Richard Afria
18. David Briars
19. William Lea
20. Richard Carver
21. Charles West

22. James Lea
23. John Allison
24. Jesse Huskey
25. Robert Herren
26. Hiram Hector
27. James Thompson
28. Wekins Nilman
29. James Braley
30. Isaac Brooks
31. Samuel Scoggin
32. John Gregory
33. Joseph Suart
34. Elijah Suirasy
35. Levi Burn
36. Robert Haney
37. John Gibbs
38. James Roach
39. Aron Bridges
40. James Hamsick
41. John Lea
42. Lewis Blanton
43. Samuel Humphries
44. Byard McCraw
45. Samuel Hamsick
46. George Blanton
47. Richard Bridges
48. Charles Durham
49. James Hall, fifer
50. Morris Quinn, drummer
51. John Blanton
52. Francis Young
53. Charles Scoggin

****

Eleventh Company,
detached from the
3rd Rutherford Regiment

1. Major R. Alexander, Captain
2. Christholm Daniel, Lieut.
3. Robert Marlan, Ensign
4. Joseph Holbert, Serg.
5. John Price, 2nd Serg.
6. Ezekiel Waldrop, 3rd Serg.
7. Aasa [sic] Hill, 4th Serg.
8. Squire Cockeran, 1st Corp.

9. William Redman, 2nd Corp.
10. Thomas Cook, 3rd Corp.
11. Jonathan Aldrige, 4th Corp.

Privates

12. James Cockeran

Page 56

13. Joseph Robins
14. Thomas Robins
15. Jacob Cantrel
16. John Martin
17. George King
18. William Owens
19. Robert Suttle
20. William McKennoy
21. John Rivis
22. John Davis
23. James Wrier
24. William Walker
25. Henry Cockeran
26. John Porter
27. James M. Erwin
28. Thomas Prater
29. John Furlly
30. John Anderson
31. Chisolm Daniel
32. James Early
33. James Hood
34. John Owens
35. John Spencer
36. John Grizzle
37. Luke Wilson
38. John Blackwell
39. Raleigh Owens
40. James Jackson
41. Jeremiah Martin
42. Patrick Scott
43. Lemuel Milcan
44. Charles Wilson
45. Solomon Blackswell
46. David Dellbuck
47. Daniel Foster
48. George Logan
49. Mathew Garrett

50. John Forster
51. John Hannon
52. Robert Thompson

****

Twelfth Company,
detached from the
2nd Rutherford Regiment

1. John C. Elliott, Captain
2.   [blank]
3. Samuel Bridges, Ensign
4. William Porter, 1st Serg.
5. James Hunter, 2nd Serg.
6. James Purrucks, 3rd Serg.
7. John Dyer, 4th Serg.
8. Joshua Hawkins, 1st Corp.
9. John Procter, 2nd Corp.
10. William Daggett, 3rd Corp.
11. Jacob Gage, 4th Corp.

Privates

12. William Wilson
13. John Waters
14. Jesse Chitwood
15. John Washburn
16. Henry Lanson
17. Samuel Gates
18. James Parks
19. Lewis Levity
20. Cazor McCurry
21. Jacob McCurry
22. Nicholas Nancy
23. Samuel Kirkland
24. Robert Rickets
25. Leroy Curruth
26. William Holeyfield
27. John McDonald
28. Joseph Nichols
29. Arthur Owenby
30. James Anthony
31. William Anthony
32. Asa Loveless
33. Marcy D. Holland
34. James G. Beatty

35. Samuel Downy
36. Samuel M. Bryer
37. Charles Y. Daggett
38. Jonathan Harder
39. Thomas Downy
40. Jesse Hill
41. John McFarland
42. Robert Lirk
43. Samuel Garland
44. Henry Workman
45. John Jarrels
46. John Hoyle
47. Thomas McReely
48. Thomas Reader
49. William Downs
50. Joseph Willis
51. James Newton
52. Abner Wilson

****

Thirteenth Company,
detached from the 2nd
and part of the 1st
Burke Regiment

1. Clinton Harthy, Captain
2. Benjamin Parks, Lieut.
3. Mathew Cox, Ensign

Privates

4. Isaac Harris
5. John Waggoner
6. John Hilemon
7. Joseph Hilton
8. William Fincannon
9. Peter Constable
10. Jacob Rample
11. Alexander Moore
12. Thomas Foster

Page 57

13. Elisha White
14. Micajah Paine
15. Leonard Keller

16. Balum Ducary
17. Abner Presnal
18. Lewis Alman
19. Reuben Henson
20. Reuben White
21. Thomas White
22. John Walkefield
23. Moses Jackson
24. James Jackson
25. Reuben Webb
26. John Gibson
27. Abner Staples
28. John Staples
29. William Farmer
30. Samuel Gibson
31. Thomas Green
32. Joseph Green
33. Thomas Sims
34. Samuel Amburn
35. William Amburn
36. John Emmett
37. Jacob Hise
38. James Host
39. John Phillips
40. James Penland
41. Reuben Parks
42. Elias Marquis
43. James Branch
44. John Gipson
45. Frederick Huffman
36. Daniel Watman
47. Daniel McFalls
48. Abram Huffman
49. Leonard Higdon
50. William Poteet
51. William Neill
52. George Duckworth
53. Jonathan Duckworth
51. Thomas Colby
53. Ephraim Evans
56. John Deal
57. Jacob Hips

****

Fourteenth Company,
detached from the

3rd and part of the 1st
Burke Regiment

1. Kenneth McKinsey, Captain
2. Jesse Brevard, 1st Lieut.
3. William Mifee, Ensign
4. John Perkins
5. Jeremiah Boon
6. William Kinkaid
7. John Boon
8. Enoch England
9. John Kinkard
10. Athan McDowell
11. James Davies
12. Joseph Little
13. Joseph Hood
14. John McClure
15. John Gribble
16. Thomas Monteath
17. Thomas Robertson
18. Alexander Harris
19. William Standford
20. Alexander Glass
21. John McDowell
22. William Hicky
23. James Warlow
24. Benjamin Wise
25. David Stroud
26. Richard Bell
27. Thomas Cripson
28. Peter Stroud, Jr.
20. Peter Epley
30. Freeman Tomberlin
31. Thomas Glass
32. William Sanders
33. John Oaks
31. Daniel Stillwell
35. Robert Childers
36. Tilman Stillwell
37. John Lowry
38. Barnard Oaks
39. Solomon Ellis
40. George Triplett
41. Josha Jones
42. William Triplett
43. Solomon Wright
44. Charles Medlock

45. William Hill
46. Charles Baley
47. William Riddisk
48. William Rickets
49. James Hunhill
50. Benjamin Allilson
51. Lemuel Paget
52. Benjamin McDowell

****

Fifteenth Company,
detached from the
1st and 2nd
Buncombe Regiments

1. Thomas Rhodes, Captain
2. Eli Merrell, Lieut.
3. Thomas Moore, Ensign
4. James Kincade
5. Francis Byers
6. John Gargely

Page 58

7. William Wilson
8. Benjamin Wilson
9. Samuel J. Murry
10. Thomas Justice
11. Cornelius Caps
12. Nathan Fletcher
13. Edward Shipman
14. Nimrod Merrell
15. John Camade
16. William Murry
17. William James
18. Henry Cary
19. Andrew Garron
20. Joshua Owens
21. Lewis Ward
22. John Drake
23. John Love
24. James Case
25. Reuben Step
26. James Abel
27. Sion Cook
28. George Story

****

29. Robert Byers
30. John Story
31. James Hickson
32. Jonathan Cinard
33. Mathew Patterson
34. David Johnston
35. Early Dasson
36. Thomas Kelley
37. James Kuchen
38. John Robertson
39. Samuel Scott
40. Benjamin Rickets
41. George D. Davis
42. Joel McKey
43. Daniel Davin
44. John Rutherford
45. Albert Amory
46. William Spivey
47. Sion Cannon
48. Charles Hayes
49. John Weaver, Jr.
50. John Plemmons
51. John Frisby
52. Joseph Black
53. John Plemmons, Jr.
54. John Plemmons
55. Andrew Plemmons
56. Stephen Rogers
57. Joseph Gudyer
58. Nathaniel Person
59. Elsey Reynolds
60. Mitchall Alexander
61. James Erwin
62. James Burns
63. John Palmer
64. John Harris
65. Jesse S-lah
66. Jacob Dunket
67. William Brown
68. William Carpenter
69. Peter Mason
70. Pendleton Underwood

****

Sixteenth Company,
detached from the

Haywood Regiment

1. Joseph Hughey, Captain
2. Robert Love, Jr. - Lieut.
3. John Anglin, Ensign
4. Samuel Brittan
5. James Avery
6. David Vance, Jr.
7. John Killian
8. Daniel Killian
9. Azia Roberts
10. John Dowell
11. William L. Dalton
12. John M. Patton
13. George C. Alexander
14. Lalas Ray
15. James Rine
16. James Welch
17. William Welch
18. Dell'd Love
19. Charles Toler
20. Marsh Coleman, Jr.
21. Henry Anderson
22. Eli N. Henry
23. Uriah Burns
24. Hezekiah Burns
25. J. Smith Armstrong
26. John Bryson, Jr.
27. Joseph Morrow
28. William Goodin
29. Martin Hepley
30. Philly Hyley
31. Garret Gardon
32. Thomas Hall
33. Benjamin West
34. Benjamin Mullen
35. Benjamin Clark
36. Josiah Crawford
37. Enos McHenry
38. John McHenry
39. Prien Adams
40. William Davied
41. David Rogers
42. George Reed
43. William Murry
44. David Elders
45. Henry Wild

46. James Carson

Page 59

47. Daniel Giles
48. John J. Wild
49. John Anderson, Jr.
50. James Greenlee, Jr.
51. George Stanton
52. John Griffith
53. Charles Hensley
54. Ephraim Piercy
55. John Baker
56. James Edwards
57. Robert Patterson
58. John Edwards
59. Joseph Shepherd
60. Jesse Radford
61. Nirain Allen
62. James Wood
63. James Redran
64. James Runnion
65. Henry Keith
66. Coleman Murry
67. John Wild
68. John Sams
69. Philip Wilson
70. John Rice
71. Isaac Rice
72. Barney Landers
78. James Thomas

****

MUSTER ROLL OF THE CAVALRY

Detached from the Militia of North Carolina, in pursuance
of a Requisition from the President of the United States
by virtue of an Act of Congress passed 10th April 1812.

REGIMENT

Edmund Jones, Lieutenant Colonel Commandant
Isham Edward, First Major
Henry Tayler, Second Major

First Company,
detached from the
Fifth Brigade

1. William G. Jones, Captain
2. William R. Bennet, 1st Lieut.
3. M - - a D. Jeffery, 2nd Lieut.
4. Frederick Jones, Cornet
5. Archibald Yarborough
6. Robert Hill
7. Samuel Thomas
8. William Jenkins
9. Robert Gill
10. Parker Murphrey
11. John K. Rey
12. Joshua Johnston
13. James Cheaves
14. Richer Hall
15. Robert Gupton
16. Benjamin Hertee
17. Charles Hayes
18. Thomas E. Hill
19. Richardson Finch
20. John F. Foster
21. Mathew Siruland
22. Benjamin Carpenter
23. Willie Williams
24. Robert C. Hall
25. Etheldred Pippin
26. David Bowers
27. Abner Cheaves
28. Clifforld Harris
29. Iasah Webb

30. Isaac House
31. William Lancaster, Jr.
32. William H. Strother
33. Allen Mumis
34. William D. Freeman
35. Jesse Pearce
36. Joseph Ballard
37. Jason Purvin
38. John Skiles
39. Arden Andrews
40. John Barnhill
41. William Cockburn
42. Henry Wyne
43. Collen Roberson
44. Darling Cherry
45. James Barner
46. Benjamin Edmonds
47. William M. West
48. Lavin Jones
49. Abner Read
50. John B. Massey

Page 60

51. Frederick Campbell
52. Robert B. Daniel
53. William Eskins
54. Pendleton B. Isbell
55. Jared Weaver
56. Hardy newell
57. Thomas Newell
58. Absalom Brown
59. Jesse Newell

60. William F. Irrard

****

Second Company,
detached from the
Sixteenth Brigade

1. Thomas Cooke, Captain
2. Leonard Cardwell, 1st Lieut.
3. Joseph Bowell, 2nd Lieut.
4. Silas High, Cornet
5. William Mallery, 1st Serg.
6. John Cheaves, 2nd Serg.
7. Hiram Taylar, 3rd Serg.
8. Robert Paine, 4th Serg.
9. John O'Brian, 1st Corp.
10. Thomas Atkins, 2nd Corp.
11, Groves Howard, 3rd Corp.
12. James Jeffers, 4th Corp.
13. Nelson Thomason, trumpeter
14. Isaac Hirter, dragoon
15. Benjamin Thomason
16. Pleasant Pearce
17. George Stroud
18. William Griffin
19. Burford Twitty
20. Jethro Lowry
21. William Williams
22. John Reaves
23. Willis Newman
24. Mathias Williams
25. Daniel S. Barringer

26. Anderson Hunter
27. Green Alfred
28. Robert H. Jackson
29. John Baxter
30. Thomas Matthis
31. William Brown
32. Hugh Cobb
33. Alexander Gray
34. Thomas Libscomb
35. Samuel Mitchel
36. Thomas Walton
37. Samuel Day
38. Benjamin Sneed
39. John Daniel
40. Charles Parrot

****

Third Company,
detached from the
Sixth Brigade

1. John Mebane, Captain
2. James Forest, Lieut.
3. Hardy Ward, 2nd Lieut.
4. Younger McListro, 1st Serg.
5. Daniel Fussee, 2nd Serg.
6. Asin Moore, dragoon
7. David Carig
8. Absalom Bulbee
9. Charles Jones
10. Jonathan Jones
11. William McMillion
12. Elam Hinton
13. Noah Rhodes
14. Samuel McBroom
15. Joseph B. Shaw
16. Elias Forte
17. Thomas Hargis
18. Alexander Mebane
19. William Thompson
20. David Patterson
21. Samuel Nelson
22. John Rogers
23. Jacob Thomas
24. William York
25. Peter Croom

26. William Elliott
27. Tobias Moser
28. Anarser Riddle
29. John Spivey
30. Anderson Williavy
31. John W. Dismaks
32. James Bell
33. William Brinkley
34. John Norwood
35. Ferrington Burnett
36. Patrick Pool
37. John Smith
38. Henry Whishenhunt

****

Fourth Company,
detached from the
Eighth Brigade

1. William Doak, Captain
2. Sampson Smith, 1st Lieut.
3. John Stewart, 2nd Lieut.
4. John Wharton, Cornet
5. Robert Woodburn, 1st Serg.
6. Leaven Ross, 2nd Serg.
7. Francis Bell, 3rd Serg.
8. David Wiley, 4th Serg.
9. Mark Gaun - -, 1st Corp.
10. Sample Garrigan, 2nd Corp.
11. W. Elam Brown, 3rd Corp.
12. Josiah Wiley, 4th Corp.

Page 61

13. Peter Monet, dragoon
14. James Gillespie
15. Abdi Gillespie
16. Ralph Forbis
17. Alexander Hanner
18. Robert Gillaspie
19. Abner Hannah
19. [sic] Eli Hannah
21. John Morrow
22. Evan Wharton
23. William Akin
24. Findley Shaw

25. Thomas Gilreath
26. Wenright Burns
27. John Gillaspie
28. Benjamin Alexander
29. James Alexander
30. John Harden
31. Thomas W. Clauds
32. Levi Huston
33. John Hannah
34. James Hendrick
35. George Sullivan
36. William Gannon
37. James Gilbreath
38. Charles Harden
39. William Dyer
40. John Alcorn
41. William Galbreath
42. Isaac Wetherly
43. Isaiah Wetherly
44. James Russand
45. Christopher Field
46. Thomas McCullock
47. Mathew Young
48. Robert Johnston

****

Fifth Company,
detached from
Seventh Brigade

1. Robert Lock, Captain
2. John Smith, 1st Lieut.
3. Francis Penny, 2nd Lieut.
4. John McCullock, cornet
5. John Brandon
6. Joshua Gay
7. John Pool, sadler
8. Thomas Smith
9. George T. Smith
10. George Lock
11. John Locke
12. Francis Lock
13. John Brandon, 4th Creek
14. David Stewart
15. Henry Verval
16. Christian Farr

17. Harman Fisher
18. Andrew Cook
19. Henry Allimony
20. Jacob Cauble
21. Elias Caruthers
22. William Henby
23. Gassaway Gaither
24. Scarlet Glascock
25. Jacob Kinkle
26. Joseph Howard
27. John Bailey
28. Peter Rupard
29. John Jones
30. Daniel Bore
31. John Hughs
32. Richmond Hughs
33. Jonathan Hunt
34. Phillip Craven
35. Elijah Daniel
36. Levi Reed
37. Jonathan Hoge
38. John Bodenhammer
39. Killion Phelps
40. James Flemming
41. John Dvidson
42. John Falls
43. John Kin
44. Ross Nesbet
45. Anguish McKinzie
46. James Hughs
47. John Crawford
48. Howell Alby
49. Ross McClenning
50. Edward Mills
51. Thomas Bell
52. William Erwin
53. Robert Johnston
54. Thomas Sloan
55. John Bell
50. Tarlton Shoemaker

****

Sixth Company,
detached from
Eleventh Brigade

1. [blank]
2. [blank]
3. [blank]
4. [blank]
5. Hugh M. McCane
6. Joseph Robeson
7. John Robison
8. Solomon Gibbans
9. John Shillington
10. James Martin
11. Henry Conner
12. John D. O. K. Pettes
13. Alexander Ross
14. William Duncan

****

Page 62

15. William Allison
16. John Knox
17. Jacob Barringer
18. George Coits
19. William Varner
20. Zeblone Ford
21. Robert Kirkpatrick
22. Jeremiah Hood
23. John Ford
24. Joseph Johnston
25. Nathan Orr
26. James Plummer
27. Isaac Price
28. B. W. Darrlson
29. Thomas Duckworth
30. Samuel Piror
31. Mathew Houston
32. Griffith Graham
33. Thomas Blewet
34. John Pemberton
35. Thomas Pemberton
36. Anguish Campbell
37. William Burton
38. John Asher
39. Edmond Almond
40. Barrum Kirk

****

Seventh Company,
detached from
Tenth Brigade

1. Henry Ramsour, Captain
2. William Green, 1st Lieut.
3. Jacob Summers, 2nd Lieut.
4. John Zimmerman, Cornet
5. John Falls, 1st Serg.
6. John Slagle, 2nd Serg.
7. Henry Smith, 3rd Serg.
8. Moses Sides, 4th Serg.
9. George Fry, Sadler
10. Ezekiel Hazelett, Trumpeter
11. Elias Bost, Dragoon
12. William Bost
13. Jacob Smoyer
14. Hiram Harbeson
15. Alexander Nail
16. Henry Smith
17. Charles Reinhart
18. Edward Sanders
19. Mathew Haynes
20. Absalom Taylor
21. Allen Wetherly
22. William Price
23. John Henry
24. Moses Heron
25. John Rhine, Jr.
26. Edward Scaboro
27. David Ramsour
28. James Grist
29. Richard Maze
30. James Knox
31. Samuel McMin
32. John Wilkinson
33. Alexander M. Corcle
34. John Cornelius
35. Hardy Abernathy
36. William Porter
37. Frederick Kimmy
38. Benjamin Suttle
39. William Hannon
40. Jeremiah Runyan
41. Timothy Hanny
42. Isaac Vanzant

****

****

Eighth Company,
detached from
Ninth Brigade

1. William P. Waugh, Captain
2. John Jones, 1st Lieut.
3. John W. Gorden, 2nd Lieut.
4. Samuel Parks, Cornet
5. Nathaniel Gorden
6. Alexander Nesbitt
7. Hugh Jones
8. Wiley G. Gorden
9. John Reynolds
10. Mechat McDowell
11. Jesse Marion [?]
12. Andrew Shepherd
13. Payten Gwyn
14. Thomas A. Gorden
15. David Waugh
16. Braxton McLiven
17. Ralph McGee
18. James Hoket
19. John Finley
20. John Johnston
21. Lancaster Cunningham
22. William F. Gamble
23. Little Hickason
24. William Laws
25. Abner Tribble
26. Joel Vaney
27. Joel Chandler
28. Samuel Wellbourn
29. John Hickeson
30. John Pumphrey
31. James M. Parks
32. Charles Adams
33. Henry Brown
34. William Hudson
35. Blewford McGee

****

Page 63

Ninth company,

detached from
Fifteenth Brigade

1. Ezebulon Baird, Captain
2. John Weaver, 1st Lieut.
3. Mathew Baird, 2nd Lieut.
4. William Alexander, Cornet
5. Samuel Semple
6. Samuel Hunter
7. George Patton
8. William Gillaspie
9. Gavid [sic] Gillaspie
10. William Greenlee
11. John Young
12. Charles Carrell
13. Nathaniel Culberson
14. William Sedford
15. Alexander Perkins
16. Charles McDowell
17. Obadiah H. Erwin
18. Thomas Flemming
19. John Harbison
20. John Kindard
21. Robert Cobb, Sergeant
22. Elisha Baird
23. Joshua Conely
21. Moses Cobb
25. Elisha Dockry
26. Henry McCall
27. John Paxton

****

MUSTER ROLL OF THE ARTILLERY

Detached from the Militia of North Carolina, in pursuance of a Requisition of the President of the United State, by virtue of an Act passed in Congress 10th April, 1812

First Company,
detached from
Wake Regiment

1. Elhannon Nutt, Captain
2. Benjamin Rogers, 1st Lieut.
3. Willis Whitaker, Ensign
4. Nathaniel Whitaker, 1st Serg.
5. Samuel Rogers, 2nd Serg.
6. Osborn Lockhart, 3rd Serg.
7. James Nance, Jr., 4th Serg.
8. Robert Nutt, 1st Corp.
9. Mark Monroe, 2nd Corp.
10. Jesse Roads, 3rd Corp.
11. Freeman Broadwell, 4th Corp
12. John A. Smith, drummer
13. Turner McInvail, fifer
14. Willie Nichols
15. Alsey Rockett
16. Jones Fowler
17. Darham Hall
18. William Rigsby
19. Robert Hall
20. Wiley Freeman
21. Britain Boykin
22. David Jones
23. Oram Ma-l-r
24. Jacob Williams
25. John Ames, Jr.
26. Alfred Acock
27. Hardy Dean, Jr.
28. Oram Tamon
29. Miles Allen
30. Elazard Moore
31. Alsey Nichols
32. Reason Rabourn
33. Kade Alfred
34. Micajah Stricklin

35. Cader Bunn
36. Israel Privett
37. James Chamblee
38. Elijah Todd
39. Jeptha Massey
40. Micajah Jordan
41. William Griffin
42. Lind-ton Ivey
43. Solomon Hartfield
44. Samuel Thompson
45. Charles Sandifurd
46. Miles Scarbrough
47. James Bell
48. James Peace
49. Bailey Alfred
50. Gilbert Alfred
51. Kinchen Medlin
52. James Lewis, Jr.
53 Joshua Beasley
54. David Beasley
55. Jacob Utley
56. Lemuel Jones
57. Robert Edwards
58. Michel Duskins, Jr.

Page 54

59. Howard Pool
60. John Hutchins, Jr.
61. Gills Brown
62. John Hull
63. Tabin Armstead
64. Arthur Reaves
65. Peteer Amget
66. William Holznd
67. Noel Norris
68. Isma Killum
69. Anthony Pilkinton

70. Miller Sexton
71. Giles J. Bledsoe
72. Darling Jones
73. John Band
74. John Watson
75. Wiley Womack
76. Tyrel Parish
77. Alvin Utley
78. Whitmill Hunter
79. Frederick Spain
80. Jesse Powell
81. Isham Holding
82. Jesse Turner
83. Robertson Ward
84. George Kith
86. Donas Yeargan
86. Aaron Shiner
87. David Geer
88. Richard Ferguson
89. Richard White
90. James Hicks
91. Elijah Kimbrough
92. David Read
93. Harbut Hobby
94. William Ladd
95. John Holloway, Jr.
96. Thomas Parham

****

Second Company,
detached from
Edgecombe Regiment

1. John Thomas, Captain
2. Lat. Vins, 1st Lieut.
3. Thomas Amosin, 2nd Lieut
4. John Bridges, Ensign

5. Theophilus Thomas, 1st Serg.
6. Benjamin Sharp, 2nd Serg.
7. William O. Carter, 3rd Serg.
8, William Williams, 4th Serg.
9. Henry C. Knight, 1st Corp.
10. James Pender, 2nd Corp.
11. Ithiel [sic] Eason, 3rd Corp.
12. William White, 4th Corp.
13. James Cobb, drummer
14. May Moore, fifer
15. John Barrow
16. Jesse C. Knight
17. Levi Long
18. Robert Long
19. John Stallings
20. Elijah Williams
21. Henry Walter
22. James Pernerter
23. Elisha Fellon
24. Benjamin Varnel
25. John Taylor
26. Reddin Thigpen
27. William Gay
28. Thomas Moore
29. Dempsey Hicks
30. Abram Coles
31. David Wollard
32. Martin B. Liles
33. Hansford Burrs
34. Hardy Simpson
35. James Moore
36. Ephraim Wooten
37. John Peele
38. Lemuel Lancaster
39. William Williams, Sr.
40. Edward Sherod
41. Daniel Land
42. John Thomas
43. Thomas Williams
44. David Thomas
45. Jehtro Weaver
46. Stephen Bullock
47. John Brantly
48. Acilles Barnes
49. Dixon Summons
50. Isaac Daniel
51. James Daniel

52. John Johnston
53. William Johnston
54. Asahel Bateman
55. Ashael Farmer
56. John Farmer
57. Reddick Barnes
58. John Barnes
59. Haman Mann
60. Enos Barnes
61. Jesse Parkey
62. John B. Cobb
63. Barnwill Moore
64. Bryant Shoots
65. Jesse Hedgepeth
66. Silas Mitche
67. Thomas Whitly
68. Richmon Cobb
69. Benjamin Sumerllin
70. Isaac Hobbs
71. Timothy Harris
72. Enoch Robertson
73. Moses Moore

****

Page 65

Third Company,
detached from
Bertie Regiment

1. Jospeh H. Bryan, Captain
2. Augustin Pugh, Lieut.
3. Lodawick Pruden, Ensign
4. William McGruder
5. Isaac Wilson
6. Henry Hunter
7. Anthony Wiggins
8. Benjamin Brogdon
9. Washington Turner
10. John A. Cordle
12. Rheuben Wilkes
12. David Harrell
13. Fred Wimberly
14. John Wilkes
15. Henry Wilkes
16. Jesse Powell
17. John Ruffin

18. Thomas Bickell
19. Turner McGlawhon
20. Edward Turner
21. Elijah C. Bryan
22. John B. Everitt
23. John Minor
24. John Stewart, Jr.
25. Richard L. Bowers
26. John Brickell
27. Linus Leonard
28. Shade Britt
29. John Brantly
30. William Brickell
31. Cader Bunch
32. Samuel Hobbs
33. Edward B. Baker
34. John Allen
35. Edward Gill
36. Edmond Fleetwood, Jr.
37. Frederick Miller
38. Reuben Lawrence
39. Wil Wilkins
40. Asa Radett
41. Levi Todd
42. Joshua P. Brantly
43. James Boswell
44. Asa Gregory
45. John Ramsey
46. Josiah Miller
47. John Rhodes
48. Haller Calway
49. Richard Bagwell
50. William H. Green
51. Nathaniel Culeper
52. Benjamin Winburn
53. James Simonds
54. Benjamin James
55. Thomas Corbett
56. William Gardner
57. David Garrett
58. Ryan Jonagon
59. Abner Aaron, Jr.
60. Samuel Martin
61. Elisha Pritchard
62. Cader Mitchel
63. Jacob Pruden
64. Levi Outlaw

56   **NORTH CAROLINA - ROSTER OF SOLDIERS IN WAR OF 1812**

****

65. David Fleetwood
66. Neal Nicholas
67, James Carley
68. Thomas Hogard
69. Lawrence Cook
70. William Roll
71. Jesse Garrett
72. George Wilson
73. Cader Hunter
74. Dred Evans
75. Silas Wilson
76. Thomas Sorrell
77. William Brogdon
78. William Hunter
79. Stephen Hymon
80. James Ryman
81. John West
82. Hardy Clements
83. Benjamin Rogers
84. William Robertson
85. Malacha Green
86. Isaac Wiggins
87. William Higgs
88. James Wilkes
89. Augt. Callum
90. West Tines
91. David Folk
92. Redden Rutland
93. George Core
94. Johnston Rutland
95. Simeon Harrell
96. Joseph Harrell
97. W. M. Bishop
98. David Outlaw
99. John Waltan
100. Nath'l Wattoman
101. William Holloman
102. John Holly
103. Moses Freeman
104. George Ward
105. Cader White
106. Hardy White
107. Miles Rollins
108. William Evans

****

Page 66

Fourth Comapny,
detached from
Carteret Regiment

1. Jacob Henry, Captain
2. William Jasper, 1st Lieut.
3. Samuel Leffers, 2nd Lieut.
4. David Wallace, Ensign
5. Thomas Howland
6. John Rigs
7. Elijah Canaday
8. John Linch
9. Joseph Fulford, Jr.
10. Anthony Davis
11. George Gibble
12. Timothy Small
13. James Johnston
14. John Simmons
15. Zacheus Green
16. Archibald Green
17. Abram Wilder
18. John Sanders
19. Elias Meadors
20. Nevil Russell
21. Elijah Gardner
22. Thomas Willis
23. John Bell
24. Benjamin Willis
25. Loftin Quin
26. Francis Gardner
27. William Lewis
28. Joseph Saller
29. Walace [sic] Salter
30. Cason Willis
31. Jacob Smith
32. James Dixon
33. William Gaskill
34. David Ireland
35. George Golding
36. John Lewis
37. Caleb Wade
38. Eliza Wade
39. John Wharton
40. Clifton Fulford
41. Benjamin Guthrie

42. George Price
43. Beliher Hakee
44. Elijah Guthrie
45. Zachariah Willis

****

Fifth Company,
detached from
Brunswick Regiment

1. [no listing]
2. [no listing]
3. John Sullivan, 2nd Lieut.
4. David Tolson
5. Richard Harris
6. Burnel Cason
7. John Cherr
8. William Pound
9. Joel Robins
10. Allegood Suggs
11. Eldred Tellers
12. William Key
13. William Hankens
14. Randal Hewet
15. John Clemons
16. Levi Swain
17. Absalom Beasley
18. William Bennett
19. Josiah Little
20. Coleman Runnels
21. Benjamin Sellers
22. Samuel Harris
23. Arthur Pinner
24. Josiah Cox
25. Alexander Campbell
26. Moses King
27. James Ellis
28. Niram Skipper
29. Jonathan Rothwell
30. Joseph Walters
31. Thomas Vines
32. Jonathan Keater
33. Benjamin Purrell
34. John Spencer
35. Daniel Bennett
36. William Gilbert

****

MUSTER ROLL OF THE RIFLEMEN

Detached from the Militia of North Carolina, in pursuance of a
Requisition of the President of the United States, by virtue
of an Act of Congress, passed 10th April, 1812

First Company,
detached from
Cumberland Regiment

1. William Loyd, Captain
2. Robert Carver, 1st Lieut.
3. George Kenedy, 2nd Lieut.
4. Richard Watson, Ensign
5. James Holmes, 1st Serg.
6. John Rhea, 2nd Serg.
7. Jesse Townsend, 3rd Serg.
8. John Dixon, Jr.

Page 67

9. Isaac Howard
10. Menas Howard
11. Allen Brown
12. Egbird Hall
13. Isham Carver
14. William Gyton
15. Elijah Ward
16. John Campbell
17. Isaiah Toler
18. Samuel Taylor
19. Daniel Pharis
20. Josiah Culberson
21. Frederick Brewer
22. Aron Smith
23. James C. Myrick
24. Jesse Ritter
25. Julius Brewer
26. John Corkman
27. Mitchel Rowland
28. John Milton
29. Gideon Moore
30. Louis Williamson
31. Louis Russell
32. Thomas D. King
33. Hardy Chesnut

34. Willie Dodd
35. Jesse Oats, 4th Serg.
36. Richard Clinton
37. Joshua Chesnut
38. William Blackman
39. Nathan King
40. Louis F. Peck
41. Daniel Cogdell
42. John Turner, Jr.
43. Travers Beddoe
44. Archibald McMillan
45. Stephen Hester
46. David Thomas
47. John Robertson
48. James Jackson
49. Cornelius Kellyham
50. Arthur Hardy
51. David M. Kemp
52. William Lewis
53. Warren Baldwin
54. John Bright
55. William Huff
56. Jonathan Cribb
57. John Graham
58. Thomas Carteret

****

Second Company,
detached from
Fourteenth Brigade

1. Nell Buie, Captain
2. William Leod
3. James McFarland
4. Malcom Gills
5. Neil Curry
6. Alexander McKay
7. Alexander McDonald
8. Malcom Yates

9. Malcom Curry
10. John Rainwater
11. Elisha Gibson
12. John Gillis
13. Hugh Gillis
14. Dugald McDuffy
15. Moses Parker
16. John Little
17. John McDuffy
18. John Turrege
19. Stephen Dees
20. Levy Dees
21. Daniel McEathan
22. William McNeil
23. Duncan Mathews
24. Alex McNabb
25. Daniel Calbroth
26. Dugald Stewart
27. Hugh Curry
28. Hector Bethune
29. Archibald Curry
30. Neil McNeil
31. Archibald McNeil
32. Duncan McGregar
33. Daniel Smith
34. Peter Livington
35. John Sinclair
36. John Wilkinson
37. Peter McArthur
38. Duncan McMillan
39. James Watson
40. Neil Ferguson

****

Third Company,
detached from the
Ninth Brigade

1. Gideon Lewis, Captain

2. Elijah Wilcoxen
3. Jonathan Taylor
4. Matthias Langly
5. Fulty Miller
6. Isaiah Miller
7. Elias Robeson
8. Theophilus Baldwin
9. David Bogan
10. Larkin Bunyard
11. Fulty Miller [2 same name?]
12. John Ray
13. James Kethborn
14. Richard Allen, Jr. - 1st Lieut.
15. Jacob Pilear
16. John Foss

Page 68

17. John Sparks, Jr.
18. Francis Kurby
19. Jacob Hoots
20. Solomon Sparks
21. Isaac Stover
22. Jeremiah Johnston
23. John N. Green
24. John Chapman
25. James Robinet
26. James Franklin, 2nd Lieut.
27. John Shipp, Ensign
28. William Oglesby, Cadet
29. Bartlet Hanmock
30. John Snow
31. Miley Cave
32. Thomas Cox
33. Thomas Oglesby
34. William Potter
35. Ephraim Witcher
36. Levi Snow
37. William Hammonds
38. Bernard Franklin

****

Fourth Company,
detached from the
Seventh Brigade

1. Francis Young, Captain
2. Samuel Young
3. William McOnnel
4. Richard Harris
5. Solomon Ellis
6. William Tomlinson
7. John Young
8. John Dobson
9. John Green
10. William Murdy
11. Fans Sharp
12. Solomon Jacobs
13. Robert Callahan
14. Thomas Francis
15. John Veark
16. James Beil
17. Enos Campbell
18. Erasmus Lazenby
19. Ezekiel Pearce
20. George Summers
21. Daniel Brown, Lieut.
22. Daniel Starns
23. Benjamin Agender
24. Jacob Trees
25. Henry Eller
26. David Butner
27. John Rainy
28. Joseph Graham
29. David masters
30. Henry Berger
31. Isaac Cummins
32. Peter Mourey
33. Jacob L. Peterson
34. Peter Agender
35. John Hartman
36. John Bose
37. Edward Burgess
38. William Glasscock
39. Jacob Booe
40. Jacob Heifer
41. Daniel Booe
42. Joshua Brinigan
43. Phillip Baker
44. Georges [sic] Graves
45. Jacob Call
46. Zedediah Jarvis
47. Jacob Hoover

48. David Larkabee
49. George Bodenhammer
50. Thomas Newcomb
51. George Miller
52. John Michel
53. John Long, Jr.
54. Andrew Yoakley
55. Jacob Sink

****

Fifth Company,
detached from the
2nd Rutherford Regiment
Tenth Brigade

1. John C. Elliott, Captain
2. William Porter, 1st Lieut.
3. Samuel Bridges, Ensign
4.   [blank]
5. James Hunter, 2nd Serg.
6. James Parrish, 3rd Serg.
7. John Dyer, 4th Serg.
8. Joshua Hawkins, 1st Corp.
9. John Proctor, 2nd Corp.
10. William Daggett, 3rd Corp.
11. Jacob Gage, 4th Corp.
12. William Wilson
13. John Walters
14. Jesse Chitwood
15. John Washburn
16. Henry Lanon
17. Samuel Gates
18. James Parks
19. Lewis Levity
20. Cazor W. Curry [McCurry ?]
21. Jacob McCurry
22. Nicholas Nancy
23. Samuel Kirkland
24. Robert Rickets
25. Leroy Curreteh
26. William Holyfield

Page 69

27. John McDonald
28. Joseph Nichols

NORTH CAROLINA - ROSTER OF SOLDIERS IN WAR OF 1812   59

****

29. Arthur Owerly
30. James Anthony
31. William Anthony
32. Asa Labeless
33. Marcus D'Holland
34. James G. Beaty
35. Samuel Downy
36. Samuel McBroyes
37. Charles Y. Dogget
38. Jonathan Harder
39. Thomas Downy
40. Jesse Hill
41. John McFarland
42. Robert Link
43. Samuel Garland
44. Henry Workman
45. John Jarrels
46. John Hoyle
47. Thomas McReely
48. Thomas Reader
49. William Downs
50. Joseph Willis
51. James Newton
52. Abner Wilson

****

Sixth Comppany,
detached from the
Eleventh Brigade

1. David Long
2. Robert Farr
3. Samuel McCurdy
4. Eli Newell
5. Peter J. Bane
6. George Sifford
7. Jacob Cruise
8. Francis Newel
9. John W. Davis
10. Jacob Stough
11. William Gray
12. Charles Juhuy [?]
13. Francis McClosky
14. Henry Fisher
15. Isaac Helms
16. Aley McCorkle

17. Robert Givens
18. Andrew Walker
19. William Campbell
20. John Campbell
21. Henry Lewis
22. John Price
23. James Todd
24. James Thompson
25. Robert Robinson
26. Milton harris
27. Cyrus Harris
28. Solomon Ballard
29. Charles Cupples
30. Thomas Frasure
31. James Haywood
32. Will Johnston
33. James Lesbury
34. Benjamin Williams
35. John Layton
36. Laban Carter
37. Zachariah Walker
38. John Hasley
39. Henry Goodman
40. John Reddell
41. Isom Williams
42. Adam Shular
43. John Ball
44. Jesse Gallimore
45. Robert C. Davis
46. David Davenport
47. John Milsaps
48. John Loftin
49. Solomon Heath
50. Jacob Myers

****

Page 70   Blank

Page 71

MUSTER ROLL

OF THE DETACHED MILITIA, ORGANIZED IN
AUGUST, 1814

General Officers designated to command in the Detachment of Militia:

MONTFORT STOKES,   Major General
JEREMIAH SLADE   }
JESSE A. PEARSON }   Brigadier Generals

First Regiment to be composed of the counties of Chowan, Currituck, Camden, Pasquotank, Perquimans, Gates, Hertford, Bertie, Northampton, Halifax, Warren and Nash.
        Officers: - Duncan McDonald, Lieutenant Colonel commandant; Andrew Joyner, Lieutenant Colonel; Joseph F. Dickerson, First Major; John C. Green, Second Major.

Second Regiment of Washington, Tyrrell, Hyde, Beaufort, Craven, Carteret, Jones, Lenoir, Greene, Pitt, Martin, Edgecombe, and Wayne.
        Officers: Simon Bruton, Lieutenant Colonel commandant; Nathan Tisdale, Lieutenant Colonel; Thomas H. Blount, First Major; James W. Clark, Second Major.

Third Regiment of Onslow, New Hanover, Bladen, Brunswick, Columbus, Duplin, Sampson, Robeson, Cumberland, Moore, Richmond and Anson.
        Officers: Maurice Moore, Lieutenant Colonel commandant; Richard Nixon, Lieutenant Colonel; Archibald McNeil, First Major; Edward B. Dudley, Second Major.

Fourth Regiment of Wake, Johnston, Franklin, Granville, Person, Orange, and Chatham.
        Officers: Richard Atkerson, Lieutenant Colonel commandant; Mourice Smith, Lieutenant Colonel; John C. Wyatt, First Major; Benjamin Chambers Second Major.

Fifth Regiment of Caswell, Guilford, Rockingham, Stokes, Surry, Wilkes, Ashe and Randolph.
        Officers: Alexander Murphy, Lieutenant Colonel commandant; Samuel Hunter, Lieutenant Colonel; James Campbell, First Major; Joseph Winston, Jr. Second Major

Sixth Regiment of Rowan, Montgomery, Mecklenburg, Cabarrus, and Iredell.
[Page 72]   Officers: Richard Allison, Lieutenant Colonel commandant; John H. Freeling, First Major; Amos Sharpe, Second Major.

Seventh Regiment of Lincoln, Rutherford, Burke, Buncombe, and Haywood.

Officers: Andrew Irwin, Lieutenant Colonel commandant; William Cathey, First Major; Nathan A. McDowell, Second Major.

FIRST REGIMENT

CHOWAN COUNTY

1. James Iredell, Captain
2. Joseph Manning, 1st Lieut.
3. John M. Roberts, 2nd Lieut.
4. Myles Wilder, Ensign
5. John D. Castillow
6. John Bond, Sr.
7. Charles Simpson
8. Jones Parish
9. James Hinsley
10. Edwin Bond
11. Hardy Morgan
12. John Evans
13. Richard Paxton
14. Nathaniel Miller
156. Sampson Wilder
16. Thomas Mires
17. James R. Crecay
18. Martin Noxon
19. Edmond Hoskins
20. Clement H. Blount
21. Samuel Charlton
22. Michael Hendrick
23. Benjamin Whidler
24. William Nickolls
25. Jackson S. Hoyle
25. Obediah Roberts
27. Jonathan Parks
28. Henry Evans
29. Isaac Boice
30. Charleston Ward
31. Joseph Winslow
32. William Jordan
33. Josiah Ward
34. Thomas Smith, Sr.
35. Michena Trulove
36. John Wilder
37. Thomas Rhea
38. Alfred M. Gatlin
39. George Waff

40. William Cheshire
41. George Mewbern
42. Edmond Bunch
43. John Ashley
44. William Todd
45. John Boyce
46. John Rhody
47. Joseph Small, Jr.
48. Jesse Mitchel
49. Stacy Floyd
50. William Ashley
51. John Reddie
52. Jethro Woodard
53. Alexander Parish
54. Julius Deale

****

CURRITUCK COUNTY

1. William Bray, Captain
2. John Baxter, 1st Lieut.
3. Phillip Dozier, 2nd Lieut.
4. Thomas Summon, Ensign
5. William Etheridge
6. Lemuel Ferebee
7. Samuel Gregory
8. Malachi Holstead
9. Charles Saoars
10. Tully Dozier
11. Samuel Glasgow
12. Peter Ferebee
13. William Spence
14. Hez Collins
15. Arthur Heath
16. Wilson Nash
17. Anthony Simmons
18. Caleb Woodard
19. Martin McBride
20. Dempsey Gregory
21. Willoougliby Boswood

22. Jordan Dozier
23. Jasper Dozier
24. Grandy Barnard
25. William Dozier
26. Willoughby Barnard
27. William Ferebee
28. William Guilford
29. John Baxter
30. Wallis Hutchins
31. Hillary Finters
32. Jeremiah Mercer, Jr.
33. Enoch Whithurst
34. Samuel Whithurst
35. Josiah Etheridge

Page 73

36. Hillary Fancher
37. John C. Glasgow
38. Cornelius Mercer
39. Branson Bell
40. William Messenger
41. Peter Parr
42. Peter Gregory
43. James Parr
44. Samuel Nicholson
45. Levi Etheridge
46. Arthur Spence
47. William Hanners
48. John Gregory
49. Jacob Aydelotte
50. Frederick Northern
51. Ralph P. Beeling
52. James Northern
53. Charles Sawyer
54. Jesse Robinson
55. James Morse
56. John Bunnell
57. Joseph Sawyer
58. John Floro
59. John Brickhouse

60. James Bunnell
61. Aaron Floro
62. Henry Bright
63. Willoughby Whally
64. William Etheridge
65. Charles Perkins
66. James Brabble
67. John W. Hughs
68. William Brumsey
69. James White
70. Jesse McClannan
71. John Lee
72. Enoch Lee
73. Joseph Tatum
74. Tatum Brabble
75. Jesse Balance
76. John Brabble
77. Bartholomew Thompson
78. Isaac Snowden
79. Dempsey Doxey
80. Matthias Bell
81. George Cason
82. Daniel Tatum
83. Maxey Tatum
84. John Caps
85. John Brabble, Jr.
86. Thomas Balance
87. James Poyner
88. Dempsey Douglass
89. Isaac Roberts
90. James Fentus
91. John Baxter
92. Alexander White
93. George Perkins
94. James Snowden
95. Samuel Payner
96. Peter Barro
97. Thomas Etheridge
98. Francis Camp
99. Spencer O'Neal
100. Reuben Taylor
101. John Forbes
102. Thomas Roberts
103. Mitchell Summons
104. Joseph Baxter, Jr.
105. Moses Cox
106. Amos Davis

107. James Lee
108. John Wilson
109. Willis B. Bentine
110. William Cilgrow
111. Henry Williamson
112. Nicholas Ellison
113. Stephen Etheridge

****

CAMDEN COUNTY

1. James S. Garlington, Captain
2. Archibald Sawyer, Lieut.
3. John H. Wright, Ensign
4. John A. Brockett
5. William Mercer
6. John Jerrell
7. Thomas Berry
8. Nathan Harrison
9. John Pue
10. Malachi Collins
11. Frederick Gregory
12. James Owens
13. Edward Cerlin
14. Cader Wright
15. Dempsey Collins
16. Malachi Knight
17. Charles Wright
18. Asa Cartwright
19. Wilson Coats
20. Miles Mercer
21. Thomas Surry
22. William Garrett
23. Thomas Bray
24. Adam Baum
25. Bradly Smith
26. Reuben Gibson
27. Job Gregory
28. William Collin
29. Elijah Staples
30. Simeon Jones
31. Forebee Sanderlin
32. Silas Forbes
33. Joseph Bell
34. Seth Wright

Page 74

35. Isaac Burges
36. Joab Bell
37. John Jones
38. Frederick Daily
39. James Sawyer
40. Frederick Kanady
41. Samuel Godfrew [Godfrey]
42. Jonathan Gregory
43. Abner Cooper
44. William Dowtey
45. Dempsey Squiers [sic]
46. Nathan Gregory
47. Miles Williams
48. James Beales
49. Henry H. Wright
50. Samuel Needham
61. Zephaniah Sawyer
52. Freeman Sawyer
53. John Godfrey
54. Josiah Sanderlin
55. Jeremiah Jones
56. James Godfrey
57. Benjamin Douge
58. Demsey Dunkin
59. Caleb Forbes
60. Peter Pugh
61. Joseph Love
62. Maxsey Sawyer
63. Jess Douge
64. Hiram Godfrey
65. James McHarney
66. Jesse Temple
67. Dempsey Riggs
68. Silas Riggs
69. Dempsey Forbes
70. Isaac Harrison
71. Cornelius Wright
72. Berket Beales
73. Joseph Seamon
74. Levi Wright
75. William Kanady
75. Abraham Cartwright
77. Joseph Barco
78. Samuel Gregory
79. Dempsey Douge

****

80. Edmond Gregory
81. Lot Needham
82. Samuel Jarvis
83. Amos Pue.

****

PASQUOTANK COUNTY

1. Carter Bernard, Captain
2. Abraham Simons, Lieut.
3. Miles Jones, Ensign
4. William Gammon
5. Henry Keaton
6. James Sawyer
7. James Turner
8. Jesse Maddux
9. Thomas Lowry
10. John Lester
11. Thomas Markum
12. Joshua Trewblood
13. Alfred Turner
14. John White
15. Richard Clayton
16. Miles Brothers
17. Caleb Brothers
18. Robert Cartright [sic]
19. David Davis
20. Malachi Davis
21. Thomas Palin
22. Cyprian Chopard
23. Jesse Walden
24. Keder Morgan
25. Richard Madrew
26. William Casey
27. James Cartwright
28. Thomas Pritchard
29. Harvey Hairis [sic]
30. James Jackson
31. Thomas Cartwright
32. William Morris
33. Isaac Williams
34. Kader Perry
35. Hezekiah Jackson
36. James Munden
37. Charles Roberts
38. Nathan Small

39. Daniel White
40. Caleb Bundy
41. William Munden
42. Daniel Spence
43. Thomas Burnham
44. Evergain Carver
45. William Cartwright
46. Joseph Haireld
47. John Hallstead
48. Harvey Stokely
49. Robert Sawyer
50. Henry Temple
51. James Williams
52. John Williams
53. Peleg Prichard
54. David Frew
55. Johnston Davis
56. William Smithson
57. Isaac Sawyer
58. Stephen Richardson
59. Adam Stafford
60. Grandy Pritchard
61. Stephen Hooker
62. Thomas Madrew, Jr.
63. Jesse Gray
64. William Allen

Page 75

65. Thomas McKey
66. William Jackson (son of
        Thos.)
57, Jabez Bright
68. Joseph Brothers (son of Jos.)
69. Joshua Pool
70. William Albertson
71. William Brumbough
72. Daniel Bray
73. Henry Pendleton

****

PERQUIMANS COUNTY

1. William R. Sutton, Captain
2. Alfred Moore, Lieut.
3. John Branch, Ensign

4. Benjamin Smith
5. Charles Elliott
6. Caleb Chappel
7. Joseph Roberts
8. Joseph Elliott
9. Jesse Elliott
10. John White
11. Foster Elliott
12. Henry Smith
13. John Rogerson, Jr.
14. Hugh Morgan
15. Joseph W. Weeks
16. Barnabus Ward
17. Francis Godfrey
18. Harrison Turner
19. James Tweedy
20. Perry Weeks
21. Thomas Feveash
22. John Jackson, Jr.
23. Nathaniel Cole
24. Robert Harrison
25. John Madre
26. Charles Hall
27. John Bunch
28. Joseph Jordan
29. James Thach
30. Willis Butter
31. John Wingate
32. William Thach
33. William Tailor
34. William Thorn
35. Charles W. Skinner
36. Seth Hendricks
37. Thomas Hasket
38. Mexum [sic] Newby
39. Josiah Smith
40. John Woodley
41. George Low
42. William Bagley
43. Hezekiah Savage
44. William Gregory
45. Willis Morgan
46. John Hasket
47. Nathan Bagley
48. Joseph Cooper
49. Dempsey Webb
50. John White (of John)

51. John Simpson
52. James Perry
53. Moses Boyce
54. William Walton
55. Asa Pelon
56. Samuel Barclift, Sr.
57. Robert Reed
58. William Humphries
59. John Stanton
60. James Needham
61. James Tatlock
62. John Stephenson
63. James Gipson

****

GATES COUNTY

1. Henry Pugh, Captain
2. Isaac K. Hunter, Lieut.
3. George Kittrell, Ensign
4. John Gordon, 1st Serg.
5. William Kitrel [sic]l, 2nd Serg.
6. John Barnes, 3rd Serg.
7. Robert Powell, 4th Serg.
8. Jonas Franklin, 1st Corp.
9. Whitmill Hill, 2nd Corp.
10. Joseph Harrell, 3rd Corp.
11. Jethro Brinkley, 4th Corp.
12. William White,
13. Elijah Lyons
14. Amos Hobbs
15. William Hofler
16. Jesse Hyett.
17. Anson Williams
18. Joseph Derden
19. James Eure
20. Timothy Spivey
21. Solomon Eason
22. William Pearce
23. William Blanchard
24. Seth Blanchard
25. Edward Briggs
26. Samuel Green
27. Robert Simons
28. Miles Knight
29. Richard Farlass

30. Francis M. Foster
31. Edward Daughtie
32. Henry Holt
33. Samuel Smith
34. Frederick Williams

Page 76

35. Kindred Parker
36. Kinchen Taylor
37. Benjamin Eure
38. Elisha Umphlet
39. Thomas Collins
40. William Crafford
41. Lewis Lee
42. Elisha Pyland
43. Jesse Parker
44. James Williams
45. Miles Williams
46. John Evens
47. Jethro Reddick
48. Shedric Pyland
49. Watson Hilley
50. William Pyland
51. Dempsey Hall
52. James Lapland
53. Kader Briggs
54. Reuben Miller
55. James Jones (of John)
56. Jesse Mathias
57. Noah Speight
58. Joshua Small
59. Robert Parker
60. Harmon Hayes
61. Robert Wilson
62. Hardy Williams
63. John Polson
64. David Brown
65. John Shearod
66. Elisha Duke
67. James Parker
68. Henry Crafford
69. Jacob Ealey
70 Joshua Lang
71. William March
72. John March
73. William Spivey

****

HERTFORD COUNTY

1. Irvin Jinkins, Captain
2. Benjamin Hill, Llieut.
3. Henry G. Darden, Ensign
4. Benjamin Brown, drummer
5. Silas Shewcraft, fifer
6. William Brown
7. James Johnson
8. Willie Willoughbee
9. Luke Hare
10. John Brown
11. Burrell Eu r
12. Jacob Overton
13. Elisha Overton
14. Jeremiah Aikin
15. William Wynns
16. Wm. W. Whitfield
17. Jeremiah D. Aikin
18. James Ratherly, Jr.
19. Allen Moore
20. William Downing
21. James Barns
22. Willie Cullan
23. Jesse Harrison
24. William Sessoms
25. George Hollomon, Jr.
26. Justin Hollomon
27. Samuel Britton
28. Jethro Sowell
29. Aaron Hare
30. Isaac Baker
31. David Welch, Jr.
32. William Sewell
33. Thomas Elerion
34. Benjamin Hocall
35. George H. Bond
36. Isaac Taylor
37. William Purnell
38. William Yeats
39. Samuel Parker
40. William Peaster
41. Benjamin Wynne
42. Samuel Ely
43. Eli Harrell

44. Boan Driver
45. John Dickinson
46. Thomas Early
47. John P. Hare
48. Stephen Howell
49. John A. Anderson
50. Benjamin Blan
51. Sterling Francis
52. Arthur Vick
53. George Whitley
54. John Seall
55. David Williams
56. James Skinner
57. Henry Brantley
58. Daniel Williams
59. James Worrell
60. Thomas Faircloth
61. Benjamin Williams
62. Lemuel Sanders
53. Gray Mabane
64. John Vinson
65. John Vaughn
66. Jonas Chiton
67. William Rodgers
68. Nelson Joyner
69. William Andrews
70. Robert Montgomery
71. William Parker
72. Mathias Cook
73. Hilary Vaughn
74. Joel Grizzard
75. Hardy M. Banks

****
Page 77

BERTIE COUNTY

1. Jonathan H. Jacocks, Captain
2. Powell Harrell, Lieut.
3. James Wilson, Jr. Ensign
4. Thomas Morgan
5. Miles Gilliam
6. William C. Terrell
7. William M. Darlett
8. Simon A. Bryant
9. William B. Mastin

10. Joseph Blount
11. Gaven Hogg
12. William P. King
13. Lewis Wimberly
14. Levi Kenaday
15. Thomas Liversage
16. James Duglas
17. William W. Johnson
18. Kenneth Clark
19. Cullen Shoolders [?]
20. Thomas Ruffin
21. William R. W. Bozman
22. Hatter Callaway
23. Asa Gregory
24. Aquilla Harden
25. Josiah Reddit
26. William Simons
27. Jasper Ward
28. William Castellow
29. Trustum Capehatt
30. Thomas I. West
31. Curry Butler
32. Josiah Bird
33. Benjamin Baker
34. Benjamin Bowen
35. John Bowen
36. Levi Jennings
37. John P. Butler
38. Silas Butler
39. Reuben Barns
40. Nehemiah Bunch
41. Cullen Bazimore
42. William K. Miller
43. Stephen Bazimore
44. James Cherry, Jr.
45. Ralph Outlaw
46. Lodowick Jenkins
47. Elisha Cook
48. James Early
49. James Williford
60. Isaac Early
51. Willie Jenkins
52. John Cobb
53. Lawrence Mizells
54. John Lassiter
55. Joshua Harrell
56. Thomas Harrell

57. Josiah Davidson
58. Isaac White
59. Peter White
60. Zachariah Ellison
61. George Mizells
62. Charles Miller
63. Meredith Harrell
64. Benjamin B. Williams
65. George White
66. James Mizell [sic]
67. Whitmall White
68. Joshua Hale
69. Charnley C. Dandalow
70. Noah Outlaw
71 Elisha Haggard
72. David White
73. Lewis Miller
74. King Mitchel
75. Willilam Griffin
76. Hatton Fleetwood
77. John Hunter
78. Timothy Mizells
79. Seth Morgan
80. Michael Mardre
81. Henry Todd
82. Luke Smithwitk [sic]
83. John Watson
84. Jeremiah Legett
85. James Baswell
86. Hardy Clements
87. Leven McTuller
88. Jonathan Zaloe
89. David Calloway
90. John Mhoon [sic]
91. John Boyd
92. Henry Lee
93. Henry Harrell
94. John Murdough
95. Dancy Harrell
95. Whitmell Ruffin
97. Moses Purvis
98. Jesse Brown
99. Jason Minton
100. John Higgs
101. Kinchen Wilks
102. Cullen Grimmer
103. James Hoggard

****

NORTHAMPTON
COUNTY

1. John F. Walker, Captain
2. Darus Parker, 1st Lieut.
3. Solomon B. Goodson, 2nd Lieut.
4. Sterling Finnie, 3rd Lieut.
5. John C. Wood, Ensign
6. Henry Adams

Page 78

7. Burges Burkett
8. Lemuel Burkett
9. Robert Baum
10. Bennet Boon
11. Brittain Brittle
12. John T. Benns
13. William Boon
14. Elijah Brewer
15. John Cornwall
16. James Day
17. Goodwin Daniel
18. David C. Dardin
19. Britain Doles
20. Thomas Deloach
21. William Draper
22. Lewis Davis
23. Jesse Deloach
24. Pink Edwards
25. Thomas Ellis
26. Williamson Edwards
27. Ricks Elliott
28. John Edwards
29. Sterling Faison
30. William Futrell
31. Enos Futrell
32. Winborne Futrell
33. Claiborne Griffin
34. Edward Gatlin
35. Joseph Griffin
36. Armstead Grizzard
37. William Gay
38. Green Hart

39. William Harriss
40. Gideon Harriss
41. Elias Harriss
42. William Hicks
43. Henry Hailey
44. Henry Hart
45. John Holmes
46. James Hill
47. Jeremiah Horton
48. Moore Higgs
49. William Ingram
50. John Jenkins
51. John Johnson
52. John Jordan, Sr.
53. Elias Johnson
54. Robert Johnson
55. Nathaniel Ingram
56. Benjamin Jenkins
57. Jesse Jones
58. George Key
59. Robert Little
60. Edwyn Liles
61. Henry Leek
62. Lemuel Lane
63. Benjamin Lawrence
64. Joshua Morgan
65. John Maughon
66. Jesse Morgan
67. Wilson Mongar
68. Bartlett McDonald
69. Samuel Norwood
70. William Naresworthy
71. Burwell Norwood
72. Everet Oliver
72. Samuel Patterson
74. William Pledger
75. George W. Pledget
76. Barnathy Pope
77. Joel Peele
78. Jesse Phillips
79. Phillip Poyland
80. James Pierce
81. Robert Roe
82. Thomas Richards
83. Willis Roane
84. Boswell Smith
85. John B. Stanback

86. Robert Snipes
87. William Short
88. Benjamin Strickling
89. Matthew Spivey
90. Benjamin Sweter
91. Henry Sweter
92. Britain Smith
93. James Sumner
94. John Thompson
95. Edmond Wilson
96. James Wheeler
97. Joseph T. Wornam
98. Sion Wheeler
99. Simeon Wood
100. Samuel Warren
101. Abraham Wall
102. Lemuel Winborne
103. Lemuel Warr
104. John E. Wallace
105. Jahn [sic] Wade (const.)

****

HALIFAX COUNTY
FIRST REGIMENT

1. William Price, 1st Lieut.
2. William Brinkley, Ensign
3. John Allen
4. Ludwell Allen
5. German Baker
6. William Curliles
7. Anderson Clardy
8. John Crawly
9. William Campbell
10. Stephen Eubank
11. John Fulgem
12. Nathaniel Gilliam
13. Alfred Harwell
14. Jesse Harlow

Page 79

15. Robert Hynes
16. Orren Harris
17. Hugh Hatheway
18. Hall Hudson

19. Joseph C. Justice
20. Willis Johnson
21. Henry Jones
22. Willis Johnston
23. Samuel King
24. William Keeter
25. Gregory Moore
26. Henry Morris
27. Willie Matthews
28. Eli Marshall
29. Eaton Morris
39. Elijah Nevill
31. William Onions
32. James Powell, Jr.
33. Benjamin Partin
34. Isham Perdue
35. John Pitts
36. Irby Powell
37. Edmond Powers
38. Allen Rainey
39. Edward Robinson
40. Jacob Sykes
41. Caleb Smith
42. Lodiman Shelton
43. Isham Sykes
44. James Shaw
45. Battie Smith
46. Peter Smith
47. Daniel L. Sturdivant
48. Joel Smith, Jr.
49. Joseph A. Sturdivant
50. Laban Vinson
51. Warren Vinson
52. Richard Vick
53. Lewis Willis
54. Samuel Weldon
55. Sharp Wright
56. James Wood
57. Joseph Williams
58. Thomas Weldon
59. Guilford Williams
60. Washington Yarborough

****

HALIFAX COUNTY,
SECOND REGIMENT

1. Jeptha A. Barns, Captain
2. John Peebles, 1st Lieut.
3. John Bradford, 2nd Lieut.
4. William Brinkley, Ensign
5. Thomas Cochran
6. Micajah Alsobrook
7. Benjamin Vick
8. Abud [sic] Gray
9. Samuel Murder
10. Henry Harris
11. Benjamin Jones
12. James Liscomb
13. Turner Brewer
14. John Sills
15. Joel Carlilsle
16. John Roan
17. Mills Parker
18. Jesse Curling
19. Josiah Fort
20. Wilson Bantly
21. William Bantly
22. David Bantly
23. William T. Bryant
24. Thomas Drew
25. John Dawson
26. Benjamin Paul
27. Cordy Drew
28. Ira Coffield
29. Edmund Wiggins
30. Whitmell Braswell
31. General Dawson
32. Marmaduke Braswell
33. Aquilla Lock
34. Dempsey P. Hillman
35. Jesse Hayes
36. Nathaniel Mullen
37. Valentine Minton
38. Edward H. Davis
39. James Northcut
40. Thomas Gall
41. Thomas Jolly
42. Richard Doggett
43. Henry Doggett
44. Thomas Lowe
45. Joseph Randolph
46. James Turner
47. Peter Brunt

48. Herbert Warner
49. Thomas Merrit
50. Landin Smith
51. John Archer
52. Ralph Skinner
53. James Bachelor
54. Matthew Holtfoot
55. Damel [sic] Glover
56. Augustin Willis
57. Elisha Euse
58. Samuel Davis
59. Joshua Manning
60. Blake Davis
61. Peyton R. Tunstall
62. James Young
63. Dempsey Pittman

****

Page 80

WARREN COUNTY

1.. Amos P. Sledge, Lieut.
2. John Monno [?] Land, Ensign
3. James Powell, Serg.
4. John Allen, Serg.
5. Wilnet Egerton, Serg.
6. William Powell, Serg.
7. James Tolley, Corp.
8. Owen F. Myrick, Corp.
9. Henry Person, Corp.
10. Doctor G. Robberson, Corp.
11. Allen Wren
12. Bird Ellington
13. Cudberth Neal
14. Charles Stewart
15. Claton Lambert
16. Daniel A. Perdue
17. Drury Thompson
18. Daniel White
19. Elish Sherren
20 Edward Patillo
21. George Hazlewood
22. Hardaway Davis
23. Henry James
24. James Edwards

25. Joseph Whaer
26. Joshua Harper
27. James Alston
28. James Thomas
29. James C. Bennet
30. James Smith
31. Joel Tolley
32. Joel Elllington
33. Jiles Carter
34. Jeptha Caps
35. Ira Allen
36. John Hawks
37. John Lancaster
38. Kinchen Williamson
39. Lemuel Mitchell
40. Lewis Sherren
41. Littleton B. Roberson
42. Lewis Ellis
43. Lanceford Baker
44. Michael Bell
45. Miles Ellis
46. Obadiah Ellis
47. Philemon Perdue
48. Peter Randolph
49. Richard Allen
50. Ransome Acock
51. Richard Davis
52. Ransome Worrell
53. Richard Brook
54. Samuel Dowton
55. Thomas Newsman
56. Thomas Walker
57. Thomas Harton
58. Thomas Davis
59. Thomas Tolley
60. William Oliver
61. Willis Person
62. William Sherren
63. William Breedfore

****

NASH COUNTY

1. Isaac Watkins, Captain
2. Joseph Vick, Lieut.
3. Willie Rick, Ensign

4. Henry Hedgepath
5. Joseph Griffen
6. James Heckworth
7. Elijah Whelas
8. William Walker
9. Solomon Thomas
10. Thomas Cobb
11. Holliday Hedgepath
12. Nelson Bowie
13. William Langley
14. Lewis Tucker
15. Robert Crickmore
16. William Ballard
17. Asberry Lindsey
18. Briant Lewis
19. Willis Hammons
20. Allen Brantley
21. Honi [?] Puchet
22. John Perry
23. John Rice
24. Joseph Bissalt
25. Reuben Strickland
26. William Colston
27. William Bunn
28. Whitmell Hicks
29. Samuel Vick
30. James W. Daniel
31. Henry Bunn
32. Valentine Chapman
33. Thomas Valentine
34. Duncan Ricks
35. Oran D. Powell
36. Thomas Pott
37. Bennet Mason
38. James Manning
39. John Williams
40. Frederick Parish
41. Henry Blount
42. Tompkins Rese
43. Thomas Aven
44. Enoch Flood

Page 81

45. Samuel Williams
46. Samuel S. Lampkin
47. Valentine Perkinson

48. Edward Strickland
49. David Hunt
50. Major Potter
51. German Mann
52. Claibourn Mann
53. Peter Prigen
54. Irwin Eatman
55. Elisha Tisdal
56. Eli Never
57. Everret Morriss
58. Griffin Lewis
59. Irvin Boykin
60. James Duck
61. Lee Horn
62. Thomas Landers
63. Thomas Williamson
64. William Landers
65. Amden Horn
66. William Braswell
67. Sion Beckworth
68. Arch G. Whitfield
69. John Harris
70. Alfred Strickland
71. Edwin Harris
72. Thomas White
73. Jesse Thorp
74. James Hunter
75. Reddick Massengill
76. Joab Tucker
77. Wright Bachelor
78. Cornelius Taylor
79. Boen Wren
80. Joseph Brown
81. William Bilbes
82. Joseph Bachelor
83. Wilson Bachelor

****

SECOND REGIMENT

WASHINGTON COUNTY

1. blank
2. blank
3. David Airs
4. Joseph H. Adams
5. Joshua Alexander
6. Anthony Alexander
7. Andrew Bateman
8. Evin Bateman
9. James Blount (3rd son of Steph.)
10. Isaac Brown
11. Reuben Carnel
12. Robert McClary
13. Richard Corprew
14. Elijah Etherige [sic]
15 Robert Everitt
16. Solomon Armstrong
17. Aaron Fagan
18. James Forlaw
19. Jacob N. Gordon
20. Josiah Haughton
21. Daniel Barns
22. Edward Hollis
23. George Harrison
24. John Jethro
25. Harman Legett
26. Downing Leary
27. Joshua Long
28. Charles Wiley
29. Aquilla Norman
30. Frederick Oliver
31. William Readit
32. Evin Phelps
33. Hezekiah Phelps
34. Willibough Phelps
35. Edward J. Ransom
36. John M. Roulhac
37. Roger Snell
38. Stephen Swain
39. William H. Star
40. James Walker, Sr.
41. Martin Walker
42. Joshua Young.

****

TYRELL COUNTY

1. Richard Hawett, Captain
2. Benjamin Clayton, Ensign
3. Jeremiah Giles
4. Daniel Ensley
5. Eli Woodley
6. Henry Mariner
7. Abel Calhoon
8. Talket Davenport
9. Samuel Davenport
10. Ebenezer Peettigrew [sic]
11. Charles Phelps
12. Uzziah Spruell
13. Willis Sawyer
14. Edward Man
15. Lewis Mydgett
16. Benjamin Mydgett

Page 82

17. Major Brickhouse
18. Gardener Alexander
19. Richard Brickhouse
20. Elixim Swain
21. John Cooper
22. Matthew Brickhouse
23. Henry Norman
24. Darius Phelps
25. Seth Sanders
26. Silas Etherige [sic]
27. Peter Wynn
28. Spence Hooker
29. Joseph Pledger
30. David Alexander
31. Joshua Swain
32. Zadock Hassel
33. William Ranton
24. Thomas Sweedy

35. Isaac Liverman
36. James McKinney
37. Joseph Swain
38. William Edwards
39. Charles Johnson
40. Josiah Jermanny
41. Carney Spinner
42. Henry Baker
43. Lilby Bilangey
44. John Cahoon (of John)
45. Benjamin Cooper
46. Thomas Clayton
47. Willis Liverman
48. Hardy Powers
49. Hardy Powers
49. Ebenezer Smith
50. Miles Sawyer
51. James Cahoon (of John)

****

HYDE COUNTY

1. Seth B. Jordan, Captain
2. Wyriott Windley, Lieut.
3. Christopher Gaskins, Ensign
4. David Paine
5. Asa O'Neal
6. Benjamin Turner
7. Henry Clark
8. Mathew English
9. William Meekins
10. Sparrow Midgett
11. Josiah Knox
12. Stephen Owens
13. Samuel Selby
14. Daniel Seabrook
15. William B. Spencer
16. Benjamin Brine
17. John Swindell
18. Thomas Mason
19. Samuel Williamson
20. Edward Rose
21. Uriah Lewis

22. Elias Mooney
23. Thomas Moore
24. Wilson Sawyer
25. Clement Daniels
26. Thomas Daniels
27. Zedekiah Swindell
28. Frisby Spencer
29. Morris Daniels
30. Henry Delow
31. Alexander Cohoon
32. Israel Henry
33. Robert Hopkins
34. Samuel Gibbs, Sr.
35. Selby Spencer
36. Thomas Sanderson
37. Jeremiah Hall
38. Stephen Gibbs
39. Washington Gibbs
40. William Cohoon
41. Thomas Gurganus
42. Zachariah Wilkinson
43. Zachariah Bishop
44. John Allen
45. Mark Smedick
46. Martin Davis
47. Henry Hobbs
48. William Eborn
49. Robert Barnett
50. John Shavener
51. Mouncen Peckham
52. Henry Blount
53. Enoch Robins
54. Zachariah Kipps
55. Richard Jordan
56. Thomas Moore
57. William Hooten
58. Lewis Blount
59. Nathan Harvey
60. Moses Windley
61. John James
62. William Barrow
63. William Fetterton
64. Richard Sadler
65. Robert Harris
66. Bartee Gibbs
67. David Gibbs
68. Josiah Harris

69. John Silverthorn
70. William Easter, Sr.
71. Solomon Easter
72. Sheldon Tonley
73. John Dixon
74. Thomas Mason
75. John Gaylard
76. William Easter, Jr.

Page 83

77. Franklin Dixon
78. Valentine Slade
79. Jeremiah Tooley
80. Timothy Parmarle
81. Hosea Tyson
82. James Loyd

****

BEAUFORT COUNTY

1. John Cox, Captain
2. Henry Williams, 1st Lieut.
3. Samuel Taylor, 2nd Lieut.
4. Wilson B. Hodges, Ensign
5. Achilles Hawkins
6. Richard Mastin
7. Jesse Godley
8. William S. Holmes
9. Allen Grist
10. William McDonald
11. Charles Holland
12. Jesse Swonner* [both
13. James Sworner*   used]
14. Christ Crandell
15. Benjamin Legget
16. Joseph Legget
17. John Brown
18. David Latham
19. Major Ball
20. Eden Beacham
21. James Gorden
22. Joel Dickenson
23. Isaac Peacock
24. Peter Demill
25. William D. Barr

26. Michael Hanrahan
27. James Kelly
28. Hugh McCullough
29. William Shaw
30. Solah Hamman
31. Levin Wallace
32. Willile Bagner
33. Alfred Bagner
34. Benjamin Braddy
35. John Wollard
36. Jacob Allegood
37. James B. Ellison
38. Littleton Hawkins
39. Nathan Cutler
40. Slamil [sic] Bagner
41. Thomas Hawkins
42. Isaac Chauncey
43. Irra [sic] Paul
44. John Seaward
45. John Pilley
46. Jacob Cordin
47. Israel Windley
48. J. Gardner
49. Thomas Floyd
50. William Fortisqua
51. John Whitley
52. Aaron Gurganus
53. Jacob Wilkinson
54. John Kelley
55. Jeremiah Garrot
56. William Sleaty
57. James Harris
58. George Harris
59. James Waters
60. Dempsey Martin
61. Elisha Harris
62. Shadric Downs
63. Noah Spear
64. John G. Hill
65. Joseph Millar
66. Thomas Morris
67. William E. Edwards
68. William N. Edwards
69. Willie Hill
70. William Telliton
71. Richard Blacklidge
72. Israel Harching

73. Uriah Slade
74. John Evitt
75. Daniel Warren
76. Hardy Rue, Jr.
77. Lott Evitt
78. William Dixon
79. Thomas Robason [sic]
80. Hilery Whitehurst
81. William Hudnal
82. Will Bond
83. Jesse Puiser
84. John Danals
85. Zadock Ives
86. David Camper
87. Frederick Watson
88. Luke Lenton
89. Zedekiah Mirow [sic]
90. Burage Linton
91. Jeremiah Slade
92. Nathaniel Woodard
93. James Jones
94. Thomas Cox
95. William Springle
96. Joshua Moore
97. Price Wm. Lewis
98. Solomon Brag
99. Archibald Wilcox
100. William Walker
101. William Thomason
102. John Roll
103. William Hollowell
104. John Dowty

****

Page 84

CRAVEN COUNTY

1. Minor Huntington, Captain
2. John S. Smith, 1st Lieut.
3. Isaac Hellen, 2nd Lieut.
4. Uriah Sandy, 3rd Lieut.
5. John Forlaw, Ensign
6. Moses H. Stephens, Serg.
7. Abner Heartley, Serg.
8. Lewis Griffen, Serg.

9. Isaac Patrick, Serg.
10.. Harvey Morris, Corp.
11. Mason Ives, Corp.
12. William Caruthers, Corp.
13. Nathaniel Clark, Corp.
14. Moses Prescott
15. Will Whitford
16. James Daniels
17. Jesse Collins
18. Joseph Stephens
19. Jesse Hampton
20. David B. Gibson
21. Michael Fisher
22. John Shipp
23. Kinchen Canaday
24. George Lane
25. Jesse Weatherington
26. Samuel Avery
27. Amos Hudler
28. William Sanders
29. Jacob Dudley
30. Levin Dunn
31. George Lewis
32. Linkfield Perkins
33. Robert Barns
34. Stephen Hawkins
35. Elisha Arnold
36. Edmund Heath
37. Henry Shute
38. Isaac White
39. John Arnold
40. Frederick Heath
41. William West
42. Cason Fell
43. Elijah Wheedleton
44. William Spikes
45. James Edwards
46. Moses Caton
47. Jos. S. Brinson
48. Rollin Dixon
49. Jordan Butler
50. John Bryan
51. Joseph Bryan
52. Lewis Warren
53. Stephen Chapman
54. Will Griffin
55. Levi Griffin

56. Jesse Griffin
57. Daniel Daughety
58. Elijah Randal
59. Louis Cox
60. William King
61. Zach Barrot
62. Shad Holloway
63. Allen Smith
64. Ervin Taunt
65. Ennis Cooper
66. William Hall
67. William Mills
68. Reding Harrison
69. John Kirk
70. Levi Gallin
71. John Taylor
72. John Sparrow
73. John Griffin
74. John S. Brown
75. John Jones
76. Nathaniel Lewis
77. Elijah Dunn
78. Evan Jones
79. Andrew Morgan
80. Thomas Hall
81. Lazarous Ipock
82. John Ipock
83. John Kemp
84. Aaron Eventon
85. Abner Gatlin
86. Henry Ipock
87. Thomas Carraway
88. Parks Ryal
89. James Masters
90. John Pittman
91. Job Smith
92. Richard Parsons
93. John Holley
94. Jephthy Simpson
95. Duran Ives
96. Isaac Reed
97. Frederick Folson
98. Peter Parris
99. William S. Brinson
100. Robert Phillips
101. Elijah Ives
102. William Harper

103. Thomas King
104. Jesse Lawson
105. James Vendick, Jr.
106. Ezekiel Simpkins
107. John Woods
108. William Williams
109. Cornelius Dixon
110. Samuel Collins
111. Thomas Hamilton
112. Lewis Dawson

Page 85

113. Murphy Trott
114. John Smith
115. Joshua Mitchell
116. Elijah V. Pittman
117. Benjamin Marriner
118. John Herrington
119. Thomas McKelro
120. Thomas Pittman
121. William Muse
122. Francis Beasley
123. Reuben Prentiss

****

CARTERET COUNTY

1. Nathaniel Pinkham, Captain
2. David A. Wallace, 1st Lieut.
3. Thomas Martial, 2nd Lieut.
4. James Chadwick, 3rd Lieut.
5. Jacob Paquanett, Ensign
6. John Paquanett, 1st Serg.
7. Jesse Prescott, 2nd Serg.
8. Alexander Hamilton
9. Samuel Sanders
10. Uriah Suggs
11. Thomas Meadows
12. Hardy Lane
13. Wilboga Prescott
14. Fama [sic] Gaskett
15. John Simmons
16. Allen Robinson
17. Samuel Piver
18. Daniel Dickerson

19. Bartoa Hendesty
20. James E. Gibble
21. Joseph Hall
22. Samuel Guthree
23. Samuel Buckman
24. John Martial
25. Logan Key
26. Zemeriah Harris
27. Jesse Haskett
28. John Weaks
29. Thomas Elliott
30. Josiah Harris
31. Samuel Gardener
32. James Piver
33. David Gould
34. Joseph Morton
35. Counsel Fealds
36. Thomas Louis
37. Archibald Louis
38. John S. Davis
39. Zephaniah Howland
40. Washington Willis
41. Newel Bell
42. William Morton
43. William Pigett
44. Williams Brooks
45. Joseph Willis
46. Uriah Gillikan
47. George Gillikan
48. Richard Arthur
49. George Linguish
50. Isaac Wade
51. Martin Chadwick
52. William Howland
53. David Gabriel
54. Joseph Willis
55. Thomas Nelson
56. Abisha Nelson
57. Littleton Willis
58. David Gaskitt
59. David Hamilton
60. Henry Saulter
61. William Smith
62. Joseph Tulcher
63. David Mason
64. James Styson
65. Reubin Willis

****

JONES COUNTY

1. Sears Bryan, 1st Lieut.
2. Jonathan Wood, Ensign
3. Jonathan Kay
4. Jones Mades
5. Aaron Eubanks
6. John Dudley
7. James Frazer
8. Theolifus [sic] Odium
9. William Foskey
10. Amos Sanderson
11. James Griffith
12. Joshua Millar
13. Joseph Wallis
14. Josiah Taylor
15. Benjamin McKinney
16. James Monford, Sr.
17. Frederick J. Becton
18. John Wilcox
19. James Reynolds
20. Robert Reynolds
21. Thomas Mackney
22. Jonathan Lee
24. Thomas McQuillar
24. Alfred Harget
25. Ivey Anders
26. Daniel Mallard
27. Adam Anders
28. Shadick Mallard

Page 86

29. Joseph Killingsworth
30. Benjamin D. Gray
31. John Overton
32. Ariel Jones
33. Daniel Smith
34. Hezekiah Alphin
35. John Shelfer
36. Lewis Kinsey
37. William Garman
38. William Wilcox
39. John Gilbert
40. Kesdon McDaniel

(son of risdon)
41. William Harget
42. James Monford, Jr.
43. Alfred McDaniel
44. Daniel Stanley
45. John Barrington
46. John McDaniel
47. James Oliver
48. Jesse Alphin
49. Abner Harrison
50. Samuel Dillahunta
51. Durant Green
52. Peter Harget

****

LENOIR COUNTY

1. Joshua Mosley, Captain
2. Richard Aldridge, 3rd Lieut.
3. Thomas Aldridge
4. William Benton
5. Silas Bowen
6. Lewis O'Bryan
7. Bartholamy [sic] Cauley
8. John Slismore
9. Jesse Slismore
10. William F. Davis
11. Reading K. Davis
12. David Evans
13. John Evans
14. Major Fields
15. Zachariah Gray
16. David Griffin
17. Samuel Hines
18. Rigdon Henry
19. William Hood
20. David Hartsfield
21. Burwell Herring
22. Kenon Hudlow
23. Josiah Horton
24. Isam Jackson
25. Isaiah Johnston
26. Isham Lassiter
27. Herod Lovit
28. Thomas Midlin
29. Kenon Meloney

30. William Moore
31. William Mosely
32. Walker Moore
33. Radner Moore
34. William Potter
35. John Phillips
36. Moses Pool
37. Farniford Pool
38. William Pearson
39. Abraham Peacock
40. Bryan Pate
41. Thomas Rows
42. Edward Smith
43. William Sutton
44. Patrick Sparrow
45. John Tilman
46. Arthur Tull
47. Jeremiah Waters
48. John Westbrook
49. Garrot Williams
50. Thomas Witherington
51. William Vause
52. Briton King

****

GREEN [sic] COUNTY

1. Henry Miller, 1st Lieut.
2. James Eastwood, 2nd Lieut.
3. Joseph Harrel, Ensign
4. John Gardner
5. John Andrews
6. Mark Taylor
7. Jonathan Parker
8. James Wasden
9. Aven Lane
10. Willis Newsom
11. John Goff
12. Henry David
13. Joel Mears
14. Gardner Jones
15. Silas Lassiter
16. Abraham Grizzard
17. William Britt
18. William Barrow
19. Joseph Williams

20. Beverly Belsher
21. John Murrah
22. Haswell Hay
23. Woody Belsher
24. James Rogers
25. Charles Tindall
26. Samuel Harrel
27. Benjamin Hardy
28. Lemuel Hardy
29. David Shirley
30. Henry Moring

Page 87

31. Nicholas Smith
32. Samuel Forrest
33. John Potter
34. Allen Stanul
35. Simon Jones
36. William Harper
37. William Farmer
38. Owen Lockhart
39. Abram Joyner
40. William Turnage
41. Jesse Cunninggem
42. Stuart Summerlin
43. Augustin Moore
44. James Hill
45. Spears Denny
46. Micajah Kenaday
47. James Edmonson
48. Fountain Ward
49. Nehemiah Garras
50. Timothy Roddick
51. Stephen Tison
52. James Ranch
53. Noah Dunn

****

PITT COUNTY

1. George Eason, Captain
2. Summer Adams, 1st Lieut.
3. Samuel Albritton, 2nd Lieut.
4. Gideon Brindon, 3rd Lieut.
5. William Briley, Ensign

6. John Stocks
7. Burrel Bell
8. John Moye
9. Jacob Rogers
10. Samuel Truss
11. James Johnston
12. Dvid Hathway
13. Kedar Randolph
14. William Whitehurst
15. Turner House
16. Jacob Moore
17. William Nichols
18. Reuben Gardener
19. Isaac Gardener
20. William Quinley
21. Stephen Quinley
22. Hardy Trip
23. Jonathan Pelt
24. James Beil
25. Jesse Cherry
26. Thomas Adams
27. John Duvol
28. John Eason
29. William Mills
30. Daniel Duvol
31. James Bryant
32. Caleb Nelson
33. Bryant Grimes
34. Jordan Nelson
35. Joseph Boyd
36. Naisby Mills
37. Naboth Nelson
38. Noah Adams
30. John Arnold
40. William Boyd
41. William Barber
42. Moses Herrington
43. Arthur Maglehan
44. Franklin Moye
45. Gilford Broom
46. Isaac Turner
47. Joab Smith
48. Noah Harris
49. Worley White
50. Ervan Dudley
51. Erandal Little
52. Hugh Telfair

53. Joseph Griffin
54. Samuel Moore
55. Silvenus Harris
56. Willie Daniel
57. James Buch
58. Amos Joyner
59. Icabod Moore
60. William Hodges
61. Sparkman Smith
62. Abner Askew
63. Absalom Page
64. Thomas Flanigen
65. David Leget
66. Willis Flemming
67. Mansel Flake
68. Miles Spier
69. Allen Moore
70. John Harriss
71. Charles Tison
72. William Bird
73. William Norriss
74. James Grist
75. John Willoughby
76. John Wallace
78. Joseph Judkins
79. John Smith
79. Richard Gammon
80. Bryant Corbet
81. Richmon Cobb
82. William Braddy
83. John Teal, Jr.
64. Samuel Williams
85. Elisha Braddy
86. Frederick Barfield

Page 88

87. Micajah Teal
88. Allen Mayo
89. William Thomas
90. Benjamin Bell
91. Simpson Meeks
92. Frederick Sommerlin
93. John Thomas
94. Alvin Mayo
95. Elisha Taylor
96. William Downs

97. Henry Jolley
98. Henry Moore
99. Solomon Harriss
100. Richard Carson
101. Amos Pelet
102. John Cox
103. James Wilson
104. Henry Cannon
105. William Emery
106. Edmond Evans
107. James Whitehead
108. William Brooks
109. Hugh Pritchett
110. John Barnhill
111. Willie Gurganus
112. Henry Barnhill
113. Edward Acrey
114. Jonathan Briley
115. John Bullock

****

MARTIN COUNTY

1. [blank]
2. [blank]
3. Lemuel Ballard
4. Obediah Bullock
5. James Belflower
6. Barnaby Brown
7. Redding Brown
8. Zachariah Browney
9. Hardie Cobb
10. Littleberry Carlisle
11. Harrod Craft
12. Jesse Cow, Jr.
13. Jonathan Callaway
14. John Douglas
15. Wight Evans
16. Michael Ellis
17. Jesse Griffin
18. Edward Griffin
19. Joshua Griffin
20. John Haislip
21. Branson Haislip
22. William Hassel
23. Joshua Hodge

****

24. Edward Hardison
25. Jesse Harrel
26. Benjamin F. Hallsey
27. Theophilus Jenkins
28. Lemmuel James
29. Lovett Lanier
30. Josephus Moore
31. Ith [?] Medford
32. Marcum Manning
33. Mathew Pickolson
34. Simon Perry
35. John Petty
36. William Pennywell
37. Hardy B. Price
38. John Quin
39 William Roebuck
40. Reddick Rawls
41. Abraham Rawls
42. Joshua Robinson, Jr.
43. Josiah Rogerson
44. Bond Stawls
45. Joel Smithwick
46. Rebuen Salenger
47. William Swain
48. James Swain
49. Samuel Spruel
50. David Wynns
51. Henry Wynns
52. George Wynns

****

EDGECOMBE COUNTY
FIRST REGIMENT

1.   [blank]
2.   [blank]
3. Abraham Taylor
4. Amos Walston
5. Allin Balton
6. Brient Evens
7. Benjamin Larder
8. Benjamin Granthen
9. Bryant Little
10. Bryant Stallons
11. Burwell Page
12. Calin Andrews

13. Dempsey Owens
14. Dempsey Gardner
15. Edwin Sherwood
16. Edward Amison
17. Eanos [sic] Askin
18. Ehisha Jones
19. Ephraim Wooton
20. George Moore
21. George H. Kilibrew
22. Henry Waller

Page 89

23. Henry Wooten
24. Isaac Scarborough
25. James Harman
26. Hillard Thomas
27. Jonathan Thomas
28. Jordan Bruce
29. Jacob Barnes
30. Jonas Williford
31. Joshua Taylor, Jr.
32. Joseph Farmer
33. Jacob Sims
34. John Evins
35. John Sharpe
36. Joseph Pittman
37. James Tart
38. Jeremiah Horne
39. Joseph Ruffin
40. John Holomon
41. John Thespin
42. Joshua Killibrue
43. Joseph Page, Jr.
44. James Ambrose
45. John Dowdin
46. Joseph Ansley
47. James Norvil
48. Jessy Morris
49. Lawrence Page
50. Lewis Peele
51. Marshal White
52. Martin B. Horne
53. Mills Harvil
54. Moses Moore
55. Perry White
56. Hobbert Coleman

57. Robert Long
58. Richard Singleton
59. Samuel R. Jenkins
60. Thomas Dixon
61. Thomas Morris
62. Thomas Barrow
63. Uriah Stallings
64. William Dixon
65. Whitmel C. Bullock
66. William Webb
67. William Singleton

****

EDGECOME COUNTY
SECOND REGIMENT

1.   [blank]
2.   [blank]
3. William P. Coleburn
4. William Savage
5. Maurice Redmond
6. John Parker
7. Stephen West
8. Robert Broadstreet
9. James Griffis
10. Berry Brown
11. Lott Killibrew
12. Laden Abrahams
13. Luke Nowells
14. Daniel Conner
15. James Cobb
16. John Anderson
17. John Moon
18. John Knight
19. Drury Mayo
20. Charles Knight, Jr.
21. Hardy Harrill
22. Geraldus Batts
23. Littlebury Edwards
24. David Pender
25. Thomas Hayner
26. James Everitt
27. William Bayton
28. James Taylor
29. James Rainer
30. Reading Crisp

31. Maulden Loops
32. Jesse Turner
33. Michael Horn
34. J. Jolly Horn
35. James Williams
36. Vincen [sic] Vaughn
37. Elijah Jackson
38. Robert Barnes
39. John Hines
40. Joseph Stallions
41. John Penney
42. David Lain
43. James Foreman
44. John Garrock
45. Jason Matthews
46. William Armstrong
47. John Sarsnot
48. James Mayo
49. Kenneth Coopper [sic]
50. Lewis Purvis, Jr.
51. Stancel Heard
52. Thomas Wiggins, Jr.
53. William Exum
54. James Petman
55. Thomas Jones
56. Bork Dickson
57. Levi Denton
58. John Lain
59. Joseph Sessums
60. Spier Bradley
61. Stephen White
62. Archibald Pope
63. Reuben Taylor
64. John Spyva
65. Thomas Strickland
66. William Kea
67. Joseph Loyd

****

Page 90

WAYNE COUNTY

1. John Flowers, Captain
2. Hillary Hook, 1st Lieut.
3. Major Blont, [sic] 2nd Lieut.

4. David Thompson, 3rd Lieut.
5. Willie Hall, Ensign
6. Henry Roberts
7. Burwell Martin
8. Jeremiah Smith
9. John Wasdon
10. Thomas Beard
11. Pearce Brogden
12. Kenrard Holland
13. Matthew Gennet
14. Bryan Bradberry
15. Joseph Smith
16. Jesse Taylor
17. Caleb Howell
18. Edward York
19. Anson Gurly
20. Raiford Wiggs
21. Lewis Forehand
22. John Hardy
23. Jethro Barns
24. Simon Barns
25. Hermant Hooks
26. Joseph Ware
27. Miles Lamb
28. William Bass
29. Cornelius Durden
30. Levi Winflet [Winslet ?]
31. Ransom Comanch
32. Samuel Barns
33. Elisha Devoun
34. Bryan Bass
35. John Mitchell
36. Lewis Powell
37. Joel Ellis
38. Noah Bass
39. Johnston Corbet
40. Michael Watson
41. John Skipper
42. Ephraim Grant
43. Kelly Creamer
44. Joseph Smith
45. Samuel Pope
46. Richard Langston
47. Miles Rodford
48. Thomas Grant
49. Richard Ivy
50. James McCullin

51. Jesse Warturs
52. Bryan Rhodes
53. Bryan Pipkin
54. Arthur Pearce
55. James Britt
56. Henry Cannon
57. William Atwill
58. Rolen Coley
59. Williams Bundy
60. Joshua Fletcher
61. William Ham
62. Taylor Smith
63. Henry Britt
64. Henry Ham
65. Wm. Landcaster
66. William Lasser
67. Isaac Hill
68. Henry Boget
69. Everit Thompson
70. Bryan Thompson
71. Richard Worrel
72. Wiley Peacock
73. Handy Alfred
74. Jesey Worrel
75. Matthew Bradford
76. John Thompson
77. James Futcret
78. Jeremiah Bunton
79. James Bartlet
80. John Elventon
81. Richard Wodel
82. Noah Peacock
83. Henry Hare
84. Elisha Cook
85. Nathan Bremon
86. William Deal
87. Simon Peacock
88. Thomas Outland
89. Arthur Bogan
90. John Heath
91. James Bridger
92. Matthew Grace
93. Joseph Herring
94. James Tindal
95. John Harrass
96. William Kelly
97. Richard Carey

98. John Cox
99. Richard Kelly
100. Jesse Peacock
101. Rheuben [sic] Mitch
102. John Bizzel
103. Sion Granthon
104. William Dunn
105. Jacob Sims

****

Page 91

ONSLOW COUNTY
THIRD REGIMENT

1. William Mitchell, Captain
2. Titus Howard, 1st Lieut.
3. Hardy Pitts, 2nd Lieut.
4. Lewis Oliver, 3rd Lieut.
5. Hilory Henderson, Ensign
6. Lott Huffman
7. George Williams
8. James Mills
9. William Calvet
10. Henry Foster
11. Henry Hyde
12. James Strange
13. Charles Cox
14. James Harvey
15. Jesse Wilder
16. Thomas Hawkins
17. Absalom Barber
18. Stephen Calvet
19. John Brown
20. Hillkiah Horn
21. Nathan Futral
22. Rigdon Whaley
23. Peter Ambrose
24. Edmund Littleton
25. William Parker
26. John Ellis
27. Isaac Simpson
28. Reuben Melton
29. James Barrow
30. Josiah Hawkins
31. Everitt Simmons

32. Edward Kellam
33. Charles Thompson
34. Benjamin Littleton
35. John Murrel
36. John Edmondson
37. Dexter Farnel
38. Hawkins Marshall
39. Kilby Henderson
40. John Eubanks
41. Otway Hawkins
42. Purnal Haskins
43. Robert Caston
41. John Marshall
45. John Morton
46. Enock Haskins
47. John Gibson, Jr.
48. Ezekiel Eubanks
49. Brice Fields
50. Henry Wells
51. Elijah Eubanks, Jr.
52. Bryan Barber
53. John Gilbert
54. Jos. Collins, Jr.
55. William Gibson, Jr.
56. William Carraway
57. John Garrett
58. Richard Simmons
59. Alexander Gray
60. Edmund Milson
61. Solomon Davis
62. Josiah Ward
63. Elijah Taylor
64. William Bell
65. Charles Scott
66. James Hurst
67. Jesse Hardison
68. John Edens
69. Samuel Nicholas
70. Peter Venters
71. Leckariah Evins
72. Laben Justice
73. Simon Hobbs
74. Whitlift Casten
75. Frederick Mills
76. John Shepard
77. James Lloyd
78. Lewis Thompson

79. Thomas King
80. Jesse Fryer
81. John Higgs
82. George Hinkley
83. William Sammons [sic]
84. John Goints
85. David Horn
86. Henry Milton
87. Edward W. Shiver
88. Hosiah Clark
89. Josiah Fayles
90. Moses Jinkins
91. James Baker
92. Obed Eason
93. William A. Pearce
94. James Oman
95. Daniel Mashborn
96. Henry Howard
97. William Orme
98. Thomas Fryer
99. John Bell
100. Samuel Howard
101. John Jones
102. David Riggs
103. James Caston
104. Jackariah Jackson
105. Amos Goints

****

Page 92

NEW HANOVER
COUNTY

1. Montesquien W. Campbell,
    Captain
2. James Nixon, Lieut.
3. Joel E. Larkins, Lieut.
4. William Lewis, Ensign
5. William McCurdy
6. Septhen Notton
7. Richard Saunders
8. James Larkins
9. Robert Rankin
10. Reuben Laving
11. John Walker

12. Joseph Jones
13. William S. Nickols
14. Donald R. McLeod
15. Jesse Scarborough
16. Jonathan J. Long
17. Moses Shellers
18. William Taylor
19. Aaron Alexander
20. Woodman S. Ledbury
21. Joshua McClammy
22. David Eddons
23. Buckner Stokely
24. Jacob Pickett
25. Jeremiah Nickols
26. Thomas Coston
27. William Nixon
28. Robert Nickols
29. Henry King
30. John James
31. Edmond Hansley
32. John Riley
33. James Ratcliff
34. William Revenbark
35. John Wood
36. William George
37. Daniel George
38. Richard Millar
39. Joseph Mumford
40. Robert Larkins
41. John Parker
42. John Beesley
43. Solomon Beesley
44. John Moore
45. John Highsmith
46. Anthony Williamson
47. Hugh lamb
48. Nickolas Boon
49. Berd Boon
50. Samuel Gerganious
51. William Gerganious
52. James Malfrass
53. John Register
54. James Bonham
55. David Bonham
56. James Busby
57. Obed Smith
58. Dempsey Powell

59. Francis Devane
60. William Corbet
61. George Corbet
62. James Lee
63. Duncan Sellars
64. Timothy Johnson
65. John Airs
66. Ross Cogdell
67. James Roe
68. Fredric Simpson
69. Luten Orr
70. John Black
71. Benjamin Moore
72. William Mathass [?]
73. George Moore
74. John B. Bourdeaux
75. Benjamin Due
76. John Bainhill
77. Timothy Rooks
78. Joseph Rooks
79. Benjamin Mott
80. Morris Bishop
81. William Adkins
82. Daniel Adkinson
83. Fredric Gerganion [sic]
84. Thomas Bishop, Jr.
85. William Robeson
86. Ensign Hinklin
87. Joseph Farrow
88. William Goodman
89. Benjamin Rockell
90. Jacob Castill
91. Alfred Wadkins
92. Lawrence Mason
93. Henry Dickson
94. James Evans
95. Daniel Bucher
96. Gilbert New
97. Hardy Bowen
98. Samuel Stranghan
99. Duncan Henderson
100. Danile Henderson
101. John Taylor
102. Matthew Johnston
103. David Paget
104. Isaac Taylor

****

BLADEN COUNTY

1. John Sellars, Captain
2. John Andrees, 1st Lieut.
3. John Andres
4. Matthew Sikes
5. James Sikes
6. Nathaniel Sutton

Page 93

7. David Sikes
8. Aaron Larkins
9. Peter Cromattee [?]
10. Beatty Sikes
11. Ever McMillan
12. Nehemiah Done
13. Charles Oliver
14. Elisha Baker
15. James Benson
16. Matthew Benson
17. Elijah Smith
18. James Counsel
19. Alfred Sikes
20. William Jones
21. Cornelius Ray
22. Samuel Smith
23. William Anderson
24. Philemon S. Hodges
25. Philip Cheshire
26. James Singletary
27. Morgan Allan
28. John Beard
29. Aaron Plummer
30. Samuel Cain
31. Neil McArthur
32. Colin Monroe
33. Joseph Allan
34. Neil Clark, Jr.
35. David Perry
36. John Robeson
37. Simon Smith
38. Duncan Clark, Jr.
39. Augus Clark
40. Willis Hudson

****

41. David Russ
42. John Mulford
43. Ever McMillian
44. Sion Callum
45. William White
46. Benjamin Singletary
47. William Wood
48. George Russ
49. Willis Singletary
50. Zadock Hillbourne
51. Samuel Pool
52. Henry Hillbourn [sic]
53. Abraham Blackw [?]
54. Jesse Jones
55. William Jones
56. William Robeson
57. Absalom Mairs
58. William McEwen
59. William Mooney
60. Archibald Robeson
61. John Bluie
62. John Lisley
63. Randolph M. Millar
64. James Rising
65. William Lewis
66. Daniel McEwen
67. Samuel Singletary
68. John Hair
69. Jonathan Lock
70. Edward Plummer
71. Brayton Singletary
72. John Martin
73. Alexander Watson
74. Richard Taylor
75. Jacob Long
76. Thomas Bedsold
77. Henry Bullard
78. Thomas Davis
79. Lewis Suggs
80. John McDonald
81. Shadrack Wether
82. William Smith
83. John New
84. Travis Bedsold
85. Daniel Sellars
86. William Simmons
87. Duke Edge

88. John Smith
89. Arthur Smith
90. John Edwards
91. John Davis
92. Daniel Melvin
93.   [blank]

****

BRUNSWICK
COUNTY

1. John Bryan, Lieut.
2. Thos. Flowers, Lieut.
3. Moses Bruton
4. John Liles
5. William Sellers
6. George Oliphant
7. James Keath
8. George Keath
9. Bennet Flowers
10. William Taylor
11. Samuel Tharp
12. Samuel Hill
13. Meady Osby
14. Henry Rainy
15. Peter Stanaland
16. James Highsmit [Highsmith]
17. John Barns
18. Henry Stanala [Stanaland ?]
19. William Gaust
20. Bryan Gause
21. Elisha Sellers
22. John Ward

****

Page 94

COLUMBUS COUNTY

1. Caleb Stephens, Captain
2. Josiah Powell, Ensign
3. William Bryan
4. Armilain Bryan
5. Meskick Wilson
6. Dothan Hammons

7. Demsey Worrell
8. William Register
9. Jonathan Dial
10. Robert Ward
11. James Campbell
12. Andrew Coleman
13. Henry Coleman
14. John Campbell
15. William Faulk
16. Asa Coleman
17. Elisha Nickols
18. John Gore
19. Levi Stephens
20. Malachiah Hews
21. Hinnant Faulk
22. Joseph Gore
23. Needham Fairfax
24. Jonathan Beech
25. William Flinn
26. Nathaniel Ward
27. William Stubbs
28. Henry Johnston
29. George Stubbs
30. James Lasser
31. John Barefoot
32. John Lasser
33. Arthur Mooney
34. Isaac Dage
35. John Wilson, Jr.
36. Thomas Faulk
37. John Billberry
38. Shadrick Wilson [enlisted]
39. Amos King
40. William Hook
41. Goldsberry Boswell
42. Reuben Stephens
43. Gilbert McKeithan
44. Eli Nobles
45. William Mooney
46. John Addison
47. James Jones
48. William Little
49. Curtis Fields
50. Henry Billbinny
51. Lewis Price
52. John Wilson [enlisted in U.S.
        A.]

53. Austin Innman
51. John Faulks

****

DUPLIN COUNTY

1. John E. Hussey, Captain
2. Amos J. Walker, 1st Lieut.
3. Abraham Glisson, 2nd Lieut.
4. John Swinson, 3rd Lieut.
5. John T. Grady, Ensign
6. Charles Bowan
7. William Streets
8. David Teachey
9. Jonathan Allen
10. Caldwell Thalley
11. George Mallard
12. Isaac Allen
13. James Norriss
14. John F. Bowey
15. Lemuel Thigper
16. Tobias Fountain
17. William Fountain
18. James Scarborough
19. James Borcy
20. Felic [Felix ?] Hancock
21. Nathan Murray
22. Henry Hollingsworth
23. Noah Lanier
24. John Bishop
25. Caleb Ostian
26. Owen Bishop
27. Joseph Brooks
28. John Farrier
29. William Sandler
30. Daniel Kenady
31. David Farrier
32. William Northcut, Jr.
33. Benjamin Pearce
34. William Farrier
35. Joseph Brooks, Sr.
36. Jonas Jones
37. Nathan Kennady
38. Reding Smith
30. Thomas Davis
40. Jesse Grimes

41. Theophilus Williams
42. James Stuart
43. Richard Matthews
44. Michael Matthews
45. Enock Quin
46. William Macner
47. Felix Sullivan
48. Stephen H. Glisson
49. William Hardison
50. Henry Deal
51. Benjamin Herring
52. Theophilus Blount

Page 95

53. John Beardan
54. William Connerly
55. Henry Moore
56. Lemuel Guy
57. Isaac Gore
58. John Pollock
59. Archibald McCaleb
60. Benjamin Rivenbark
61. John Bennet
62. Solomon Kenady
63. Joel Burnham
64. Daniel Parker
65. John Barfield
66. Bennet Millard
67. Lewis Rouse
68. Daniel Jones
69. Dickson Sullivan
70. Henry Sommerlin
71. Thomas Jones
72. Daniel Swinson
73. Thomas Brock
74. John Swinson
75. Reading Bowden
76. Joseph Sollace
77. Jesse Brock
78. Henry Boyt
79. James Wade
80. Moses Bourdeaux
81. Elam Lea
82. Allen Jones
83. John Hines
84. David Floan [Sloan ?]

85. Alexander Heath
86. David Brock
87. James Morris
88. John Miller, Jr.
89. Jacob Mallard
90. Samuel Chambers
91. George Cummings
92. Patrick Ezell
93. Nicholas Rogers
94. Isaac Taylor
95. Samuel Grier
96. Nathan Jones
97. William White
98. Isaac Wilson
99. Byrd Williams
100. John Oneal
101. Stephen Noles
102. Joseph Waller
103. Jacob Taylor
104. Elijah Jones
105. Daniel Cannon

****

SAMPSON COUNTY

1. Payton R. Parker, Captain
2. Thomas Sutton, 1st Lieut.
3. Ira Tucker, 2nd Lieut.
4. Burrel Register, Ensign
5. James Pennington
6. John Brewer
7. Zachariah Parker
8. Thomas James
9. Cornelius McKay
10. John Cook, Jr.
11. Levi S. Mars
12. Joshua S Mars
13. Zepheniah Parker
14. Felix Merritt
15. Levi Register
16. Manassah Williams
17. Lewis Williams
18. Michael Shurly
19. Aaron Marlin
20. Lowamy Flowers
21. Whitfield Sutton

22. Wiley Merrit
23. Philip Flowers
24. Wm. Hope
25. Gabriel Peterson
26. Wm. Stephens
27. William Robinson, Jr.
28. George Robinson, Jr.
29. William Edge
30. Allen Jones
31. Needham Watkins
32. James Chesnut
33. Joseph Chesnut
34. Joseph Kelly
35. John Boon
36. Abraham Joiner
37. Robert Wilkins
38. James Hall
39. Cornelius Autrey
40. Ezekiel Owens
41. Sherrod Simmons
42. John Faircloth
43. Isom Faircloth
44. Raphial Faircloth
45. Curtis Nillens
46. Juni [?] Pope
47. Thomas Owens
48. John McLewinnen
49. Jesse Carr
50. Thomas Britt
51. Stephen Pope
52. Jonathan Carrold
53. John W. Turner
54. Martin Hare
55. Thomas Howard
56. Nathan Williams

Page 96

57. Nathan Strickland
58. William Stewart
59. Tobias McGee
60. James Faircloth
61. Martin Strickland
62. Matthew Porter
63. Elbert Strickland
64. Henry Hall
65. Drew Daughtrey

66. William Goodwin
67. Hardy Daughtrey
68. David Strickland
69. Jonas Quimby
70. Michael Hobbs
71. Henry Woods
72. John Royals [Owin's son]
73. Robert Dardin
74. Nias Waters
75. Uriah Westbrook
76. Green Hill
77. Jordan Coats
78. Barney Blackman
79. Young Wood
80. John Tallow
81. John Tart
82. David Rainer
83. James Wilson
84. Felix Bass
85. William Williford
86. James Anderson
87. Hardy Warrick
88. Duncan Peterson
89. Joseph Lorraman
90. Clemm Sales
91. Robert Wilson
92. Malcom McCorquadale
93. David Dudley
94. Hugh McQueen
95. Neil Stewart
96. Lurrel Mobley
97. James Rench
98. John Hare
99. James Rainer
100. Ervin Jackson
101. William Chesnut
102. John Royal [Isom's son]
103. Bailey Chesnut
104. Owen Page.

****

ROBESON COUNTY
FIRST REGIMENT

1. John McPhattair, Captain
2. Duncan Murphy, 1st Lieut.

3. James McRee, 2nd Lieut.
4. Jacob Little, 3rd Lieut.
5. John McPhaul, Ensign
6. Archibald McIntyre
7. Stephen Cumboe
8. Neil McMillan
9. Jesse Manuel
10. Jesse Pittman
11. Dempsey Powell
12. Aaron Braswell
13. William Shipwash
14. Elias Bullard
15. Richard Bullard
16. Anderson Taylor
17. Henry Trawick
18. James Brassie
19. Charles Williams
20. John McNeil
21. John McDonald
22. John Walker
23. James Watson
24. Peter Nickolson
25. Peter Monroe
26. Malcom McEachern
27. Duncan McEachern
28. Lauchlin McLauchin
29. Stephen Powell
30. Henry Bullock
31. Sterling Powell
32. Stephen Ammons
33. Lalathel [?] Pipppin
34. Willis Jones
35. Richard Watson
36. Richard Small
37. John Townsend
38. Burwell Britt
39. Stephen Land
40. John Philips
41. James Wilcox
42. Benjamin Lovet
43. William Histers
44. Zachariah Pate
45. Reuben Musslewhite
46. Charles Pate
47. Michael Baxley
48. Joel Stephens
49. John Hammons

50. Cade Barfield
51. Albertain Barnes
52. Erick Legget
53. Asa Daniel
54. James Taylor
55. Burwell Lee
56. Giles Herring
57. Elijah Pittman
58. Needham Barfield
59. John Parnell
60. John Powers
61. Moab Willis
62. Paul Allen
63. Thomas Wilson
64. James Bourne
65. Hardy Cox

****

Page 97

ROBESON COUNTY
SECOND REGIMENT

1.   Blank
2.   Blank
3. Willis Baslay
4. Neill Thompson
5. Malcom McRainey
6. Edward Malloy
7. Robert McAlpin
8. James McMillan
9. John McMillan
10. Neel McKennon
11. John Davis
12. Daniel Stewart
13. Daniel McAlpin
14. Hugh Carmickdet
15. Hugh Mathews
16. John Shaw, Jr.
17. Daniel Ruthoen
18. Elijah Wilks
19. Duncan Smith
20. Hugh McKenzie
21. John McKay
22. Neill Wilkinson
23. Alex McNeill

24. Alex Johnson
25. Archibald McNeel
26. Angus McAlpin
27. Gadi[sic] Strickland
28. James Furguson, Jr.
29. Malcom McAlpin
30. Neil McNeill
31. Daniel Buie
32. Marsh Barlow
33. Hugh McKay
34. Daniel McNeill
35. Hugh McPherson
36 John Smith
37. John Powell
38. John Currie
39. John Farrell
40. Malcom Smith
41. Malcom McLoud
42. Peter McEacheron

****

CUMBERLAND COUNTY
SECOND REGIMENT

1. John Burt, Captain
2. John Armstrong, 1st Lieut.
3. Murdoch Ochiltree, 2nd Lieut.
4. Neil McArthur
5. James Cameron
6. Wm. Kennaday
7. Archibald Patterson
8. Malcom Clark
9. Duncan McLean
10. Archibald McGregor
11. Murdock McLeod
12. John Morrison
13. Hugh McLean
14. James Huckaby
15. James Ferguson
16. Lea Parker
17. Lewis Walker
18. John Dollihit
19. Young Blanchet
20. Jones Stephen
21. John Knight
22. James Stewart

23. Asey Pearson
24. Asa Matthews
25. Durham Aven
26. Elijah Spencer
27. Henry Urquhart
28. John Eley
29. James Christian
30.. Tapley Johnston
31. William Watson
32. Duncan McDongald
33. Hardy Parker
34. Duncan Dorman
35. Wm. Smith
36. James Campbell
37. Neil McAllister
38. James Dean
39. Alex McAllister
40. John Evans
41. James Kellin
42. Allen Godwin
43. David Balentine
44. Daniel McLeod
45. George Learcey
46. John Avery
47. John Johnston
48. Jonathan Smith
49. Levie Ennes
50. Lemi Searcy
51. Norman Urquhart
52. Norman Urquhart [sic]
53. Sam'l Card

****

MOORE COUNTY

1. Wm. Dowd, Captain
2. John Oats, 1st Lieut.
3. Alex McNeill, 2nd Lieut.
4. John Stuart, Ensign
5. Archibald Graham
6. John Blackman

Page 98

7. Kenneth Black
8. Ezra Russel

9. Martin Eagle
10. Wm. Barrot
11. John Moore (drummer)
12. Merriman Ball (fifer)
13. James Spicer
14. Daniel Kelley
15. John MacBeth
16. Benjamin Siler
17. Abner Hawser
18. Alex Curry
19. James Curry
20. Peter Kelly
21. Burwell Maples
22. James Ringstaff
23. John Hancock
24. Henry Philips
25. Hugh Kelly
26. Thomas Muse
27. Joseph Johnston
28. Henry Stuts
29. Malcom McCrommon
30. Duncan McLanchlin
31. Kindrick Brickhead
32. William Jinkins
33. John MacDonald
34. George Ritter
35. Neil Black
36. George Fry
37. John Rouse
38. John McLane
39. Duncan McInnish
40. Angus McNeill
41. Peter Blue
42. Neil McMillan
43. Malcom Bachan
44. John Black
45. Neil Sullivant
46. Joseph Robeson
47. John Morris
48. Martin Thomas
49. John MacIver, Jr.
50. James Walker
51. Duncan Baker
52. Edward Walker
53. Robert McIver
64. Malcom MacFarland
55. Martin Dye

56. Bartholomew Dunn
57. Wm. Smith, Jr.
58. John Gibson
59. Thomas Dunn
60. John Smith
61. William Britt
62. Angus McKennon
63. Wm. Jones
64. Daniel Buchan
65. Thomas Keyson
66. Alexander MacLane
67. John Nickolson
68. Dahald Campbell
69. Allen McLeod
70. Wm. Milton
71. Daniel Buie
72. Duncan Thompson
73. Duncan McDuffee
74. Wm. Brown
75. Gardener Rowling
76. Joseph Owens
77. Wm. Smith
78. John Dunlop
79. William Brewer, Jr.
80. Kindrick Williamson
81. Jacob Ormand
82. Moses Myrick
83. Isaac Teaque
84. Robert Brady

****

RICHMOND COUNTY

1. Pleasen M. Mask, Captain
2. Henry Thomas, 1st Lieut.
3. John MacKinnon, 2nd Lieut.
4. John Carmichael, 3rd Lieut.
5. Shelsby Cobman, Ensign
6. Thomas H. Lewis
7. David D. Tedder
8. John Steele
9. John Buck
10. John Kelly
11. Absalom Wall
12. James Gorden
13. William Robeson

14. Joseph Dark
15. Daniel Smith
16. Thomas Cope
17. William Long
18. Isham Shepard
19. Thomas Shepard
20. Culiver Britt
21. Daniel Laslie
22. Israel Luced
23. Moses Overstreet
24. Daniel McLeod
25. Lewis Thomas
26. William Scott
27. Burrel Graham
28. Stephen Herring
29. Benjamin Scott
30. Nehemiah Hadder
31. John Pate
32. Archibald Macgee

Page 99

33. Silas Norton
34. Benjamin Watkins
35. Richard Welsh
36. John Webb, Jr.
37, Jacob Lampley
38. Alexander Oliver
39. Moses Watkins
40. Thomas Serjiner
41. Daniel Munroe
42. Malcom Morrison
43. John Quick
44. Neill Laslie
45. Alexander McCall
46. Alexander Martin
47, Archibald McCattum, Jr.
48. John MacDonald
49. Dugal MacDuffie
50. Archibald Graham, Jr.
51. John Leech
52. Dugal Leech
53. John Morrison
54. John McQuain
55. Miles K. Well
56. Norman Campbell
57. Alex Cunningham

58. Noah Sanderford
59. Vincent Rainwater
60. Roland Hammons
61. John Powell
62. Eli MacDonald
63. John MacInnis
64. Gooden Capell
65. Huncan [Duncan ?]MacRae
66. Alfred Balding
67. George Dawkins
68. Duncan Cunningham
69. Alexander Gordon
70. Landerford Loving
71. Briant Loving
72. Archibald McCabler
73. Alex Cunningham
74. John Stewart
75. Isham Scott

****

ANSON COUNTY
FIRST REGIMENT

1. Benjamin A. Laniere, Captain
2. Thomas Godfrey, 1st Lieut.
3. Gideon Threadgill, 2nd Lieut.
4. John Lockhart, 3rd Lieut.
5.   [blank], Ensign
6. Nathaniel Hales
7. John Legoe
8. Micajah Dawkins
9. James Runnols
10. Joshua Legoe
11. Hugh Monroe
12. John Martin
13. John F. Russell
14. Theophilus Hopgood
15. Joseph Parish
16. Ezekiel Wynn
17. Abner Beverly
18. Emanuel Courtney
19. Henry Gullidge
20. Leroy Pounds
21. Isaac Boggaw
22. Thomas Ward
23. William Davis

24. William Taylor
25. Philip Gathings
26. William Howell
27. John Howell
28. John Patterson
29. Daniel McKay
30. Willis Struter [Streater ?]
31. William Dilport
32. James Short
33.. John Hopkins
34. John Hinson, Jr.
35. John Harrington
36. Daniel May
37. Daniel MacRae
38. John Punkett
39. John Launcan
40. Daniel Murphy
41. Elias Best
42. Charles Gathings
43. William Johnson
44. Axum Turner
45. Burwell Messer
46. Freeman Winkfield
47. Jeremiah Messer
48. Jacob Pope
49. Peyton Lunsford
50. Richard McBride
51. Shadrick Brazil
52. Wright Lee
53. John Lockhart
34. John Gowin
55. John Ingram
56. Thomas Smith
57. Wm. Vandiford
58. Angus Murchison
59. Joel Hamn
60. John Morel
61. William Wallace
62. Jonathan Boggan
63. Jesse McLindon
64. Jesse Little

Page 100

65. Wm. Bailey, Jr.
66. Colin Evans
67. John Cockran

68. Ashur Myres
69. William Rivers
70. William McDonald
71. Needham Eddins
72. Enoch Little
73. Levi Medor
74. John H. German
75. Isaac Morce

****

ANSON COUNTY
SECOND REGIMENT

1. Obadiah Curbee, Captain
2. Solomon Trull, 1st Lieut.
3. James White, 3rd Lieut.
4. Stephen Rushing, 3rd Lieut.
5. Hardy Harton, Ensign
6. Abraham Griffin
7. Saunders Taylor
8. John Parker
9. William Trull
10. William Gurly
11. Solomon Tragall
12. Thomas Trull
13. Joel Williams
14. Charlton Joiner
15. Enock Griffin
16. Moses Pearce
17. Horantio Rosser
18. Reuben White
19. Thomas Jones
20. John Meggs
21. John Jones
22. Asa Pearce
23. John lassiter
24. John Davis
25. Jesse Green
26. John Wm. Thomas
27. Philip Hagler
28. David Tomerlin
29. Nathaniel Bibby
30. William Shelby
31. David Medcalf
32. Joseph Price
33. Jordan Drake

34. Joshua Hudson
35. Wyatt Nance
36. William Hatcher
37. James Bawcom
38. Jephthah Beverly
39. James Dunn
40. Hausel Horn
41. George Hobbs
42. Isaac Williams
43. John Hyatt
44. James Hill
45. George Nash
46. Willis Williams
47. David Allen
48. John Wilkerson
49. William Morgan
50. Elijah Cook
51. John Holifield
52. Joel Meador
533. George Duran
54. Thomas Moss
55. Isham Harrell
56. David Prince
57. Robert Leonard
58. George Williams
59. Elijah Carthodge
60. Wm. McMillan
61. Jeremiah Anderson
62. John Jones
63. Charles Trull
64. Stephen Williams
65. David Brumblow

****

FOURTH REGIMENT

WAKE COUNTY, FIRST REGIMENT

1. John Bell, Captain
2. William Battle, Lieut.
3. Zenas O'Kelly, Ensign
4. Joel H. Lane
5. Wm. W. Mason

6. William Wiggins
7. Dennis Wilson
8. William M. White
9. Charles Gilliam
10. Thomas Hill
11. Thos. R. Cooke
12. John Vandigriff
13. John Terry
14. Hardy Dodd
15. Charles Stewart
16. Newton Wood
17. Benjamin Brantly
18. Charles Johnson
19. Williams Damsell
20. James Reddish
21. John Luced
22. John Smith

Page 101

23. John Andrews
24. John Cooke
25. Isham McGee
26. Wm. Buffalo
27. Thomas Neal
28. Lewis Bunn
29. Harris Liles
30. Robert Hicks
31. Bennet Brown
32. Reuben Mitchell
33. Thomas Williams
34. Micajah Wall
35. Charles Horton
36. William Learcey
37. Berry Ambrous
38. John Butter
39. Hardy Peane
40. William Boyakin
41. Budd Bagwell
42. Dickson Jordan
43. Burwell Fowler
44. William Hopkins
45. Mark Cole
46. Reddick Massey
47. Jedemiah Pulley
48. John Jones
49. Isaac Massey

50. Benjamin Marriott
51. William Reddish
52. Jerrod Chamblee
53. Budd Bunn
54. Wm. Philips
55. John Perry
56. Henry Culpepper
57. Robert B. Williams
58. Seth Jones
59. Hinton Pugh
60. John Leopard
61. Elie Alford
62. Samuel Landiford
63. Bennet Perry
64. William Clark
65. William Reaves
66. Thomas Garrott
67. Shadrack Bolar
68. Josiah Battle
69. Brittain Acock
70. Thos. Alston
71. David Williams
72. Simon Williams
73. Peter Porter
74. James Williams
75. Samuel Sugg
76. Acril Myatt
77. Ephraim Messer
78. Wm. Rand
79. Wm. Roads
80. Hardy McGuffe
81. Willie Pollard
82. Wm. Canwadd
83. Samuel Slaughter
84. Jacob Baltin
85. Henry Smith
86. Osbourn Jordan
87. Bryan Ferrill
88. Hardy Lewis
89. Ansel Price
90. Brittain Deloach
91. Bennet Bawcom
92. David Hutchins
93. William Todd
94. Jesse Fason
95. John Traywick
96. Simon Stephens

97. Joseph Shaw
98. Johnson Britt
99. Samuel Jones
100. David Slawson
101. Allen Parker
102. William King
103. Thomas Spiar

****

WAKE COUNTY
SECOND REGIMENT

1. John Green, Captain
2. Willis Whitaker, 1st Lieut.
3. Joseph Barbee, 2nd Lieut.
4. Jephthah Tyrell, 3rd Lieut.
5. John W. Lee, Ensign
6. Alexander Smith
7. Allen Jones
8. Aaron Matthis
9. Alsey Yates
10. Anda Burges
11. Asa Blake
12. Abner Green
13. Anthony Bledsoe
14. Alfred Wilkins
15. Absalom Hayes
16. Aquilla Hubbard
17. Bradford Jones
18. Burwell Brown
19. Britain Smith
20. Benjamin Ashworth
21. Britain Mills
22. Benjamin Davis
23. Christopher Woodard
24. Christopher Spier
25. Daniel Jackson
26. Daniel Matthis
27. Dawson Adkinson
28. Eldah Brown

Page 102

29. Edward Bledsoe
30. Ewell Watts
31. Francis Jones

32. Gideon Vaughn
33. Green Hill
34. Hillsman King
35. Henry Haley
36. Hillsman Parish
37. Hinton Courtis
38. Henry Moore
39. Harwell Sims
40. James King
41. John Tedrick
42. Jacob Vandigriff
43. Isham Oliver
44. Joseph H. Hill
45. Joseph Woodard
46. John W. Lee
47. John Crocker
48. John Peddy
49. John Betts
50. John Fadgett
51. John Surls
52. Jacob Sorrel
53. John Luallen
54. James Walker
55. Johnston Loyd
56. John Carpenter
57. John Moore
58. John Jarral
59. James Thompson
60. Jonathan Hall
61. James Estes
62. John Geer
63. John Holloway
64. John Ward
65. Isham Goodwin
66. John Marshall
67. James Rigsby
68. John Edwards
69. Kitchen Griffin
70. Laban Jones
71. Martin Mann
72. Mordecai Joplin
73. Matthews Goodwin
74. Major Bradley
75. Nash Standley
76. Neal Womble
77. Peyton Norris
78. Robert Ray

79. Robert Glenn
80. Stephen King
81. Samuel Narris
82. Sion Uutly [?]
83. Stephen Seagroves
84. Seth Sexton
85. Stephen Pearson
86. Samuel Reaves
87. Timothy W. Jones
88. Thomas Dennis
89. Thomas Edwards
90. Thomas Laffoon
91. Wm. Evans, Jr.
92. William Silvey
93. Westley Jones
94. William Woodard
95. William Braker
96. William Eves
97. William Yates
98. Ridley Jones
99. William King
100. Walter Marshal [sic]
101. William Harris
102. Willie Harrison
103. Woodson Allen
104. William Marshall
105. Young Allen, Jr.

****

JOHNSTON COUNTY

1. Harry Bryan, Captain
2. Thomas J. Walton, 1st Lieut.
3. David Bryan, 2nd Lieut.
4. Hardy Pool, Ensign
5. Hartwell Ivey, 1st Serg.
6. Young Allen, 2nd Serg.
7. David Bridgers, 3rd Serg.
8. Godfrey Stansill, 4th Serg.
9. Rice Price, Fifer
10. Futrill Cockrett, Drummer
11. Ambrose Ingram
12. William Johnson
13. Averytt Holston
14. Nelson Andrews
15. Burwell Blackburn

16. Thomas Price
17. Allen Watson
18. Martin Price
19. James Smith
20. Bridgers Porch
21. John Brown
22. William Pullen
23. Larkin Smith
24. Joel H. Atkinson
25. Dixon Philips
26. William Willons
27. John Patterson, Jr.
28. John Evans
29. Henry Capps
30. William Braddy, Jr.
31. William Edwards
32. Noel West

Page 103

33. John Hobby
34. Hartwell Ivey
35. William Jones
36. James Ivey
37 Elisha Stanley
38. Benjamin Stephens
39. James Dozier
40. John Woodall
41. Moses Johnson
42. Alexander Woodall
43. Sion Hill
44. Samuel Wilder, Jr.
45. John Nawl
46. Eunuch Whitley
47. James Hinton
48. Theophilus Biddingfield
49. John Cooper
50. John Pallen
51. Wm. Cockrill
52. Isaac Keen
53. Stephen Williamson
54. William Watson
55. Edmond Balance
56. Arthur Pearce
57. Stephen Lasser
58. John Lamb
59. Silas Horn

60. Nathan Morris
61. Samuel Mitchiner
62. Wm. Thompson
63. Wm. Farrow
64. Asa Learcey
65. Osborn Howell
66. John Powell
67. Samuel Learcey
68. Nathaniel Hood
69. Lewis Tiner
70. Irvin Price, Jr.
71. George Bayett
72. Micajah Oneal
73. Jacob Peacock
74. Willie Price
75. John Eatman
75. Stephen Oneal
77. Stephen Price
78. Willie Hall
79. John Stansill, Jr.
80. Jonathan Austin
81. Nathaniel Jones
82. Alexander Franklin
83. Jacob Vincent
84. Zadock Gower
85. Willis Hayes
86. Benjamin Stephenson
87. William Stephenson
88. Wm. Snipes
89. Thomas Frail
90. Jonathan Baker
91. Willie Junigan
92. Nathan Almond
93. John Jordan
94. Joseph Bryan
95. Edward Stevens
96. James Brown
97. Lewis Smith
98. William Noals
99. John Warwick
100. John Kelly, Jr.
101. John Turner, Jr.
102. Abner Smith
103. Jesse Ellington
104. Theophilus Pool
105. Reddin Johnson
106. Isaac Pinney

107. Alsey Busby
108. Elisha Regging
109. James Pool
110. William Jones

****

FRANKLIN COUNTY

1. Jones Cook, Captain
2. Sherrod Sanders, Lieut.
3. Benjamin Carpenter, Ensign
4. Hicks Wynne
5. Nathan Patterson
6. Jeremiah Solomon
7. John B. Debnam
8. Richard Caisar
9. Micajah T. Cotten
10. Samuel Johnson
11. William Asque
12. James Langon
13. Peter Denton
14. William Denton
15. Solomon Perry
16. MacKollach Stone
17. Thomas Gay
18. Charles Hines
19. Willis Peale
20. Arthur Fassel
21. Charles Coppage
22. John Nelms
23. Jones Walker
24. Jesse Winston
25. Robert Robertson
26. Nathaniel Nickolson
27. William Duke
28. Ransom Brogdon
29. William Browning
30. Reuben Neale
31. David Cook
32. Benjamin Priddie

Page 104

33. John Arnolds
34. Benjamin Thomas
35. Joseph Bledsoe

36. George Bledsoe
37. William Murphree
38. Patrick Bledsoe
39. Miles King
40. Thomas Driver
41. James Upchurch
42. William Owens
43. John Bell
44. Isaac Griffin
45. Banister Peppin
46. Berkely Upchurch
47. Richard Spivey
48. Wm. T. Hollingsworth
49. Elisha Sandeford
50. William Phelps
51. James Medlin
52. William Sanders
53. James Cooley
54. John Harriss
55. Jos. Young
56. Jacob Alford
57. Henry Harriss
58. Nathaniel Williams
59. John Douglas
60. Isaac House
61. John B. Bobbit
62. John Dickson
63. James H. Murry
64. James Graham
65. Sugar McLemore
66. James Moore
67. Wm. Loyd
68. John Merrit
69. Wm. Pulliam
70. Thomas Wise
71. James Wiggins
72. Joseph Pleasants
73. Joseph Heltan
74. John Fuller
75. John Hornsby
76. Malachi Simmons
77. Jeremiah Cook
78. James C. Jones
79. Caswell Finch
80. Josiah Jackson
81. Dickson Cour
82. Oram Jackson

83. Peyton Tunstall
84. John Gill
85. Turner Cupton
86. James Nelms
87. Jacob Gupton
88. John Cook
89. Joel Parish
90. Benjamin Hamm
91. William Alford
92. John Farmer
93. Robert Cary

****

GRANVILLE COUNTY
FIRST REGIMENT

1. Willis Johnson, Captain
2. Wm. Nailing, Lieut.
3. William Mann, Ensign
4. Absalom Parish
5. Lemuel Kittrell
6. Micajah Harris
7. John Inscore
8. Anthony Moore
9. Malachiah Frazer
10. Edward Sutton
11. Richard Harris
12. Harrel Wiggins
13. John Wiggins
14. James Conway
15. Beriman Ham
16. Wm. W. Reavis
17. Alfred Hicks
18. Joshua Archer
19. Edward Bryant
20. James Bryant
21. David McGlanklin
22. William Warrels
23. Reuben Harris
24. Egrippy Nance
25. Gideon H. Macon
26. Thomas White
27. James Tate
28. John Floyd
29. Green B. Walker
30. Dick H. Dalby

31. Zackariah Lyon
32. James Bowers
33. Taswell Spain
34. Littleton Spain
35. Alexander Walters
36. Nathaniel M. Taylor
37. James Suite
38. Joseph Hister
39. Wm. Brogdon
40. Leonard Bullock
41. John Haley
42. James Arnold
43. Ezekiel Wheeler
44. Gideon Davis
45. Edward Chappel
46. Joseph Lysle
47. Burges Walls
48. John Stephenson

Page 105

49. Samuel Forsythe
50. Archibald Mitchell
51. Wm. McFarland
52. Micajah Dally
53. Thomas Forsythe
54. Jeremiah King
55. John Adams
56. William Adams
57. John Fuller
58. Abner Fletcher
59. Hezekiah Jones
60. James Allison
61. Gilliam McGehe
62. James Cook
63. Gilford Ball
64. Washington Womouth
65. Dempsey Brown
66. Willie Jones
67. Winkfield Morgan
68. Gideon Gill
69. Isham Huskey
70. Barnett Jeter
71. John W. Finch
72. William Hitlin
73. James B. Eustia

****

GRANVILLE COUNTY
SECOND REGIMENT

1.   Blank
2.   Blank
3.   Blank
4. George Parker
5. John P. Beasly
6. Matthew Chandler
7. Robert Blackwell
8. Anderson Satterwhite
9. William Amos
10. John Whitamore
11. Francis Oliver
12. Robert Hester
13. James Smith
14. George Lumpkin
15. Joseph Ames
16. Graves Hart
17. Robert Knott
18. James Falconer
19. John Finch
20. Bird Lofter
21. Robert Lewis
22. Samuel Lewis
23. Bussee Lewis
24. Charles Vancey
25. Samuel Daniel
26. John Royster
27. John J. Inge
28. Wm. Martin
29. James Lewis, Jr.
30. Richard Brown
31. Willis Hanks
32. Thomas Grissom
33. Thomas Terry
34. Nathaniel Roberson
35. John Hanks
36. John Dorch
37. Laban Grissom
38. John Cretcher
39. Archibald Gordon, Jr.
40. Allen Jones
41. Wm. Longmire, Jr.
42. William Frazier

43. Larkin Curren
44. Thomas Morris
45. John Sander
46. Alfred Hester
47. Richard Lemay
48. Samuel Ussery
49. Thomas Rice
50. Evan Raglin
51. Richard Ball
52. Abner Hicks
53. James K. Clark
54. Pumphrett Gooch
55. Abraham Eastwood
55. Simon Clements
57. John Hopkins
58. Riley Meadows
59. Elkanah Lyon
60. John Dodson
61. Young Montague
62. Bennet Foster
63. Ephraim Frazier
64. Thomas Hunt
65. John Cobs
66. Anthony Wood
67. John Duncan
68. Woodson Washington
69. Daniel Tucker
70. John Bowls
71. Jordan Bowls
72. Thomas Hayes
73. Benjamin Hester

****

PERSON COUNTY

1. John Bradshaw, Captain
2. William Bagley, 1st Lieut.
3. Bradshaw Fuller, 2nd Lieut.
4. Jeremiah Dixon, Ensign

Page 106

5. John Scoggin
6. Morgan Fitts
7. Elijah O'Briant
8. Robert Carter

9. Samuel Wheeler
10. John Russel
11. Downey Wade
12. John Riggs
13. Samuel Burke
14. Richard Broach
15. Robert Jones
16. Churchwell Jones
17. Anderson Jones
18. James Jones
19. Mark Glenn
20. Daniel Meadows
21. Richard Farrar
22. Samuel Mangrum
23. Riley Suit
24. Caswell Vaughan
25. Jeremiah Roberts
26. Wm. Cates
27. Seth Coleman
28. James Cozort
29. Daniel Hicks
30. Ambrose Day
31. Ambrose Dary
32 Archibald Day
33. Grant Allen
34. James Hay
35. John Parrot
36. Wyatt Painter
37. Wm. Bumpass
38. Thomas Gill
39. Wm. Elliot
40. Josiah Oliver
41. Gilliam Mitchell
42. Peter Warren
43. Pleasant Hall
44. John Harralson
45. Archibald Harralson
46. Wm. Martin
47. George Berry
48. Edward Johnston
49. James Johnston
50. Richard Jones
51. David Bell
52. James Bradshaw
53. Henry Worsham
54. Henry Lipscomb
55. James Dollerhide

****

56. Vincent Bradshaw
57. Vincent Lea
58. McFarland Oakley
59. Samuel Winstead
60. Wm. Royster
61. Reuben Lea
62. Wm. Southward
63. Richard Harris, Sr.
64. Drury A. Pulliam
65. Thomas Marit
66. Joseph M. Stanfield
67. Ransom Austin
68. John Brooks
69. Samuel Bull
70. Drury Pulliam
71. Daniel Rease
72. John Jas. Brooks
73. Allen Green
74. Henry Bailey
75. John Buckanan
76. Daniel Walker
77. Thos. Townsend
78. Wm. Buckanan
79. Wyatt Ford
80. John Wilkerson
81. Hastin Blalock
82. Wm. Mann
83. Wm. Hill
84. Benjamin Sampson

****

ORANGE COUNTY
FIRST REGIMENT

1. John Young, Captain
2. Arthur Bobbit, Lieut.
3. Isaiah Davis, Ensign
4. James Linsey
5. Elijah Hunt
6. Alfred McDaniel
7. John Cummins
8. Thos. Ward
9. Wm. Ringstaff
10. James Guttis
11. John Crabtree
12. Wm. Wilson

13. Lemuel Carrol
14. Green Williams
15. Joseph Proctor
16. Levy Cole
17. Timothy Cate
18. Isaac Wood
19. Archibald Carrington
20. Thomas Cate
21. Wm. Carrington
22. Zilmon Allison
23. Jos. McCullock
24. John I. Woods
25. Jesse Clark
26. John Jordan
27. David Ray
28. Green Richards
29. James Lindsey
30. Wm. Herndon

Page 107

31. Edmond Linch
32. John Browning
33. John Carden
34. Bartlet Hinchey
35. May Desern
36. John Scarlett
37. John Hitchins
38. James Raney
39. Daniel Boothe
40. George Nickolas
41. Wm. Woods
42. Hugh Riggs
43. John Woods
44. Bradley Collins
45. Robert Turrentine
46. Jesse McGee
47. Carter Garrard
48. Wilie [sic] Sweaney
49. Mark Oakley
50. Harrison Parker
51. George Moore
52. John Taylor
53. Willis Roberts
54. Amos Nickolas
55. John Garrard
56. Arthur Stephens

57. Charles Roberts
58. Ephraim Carrington
59. Thornton McFarland
60. James Stagg
61. John Roberts
62. James Parish
63. Levi Owens
64. John Tilly
65. Robert Clinton
66. Wiley Glenn
67. Canady Horton
68. Joshua Horton
69. Westly Rhodes
70. Lewis Hutchins
71. Moses Dorsett
72. Delamy Chizenhall
73. Daniel Holden
74. James Browning
75. Laney Chizenhall
76. Samuel Strayhorn
77. Anderson Whitehead
78. Benjamin Haswell
79. Newcomb Thompson
80. Pleasant Herndon
81. James Whithead
82. Edward McDade
83. Thomas Ruffin
84. James Thompson
85. Morris Henderson
86. Thomas Walker
87. David Strain
88. Thomas Gattis
89. Joseph Dawson
90. Bennet Pattin
91. Patterson Yeargin
92. Wm. Kirkland
93. Lewis Pattin
94. Andrew McCanley
95. James Woods
96. Willis Marcomb
97. Drury Leigh
98. John Browning
99. Asa Brown
100. Thos. Luter
101. James Shepard
102. Daniel Holden
103. Willie Marcomb

****

ORANGE COUNTY
SECOND REGIMENT

1. David Tate, Captain
2. Joseph Allison, Lieut.
3. Egbert Shepherd, Ensign
4. Wm. Mabane
5. George Mebane
6. Henry Mulhollan
7. Allan Mebane
8. Thomas Tinnon
9. Burk Walker
10. Robert Smith
11. Robert Shanklin
12. Samuel Gilston
13. Alex Criswell
14. Thomas Finnen
15. Thomas Woods
16. Hunter McCulloch
17. Will Campbell
18. Joseph Smith
19. Larkin Sanders
20. Thos. McClushy
21. John Bain
22. Walter Murray
23. John Wilson
24. Wesley Carson
25. Walker Pickett
26. James Davis
27. Rob't Dickee
28. Barnabas Perry
29. William Wilson
30. William Price
31. George Jordan
32. Frederick Bason
33. Sterling Price
34. Alex Lasly
35. John Woody
36. James Grimes

Page 108

37.Wm. Clendinen
38. Wm. Stewart
39. Elisha Pickhart

40. John Thompson (miller)
41. James Pindar
42. James Thompson, Jr.
43. Thomas Rhadshaw, Sr.
44. Simon Buckum
45. Matthew Tutral
46. David Ray
47. Jesse Ray
48. Samuel Kirkpatrick
49. Berry Duke
50. Stephen Glass
51. Alex Patten
52. James Webb
53. Erasmus Compton
54. Leroy Acros
55. Alfred Compton
56. Jeremiah Compton
57. Bobert [sic] Faucett
58. Eli Faucett
59. Anderson Faucett
60. Thos. Millington
61. Andrew Murray
62. Peter Belvin
63. Joshua Ward
64. Thomas Ward
65. Richard Hayes
66. Jesse Pickhart
67. Thos. Durham
68. Benj. Cruchfield
69. Richard Cate
70. Richard Workman
71. Green O. Daniel
72. James Minnis
73. Wm. Workman
74. Alex. NayBo [sic]
75. Alex. NayUts [sic]
76. Reuben Owens
77. Thos. Moore
78. Thos. Durham
79. Thos. Williams
80. James Weaver
81. Wm. Beaver
82. George Haywood
83. James Crabtree
84. Wm. Caven
85. Wm. Ivey
86. James Miles

87. Wm. Brewer
88. Thos. Cate
89. Anderson Blackwood
90. Benj. Bridges
91. Jasper Glawson
92. John Fowler, Drummer
9 3. John Webb, Fifer

****

ORANGE COUNTY
THIRD REGIMENT

1. James Grahams, Captain
2. Wm. Holt, Lieut.
3. Absalom Harvey, Ensign
4. Henry Holt
5. Thos. Powell
6. David Parks
7. Isaac Rainey
8. Jacob Whitsell
9. Richard Wilkins
10. Jeremiah Grant [son of John]
11. James Faddis
12. Jacob Albright
13. Charles Webster
14. Alex McDaniel
15. Joseph Albright
16. John McDaniel
17. George Ephland
18. Wm. Hashford
19. Wm. Caps
20. Joseph Smith
21. Nickolas Troxler
22. John Troxler
23. John Coe
24. James Wilson
25. Barney Troxler
26. Oliver Powell
27. Anderson Thompson
28. Simpson Harris
29. Avery Coe
30. Daniel Theek
31. George Spoon
32. Frederick Moser
33. John Wells
34. John Kimbro

35. Stephen Wells
36. Wm. Thompson
37. John Ray
38. Philip Rose
39. Ezekiah Hendley
40. George Martinn [sic]
41. Robert Fausett
42. Wm. Cooke
43. Thos. Rumbley
44. Wm. Jones
45. Joseph West
46. Nathaniel Jones
47. Robert Lackey
48. Joseph Hughes
49. George McCulley
50. Andrew McCulley
51. Edmund Branock
52. Alfred Moore

Page 109

53. Wm. Dickey
54. James Jackson
55. James Busick
56. James Burnet
57. Levi Kilton
58. James McPherson
59. Jos. Marshall
60. Wm. Carter
61. Richard Cambel
62. Timothy Weaver
63. George Stafford
64. Caleb Busick
65. Boston Tiley
66. James Melvan
67. Daniel Johnston
68. Jacob Huffins
69. Stephen Willis
70. Zacheriah Philips
71. John Cocke
72. Matthew Cotner
73. Jacob Cockeleress

****

CHATHAM COUNTY

1. Aaron Evans, Captain
2. Richard C. Cotten, Lieut.
3. Isaac Headen, Ensign
4. Mial [sic] Ramsey, 1st Serg.
5. John Taylor, 2nd Serg.
6. Wm. Underwood, 3rd Serg.
7. Wm. Duty, 4th Serg.
8. Thomas Craver, 1st Corp.
9. Stephen Cruchfield, 2nd Corp.
10. Asa Stone, 3rd Corp.
11. Rufus McMasters, 4th Corp.
12. Alex Boyd, Drummer
13. Henry Harris
14. George Harman
15. Ira Rosson
16. Thos. Beal
17. Thos. Clark
18. David Blalock
19.   blank
20. Jephthy Fooshee
21. Reuben May
22. Allen Goodwin
23. Bennona Rosson
24. Jonathan Lindley
25. John Lewis
26. Jos. Blaylock
27. Peter Quakenbush
28. George Rodgers
29. Wm. Lea
30. Sam'l Jackson
31. John Powell
32. Edward Caudle
33. Nathaniel Roberson
34. Richard Cates
35. James Crow
36. Hasten Poe
37. Jos. Wilkerson
38. John Glass
39. John Fields
40. Jos. Glass
41. Jonathan Green
42. Jonathan Miles
43. Tabner Beal
44. Wm. Tilman
45. James Jones
46. Joel Edwards
47. Jesse Bray

48. Samuel Elkins
49. James Limbory
50. John Moorey
51. Eli Bone
52. John Purvis
53. John Mann
54. John Brown
55. John Brigat
56. Asa Gunter
57. Alex Lassiter
58. Wm. Thomas
59. Jourdan Davis
60. Archibald Little
61. John MacIver
62. Thomas Bland
63. Burwell Williams
64. John Clegg
65. Whitmil Little
66. James Ward
67. Charles Johnston
68. Abner Minter
69. Wm. Lassater
70. George Drake
71. Alfred Buckannan
72. Robert Wicker
73. Wm. Hinton
74. Benj. Teddar
75. Stephen Loot
76. Wm. Smith
77. Harman Cox
78. Jos. Pearson
79. Benj. Phillips
80. Jesse Hicks
81. Claiborn Deaton
82. Gambol Powers
83. Daniel Brown
84. Tyson Womble
85. Jesse Highland
86. Aaron McMasters
87. Wm. Perry
88. Isaac Phillips

Page 110

89. Isaac Harrington
90. Jos. May
91. Ephraim Oldham

****

92. Henry Fields
93. John Gilman
94. Peter Smith
95. James Burns, Jr.
96. Wm. Smith
97. Joseph Holliday
98. Reuben Reeves
99. Jos. Whitehead
100. Elisha Harris
101. Frederick Philips
102. Henry Smith
103. Daniel Smith
104. Rufus MacMasters
105. Nickolas Fox, Sr.
106. David Vestal, Sr.
107. Jesse Nelson
108. Nathaniel Whitehead
109. Amos Ward
110. Joseph Allen
111. James Smith
112. John Norwood
113. Hiram Burns [112] [?]
114. John Wesley Bynum, Lieut.
115. John Cocke, Ensign
116. John Smith, 1st Serg.
117. Avent Cotten
118. James Thomas
119. Rora [sic] Womack
120. John Bowers
121. Thos. Williams
122. Joseph Mims
123. Richard Holt
124. Ransom Byrum
125. John Bishop
126. Henry Williams
127. James Boling
128. Thomas Garner
129. Allen Riddle
130. Guilford Garner
131. Green Straughan
132. Samuel Brewer
133. Elbert Williams
134. Watson Mitchell
135. Henry Wilson
136. Wm. Pennington
137. Thos. M. Sturdivant
138. Samuel Wilson

139. Elijah Willis
140. Wilson Willis
141. John Parker
142. Britain Hatley
143. Elijah Bell
144. Jacob Womble
145. Allen Parker
146. John Clark
147. Ruffin Upchurch
148. Allen Rhodes
149. Nickolas Long
150. Robert Council
151. Britain Harwood
152. John A. Mason
153. Thomas Oliver
154. Presley Moore
155. James C. Barbee

****

FIFTH REGIMENT

CASWELL COUNTY

1. James Holder, Captain
2. John Johnston, Lieut.
3. John Roan, Ensign
4. Francis H. Burton
5. Wm. Eddins
6. James Darby
7. Drucis Briggs
8. Wm. P. Jackson
9. Thos. Dameron
10. Adam Stafford
11. John Tirrell
12. Spencer Ball
13. Wm. Nelms
14. Harbert Samuel
15. Archibald Samuel
16. Edward Kersey
17. James Gordon
18. Samuel Johnston
19. Timothy Warren
20. John Hodge
21. Wm. Johnston

22. James Johnston (son of Jas.)
23. Alex Jackson
24. Charles Connally
25. Giddal Gillaspie
26. Thos. Evans
27. James White
28. John Gunn
29. James Ingram
30. Thos Pittard
31. Birditt Escridge
32. Dempsey Sargent
33. Abraham Price
34. James Florence
35. Wm. Murry
36. Absalom Burton
37. Christopher Matthews
38. John Love

Page 111

39. Wm. Tolloch
40. Eli Stafford
41. James McCain
42. Noel Burton
43. John Farley
44. Newman Durham
45. David Ball
46. Bird Wisdom
47. Virgil M. Rainey
48. James Swann
49. Laban Farland
50. Wm. Tirrell
51. Williamson Moore
52. Lewis Tirrel
53. Paul Tirrel
54. Henry Wilson
55. Major Stanfield
56. Henry Mahoon
57. Robert Malone
58. John N. Fuller
59. Peter P. Stublefield
60. Levi Simpson
61. Thos. Brinsfield
62. Philip Eubank
63. Richard Gates
64. James Baldridge
65. Benj. B. Nelson

94   **NORTH CAROLINA - ROSTER OF SOLDIERS IN WAR OF 1812**

****

66. Luke Sanders
67. John Norris
68. Thos. Hobbs
69. Matthew Walker
70. Wiley Mason
71. James Nighton
72. Jos. Swann
73. James H. Pass
74. Wm. W. Price
75. John Thompson
76. Rob't Ware
77. Thos. Penix
78. Joseph Burroughs
79. Thomas Swann
80. David Farley
81. Nathaniel Lea
82. Christopher Dameron
83. John Wray
84. James Thompson
85. Lewis Samuel
86. Abraham Montgomery
87. John Montgomery
88. Rowzee Samuel
89. Wm. Randolph
90. George Finlay
91. Thos. Turner
92. Isaac Patterson
92. Edley Campbell
94. Wm. Fullington
95. Christopher Spencer
96. Jos. Swann, Jr.
97. Rob't Yealock
98. John Covington
99. John Mansfield
100. Gabriel B. Lee
101. John Woods
102. Nickolas Thompson
103. Anderson Smith
104. Stephen Stuart
105. John Stuart
106. Sandy Smith
107. Wm. Culberson
108. John Fitch
109. James Johnston
110. Jesse Corbith
111. David Culberson
112. David Mitchell

113. Oney Randolph
114. Rob't Randolph
115. James Underwood
116. Wm. Jones
117. Edw. Moore
118. Jonson [sic] Brooks
119. Edward Wattington
120. James Rozwell
121. Henry Willis
122. Edward Jones
123. James Holdesnes
124. George Brooks, Jr.

****

GUILFORD COUNTY
FIRST REGIMENT

1. Rob't McEniston, Captain
2. Moses Owen, 1st Lieut
3. Wm. McBride, 2nd Lieut.
4. Jesser McCurston, Ensign
5. John Grogan
6. Levi Forbers
7. Samuel Hillmon
8. James Donnel
9. John McCurston
10. John McCain
11. Wm. Adams
12. John Hoskins
13. Amos Page
14. Nathan Lester
15. Caleb Hillmon
16. Wm. McCuiston
17. Samuel Kellum
18. Jos. Hoskins
19. James Lap
20. Thos. Hister
21. Elijah Owen
22. Wm. Hutchison
23. Elisha Coffin
24. Joshua Hillmon

Page 112

25. Daniel Caulk
26. Aaron Binny

27. Tilmon Clark
28. Robert Burney
29. John Nickolson
30. Wm. Claton
31. Lemmuel [sic] Oaks
32. James Hutchinson
33. James Bevill
34. Taylor Holloway
35. Moses Elliott
36. Henry Bevill
37. James McCuiston
38. Hartwell Knight
39. Turner Irby
40. Jos. Simmons
41. Alexander Hutchinson
42. James Loar
43. Ellis Hoskins
44. Isaac White
45. Wm. Wilson
46. Wm. Dennis
47. Agbert Landingham
48. Wm. Knight
49. Robert Spivert
50. Mark Caps
51. Tandy Bell
52. John Starnt
53. Benj. Allen
54. Shadrach Allen
55. James Brown
56. Electris Johis
57. Robert Flemming
58. John Perdue
59. Henry Anthony
60. Nickolas Edwards
61. James Tobin
62. Marmon Strawn
63. David Burney
64. Robert Middleton
65. Abraham Burt
66. George Kinnodle
67. Beniah Fleming
68. Hugh McCain
69. Amous Wilson
70. David Madaris
71. Thos. Daugherty
72. James Clark
73. Harvey King

74. John Pegram
75. Henry Wilson
76. Garrison Justice
77. Jesse Knott
78. Hooper Caffer
79. James Ross
80. Jasper Gent
81. William Shelby
82. Thomas Parker
83. David Loyd
84. Adam Boyd
85. David Edwards
86. Elias Morgan
87. Robert Russel
88.. Samuel Barney
89. George Donner
90. David Allin
91. Henry Clark
92. Wm. York
93. Harbert Brown
94. Sutton Taylor

****

GUILFORD COUNTY
SECOND REGIMENT

1. Wm. Clapp, Captain
2. Henry Humphreys, Lieut.
3. Robert Ervin, Ensign
4. Aaron Williams
5. Andrew Garenger**
6. Adain Trollenger
7. Andrew Gamble
8. Daniel Geringer**
   [**= both spellings used]
9. David Edwards
10. Ephraim Burrow
11. Enos Frazer
12. Francis Simpson
13. George Sullivan
14. George Stephens
15. Henry Weatherly
16. Henry Camplain
17. Isaac Wolfingtan
18. Isaac Lamb
19. Isaac McDill

20. Jesse Forbes
21. Jacob Hager
22. John Rarden
23. John Amick
24. Jos. Shaw
25. Jacob Coble
26. Jacob Greason
27. John Kinman
28. John Fogleman
29. James Foster
30. Zedekiah Smith
31. Jesse Shaw
32. James Grissom
33. John Dickson
34. Jesse Holton
35. Joel Lowden
36. John Boyd
37. John Tucker
38. Joseph Quaits
39. John Ingle
40. Jonathan Short

Page 113

41. John Murphy
42. James Suduth
43. John Hemphill
44. Leonard Phillippie
45. Major Underwood
46. Martin Fifer
47. Moses Job
48. Michael Swain
49. Moses Gibson
50. Nehemiah Whittington
51. Obed Gardner
52. Richard Williams
53. Robert Morgan
54. Reuben Dick
55. Robert Wood
56. Robert Wilson
57. Robert Field
58. Robert Patterson
59. Solomon Burrow
60. Samuel Dick
61. Samuel Irwin
62. Wm. Thomas
63. Wm. Fryer

64. Wm. Simmons
65. Wm. Swain
66. Wm. Richardson
67. Whittenton Sullivan
68. Wm. Fifer
69. Winwright Barns
70. Wm. Humphries
71. Wm. Watson
72. Wm. Suits
73. John Humphreys

****

ROCKINGHAM COUNTY

1. Geo. W. Barker, Captain
2. Howel Harris, 1st Lieut.
3. David Smith, 2nd Lieut.
4. James Fewel, Ensign
5. Joel Cardwell
6. John Gay
7. John Smith
8. George Jackson
9. Pleasant Dearing
10. Pleasant Tod
11. Reuben Lindsay
12. Dillard Allen
13. Josiah Settle
14. Leonard Carney
15. Alfred Bethell
16. Absalom Wall
17. Philip Gates
18. Wm. Wall
19. John Scales
20. Geo. W. Jennings
21. Samuel Dalton
22. Alfred Scales
23. Green Vernon
24. Wm. H. Rice
25. Jos. G. Porter
26. John J. Wright
27. Zack Strong
28. Elisha Hancock
29. Zack Fewee
30. Zack Wall
31. Thomas Smith
32. James Wall

33. James Webster
34. John C. Overton
35. John Webster
36. Thos. Barker
37. John Gilliland
38. Silas Padge
39. Joel Fagg
40. John Barker
41. Martin Roberts
42. Robert Hall
43. James Vaughan
44. Wm. Whitworth
45. Jonathan Aldridge
46. Pleasant Black
47. Pleasant Webster
48. Samuel Vernon
49. Robert Joyce
50. Philip Ision
51. Jacob Crawford
52. Jeremiah Barns
53. Wm. Reynolds
54. John D. Vernon
55. Josiah Vernon
56. Bartlet Edwards
57. John Sharp
58. Willie Dearing
59. John Parish
60. Shelton Foster
61. Thos. Robertson
62. And. Robertson
63. John Vaughan
64. Hardiman Strong
55. Samuel Page
66. Samuel Moxley
67. John Cody
68. James Walker
69. Milton Grant
70. Powhattan May
71. Wm. Duncan
72. Francis Hains
73. John Wilson
74. John Carter
75. John Geesling
76. Fountain Purrell

Page 114

77. Thos. Carter
78. James Andrews
79. Wm. Gedsey
80. Robert Hudson
81. Wm. S. Tucker
82. Freeman Greer
83. John Tucker
84. Isaiah Hancock
85. Alam [sic] Boak
86. Pleasant Gorman
87. Peter Lyon
88. Isaac Philips
89. David Kellan
90. Lee Bondusant
91. Stephen Gibson
92. Wm. Mangham
93. Stephen Pratt
94. Robert Gibson
95. Rob't H. Coats
96. Anth'y N. Millar
97. Cooper Jordan
98. Signor Ahorn
99. George Wright
100. James Underwood
101. John Robertson
102. John Kelly
103. Benjamin Ladyman
104. Thos. Underwood
105. Wm. Small
106. Edward King
107. John B. Curry
108. Noah Cardwell
109. James Norman
110. John Smith
111. John Joyce, Jr.
112. Pleasant Gibson
113. John Claridge
114. Eli Hancock
115. Jos. Bishop
116. John Dillard

****

STOKES COUNTY
FIRST REGIMENT

1. Sam Martin, Captain

2. Thos. Smith, Lieut.
3. Newton Ladd, Ensign
4. Elijah Nelson
5. Jacob Nelson
6. Jeremiah Cloud
7. James Lawson
8. Larkin Burge
9. Joel Ketchum
10. Edward Yates
11. Ezekiel Collins
12. Wm. Blanchet
13. Benj. Fry
14. Jas. G. Lyon
15. Wm. Johnson
16. Thomas Doss
17. Bartlet Shipp
18. Joseph Martin
19. Wm. Shipp
20. John Cox
21. Reuben Tilley
22. Lambert Dodson
23. Wm. Stanly
24. James Hutchers
25. Benj. Thomas
26. James Perkins
27. Matthew Moore
28. Wm. Young
29. George Breedlove
30. Hansford Pollard
31. John Pollard
32. Floyd Webb
33. John Jones
34. Wm. Cannon
35. Jeremiah Cisk
36. George Neele
37. Samuel Angel
38. Wm. Ladd
39. James Powers
40. Benj. D. Angle
41. Wm. Carr
42. Wm. Gibson
43. Robert Neele
44. David D. Bostick
45. Thos. Martin
46. Wm. Poindexter
74. John Tilley
48. Wm. Slaughter

NORTH CAROLINA - ROSTER OF SOLDIERS IN WAR OF 1812   97

****

49. George Booth
50. Richard Flynt
51. James Davis
52. Wm. Welch
53. Thomas Evans
54. John Harvey
55. John Hoover
53. Thos. Reddick
57. Henry Spainhower
58. James Ridley
59. Jacob Wolf
60. Jacob Helsepeck
61. John Brabin
62. Jesse Brown
63. John Edwards
64. Jacob Fiscus
65. John Prater
66. David Spainhower
67. Frederic Fulk
68. Wm. Childress
69. Shadrack Reddick
70. James Merrit

Page 115

71. John Kances
72. Isaac George
73. John Hooker
74. Jacob Denton
75. James Bowleyjack
76. Samuel Riggs
77. John Neal
78. Samuel Neale
79. Jesse Dunlap
80. Kelly Shirley
81. Jesse Banks
82. John Brown
83. Arthur Muskram

****

STOKES COUNTY
SECOND REGIMENT

1. John L. Hausar, Captain
2. Benj. Briggs, Lieut.
3. Solomon Fulps, Ensign

4. Duncan C. McCocklin
5. Alex McKay
6. Wm. G. Parish
7. Peter Shamell
8. David Jean
9. Jacob Neel
10. John Myers
11. Thos. Snow
12. John Snow
13. Matthew Marshall
14. Martin W. Marshall
15. James Allen
16. John Boswell
17. Thos. Marshall
18. John Bibee
19. Christian Waggerman
20. Stephen McFerson
21. Wm. Frazier
22. Matthias Maston
23. Thos. Walker
24. Owen Walker
25. Israel Robinson
26. James Lawrey
27. Elijah Harrell
28. Fredrick Millar
29. Fracis [sic] Rose
30. Jacob Huphines
31. Charles Vest
32. Wm. Blackburn
33. Thos. Jinkens
34. Robert Cornelious
35. Henry Fidler
36. John Oens
37. John Karney
38. John Strape
39. John Haning
40. Jacob Shamel
41. Daniel Hauser
42. Abram Lash
43. Henry Ripple
44. John Fidler
45. John Rell
46. Thos. Rell
57. Charles Chube
48. John Todd
49. Philip Huffman
50. Abram Johnson

51. Elisha Johnson
52. Jonathan Sell
53. John Styers
54. John Johnson
55. Richard Clampit, Jr.
56. Joseph Idol
57. John Whitehead
58. Hampton Bynum
59. Julius Patterson
60. John Blume
61. Christian Ebert
62. David Patterson
63. John D. Salmons
64. Wm. Golding
65. Andrew Bowman
66. Thos. Westmoreland
67. Elijah Fowler
68. Seth Hamm
69. George Lenville
70. Moses Lenville
71. John Forrester
72. John Campbell
73. Wm. Branson
74. Lawrence Angel
75. John Sprinkle
76. Wm. Branson
77. Godfrey Millar
78. Isaac Church
79. Robert Hill
80. John Cornelius
81. Harman Millar
82. Mickael Sailer
83. Henry Doub

****

SURRY COUNTY
FIRST REGIMENT

1. David Freeman
2. Joseph Bunham
3. Michael Teag
4. Enock Stone

Page 116

5. Henry Fults

6. Joel Bray
7. Joseph Chandler
8. Ezekiel Denny
9. Jesse Lam
10. Jesse Peal
11. James Martin
12. Edmund Fleming
13. Mordecai Fleming
14. John M. Fleming
15. James Bays
16. Wm. B. McCraw
17. James Roberts, Jr.
18. Wm. Williams
19. Coleby Cruid, Jr.
20. Abraham Cruid
21. Hail Snow
22. Thos. Snow
23. Elijah Aubury
24. Jesse Prichet
25. Wm. Golden
26. Matthew Davis
27. Robert Ship
28. James Cockram
29. James Smyth
30. Charles Tucker
31. James Smith, Jr.
32. Solomon Center
33. Isaac Bartlett
34. Elijah Thompson
35. John Thompson
36. Stephen Potter
37. Henderson Thompson
38. Barnard Franklin
39. Joel Canada
40. Andrew Willlie
41. Wm. Mash
42. Thos. Franklin
43. John Mash
44. Wm. Paul
45. Jesse Burch
46. Lemuel B. Jones
47. John Collins
48. John Whitlock
49. Jacob Jones
50. Aaron Andres
51. Isaac Winfrey
52. James Kyle

53. Jacob Dubbins
54. Jesse Jones
55. John Thomason
56. Wm. Car
57. Jesse Whitaker
58. Achilus Key
59. Littleton Isbell
60. James Fitzgerald
61. Lawrence Morris
62. James Harrison
63. Asa Earley
64. John Aulberty
65. Wm. Whitaker
66. Isaac Whitaker
67. Charles Hunn
68. James McDonald
69. Richard Studard
70. Daniel Griffith
71. Zachariah Clandler
72. Barajah [sic] Reynolds
73. David Love
74. James Rorden
75. Lewis Forkner
76. Isaac Norman
77. Eli Tansey
78. Jeremiah Rorden
79. Robert Blackville
80. Wm. Holifyeld
81.   Blank
82.   Blank

****

SURRY COUNTY
SECOND REGIMENT

1. Abner Carmichall, Captain
2. John Welch, Lieut.
3. George Hudspith
4. Richard Walker
5. Wm. Petty
6. George Debode
7. Willie Harp
8. Daniel Brandle
9. Henry Millar
10. Aaron Nooton [sic]
11. Samuel Speak

12. John Parks
13. Benj. Brewer
14. George Tipps
15. John Brown, Jr.
16. Wm. Sparks
17. Joel Sparks
18. Stephen Denny
19. Joshua Fenny
20. Joseph Horton
21. Nathan Ratcliff **
22. Jonathan Ratliff **
    [** Both spellings used here.]
23. Wm. Hunt
24. Abraham Swann
25. Davis Bagley
26. Hawkins Cook
27. Nickolas Cook
28. Hempley Hart
29. Jesse Collins
30. John Southan
31. Levy Johnson
32. Thomas Hampton

Page 117

33. John Castephens
34. Neal Bohannen
35. Isaac Vestal
37. Joseph Carter
38. Berry Patterson
39. Charles Davis
40. George Hobson
41. Jonathan Hinshaw
42. Lewis Wyles
43. Henry Hoots
44. John Frady
45. Charles Stedman, Jr.
46. Fredric May
47. John Rutledge
48. Matthew Johnson
49. Edmond Loveleps
50. Wm. Eaperson
51. Henry Peace
32. Benj. Pitell
53. Wm. Lane
54. Benj. Glenn
55. Bennet Philips

****

56. Henry Shore
57. Wm. Robertson
58. Edmund Phillips
59. Isaac Jarrat
60. Francis A. Poindexter
61. James Ball
62. Benj. Kelly
63. John Spillman
64. Henry Skidmore
65. George Ball
66. John Pilcher
67. Francis Moreland
68. Thos. Thornton
69. Giles Coe
70. John McGuire
71. Peter Vest
72. Peter Sprinkle

****

WILKES COUNTY

1. Ambrose Carleton, Captain
2. Andrew Vannoy, 1st Lieut.
3. Sam'l Johnston, 2nd Lieut.
4. Elijah Coffey, 3rd Lieut.
5. Lewis Walters, Ensign
6. David Allison
7. Hiram Pipes
8. Martin Livingston
9. Moses Stansberry
10. Samuel Brown
11. Samuel Neathery
12. Thos. Barlow
13. Wm. Hagler
14. Thomas Steed
15. Hughs Napper
16. Thos. Potts
17. John Allen
18. John Ferguson
19. Joel Watters
20. Edward Watkins
21. Benj. Foster
22. Christopher Gullet
23. Daniel Gullet
24. Eli Hamby
25. Jacob Lipps

26. John Craine
27. Joel Vannay
28. Thos. Summers
29. Wm. Church
30. James Bradley
31. Hezekiah Paisley
32. Cewen Humphry
33. Isaac Hogler
34. Joshua Hendrickson
35. Peter Elerod
36. John Coffey
37. Archibald Brown
38. Wm. Murphy
39. Joshua Brown
40. Elijah Barns
41. Solomon Saunders
42. John Barns
43. Joon [? John ?] Pearson
44. Larkin Kerly
45. Samuel Newsom
46. Simon Shaw
47. Charles Vickers
48. George Gilbreath
49. Helen H. Gilbreath
50. Frederic Tyser
51. Javan Ball
52. Marshall McDaniel
53. Allen Robinett
54. Hiram Gilbreath
55. John Rains
56. Gideon Gilbreath
57. Hiram Smoot
58. Wm. Smith
59. John Norris
60. Joel Johnson
61. Reuben Hamby
62. James Morgan
63. Daniel Holderfield
64. Sylvester Adams
65. Benj. Treble
66. George Barns
67. Wm. Morgan
68. Larkin [?] Sheppard
69. Gibson Adams
70. Whitfield Brown

Page 118

71. Eli Brown
72. Isaac Adam
73. David Trusty
74. John Bruce
75. Daniel Hayes
76. John Robards
77. John Brown
78. Wm. Walsh
79. Peter Brown
80. Wm. Amburgy
81. Malachai Lawrence
82. John Sparks
83. George Crouse
84. John Dunkin
85. Thos. Rigsby
86. George Sparks
87. Jeremiah Caudill
88. Wm. V. Lyon
89. John Gilliam
90. James Tucker
91. Thos. Wood
92. John Bensel
93. Wm. Toliver
94. Joshua Parks
95. Elisha Brown
96. George Sparks
97. Joseph Gregory
98. Robert Layle
99. Wm. Gray
100. Joseph Brown
101. Elisha Felts
102. Robert Perdue
103. Ramsome Shore
104. Jonathan Sparks
105. Daniel McDaniel
106. Presly Bussill
107. Daniel Norman
108. Levi Wilson
109. Charles Bewsey
110. James Lewis
111. James Morgan
112. George Norman
113. Luke Rash
114. Wm. Combs
115. Wm. Darnall
116. Ezekiel Brown
117. Hezekiah Sebastian

118. Jonathan Walsh
119. Jesse Adams
120. Hopkins Pratt
121. Edward Turner
122. Samuel Spier
123.   Blank

****

ASHE COUNTY

1. Gideon Lewis, Captain
2. Isaac Weaver, Lieut.
3. Wm. Toliver, Ensign
4. Henry Graybeal
5. Eli Ragon
6. Henry Millar
7. James Duncan
8. David Graybeal
9. David Carpenter
10. Samuel Griffith
11. Isaac Taylor
12. Frederick Staley
13. Isaac Lewis
14. Wm. Morefield
15. Abraham Miller
16. John Millar
17. Mark Weaver
18. Peter Hart
19. Absalom Bower
20. John Faw
21. Jacob Mikel
22. David Hartzog
23. Aaron Owens
24. Peter Feese
25. Andrew Shearer
26. Wm. Cox
27. Isaac Smith
28. Wm. Mink
29. Edmond Tilley
30. Joshua Pennington
31. David Horton
52. Phineas Horton
53. Reuben Hartley
34. Lewis Fairchilds
35. Jacob Ingerham
36. Levi Blackburn

37. John Shearer
38. Joel Dugger
39. David Dugger
40. Thomas Swift
41. Henry Hately
42. John Vanderpool
43. Wm. Brewer
44. Jacob Brinegar
45. John Hoppass
46. John Brower
47. Wm. S. Edwards
48. Young Edwards
49. Alex. T. Conley
50. Enock Passmore
51. Joel Rose
52. Richard Perry
53. Wm. Vanover
54. Joseph Colwell

Page 119

55. Enock Baldwin
56. John Rutherford
57. John Quinley
58. John Williams
59. William Taylor
60.   Blank
61.   Blank
62.   Blank

****

RANDOLPH COUNTY
FIRST REGIMENT

1. Zebidee Rush, Captain
2. Wm. Welborn, Lieut.
3. [blank]   ,Ensign
4. Isaac Elliott
5. Laza Merril
6. John McGee
7. Seth Dickson
8. Isaac Hannah
9. Matthew Davis
10. Mark Stud
11. Solomon Hannah
12. Wm. Crawford, Jr.

13. Wm. Morris
14. John Hannah
15. Wm. Coggin
16. Solomon Farmer
17. Jeremiah Bailey
18. Benj. Fuller
19. James Skeen
20. Stephen Hulgan
21. John Gibson
22. Richard Gallimore
23. Jos. Nicolson
24. James Harvey
25. John Mills
26. Jesse Blair
27. Robert Gray
28. Andrew Johnston
29. Benj. Sanders
30. Nathan Hoedridge
31. Lewis Walton
32. Isaac Coltrane
33. Thos. White
34. Reuben Rush, Serg.
35. Thos. Pearce
36. Wm. Varner
37. Benj. Cooper
38. Andrew Fonts
39. Whitlock Crage
40. Jacob Lamn
41. Reuben Alexander
42. Benj. Wright
43. Enock Spinks, Serg.
44. Branson Lawrann, Serg.
45. Enock Tucker
46. Wm. Pearce
47. Michael Cole
48. Daniel Cast
40. John Bowdown
50. John Haskitt
51. Wm. Swafford
62. Joseph Hinson
53. John Wormington
54. Micajah Brewer
55. Jonathan Moffet
56. Wm. Macon
57. Doran Yeorgan
58. Thos. Yeorgan
59. Thos. Pain

60. Samuel Milliken
61. Thos. Clark
62. Daniel Robins
63. John Miller
64. John Jordan
65. Nathan Goddin
66. George Williams
67. Wm. Presnall
68. Barnabas Hobbs
69. Johnson King
70. Benj. Page
71. Isham Hancock
72. Jos. Luther
73. Wm. Laitham

****

RANDOLPH COUNTY
SECOND REGIMENT

1. John Ramsour, Captain
2. Minos Ward, Lieut.
3. Richard Richardson, Ensign
4. Elias Hayes, Serg.
5. Ivy Richardson, Serg.
6. Aaron Moffet, Serg.
7. Nathan Swafford, Fifer
8. Enock Swafford, Drummer
9. Samuel Aldridge
10. Christian Bower, Jr.
11. David Ameek
12. Samuel Royer
13. Aaron Kivet
14. Jabaz York
15. Goshen Gennings
16. Timothy Cude
17. Reuben Alfred
18. Adam York
19. Wm. Lochlan
20. James Lowe
21. John Wren
22. Isaac McCollum

Page 120

23. David Campbell
24. Wm. Norman

25. Samuel Russell
26. Moses Johnston
27. Wm. Underwood
28. Daniel Smith
29. Charles Jones
30. Vestal Beeson
31. Thos. Underwood
32. Iri Richardson
33. Joseph Lamb
34. Gabriel Lamb
35. Michael Swean
36. John Robbus
37. Marmaduke Vickery
38. Wm. Robbins (of Dan'l)
39. John Ruston
40. Benjamin Johnston
41. James Philips
42. Henry Williams
43. Richard Caveness
44. James Warren
45. Joshua Brown
46. James Cruthes
47. Ezekiel Matthews
48. Henry Moffet
49. John Cravan
50. Eli Lambert
51. John Deaton
52. Wm. Vestal
53. Gabriel Lamb

****

SIXTH REGIMENT

ROWAN COUNTY
FIRST REGIMENT

1. Thos. Matthews, Captain
2. Truth Wood, Lieut.
3. Johnsten Neblock, Lieut.
4. Richman Hughes, Lieut.
5. David Cowan, Ensign
6. Thos. Allison
7. Michael Braner
8. John Albright
9. Henry Allemony
10. Jos. Daniels

11. Zekial Dekison
12. Jacob Delow
13. John Weaver
14. Jos. Chamblers, Sr.
15. Thos. Reaves
16. Joseph Agnor
17. George Dunn
18. Wm. Gardnor
19. Samuel Bunch
20. Littleton Rainey
21. Philip Rumple
22. Wm. Rogers
23. Daniel Murphy
24. Caleb Curfuse
25. Christ. Blackwelder
26. Jacob Corisher
27. Judson Brown
28. John Minster
29. Michael Biley
30. Wm. Williamson
31. Elijah Marlin
32. Wm. Thompson
33. Wm. Rice
34. Peter Traxler
35. Levi Mays
36. Wm. Henlin
37. Jos. Marlin
38. James Sammons
39. John Yost
40. Adam Eddleman
41. Andrew Boston
42. John Shulleberger
43. Wm. Rose
44. Abraham Zickler
45. Henry Arenhart
46. Henry Snider
47. Nathan Morgan
48. Jonathan Miller
49. John Paim
50. Noah Parks, Jr.
51. Jacob Shover
52. Michael Pittman
53. James Hutson
54. George Knox
55. Joseph Clotfelter
56. John Mills
57. Samuel Graham

****

58. Samuel Reaves
59. Zekiah Cowan
60. John Cowan
61. Reuben Yearborough
62. Kisman Linn
63. John H. Brandon
64. Henry Hill, Jr.
65. Wm. Anderson
66. Henry Stillar
67. Enock Philips
68. Fred Menos
69. Wm. Barber
70. Jos. Cowan
71. Walter Rigdon
72. Barrage Davenport
73. John McConniherty
74. John Craig

Page 121

75. Thomas Willis
76. Jacob Weant
77. Jacob Cross
78. Thomas Craig
79. William Long
80. Samuel Anderson
81. Solomon Hall
82. William Anderson
83. William Price
84. Matthias Phifer
85. John Weab
86. Thomas Renshaw
87. Wilson Nibleek
88. Daniel Bogar
89. Martin Clutz
80. Anthony Pealor
91. Peter Cruse
92. John Lippert
93. John Wasnor
94. Jacob Poole
95. John Thomas
96. Volentine Rimer
97. George Waller
98. Thomas Cunningham
99. Hermon Walton
100. Peter Brown
101. Jerry Arey

102. George Smithall
103. John Crotzer
104. John Hartman
105. George Eller
106. Peter Agnor
107. John Gardenor
108. Daniel Swink
109. Jacob Thomas
110. Henry Castor
111. Philip Edlinian
112. George Agle
113. Christian Rinehart
114. Fred Holshansen
115. Jacob Fulwider
116. Joseph Cowan, Sr.
117. Joseph Cowan, Jr.
118. Timothy McNealey
119. David Cooper, B.S.
120. Samuel McLaughlin
121. James Short
122. James McLaughlin, Sr.
123. James Brigs
124. James Locke

****

ROWAN COUNTY
SECOND REGIMENT

1. George Smith, Captain
2. George Miller, 1st Lieut.
3. John Wilson, Ensign
4. David Billiny
5. Samuel Spafford
6. Elisha Word
7. Peter Frank
8. Henry Workman
9. Isaac Kinney
10. George Gregson
11. Peter Whitaker
12. John Gregor
13. William McCarn
14. William Jarrat
15. John Garvay
16. Lennard Smith
17. William Peacock
18. James Jackson

19. Jesse Pealer
20. John Houser
21. Walter Northern
22. Mashack Green
23. John Goss
24. John Briggs
25. Jonathan Barclay
26. Joseph Goss, Jr.
27. Isaac Cobble
28. Isaac Margan
29. Alex. Yarborough
30. Joseph Clark
31. William Stout
32. Jessee Harris, Jr.
33. Edward Davis
34. Peter Riley
36. William Hughs
36. Joseph Shoulse
37. David Garner
38. James Hughes
39. Jonathan Coggins
40. Isaick Russell
41. Cornelius Loftin, Jr.
42. Edmond Smith
43. Henry Shemeel
44. Isaac Thompson
45. James Johnston
46. John Shipton
47. John Davis, Jr.
48. Robert Lacey
49. James Morgan
50. William Sorrat, Jr.
51. James Davis
52. Abraham Owen
53. James Wiseman
54. David Smith
55. James Elliot
56. Ebenezer Moore
57. Noah Hunt
58. Ezekiah Owen
59. David Grub
60. John Shoaf

Page 122

61. Martin Owen
62. James Womack

****

63. Warren Roberts
64. Hugh Cunningham
65. George Grub
66. Michael Sink
67. Thismothy [sic] Wiseman
68. John Macray
69. Thomas Sullivan
70. Joseph Black
71. David Bower
72. Adam Black
73. Ruedolph [sic] Yonce
74. John Wortman
57. Philip Myre
76. William Goodman
77. John Moss
78. Daniel Myre
79. Michael Myre
80. Matthew Byrns
81. Christopher Hepler
82. Nathan Lambeth
83. Philip Hapler
84. John Beck
85. Jacob Hasby
86. Thomas Owen
87. Lewis Robling
88. Peter Winklar
89. William Ball
90. John Hill
91. James Pickler
92. James Dedman
93. James Coaths

****

ROWAN COUNTY
THIRD REGIMENT

1.   Blank
2.   Blank
3.   Blank
4. Thomas Mumford
5. Ishmael Cordle
6. Jacob Lam
7. Daniel Click
8. William Call
9. James O'Neal
10. Jesse Hendricks

11. Drury Jones
12. Abraham Allen
13. Enoch Ellis
14. John Peck
15. David Harris
16. William Guy
17. Thomas Skinner
18. William Dulin
19. Stephen Williams
20. William Edwards
21. Samuel Poyner
22. Joshua Hindrix
23. Isaac Twoney
24. Jesse Swan
25. John Hare
26. William Madden
27. Samuel Gray
28. Joseph Forcum
29. John Taylor
30. John Brandon
31. Joseph Beal
32. William Dockins
33. Saul Price
34. Thomas Smoot
35. Laurence Hudson
36. John Gabard
37. Alfred McCullock
38. George Wilson
39. Charles Detheridge
40. John Smart
41. Thomas Hendrix
42. Christopher Killer
43. Frost Nelson
44. John Ijams
45. Daniel Earnest
46. Johnsey Gaither
47. Daniel Helfer
48. William Nelson
49. Jacob March
50. Wilson Austin
51. John Bryan
52. John Douge
53. Peter Mock
54. John Etchison, Jr.
55. Henry Brickhouse
56. Jesse Bowden
57. William Chapman

58. Elijah Adams
59. John West
60. Isaac Creff
61. Samuel Ward
62. Smith Cox
63. Thomas Chaffin
64. John Renair
65. Hamilton Gatton
66. William Foster
67. Thomas Foster}
68. Thomas Foster} [sic]
69. Ignatius McDonnell
70. John Philips
71. William Hainline
72. Abraham March
73. Thomas Owens
74. William Batey
75. Elisha Leach
76. Henry Hendrix
77. Jonothan [sic] Cronfell
78. Jonathan Jones

Page 123

79. John Pierce
80. John Johnson
81. William Humphries
82. William Holomon
83. Abijah Irwin
84. Conrad Mires
85. Anthony Silvey
87. John Sparks
88. David Sheets
89. John Thornton
90. George Howard
91. Samuel Brannock
92. Henry Call
93. William Johnson
94. John D. Ballard

****

ROWAN COUNTY
FOURTH REGIMENT

1. Moses Welborn, Captain
2. Moses Welborn, Jr., Lieut.

3. Adam Huffman
4. Christian Zimmerson
5. Cage Ferril
6. David Bodenhamer
7. David Clinard
8. Daniel Motsingen
9. David Weer
10. David Michael
11. Emsley Burton
12. George Zink
13. George Grimes
14. George Jush
15. Henry Little
16. Henry Sawers
17. Henry Wood
18. Henry Mires
19. Hugh Robertson
20. Henry Barrier
21. James Pope
22. James Evans
23. James Jeague
24. John Pain
25. Jesse Farabe
26. Joseph Stone
27. John Weer
28. John Jush
29. John Charles
30. Jacob Mailer
31. Jacob Hague
32. Jacob Bominger
33. John White
34. Jacob Snider
35. John Hague
36. John Frits
37. Jacob Myers
38. Jacob Lopp
39. John Miller
40. John Markland
41. John Clemmons
43. John Lockinbill
44. Moses Stokes
45. Moses Teague, Sr.
46. Michael Easter
47. Moses Teague
48. Michael Worlaw
49. Philip Cecil
50. Philip Leonard

51. Phillip Mock
52. Stephen Dowthard
53. William Hayworth
54. William Cook
55. William Bodenhamer
56. William Robertson
57. William Brookshire
58. William Danaway
59. Wilson Rodes
60. Thomas Phelps
61. Samuel Bird
62. Zachariah Stout
63. Basdel Burton
64. Ice Long
65. Thomas Hartie
66. Daniel Wood, Jr.
67. Robert Green
68. William Sweeney
69. Jacob Bodenhamer
70. John Gobbel
71. John Farabee
72. Thomas Cecil

****

MONTGOMERY COUNTY
FIRST REGIMENT

1. Willis Haris [sic], Captain
2. blank, 1st Lieut.
3. William Lilly, 2nd Lieut.
4. blank, Ensign
5. John Hunt
6. Basel Denton
7. James Parson
8. Edward Mund
9. Daniel Garriot
10. Thomas Deaton
11. Malcom Gillis
12. John Yarborough
13. William Russel, Sr.
14. - - pry, Reavis
15. Joseph Russel
16. Hugh Steward
17. Levi Coggins
18. Joseph Steward

Page 124

19. John Steward
20. James Taylor
21. John Partin
22. Jarrett Russell
23. Abraham Beaman
24. William Green
25. George Allen
26. John Townsend
27. Noah Randle
28. Reuben Smith
29. David Taylor
30. George Calicoat
31. Talton Johnson
32. William Spencer
33. William James
34. John Arnet
356. Nicholas Rynalds
36. David Beamon
37. John Holton
38. Jonathan Harris
39. Samuel Webb
40. Elisha B. Smith
41. Jeptha Harris
42. Levi Reddin
43. Anguish Chisholm
44. Isaiah Hogan
45. Daniel Manus
46. Moses Yarborough
47. Welcome Ussery
48. Wilson Andress
49. John Chisolm
50. Thomas Parsons
51. Joel Harris
52. John Alley
53. John Wilson
54. John Hill
55. Aaron Russell
56. James Ussery
57. James Cook
58. James Mills
59. Levi Russel
60. Martin Russel
61. Thomas Bledsoe
62. Willie Scarborough
63. William Seagraves

64. William Christoon
65. Wiley Johnston
66. Andrew Dennis
67. Malcom McCollum
68. Bannet Brown
69. Cobelas Hunley
70. Elisha Smart
71. George Coggins
72. Harbert Suggs
73. John Calicoat
74. James G. Mask
75. Moses Steel
76. Peter Edward
77. William A. Scott
78. William Russel
79. Eli Townsend
80. Thomas Kirk
81. Samuel Scarborough
93. Benjamin Merrit
83. John Rolins
84. Thomas Davis
85. Charles Reynolds
86. John Townsend
87. Lovin Bennet
88. David Sedberry
89. Jacob Luken
90. John Mills
91. Jesse Haygood
92. Kenneth McClenon
93. Thomas Williams
94. Moses Batton

****

MONTGOMERY COUNTY
SECOND REGIMENT

1. David Green, 1st Lieut.
2. Charles Culpepper, 3rd Lieut.
3. George Little, Ensign
4. Burwell Braswell
5. William Buress
6. Andrew Bird
7. Stephen Crump
8. Abraham Cooper
9. Washington Coaley
10. Leonard Cagle

11. Thomas Cox
12. George W. Davidson
13. James Floyd
14. Daniel Ford
15. Richard Greene
16. Isham Honeycut
17. Sarquel Honeycut
18. George Hearn
19. Philip Hegler
20. Reuben Honeycut
21. Jacab [sic] Hartsell
22. Leonard Hartsell
23. Willie Harris
24. John S. Kindall
25. Henry Kimry
26. Henry Kipley
27. Stephen Kirk
28. William Lyerly
29. Joseph Milton
30. Frederick Mossman
31. William Moss
32. Jonathan McDonald
33. Mathew Parham
34. George Poplin

Page 125

35. Jarret Pritchard
36. Jesse Poplin
37. Michael Richie
38. George Read
39. Joel Rowland
40. Jordan Russel
41. George D. Smith
42. John Smith
43. Richard Stoker
44. George Sydes
45. James Townsell
56. William Tomlinson
47. Jonathan Wilkerson
48. Hewet Weaks
49. John Walker
50. George Whitley
51. George Palmer
52. Farley Hopkins
53. Bennet Solomon

****

MECKLENBURG COUNTY
FIRST REGIMENT

1. James Wilson, Captain
2. Thomas Boyd, Esq. 1st Lieut.
3. Joseph Blackwood 2nd Lieut.
4. Isaac Price 3rd Lieut.
5. Charles Hutchinson, Ensign
6. William Carson
7. John Wynens
8. Barzilla Garner
9. James McCombs
10. John Barnett
11. William McKelvia
12. John Hawkins
13. Amos Barnett
14. Ezekiel Alexander
15. William Shelvey
16. John C. Garrison
17. James Means
18. Thomas Hope
19. Robert Coldwell
20. John Price
21. John Parkes, Sr.
22. Samuel Johnston, Jr.
23. William Wolles, Jr.
24. Mathew Wallis, Jr.
25. Samuel Parks
26. Robert Coldwell, Jr.
27. Ann Wynns
28. John Sadler
29. John Barnhill
30. Jacob Julin
31. James Henderson
32. Elisha McCracken
33. Christopher Love
34. Robert Dunn, Jr.
35. Andrew M. Parish
35. William Dunn
37. Andrew Lewing, Jr.
38. Francis Perry
39. John Farra
40. John Lewing
41. James Carothers
42. James Dinkins

43. Robert Bigham, Jr.
44. John Johnston
45. William Johnston
46. Samuel Neeley
47. David Reed
48. Joseph Whiteside
49. Augustus Miles
50. Mathew West
51. Thomas Connel
52. William Benhill
53. Robert McKnight
54. Michael Baker
55. Abel Baker
56. Hugh McDowel
57. William Kerr
58. John Towd
59. Aaron Baker
60. Andrew Walker
61. James Porter
62. John Beaty
63. Samuel Bigham
64. Simon V. Pelt
65. John Beaty
66. Peavon Jackson
67. John Blackburn
68. John Wilson, Jr.
69. John Brown
70. William S. Norman
71. Daniel Baxter
72. Benjamin Wilson
73. Thomas Elliott
74. James Conner
75. Daniel Davis
76. William Elliott
77. Richard Hartley
78. George Duckworth
79. James Meek
80. James Alexander
81. Joel Jones
82. James Sloan
83. Isaac Morrison, Jr.
84. John Parker
85. James Mentith
86. Joseph Williams
87. Andrew Prim
88. Robert A. Orsburn
89. John White

90. Michael Channels

Page 126

91. Gabriel Ferrel
92. Giles Irwin
93. John Ferrel
94. Joseph Wallis
95. Henry Hunter, Jr.
96. William Ferrel
97. James Steele
98. Nelson Gray
99. John Steel
100. Robert Montgomery
101. Richard Peoples
102. James A. Braddy
103. Joseph McKellerand
104. George Goforth
105. John D. Alexander

****

MECKLENBURG COUNTY
SECOND REGIMENT

1. David Moore, Captain
2. John Wilson, 1st Lieut.
3. Solomon Reed, 2nd Lieut.
4. William John, 3rd Lieut.
5. Albertes Alexander, Ensign
6. Richard Barflet
7. Mathew McCall
8. James McCall
9. Henry Thompson
10. Alexander Stewart
11. William Cheery
12. James Robertson
13. Samuel Yandles
14. James Harbeson
15. William Shelby
16. Gideon Freeman
17. John Morrison
18. John Allen
19. John Forsythe
20. Games Barnes
21. Moses Purser
22. Micajah Barns

23. Osburn Wilkinson
24. Robert Allen
25. Groves Vinson
26. William Helmes
27. Charles Helmes
28. Frederic Starns
29. Nathaniel Starns
30. Morris Shehorn
31. William Yerby
32. James Rone
33. John Belk
34. Dan'l Rich
35. John Junderbusk
36. Henry Flowers
37. David B. Yandles
38. Salamachus Alexander
39. Abdon Alexander
40. Osburn Smart
41. Elisha Smart
42. John McCullock
43. Robert Cook
44. Stephen Hanson
45. Moses Craig
46. Wm. McCoy
47. Robert Howood
48. William Woodall
49. Jacob Gray
50. Aaron Howie
51. Andrew King
52. Joshua Finsher
53. Samuel Rape
54. Samuel Rener
55. James Hambleton
56. Moses Vick
57. John Philips
58. James Train
59. George Berns
60. William Fisher
61. Daniel Button
62. Hugh McAlroy
63. Jess Ivey
64. John Hauley
65. Benjamin Spravey
66. Joseph Reed
67. Adam Karr
68. John Mathews
69. George Parke

70. William Reed
71. Wm. Downs
72. Wilson Taylor
73. John Maglanchlin
74. Joseph Hall
75. William Maygeehee
76. Henry Hargett
77. William Hargett
78. Joel Helmer
79. John Crowel
80. Peter Chainey
81. David Harkey
82, George Tuter
83. Elias Stilwell
84. James Morrison
85. Moses Tomberlin
86. Edward Reak
87. Neel Morrison
88. James Costley
89. Thomas S. Cochran
90. Wm. Housten, Jr.
91. Robert Cochran
92. Hugh Wilson
93. Reuben Hood
94. Charles Dennie
95. Samuel Neele
96. John Harkey

Page 127

97. James Rogers
98. Rob't Harrison
99. John Hodge
100. Richard Lambert
101. David W. Story
102. John Fuller
103. James Shaw
104. Lewis Webb
105. James Story, Sr.

****

CABARRUS COUNTY

1. Even S. Willey, Captain
2. George Fogleman, Lieut
3. Christopher Milken, Ensign

4. Alexander W. Harris, 1st Serg.
5. Ozni Rogers, 2nd Serg.
6. John Long, 3rd Serg.
7. Andrew Kemirons, 4th Serg.
8. Peter Alles, 1st Corp.
9. John Drye, 2nd Corp.
10. Daniel Drye, 3rd Corp.
11. Andrew Trulman, 4th Corp.
12. Daniel Mooss [sic]
13. Daniel Ritengous
14. Henry Hover
15. Andrew Blackwater
16. John Nusman
17. John Goger
18. Jacob Overcast
19. Jonathan Stanford
20. Alexander Bain
21. Methias [sic] Passenger
22. Jacob Stirwatt
23. William Bell
24. John Hall
25. William Pelt
26. Samuel Neel
27. James Ross
28. George Long
29. James Gray
30. George Kegle
31. David White
32. John Mathews
33. James Love
34. James McMahew
35. John Haskey
36. Adam Ritchey
37. George Trutman
38. James Buchanon
39. John Snider
40. George Miller
41. Moses Conel
42. Andrew Yaw
43. Jacob Bager
44. John Bager
45. David Nisler
46. William Scott
47. Jacob Croner
48. Christopher Hattaman
49. John Mitchell
50. Peter Walter

51. Paul Walter
52. Charles Hartman
53. George Lefort
54. Jacob File
55. Cirus Alexander
56. Silas McCinlay
57. Richard D. Plunkett
58. James Welch
59. John Eliot
60. Andrew Walker
61. John Clay
62. John Davis
63. John Morris
64. Robert Dixon
65. Isaac McClerland
66. Hugh Dixon
67. Hezekiah Davis
68. Jacob Goodman
69. John McGinley
70. John Bradshaw
71. Isaac Howell
72. John Johnson
73. William Houston
74. John Mullen
75. John Green
76. William Simons
77. John McLain
78. Joel S. Houston
79. Henry Petery
80. Jacob Cline
81. Tobias Mesthinghams
82. James Hadley
83. James Nicholson
84. John Davis
85. William G. Harris
86. David Winecof
87. Samuel Holebrooks
88. Cirus Wedenton
89. George Goodnight
90. David McRee
91. William Houston
92. Tobias Goodman
93. Joseph G. Spires
94. John Garman
95. Beverly Gray
96. John Sossiman
97. Christopher Osburn

98. Durum Cuzine
99. Caleb Blackwater
100. Moses Archabb

Page 128

101. Samuel H. Cochran
102. John Cuzine
103. David Linker
104. Adam Cariker
105. David Miskingham
106. Jacob Tucker
107. Jacob Hegles
108. Jacob Fune
109. Daniel Fune
110. David Fink
111. Matthias Miskingham
112. Henry Himpman
113. George Barnhart

****

IREDELL COUNTY

1. John McKee, Captain
2. William Kerr, Lieut.
3. Thomas Forterner, Ensign
4. Andrew McKenzie
5. William Hicks
6. Charles Summers
7. Alexis Alexander
8. James Crawford
9. William Jacobs
10. John Bone
11. Alexander Watts
12. John Freeland
13. Alexander Hall
14. Andrew W. Davidson
15. John Woodard
16. Daniel Brawley
17. Aaron Downs
18. James McKnight
19. John Sloan
20. John Huggins
21. John Atwell
22. James Maulholland
23. Robert Brawley

24. Ruel Walles
25. Hiram Lawson
26. James McRee
27. John McDate
28. Robert Elliott
29. David McRee
30. Jeremiah Whiley
31. James B. Thomas
32. Angus McRoy
33. Robert McFarland
34. Samuel McFarland
35. Ralph Stewart
36. Henry Morrison
37. James Alexander
38. Jacob Bostion
39. John Carter
40. John Wilkinson
41. Tobias Miller
42. Martin Cryder
43. Thomas Elliott
44. Hamelton McClatchy
45. Abner Feamster
46. George Erwin
47. James Gilley
48. William Morrison
49. Jaran Fortune
50. Joseph Wright
51. Andrew Davis
52. Rhoda Westmoreland
53. Abner York
54. Samuel Honeycutt
55. Alfred Kerr
56. Robert Timpleton
57. Richard F. Houston
58. James Alley
59. Peterson Westmoreland
60. William Mayhew
61. Joseph Rogers, Jr.
62. James Randels
63. John Lippard
64. Joseph Parks
65. Mathew Calaher
66. Windle Holshouser
67. Abraham Ritchey
68. David Clodfelter
69. Neal McKay, Jr.
70. John Wilson

71. Neal McKay, Sr.
72. Andrew Neil
73. John Fleming
74. James Morten
75. John Erwin, Sr.
76. John Steel
77. William Lipperd
78. William King
79. John Harchie
80. William Allison
81. William Gay
82. Samuel Archibald
83. Ninia Steel
84. Robert McGuire
85. Thomas Allison
86. Maxwell Chambers
87. George Mair
88. Samuel Timpleton
89. Daniel Lewis
90. Kinchen Walls
91. Robert Lazenby
92. Lebishes Gaither
93. Greenberry H. Johnston
94. John Fitzgerril
95. David Holleman
96. Leonard Wishon

Page 129

97. William Mason
98. Solomon Sumners
99. John McLelland
100. John Claggett
101. William Summers
102. Humphrey Tomlinson
103. Thomas Kerney
104. James Thompson, Captain
105. Isaac Smith, Lieut.
106. Perry Tomlinson, Ensign
107. Ezekiel Morgan
108. Jacob Privit
109. William Mitchell
110. James Williams
111. John Mears
112. Robert Coleman
113. Mark Marlow
114. Gideon Deboard

****

115. Anderson Johnson
116. Ezekiel Mires
117. William Bogle
118. Charles Hatton, Jr.
119. Elisha Farmer
120. Isaac Hena
121. James Bogle
122. James Reynolds
123. Elias King
124. James Hardin
125. Lemuel Leecham
126. Samuel Meadows
127. William Jolley
128. David Roberts
129. James Barnard
130. Henry E. Williams
131. Enock Gaither
132. John Dilliard
133. Adam Campbell
134. William Marlow
135. Archibald Cast
136. Plesabo Hueston
137. Isaac Wailes
138. David Marmon
139. Thomas Marmon
140. John Maiden
141. Joseph Milsaps
142. Alexander Lackey
143. Dearling Allen
144. Elihugh King
145. John Gaider
146. Nathan Guiltney
147. William Guiltney
148. Robert Guiltney
149. Wallis Privit
150. John S. Patterson
151. John Griffith
152. Ruton Jordan
153. Ezekiel Edis
154. George Flowers
155. James Dishman
156. Richard Cook
157. James Bentley
158. John Arrington
159. Alexander McHague
160. Arnold Holland
161. John Maxwell

162. Joseph Shelby
163. Alexander Long
164. James King
165. James Gregory
166. John King

****

LINCOLN COUNTY
FIRST REGIMENT

1. James Finley, Captain
2. William J. Wilson, Lieut.
3. Richard Cowan, 2nd Lieut.
4. Andrew Berry, 3rd Lieut.
5. John Beard, Ensign
6. Ambroze [sic] Gaullney
7. Andrew Sankard
8. John Hagan
9. Henry Sadler
10. George Berry
11. Jacob Trentman
12. William Short
13. James Graham
14. Isaac Murrell
15. John Hunt
16. Benedict Jetton
17. Benjamin Proctor
18. John Litz
19. William Little
20. Richard Proctor
21. William Nance, Jr.
22. James White
23. William Nance
24. William Tucker
25. Ambrose Cobb
26. Jacob Cloninger
27. Samuel Pew
28. Thomas Sadler
29. Needam Wingate
30. David Smith, Jr.
31. Robinson Moore
32. William Meginess
33. John Rhodes
34. John Meginess
35. William Sutton
36. John Mahew

37. Bedford Childers
38. Thomas Tucker

Page 130

39. Samuel Abernathy
40. Red Errowood
41. Rob't Lucky
42. Charles Edwards
43. Anthony Long
44. Freeman Shelton
45. Reuben Grice
46. John Bynum
47. William Hill
48. Willis Ballard
49. William Killian
50. Robinson Harris
51. Anthony Hinkle
52. Ashman Gwin
53. James Hicks
54. Daniel Killian
55. Frederic Killian
56. Edward Carroll
57. John Jinkens
58. Thomas Dickson
59. John Venable
60. Austin Ford
61. Peter Titman
62. James McCarver
63. William Rockford
64. Robert Alexander
65. William McCarver
66. Wiett Jenkins
67. Reuben Jenkins
68. Jacob Rhine
69. Adam Rhine
70. Solomon Rhine
71. John Rhodes
72. John Bynum
73. David Costner
74. Jacob Smith
75. George House
76. Amos Robeson
77. Alex'r McCullock
78. Keece Price
79. Moses Grissom
80. Thomas Groves

81. Hiram Harris
82. James Shannon
83. Jacob Fite
84. Ezekiel McClure
85. John Merner
86. Samuel Williams
87. James McClure
88. William Lettimore
89. John Damon
90. Anderson Wells
91. William Hamilton
82. John Leeper
93. John Glover
94. Alexander Rankin
95. William Reed
86. Steward Jinkens
97. William Bluford
98. John Hanks
99. Ebner Rumfelt
100. John Carthy
101. Jacob Kenedy
102. John Oats
103. John Parmer
104. William Adams
105. John Blackwood

****

LINCOLN COUNTY
SECOND REGIMENT

1. Daniel Hoke, Captain
2. John B Harris, 1st Lieut.
3. Gilbert Milliken, 2nd Lieut.
4. Isaac Manney, 3rd Lieut.
5. Peter Hoke, Ensign
6. John Carpenter
7. Henry Huffsteddler
8. Moses Barr
9. Jacob Hook [?]
10. William Carpenter
11. Joseph Black
12. William Ferguson
13. Cudias Smith
14. Jonas Rudsil
15. Peter Manney
16. David Kezer

17. Peter Eaker
18. George Seller
19. Peter Costner
20. John Huffsteddler
21. William Guntlesey
22. Daniel Glotfelder
23. Elias Glotfelder
24. John Teague
25. George Glotfelder
26. Rudolph Glotfelder
27. Lewis Huet
28. Phillip Skerd
29. Thomas Smith
30. John Bumgarner
31. Willie Heps
32. Archibald Cobb
33. Elisha Saunders
34. Joshua Hunter
35. Comrade Heldebreand
36. Peter Reymer
37. Bostian Best
38. John Heuser
39. Solomon Shoup
40. Samuel Bigham
41. William Willis
42. Charles Williams
43. James Chapman
44. Nathaniel Pew
45. Jacob Houser
46. John Watterson

Page 131

47. Joseph Wear
48. James Patterson
49. Preston Goforth
50. Hugh Spurlin
51. Isaac Mullinax
52. James Elliott
53. Thomas Earwood
54. George Goforth
55. Jacob Harman
56. Robert Barber
57. Young Marder
58. Thomas Black
59. David Dickson
60. Hardy Long

61. Solomon Childers
62. Christopher Carpenter
63. James Endsley
64. Anthony Clerk
65. David Backout
66. Archibald Endsley
57. James Wright
68. Thomas Crags
69. Philip Hayness
70. John Whitworth
71. Joshua Howell
72. Samuel Collins
73. John Monser
74. Casper Bolick
75. George Bowman
76. Henry Lickman
77. Mathew Boovey
78. Charles Ward
79. William Harman
80. David Huntley
81. Martin Lickman
82. George Turner
83. Abraham Tray
84. Henry Lickman, Jr.
85. Samuel Sullivan
86. Christian Bollinger
87. Christopher Hope
88. Michael Ingle
89. William Cline
90. John Shafer
91. Henry Houser
902. Ransom Husky
93. Matthis Barringer
94. Michael Dillenger
95. Daniel Blacksburn
96. Jacob Harner
97. Aaron Moore
98. David Dick
99. Joseph Heldebrand
100. Joseph Lenhart
101. James Lemons
102. Daniel Fullbright
103. Francis Summitt
104. Daniel Summitt
105. Nicholas Carpenter
106. Peter Lorance
107. Joseph Ashe

108. John Earncy
109. Alfred Sherril
110. Elias Shine
111. Conrade Ward
112. Avery Guant
113. Andrew Yant
114. Phillips Hedrick
115. Benedict Levant
116. John Cowan
117. George Shook
118. Jacob Fullbright
119. Leonard Kagle
120. Ephraim Christopher
121. William Echard
122. John Hadrick
123. Aaron Dawnson
124. Peter Keller
125. Gabriel Isaac
126. Samuel Peterson
127. Frederick Knup
128. Francis King
129. Peter Raby
130. Michael Sattenfield
131. Jonathan Robinson
132. Miles Abernathy
133. David Hawn
134. Valentine Taylor
135. John Stamy
136. Peter Frey
137. James Gilleband
138. John Snyder
139. James Bridges
140. James Jones
141. Benjamin Newman
142. Sterling Singleton
143. John Ward
144. John Glotfelder
145. James Fisher
146. Samuel Setton
147. William Black
148. David Warlie
149. Elisha Winson
150. Nimrod Winson
151. Henry Killian
152. Solomon Killian
153. Daniel Coulter
154. Henry Coulter

155. John Shufford.

****

Page 132

RUTHERFORD COUNTY
FIRST REGIMENT

1. John Oliver, Captain
2. John Moore, 1st Lieut.
3. Joseph Taylor, 3rd Lieut.
4. Lindsey Fortune, Ensign
5. Adam Hampton
6. Vincent Wood
7. John McHan
8. James Hill
9. Jonathan Mullens
10. William Hicks
11. Jonathan Hampton
12. Harbert Herton
13. Ransom Edgarton
14. David Wamock
15. Hamilton Freeman
16. Carter Johnston
17. Beuben [sic] Melton
18. Robert Webb
19. Leonard Deck
20. John Melton
21. Richard E. Allen
22. Thomas Wamock
23. Jeremiah Webb
24. Asaph Hill
25. Moses White
26. Samuel Bickerstaff
27. Robert Johnston
28. John Crow
29. Thomas Stockton
30. John Bradey
31. Josiah Jones
32. Isaac Rhom
33. Benjamin Grayson
34. William Grayson
35. William Melton
36. Elijah Pool
37. William Hunt
38. Elijah Sparks

39. Thomas Braskett
40. Simon Steel
41. William Hutchins
42. William Street
43. James Taylor
44. Hugh Watson
45. Daniel Watson
46. William Reed
47. John Guffey
48. Archy Reed Guffey
49. James S. Guffey
50. Jesse W. Grove
51. Benjamin Andrews
52. James Thompson
53. James Moore
54. George Ross
55. James Irvine
56. William Sprat
57. Richard Neweam
58. David Hodge
59. Rea Hid
60. Henry Camp
61. Noah Sergant
62. Benjamin Keter
63. Wade Biles
64. Eli Hanes
65. James Keter
66. William Marshall
67. Malajah Bankenship
68. James Nancy
69. Ephraim Cook
70. William Wallace
71. Jacob Veazant
72. John Cook
73. Howard Williams
74. Henry Morris
75. Zedekiah Harris
76. William Whitesides
77. Sterling Lewin
78. John Hunter
79. Mari Moore
80. William Harris
81. Andrew H. Eliot
82. James Ward
83. Miner Winn
84. Jesse Morgan

****

RUTHERFORD COUNTY
SECOND REGIMENT

1. Abram Irvine, Captain
2. John Fonstren, Lieut.
3. Joseph Willis, Ensign
4. Micajah Davis
5. John Blanton
6. Byard McCraw
7. James Wilkins
8. Jesse Blanton
9. John Rippy
10. Elijah Hamrick
11. Richard Bridges
12. Samuel Fonstren
13. Absalom Ellis
14. Nehemiah Padgett
15. Benjamin Burns
16. Valentine Martin
17. Richard Lea
18. George Bridges
19. Jesse Rippy
20. Samuel McIntire
21. Robert Smith
22. Joseph Luguire

Page 133

23. Henry Ledbetter
24. David King
25. James McClure [?]
26. Henry Wilson
27. Thomas Downey
28. James Wilson
29. Alfred [?] Moore
30. James Crains [?]
31. Samuel Wilson
32. Jesse Braddy
33. Solomon Harralson
34. David Lissum
35. John Bailey
36. Henry Waite
37. Alfred Moore
38. Constant Brooks
39. James Wilson

40. James Dickns [sic]
41. Jenky Jenkins
42. Lewis Johnson
43. Elias Story
44. William Holland
45. Zeckeiah McDaniel
46. John Green
47. Darlin Webbs
48. Gilbert Harrel
49. Richard Bostick
50. Henry Grigs
51. Jacob Willis
52. Jacob McKinney
53. John White
54. Henry Workman
55. William Newton
56. John Rooker
57. Hugh McRannolds
58. William York
59. Blueford Randal
60. James Arrowood
61. Jesse Grigs
62. Samuel - -
63. R - - - - -
64. William Wilkey
65. Moses Black
66. Samuel John
67. Jabez Matey
68. John Smith
69. John Barker
70. James Clifwood
71. Jesse Ledford
72. Thomas Hill
73. Abel Beaty
74. William Dedman
75. Amos Martins
76. John Hindcastle
77. Martin Beam
78. Samuel Made
79. Thomas Casher
80. William McEntire
81. Isham John
82. John Alexander
83. Elijah Hohfield
84. P - -   Scruggs
85. Joel Williams
86. Abraham Padgett

87. William Lea
88. - - Scruggs
89. John Robeson
90. David Bekeler
91. John Amos
92. David Pope
93. Arther [sic] Clarke

****

RUTHERFORD COUNTY
THIRD REGIMENT

1. Ephraim Carruth
2. James Braden
3. William Newman
4. Andrew Thompson
5. Leander P. Carruth
6. James Ruth
7. Joseph Wood
8. Robert Baiely
9. William Coller
10. James Crawford
11. Noah Hampton
12. Austen Musuck
13. Thomas Prator
14. Gabriel Wilmath
15. John Ownsby
16. Sims Ownsby
17. John Lawther
18. Isaac Goforth
19. Cornelius Clemmons
20. Greenbury Griffen
21. John Dalton
22. David Trully
23. John Going
24. William Wooten
25. Charles Edwards
26. Pleasant Whirly
27. Elijah Dolten
28. Thornton Randal
29. Dennis Duff
30. Edward McGuin
31. Ephraim Jackson
32. Luke Woldson
33. John Eaflin
34. Samuel Thompson

35. John Skipper
36. Burges Smith
37. Jonathan Ellison
38. George McKinney
39. Jeremiah Smith
40. William Thompson

Page 134

41. Robert Cockrun
42. Joseph Studman
43. James Menice
44. John Sutton, Jr.
45. Thomas Dills, Sr.
46. James Henderson
47. William Giles
48. William Sutton, Jr.
49. John Logan
50. James Miller Erwin
51. William Wilson
52. William Clinton
53. Edley Hambleton
54. George Musick
55. Archibald Sohlar
56. An'd Young
57 Claton Brown
58. William Ownby
59. John Dillbark, Jr.
60. Burrel Utly
61. Thomas Blackurl
62. George Fry
63. Caleb Williams
64. Joshua Wells
65. Thomas Steedman
66. Solomon Blackurl
57. Richard Sisemore
68. Joseph Willson
69. John Smith
70.   blank
71.   blank
72.   blank

****

BURKE COUNTY
FIRST REGIMENT

1. Frederick Sluillel, Captain
2. Elrod Pobete, 1st Lieut
3. John F. O'Neill, 2nd Lieut.
4. John Rill, Ensign
5. William Brittain, 1st Serg.
5. Jacob Keller, 2nd Serg.
7. John Walker, 3rd Serg.
8. Henry M. Oneal, 4th Serg.
9. Swinton Lowdor, Drummer
10. Stephen Ballow, Fifer
11. Ezekal England
12. Peter Wisinghunt
13. John Williams
14. Peter Mull
15. Frederick Bottles
16. Garrat Garratson
17. James Largant
18. Thomas Moody
19. Philip Pitts
20. William Sorrals
21. Joseph Thompson
22. James McFalls
23. Reuben Walker
24. Samuel Lockrage
25. William Oglesby
26. Archibald Oglesby
27. Thomas Michaels
28. Robert Good
29. William Reed
30. Andrew England
31. Joseph Baker
32. John Bottles
33. Elijah Walker
34. John Good
35. William Hartley
36. Joseph Murphy
37. John H. Singling
38. Philip Shufler
39. Joseph England, M [?]
40. William England, Jr.
41. Solomon Good, Jr.
42. John Powell
43. Michael Wisinghunt
44. Demmon Dossey, Jr.
45. John Derryburry
46. Alexander Deal
47. Henry Deal

48. John Jones
49. John Poteete
50. Peter A. Bey
51. Michael Wehunt
52. John Martin
53. William Deal
54. John Black
55. John Kennedy
56. John Hartley
57. Abraham Deal
58. William Brackett
59. John Airwood
60. George Reider
61. William Wenters
62. John Eavins
63. Elijah Powell
64. Lewis Powell
65. Henry Wilds
66. John Bial
67. Jacob A. Bey
68. Andrew Kincald
69. James McDowell
70. John Hayse
71. Elijah Hayse
72. Isaac Tunmire
73. Henry Winkler
74. John Killan
75. John Purson
76. Thomas Bryant
77. Perian Daniel
78. Jesse Smith

Page 135

79. John Smalley
80. Henry Kyles
81. William Pyott
82. Archibald Gibbs
83. James Hill
84. Micajah Lisk

****

BURKE COUNTY
SECOND REGIMENT

1.   blank

2.   blank
3.   blank
4. Larkin Kerby
5. Andrew Reid
6. Joel Williams
7. William Turner
8. William Roberts
9. James Collins
10. John Fincannon
11. Thomas Bean
12. Jesse Berry
13. Abraham Melone
14. Samuel Smith
15. John Bevey, Jr.
16. John King
17. Leps Helton
18. Joshua Harshaw
19. Henry Cook
20. Alexander Campbell
21. John Ernest
22. Solomon Crisp
23. James Fletcher
24. William Coffey
25. Colbert Hays
26. John Harriss
27. Reuben Coffey
28. James Gilbert
29. John Sumpter
30. Joseph Owens
31. John Prock
32. Alexander West
33. Samuel Howell
24. Thomas Blair
35. Justice Beech
36. Frederick Tucker
37. John Brown
38. Christian Hass
39. John Litten (in dispute)
40. Robert Riner
41. Philip Rough
42. Joseph Kerby
43. Jonathan Penly
44. Lemuel Holt
45. John Fritt
46. William Reed
47. Matthew Winkler
48. Daniel Whittenburg

49. Thomas King
50. Enock Presnill
51. Thomas Dorsett
52. Eli Justice
53. Thomas Forrester

****

BURKE COUNTY
THIRD REGIMENT

1. Jason Carson, Captain
2. James Burgen, Leiut.
3. Pleasant Cashin
4. Burret Rickets
5. James Smith
6. Jonathan Allison
7. John Ross
8. Dennis Ross
9. Ben. Curtis
10. Livender Fortune
11. George Darnald
12. Alexander Porter
13. George Edmison
14. Johnson Allison
15. Samuel Cockhorn
16. William Barley
17. Swinefield Hell
18. Henry Crown
19. William Guy
20. Jesse Henil
21. William Hughs
22. Andrew McKinly
23. Abner Devenporte
24. William Waldriss
25. Elis Waldriss
26. Thomas Devenporte
27. Manual Lamb
28. William Dickson
29. William Vonn
30. Austin Pack
31. William Bright
32. Joab Goodbread
33. Joseph Lanner
34. Thomas James
35. Thomas Gribils
36. Mitchel Parham

37. William Henderson
38. Joseph Civins
39. John Queen
40. John Morris
41. William Duncan
42. John W. Carson
43. Stogdol Wilson
44. David Curtis

Page 136

45. Man Shote
46. Thomas Hancy
47. Daniel Morrow
48. John Biddicks
49. James Reves
50. Jacob Martin
51. William Jones
52. William Lackey

****

BUNCOMBE COUNTY
FIRST REGIMENT

1. Clayton Neel, Captain
2. Andrew Wilson, Lieut.
3. John Sutton
4. Samuel McCarson
5. Charles McLain
6. Lewis Herrin
7. William Wilson
8. James Brevard
9. Robert Wilson
10. Thomas Jones
11. Charles Adams
12. James Erwin
13. Cajer Smith
14. Abraham McGuffee
15. George Justin
16. James Jones
17. Nathan Fletcher
18. John Justice
19. Jesse Case
20. Andrew Lockhart
21. James Maxwell
22. William Justice

NORTH CAROLINA - ROSTER OF SOLDIERS IN WAR OF 1812   115

****

23. William Case
24. Andrew Lockart
25. James Maxwell
26. Archibald Edmiston
27. James S. Smith
28. Jesse Causby
29. William Carn
30. Davis Rhodes
31. Ninnion Edmeston
32. Willliam Cincard
33. Ezekiel Sandelin
34. John Osborn
36. Jeremiah Osborn
36. Daniel Allen
37. Henry Studer
38. Matthias Little
39. Samuel Corn
40. James Tweed
41. Hugh Johnston
42. David Evins
43. Enock Williams
44. Robert Orr
45. James Nickolson
46. Peter Sheperd
47. William W. Lain
48. Richard Scentill
49. Daniel Hefner
50. Eli Merrill
51. Ballard Lake
52. John Clayton
53. George D. Davis
54. David Fains
55. Burges Lake
56. George Erwin
57. Samuel King
58. Walter Burwell
59. James Clark
60. Mathew Wilson
61. James Kitchins
62. David Johnson
63. Alexander Jordan
64. Jonathan Lincard
65. Grady Johnson
66. Solomon Farker
67. John Galloway
68. Lewis Ransom

****

BUNCOME COUNTY
SECOND REGIMENT

1.   blank
2.   blank
3. John Smith
4. John Hawkins
5. Aaron Javette
6. Elsy Rundles
7. Joseph Gudger
8. John Gooch
9. Joseph Wright
10. Nimrod Merrill
11. Amos Lanning
12. Eli Rimon
13. Aaron Banks
14. Andrew Gorran
15. Thomas Spolson
16. Thomas Rogers
17. George Lindsey
18. John Frishy
19. William Spivey
20. David Rogers
21. David Vance
22. James Wever
23. William Botton
24. David E. Baly
25. George Corn
26. Richard Duff
27. James Dillard
28. Robert Britton
29. James Rogers
30. Jacob Carber

Page 137

31. Joseph Carver
32. Joseph Millsaps
33. William Mason
34. David Millar
35. Malley Reeves
36. Thomas Jones
37. Irea Javiette
38. Joseph Hays
39. George Brock

40. Elisha Spivey
41. Jacob Fortunberry
42. Abraham Penland
43. Aswell Phillips
44. James Rice
45. William Crage
46. Samuel Mafee
47. William Murray
48. John M. Patton
49. William Wafer
50. John Henry
51. John Palmer
52. Andrew Garron
53. John Gearron
54. William H. Murrey
55. M. Haustin Patton
56. Jacob Jaron
57. William Gudger
58. Thomas Murry
59. Thomas Taylor
60. Samuel Jinkins
61. Adam Garron
62. John Patton
63. Cilas Rhea
64. Azra Jinkens
65. Samuel J. Mavey

****

BUNCOMBE COUNTY
THIRD REGIMENT

1. Levi Bailey, Captain
2. Joseph Shepard, 1st Lieut.
3. David Hughey, Ensign
4. William Keith
5. Henry Keith
6. James Wood
7. Mark Roberts
8. Thomas Roberts
9. Edward Robertson
10. Reuben Keith
11. John Cody
12. Travner Moore
13. Joseph Ponder
14. Thomas Gaines Roberts
15. Nimrod Buckner

16. Robert Roberts
17. Jesse Giles
18. John Green
19. William Carson
20. John Greenwood
21. James Hurstle
22. Samuel Hughey
23. Shadrack Guthry
24. Garrat Deweese
25. William Williams
26. Augustine Prestwood
27. John Lams
28. James Lams
29. Britain Williams
30. John Arrowood
31. Benjamin Webb
32. Richard Holland
33. Joseph Callihorn
34. Absolom Medcalf
35. Sperlin Bowman
36. John Cornwell
37. John Garrett
38. John Stanton
39. John Stanton [sic]
40. George Stanton
41. John Randolph
42. George Robertson
43. William Byrd
44. John Edwards
45. Samuel Byrd
46. William Dayton
47. James Edwards
48. William Taylor
49. Jacob Silver
50. James Angel
51. Jacob Killian
52. James McMahan
53. Maxamillan Harriss
54. Uriah Honeycutt
55. Angel Cook
56. John Anglin
57. John Poteet
58. James Poteet
59. William Calliway
60. Abner State
61. Jesse Radford
52. Edmond Edwards

63. Thomas Wilson
64. Thomas Lawson
65. Joseph Ray

****

Page 138

HAYWOOD COUNTY

1. John McClure, Captain
2. Elijah Dever, Leiut.
3. John Dever, Ensign
4. John Welsh
5. Joseph Cathey
6. Jethro Cathey
7. Christian Howel
8. Benjamin Hatfield
9. Jonathan Hains
10. James Campble
11. Andrew McClor
12. William McClure
13. Benjamin McMullen
14. Charles Evenes
15. Richard Clark
16. Abraham Eaton
17. William Goodwin
18. Lazarus Eaton
19. James Chambers
20. William Chambers
21. James McFarland
22. Bailey Fleming
23. Champ Langford
24. David Elder
25. John Dillord
26. John Oliver
27. Benjamin Enloe
28. Edward Coiter
29. Jesse Enloe
30. James A. Ellis
31. George Penland
32. William Rogers
33. James Williams
34. John Telley
35. Robert Penland
36. Hirom Gray
37. William Murry

38. William Crawford
39. Josiah Crawford
40. Joseph Chambers
41. John Lord
42. Andrew McLon
43. Joseph Dunn
44. John Bell
45. Andrew Bryson
46. John Middleton
47. Jonas Denton
48. Andrew Hopper
49. Jonathan Deaton
50. James Peterson
51. Malachai Boland
52. John Middleton
53. William Watson
54. John Nelson
55. Henry Anderson
56. Martin Hefley
57. Nicholas Massey
58. William Montgory
59. George Hiffley
60. John Anderson
61. Isom Gurly
62. James Welsh
63. Hugh Donalson
64. Mark Colmer
65. Elisha Foller
66. John Mann
67. John Toller
68. Samuel Corter
69. Samuel Robeson
70. Thomas Watson
71. John Watson
72. James Love
73. Loyd Heyson

****

NORTH CAROLINA - ROSTER OF SOLDIERS IN WAR OF 1812   117

****

MEMORANDA

The following Counties of the Detached Militia of 1814, were called into office at Norfolk, in Virginia, by orders and issued in September, A.D. 1814, to wit: Granville, Wake, Johnston, Franklin, Warren, Halifax, Northampton, Nash, Edgecombe, Martin, Bertie, Hertford, Gates, Chatham, Orange, Person.

N.B. The detached of Militia form the Counties of Chatham, Orange and Person were ordered to return to their respective homes before they arrived at Gates Court House, the place of rendezvous.

The Detached Militia from the following Counties were called into service at Wilmington, North Carolina, by orders issued September 29th, A.D. 1814, to wit: New Hanover, Brunswick, Bladen, Columbus, Robeson, Cumberland, Duplin, Sampson.

The following Counties of the Detached Militia were called into service at Newbern, North Carolina, by orders issued September 17th, A.D. 1814, to wit; Wayne, Greene, Jones, Lenoir Craven, Beaufort.

The detached Militia from the following Counties were called to Hillsboro, the place of rendezvous, on the 28th of November , A.D. 1814, where they were organized and from thence they were marched to Norfolk, in the service of the United State, agreeable to the requisition made by the President and Governor of the State: The Counties to wit: Orange, Chatham, Person, Caswell, Rockingham, Guilford, Randolph, Stokes, Surry, Wilkes.

The officer of the regiment were:

Richard Atkerson, of Person, as Lieutenant Colonel Commandant

Samuel Hunter, of Guilford, as Lieutenant Colonel

- - ies Campbell, of Rockingham, 1st Major

Joseph Winston, Jr. Of Stokes, 2nd Major

Requisition was made by Major General Thomas Pinkard for one Regiment to march to the defense of the Southern Frontier of the sixth District of the United States. In consequence of which order we made at this office, calling for the Detached Militia from the following counties to wit: Anson, Richmond, Moore, Cabrass, to rendezvous at - - -burgh, in Anson County, on the 24th Febraury, A.D. 1815. Also, the counties of Wilkes, Burke, Rutherford, Buncombe, Haywood, to rendezvous at Wadesburgh in Anson County, on Wednesday the 1st day of March, A.D. 1815. Of the Regiment the following officers were designated to the command.

Andrew Irwin, as Lieutenant Colonel Commandant

- - - McGrmusey, of Burke, as Lieutenant Colonel

- - se Allen, of Wilkes, 1st Major

- - - mias Lenoir, of Haywood 2nd Major

N.B. The orders from this office were dated on January 25th, A.D. 1815

Page 140   Adjutant General's Office
                      Raleigh, march 22d 1851

I do hereby certify, on the best of my knowledge and belief, that the foregoing is a true copy of the names of the Officers and Soldiers of the Detached Militia of north Carolina, in pursuance of a Requisition of the President of the United States, in virtue of an act of Congress, passed 10th April, 1812.

                      Robert W. Haywood,
                      Adjutant General of the
                      Militia of N. Carolina.

NOTE BY THE PUBLISHER

The names of the Soldier are spelled just as we find them on the Muster Roll which will account for the seeming inaccuracies in the list, according to the present orthography of proper names.

****

INDEX OF REGIMENTS IN COUNTIES IN 1812-1814

A

Aaron, Abner, Jr. 55
Abbot, Samuel 9
Abel, James 48
Abernasty [sic], Frederick 44
Abernathy, Ezekiel 44
  Hardy 52
  Iasiah [sic] 45
  Joshua 44
  Miles 111
  Moses 44
  Samuel 109
Abington, James 15
Abrahams, Laden 75
Abshire, Jeremiah 43
  John 43
Acborn, Will 27
Acer, Christopher 45
Acock, Alfred 54
  Brittain 85
  Jesse 29
  Ransom 18
  Ransome 68
Acrey, Edward 74
Acros, Leroy 91
Adain, William 46
Adam, Isaac 99
  William 10
Adams, Andrew 13
  Benjamin 43
  Bryan, Jr. 11
  Charles 53, 114
  Elijah 103
  Gibson 99
  Hardy 11
  Harman 24
  Henry 66
  Isaac 43
  Jacob 11
  Jesse 100
  John 43, 88
  Joseph H. 69
  Laban 43
  Martin 29
  Noah 74
  Prein 49
  Summer 73
  Sylvester 99
  Thomas 74
  William 88, 110
  Wm. 94
Adcock, Henry 24
  Jese [sic] 30
  William 30
Addison, John 79
Adkins, George 34
  William 78
Adkinson, Daniel 78
  Dawson 86
Adkison, Willie 19
Afria, Richard 46
Agender, Benjamin 58
  Peter 58
Agle, George 102
Agnor, Joseph 101

Peter 102
Ahorn, Signor 96
Aikin, Jeremiah 64
  Jeremiah D. 64
Aire, William K. 37
Airs, David 69
  John 6, 78
  Richard 17
Airwood, John 113
Akin, William 51
Alberly, Henry 35
Albertson, William 63
Albird, William 7
Albright, Jacob 91
  Joel 27
  John 26, 101
  Peter 36
Albritton, John H. 10
  Samuel 73
  Simeon 10
Alby, Howell 52
Alcorn, John 51
Aldridge, Jonathan 47, 96
  Richard 73
  Samuel 101
  Thomas 73
Aldrige, Samuel 34
Alexander, Aaron 78
  Abdon 106
  Albertes 106
  Alexis 108
  Anthony 69
  Benjamin 51
  Cirus 107
  David 39, 69
  Eli 39
  Ezekiel 105
  Gardener 69
  George C. 49
  Harman 6
  James 51, 106, 108
  John 40, 46, 112
  John D. 106
  Johnston 32
  Joseph 39
  Joshua 69
  Laid 40
  Major R. 46
  Mitchall 49
  Palau [sic] 40
  Reuben 100
  Robert 109
  Salamachus 106
  Thomas 27
  William 6, 33, 53
  Willis 43
Alford, Elie 85
  Jacob 88
  Julius 19
  William 19, 88
Alfred, Bailey 54
  Gilbert 54
  Green 51
  Handy 76
  Kade 54
  Macomb 19
  Reuben 101
Allan, Joseph 78
  Morgan 78
Allegood, Jacob 70

Allemony, Henry 101
Allen, - -se [?] 117
  Abraham 103
  Amos 23
  Benj. 94
  Charles 18
  Daniel 115
  David 12, 85
  Dearling 109
  Dillard 95
  Eaton F. 15
  George 104
  Grant 89
  Icy 18
  Ira 68
  Isaac 80
  James 29, 97
  John 11, 18, 55, 66, 67, 70,
    99, 106
  Jonathan 80
  Joseph 93
  Ludwell 66
  Miles 54
  Nirain 49
  Paul 82
  Richard 68
  Richard E. 111
  Richard, Jr. 58
  Robert 26, 106
  Shadrach 94
  Thomas 2-4, 39
  Vine 8
  Walter 9
  William 6, 26, 63
  Woodson 86
  Young 86
  Young, Jr. 86
  Zachariah 15
Alles, Peter 107
Alley, James 108
  John 104
Allimony, Henry 52
Allin, David 95
Allison, Benjamin 48
  David 99
  James 88
  John 46
  Johnson 114
  Jonathan 114
  Joseph 91
  Richard 60
  Robert 39
  Thomas 108
  Thos. 101
  William 52, 108
  Zilmon 90
Alloway, William 43
Alman, Lewis 48
Almond, Edmond 52
  Nathan 87
Alphin, Frederick 5
  Hezekiah 72
  Jesse 73
  John 5
  Thomas 13
Alsobrook, James 16
  Micajah 67
Alson, James 68
Alston, James 18
  John 15

Joseph 28
  Thos. 85
Ambrose, James 75
  Jehu 6
  Levi 6
  Peter 77
Ambrous, Berry 85
Amburgy, Wm. 99
Amburn, Samuel 48
  William 48
Ameek, David 101
Ames, John, Jr. 54
  Joseph 89
Amget, Peteer [sic] 54
Amick, John 95
Amis, Benjamin 17
  John 17
Amison, Edward 75
Ammonds, John 9, 21
Ammons, Stephen 81
Amory, Albert 49
Amos, John 112
  William 89
Amosin, Thomas 54
Amyett, Darius 8
Ananias, William W. 29
Anders, Abner 13
  Adam 72
  Ivey 72
Anderson, Andrew 22
  Charles 34, 37
  Francis 15
  George 22
  Henry 49, 116
  James 81
  Jeremiah 30, 85
  John 47, 75, 116
  John A. 65
  John, Jr. 49
  Reuben 32
  Samuel 102
  Scarlet 30
  William 13, 20, 23, 78, 102
  Wm. 102
Andrees [sic], John 78
Andres, Aaron 98
  John 78
Andress, Wilson 104
Andrew, Hezekiah 27
Andrews, Arden 50
  Benjamin 111
  Calin 75
  James 96
  John 9, 73, 85
  Nelson 29, 86
  Vensten 9
  Warren 8
  William 6, 65
Angel, James 116
  Joshua 42
  Lawrence 97
  Peter 28
  Samuel 96
Angle, Benj. D. 96
Anglin, John 49, 116
Ansley, Joseph 75
Anson, Jesse 20
Anthony, David 42
  Henry 94
  James 59

William 47, 59
Applewhite, Thomas 14
Applin, William 17
Archabb, Moses 108
Archer, David 33
   Elijah 6
   James 33
   John 67
   Joshua 88
   Mathuel [sic] 6
   Moses 28
Archibald, Samuel 108
   Thomas 39
   William 7
Archland, Thomas 1
Archlin, Bryan 8
Arendel, Thomas B. 19
Arenhart, Henry 101
Arey, Jerry 102
Argee, Joseph 27
Armond, James 10
Armstead, Tabin 54
Armstrong, Andrew 6
   J. Smith 49
   John 82
   Matthew 44
   Samuel 44
   Selby 6
   Solomon 69
   William 76
Arnet, John 104
Arnett, Asbury 35
Arnold, Edward 8
   Elisha 71
   James 88
   John 5, 71, 74
Arnolds, John 87
Arrenton, Edward 4
   Joseph 4(2)
   Thomas 4
Arrington, John 109
   Levi C. 17
Arrowood, James 112
   John 116
Arthur, Richard 72
   William 39
Artis, Cullen 16
   Kinchen 16
Asbrige, Joseph, Jr. 34
Asbury, Francis 45
Ash, Halvin 15
   James 15
   Thomas 45
Ashe, Joseph 110
Asher, John 52
Ashley, James 26
   John 61
   William 61
Ashworth, Benjamin 86
Asken, George 5
Askew, Abner 74
Askin, Eanos [sic] 75
Askins, Ezekiel 13
   Josiah I. 5
Asque, William 87
Atherly, James 9
Atkerson, Richard 60, 117
Atkins, James 31
   Jonas 5
   Thomas 50

Atkinson, Dawson 29
   Joel H. 87
   John 31
   Richard 25
   William 21
Atkius [Atkins ?], Jacob 18
Atwater, Moses 26
Atwell, John 108
Atwill, William 76
Aubury, Elijah 98
Aulberty, John 98
Austin, Jonathan 87
   Ransom 90
   Wilson 103
Auston, Cornelius 2
   Moses 2
Autrey, Cornelius 81
Autry, Frederick 22
Aven, Durham 82
   Thomas 68
Avera, Jacob 11
Averhart, Jacob 38
Averit, Thomas 19
Avery, Henry 29
   Isaac 2
   James 49
   John 82
   Samuel 71
Aycock, James 11
Aydelotte, Jacob 61

B

Baber, Robert 42
Bachan, Malcom 83
Bachelor, Daniel 18
   James 67
   Joseph 68
   Wilson 68
   Wright 68
Backout, David 110
Backwith, Armor 18
Badget, John 31
Bager, Jacob 107
   John 107
Baggett, Abram 45
   Asa 23
   Drury 45
Baglen, Joseph 2
Bagley, Davis 98
   Joseph 3
   Nathan 4, 63
   William 63, 89
Bagly, Etheldred 11
Bagner, Slamil [sic] 70
   Willile [Willie?] 70
Bags, Hall 12
Bagwell, Budd 85
   Richard 55
Baiely, Robert 112
Bailey, David 11, 45
   Henry 90
   Jeremiah 100
   John 52, 112
   Jonathan 16
   Levi 115
   Wm., Jr. 84
Baily, John T. 9
Bain, Alexander 107
   John 91
Bainhill, John 78

Baird, Elisha 53
   Ezebulon 53
   Mathew 53
Baiter, Arthur 19
Bake, Samuel 29
Baker, Aaron 106
   Abel 106
   Benjamin 42, 65
   Blake 15
   Duncan 25, 83
   Edward B. 55
   Elisha 78
   German 66
   Henry 35, 69
   Isaac 64
   James 77
   John 1, 5, 19, 23, 49
   Jonathan 87
   Joseph 113
   Lanceford 68
   Martin 43
   Michael 106
   Nathan 5, 38
   Phillip 44, 58
   Robert 46
   William 4, 19, 44
Balance, Edmond 87
   Jesse 62
   Thomas 62
Balding, Alfred 84
Baldridge, James 93
Baldwin, David 23
   Enock 100
   James, Jr. 23
   Theophilus 58
   Warren 57
Balentine, David 82
Baley, Charles 48
   Drury 11
Ball, David 93
   George 99
   Gilford 88
   James 99
   Javan 99
   John 59
   Major 70
   Merriman 83
   Richard 89
   Spencer 93
   William 103
   Wilson 26
Ballance, Merrit 1
   William H. 15
Ballard, Drewry 26
   Edwin 4
   Gardner 26
   John 45
   John D. 103
   Joseph 50
   Lemuel 74
   Solomon 59
   William 25, 68
   Willis 109
Ballenger, Allen S. 11
Ballester, William 5
Ballie, Mills 24
Ballow, Stephen 113
Baltin, Jacob 85
Balton, Allin 75
   James 41

Baly, David E. 115
Bambow, Paten 40
Band, John 54
Bandy, Thomas 45
Bane, Peter J. 59
Bankenship, Malajah 111
Banks, Aaron 115
   Hardy 5
   Hardy M. 65
   James 1
   Jesse 97
   John 6
   William 7
Banley, Stephen 25
Bantly, David 67
   William 67
   Wilson 67
Bar, William 36
Barbage, George C. 7
Barbee, James C. 93
   Joseph 86
Barber, Absalom 77
   Brittain 11
   Bryan 77
   David 26
   John 11, 24
   Johnston 28
   Robert 110
   William 74
   Wm. 102
Barclay, Henry 45
   Jonathan 102
Barclift, Samuel, Sr. 64
Barco, Baley 2
   Joseph 62
Bardford, Joseph 25
Barefoot, John 79
   Noah, Jr. 11
Barelipt, Samuel 4
Barfield, Allen 23
   Benjamin 17
   Bryan 10
   Cade 82
   Frederick 74
   Henry 10
   John 80
   Needham 82
   Thomas 33
Barflet, Richard 106
Barham, Nathan 32
Barker, Daniel 42
   Geo. W. 95
   James 27
   Jeremiah 27
   Jethro 14
   John 96, 112
   Robert 28
   Thos. 96
Barley, William 114
Barlow, Marsh 82
   Thos. 99
Barnard, Grandy 61
   James 109
   Willoughby 61
Barncastle, Francis 38
Barnell, Danil [sic] 33
Barner, James 50
   Richard 7
Barnes, Acilles 55
   Albertain 82

David 16
Enos 55
Games 106
Jacob 75
John 40, 55, 64
Pleasant 33
Reddick 55
Robert 33, 76
William 30
Barnett, Amos 105
Jesse 23
John 2, 7, 29, 105
John, Jr. 29
Luke 24
Robert 70
Barney, Samuel 95
Simon 8
Barnhard, John 41
Barnhart, George 108
John 32
Barnhill, Henry 74
John 50, 74, 105
Robert 25
Barnrd [Barnard?], Reuben 38
Barns, Daniel 69
Elijah 99
George 99
James 64
Jeptha A. 67
Jeremiah 96
Jethro 76
John 79, 99
Micajah 106
Reuben 65
Robert 71
Samuel 76
Simon 76
William 40
Winwright 95
Barr, John 34
Moses 110
William D. 70
Barratt, Asa 6
Barrett, William M. 39
Barrier, Henry 104
Barringer, Daniel S. 50
Jacob 52
Matthis 110
Barrington, Jesse 9
John 73
Lemuel 3
Barro, Peter 62
Barrot, Wm. 83
Zach 71
Barrow, Benjamin 13
James 19, 77
John 7, 55
Jorden 18
Thomas 75
William 70, 73
Barry, David 34
James 34
John 34
Bartholomew, Jacob 15
Bartlet, James 76
Bartlett, Isaac 98
Baslay, Willis 82
Bason, Frederick 91
Bass, Bryan 76
Cader 18

Felix 81
Guilford 19
Horatio 30
Jesse 10
John 29
Moses 25
Noah 76
William 10, 76
Baston, David 17
Baswell, Edward 26
James 65
Matthew 26
Bate, Freeman 37
Bateman, Andrew 69
Asahel 55
Benjamin 4
Cornelius 8
Evin 69
Hardy 4
Jeremiah 8
Lemuel 4
Baten, Thomas 16
Batey, William 103
Batten, Amos 11
Hardy 11
William 11
Battle, Josiah 5, 85
William 85
Batton, Moses 105
Batts, Geraldus 75
Lott 12
Baum, Adam 62
Robert 66
Bavick, James 35
Bawcom, Bennet 85
James 85
Baxley, Michael 81
Baxter, Daniel 106
John 51, 61, 62
Joseph, Jr. 62
Joshua 2
Bayett, George 87
Bays, James 98
Bayton, William 75
Bazimore, Cullen 65
Stephen 65
Beach, John 17
Richard 18
William 17
Beacham, Eden 70
Beal, Joseph 103
Tabner 92
Thos. 92
Beale, Robert 44
Beales, Berket 62
James 62
Beals, Josiah 2
Beam, Martin 112
Beaman, Abraham 104
Samuel 37
Beamon, David 104
Bean, Thomas 114
Beane, Nathaniel 25
Bear, John 44
Beard, John 36, 78, 109
Lewis 36
Thomas 76
Beardan, John 80
Beasel, Elijah 33
Beasley, Absalom 56

David 54
Francis 72
James 35
Joshua 54
Samuel 1
William 1
Beasly, John P. 89
Beason, David 33
William 35
Beatty, James G. 47
Beaty, Abel 112
Isaac 39
James G. 59
John 106(2)
Beaver, Wm. 91
Beck, Abram 34
John 103
Becketh, John 37
Beckwith, Thomas 17
Beckworth, Sion 68
Becton, Frederick J. 72
Bector, John 39
Beddoe, Travers 57
Bedsold, Thomas 79
Travis 79
Beech, Jonathan 79
Justice 114
Beeling, Ralph P. 61
Beem, Peter 45
Beesley, John 78
Solomon 78
Beeson, Vestal 101
Beil, James 58, 74
John 39
Beill, Reasoon 38
Walter 38
Bekeler, David 112
Belcher, George 10
Belflower, James 74
Belinger, Julian D. 3
Belk, Brelon 40
John 106
Bell, Benjamin 74
Branson 61
Burrel 74
David 89
Elijah 93
Francis 51
George W. 33
Hillary 2
James 51, 54
Jeremiah 29
Jesse 42
Joab 62
John 52, 56, 77, 85, 88, 116
Joseph 62
Joshua 7, 21
Matthias 62
Michael 68
Newel 72
Reason 39
Richard 48
Tandy 94
Thomas 52
William 29, 77, 107
William W. 29
Belsher, Beverly 73
Woody 73
Belvin, Peter 91
Bendon, Charles 10

Benge, James 43
Benhill, William 106
Benion, John 16
Bennet, Charles 18
James C. 18, 68
John 80
Lovin 105
Mereday 35
William R. 50
Bennett, Benjamin C. 23
Daniel 10, 56
Drury 41
James 41
Luke 17
Thomas 12
William 45, 56
Bennik, Jeremiah 46
Benns, John T. 66
Bensel, John 99
Benson, James 78
Matthew 78
Benthall, John 5
Bentine, Willis B. 62
Bentley, James 109
Bently, Benjamin 8, 38
Benton, Abbey 5
David 5
Francis 9(2)
Henry H. 5
Jacob 5
Jethro 5
Joseph 31
Joshua 3
William 5, 73
Berbank, Paul 9
Bereman, Kader 5
Berger, Henry 58
Bernard, Carter 63
Berns, George 106
Berring, William 14
Berry, Andrew 109
David 12
George 89, 109
Isaac 2
Jesse 114
Joseph 34
Miles 2
Thomas 62
Timothy 2
William 2, 7
Berryman, Stephen 22
Berton, Robert 41
Berwick, William 33
Beson, Samuel 27
Best, Bostian 110
Elias 84
Henry 17
Theophilus 13
William 12
Betha, Jesse 20
Bethell, Alfred 95
Bethune, Hector 57
Betts, John 86
Beverly, Abner 84
Jephthah 85
Bevers, Thomas 27
Bevey, John, Jr. 114
Bevill, Alexander 32
Henry 94
James 94

Phillip 32
Robert 33
Thomas 32
Bewsey, Charles 99
Bey, Jacob A. 113
  Peter A. 113
Bial, John 113
Bibby, Nathaniel 84
Bibee, John 97
Bickell, Thomas 55
Bickerstaff, Samuel 111
Bickle, Samuel 14
Biddicks, John 114
Biddingfield, Theophilus 87
Bierly, David 37
Biggers, Johnston N. 41
Biggoner, Fredrick 11
Biggs, Davis 6
Bigham, Robert, Jr. 106
  Samuel 106, 110
Bilangey, Lilby 69
Bilberry, James 16
Bilbes, William 68
Biles, Wade 111
Biley, Michael 101
Billard, Lewis 31
Billberry, John 79
Billbinny, Henry 79
Billingsby, Hezekiah 23
  William 33
Billiny, David 102
Bince, Felix M. 33
Bingham, Joseph 39
  William 43
Binkley, John 34
Binny, Aaron 94
Bird, Andrew 105
  Bright 11
  James 25
  John 21, 22
  Joseph 25
  Joshua 9
  Josiah 65
  Nathan 9
  Raphael 10
  Samuel 104
  William 19, 45, 74
Birkhart, George 36
Bishop, John 80, 93
  Jos. 96
  Morris 78
  Owen 80
  Thomas, Jr. 78
  W. M. 56
  William 26
  Zachariah 70
Bissalt, Joseph 68
Bissent, William 37
Bizzel, John 77
Bizzett, John 6
Black, Adam 103
  Alexander 22
  David H. 41
  George 28
  John 24, 40, 41, 78, 83, 113
  Joseph 49, 103, 110
  Kenneth 82
  Moses 112
  Neil 83
  Pleasant 96

Thomas 110
William 111
Blackburn, Asa 15
  Burwell 86
  Daniel 110
  Jesse 15
  John 17, 43, 106
  Levi 100
  Wm. 97
Blackenship, William 38
Blacklidge, Richard 70
Blacklock, David 28
Blackman, Barney 81
  Jeremiah 11
  John 82
  William 57
Blackswell, Solomon 47
Blackurl, Solomon 113
  Thomas 113
Blackville, Robert 98
Blackw [?], Abraham 79
Blackwater, Andrew 107
  Caleb 108
Blackwelder, Christ. 101
Blackwell, John 22, 47
  Robert 89
Blackwood, Anderson 91
  John 110
  Joseph 105
Blair, Jesse 100
  Thomas 114
Blake, Asa 86
  Etheldred 41
  Joseph 41
Blallock, David 41
Blalock, David 92
  Hastin 90
  John 44
  Terrel 41
Blan, Benjamin 65
Blanchard, Dempsey 5
  Jeremiah 31
  John 5, 12
  Reuben 12
  Seth 64
  William 64
Blanchet, Wm. 96
  Young 82
Bland, George 8
  Thomas 92
Blankinship, Archibald 44
Blanks, William 30
Blanton, George 46
  Jesse 112
  John 46, 112
  Lewis 46
Blaylock, Jos. 92
Bledsoe, Anthony 86
  Edward 86
  George 88
  Giles B. 28
  Giles J. 54
  John 23
  Joseph 87
  Patrick 88
  Thomas 104
Blewet, Thomas 52
Blont [sic], Major 76
Blount, Benjamin 25
  Clement H. 61

Ezekiel 6
Henry 68, 70
James 69
John 22
Joseph 25, 65
Lewis 70
Reading 25
Steph. 69
Theophilus 80
Thomas H. 60
Warren 12
Blue, Archibald 22
  Collin 13
  Duncan 22
  John 22, 24
  Peter 83
Bluford, William 110
Bluie, John 79
Blume, John 97
Boak, Alam [sic] 96
Bobbit, Arthur 90
  John B. 88
Bodenhamer, David 104
  Jacob 104
  William 104
Bodenhammer, George 58
  John 52
Bodiford, William 25
Bogan, Arthur 76
  David 58
Bogar, Daniel 102
Boget, Henry 76
Boggan, Jonathan 84
Boggaw, Isaac 84
Bogle, James 109
  William 109
Bogleman, Archibald 23
Bogue, Josiah 4
Bogus, Jonathan 4
Bohannen, Neal 98
Boice, Isaac 61
Boid, Major 8
  Robert 40
Boland, Malachai 116
Bolar, Shadrack 85
Bolick, Casper 110
Boling, James 93
Bolling, Henry 35
Bollinger, Christian 110
Bominger, Jacob 104
Bond, Edwin 61
  George H. 64
  John 4
  John, Sr. 61
  Will 71
Bondurant, John 33
Bondusant, Lee 96
Bone, David 20
  Eli 92
  John 108
  Richard 20
Bonham, David 78
  James 78
Bonner, John 7
  Richard 7
Bonney, Gideon 1
Booe, Daniel 58
  Jacob 58
Book, William 29
Booker, Richard 38

Boon, Abraham 6
  Bennet 66
  Berd 78
  David 15
  Elisha 15
  Jep 16
  Jeremiah 48
  John 28, 48, 81
  Joiner 16
  Kinchen 19
  Lewis 6, 16
  Nickolas 78
  Owen 20
  Samuel 6
  West 6
  William 16, 66
Booth, Alexander 5
  Arthar [sic] 5
  George 97
  Zachariah 37
Boothe, Daniel 90
Boovey, Mathew 110
Borcy, James 80
Bore, Daniel 52
Bose, John 58
Boss, Henry 27
Bost, Daniel 40
  David 45
  Elias 52
  Matthias 41
  William 52
Bostick, David D. 96
  Richard 112
Bostion, Jacob 108
Boston, Andrew 101
Bostwick, John 24
Boswell, Goldsberry 79
  Gustavous 37
  James 55
  John 1, 97
Boswood, Willougliby [sic] 61
Bottles, Frederick 113
  John 113
Botton, William 115
Botts, Thomas 33
Bourdeaux, John B. 78
  Moses 80
Bourne, James 82
Boushel, Robert 2
Bowan, Charles 80
Bowden, Jesse 103
  Reading 80
  Thomas 29
Bowdown, John 100
Bowell, Joseph 50
Bowen, Benjamin 65
  Elias 32
  Hardy 78
  John 12, 65
  Lewis 12
  Silas 73
  Thomas 20
Bower, Absalom 100
  Christian, Jr. 101
  David 103
  Lewis 35
Bowers, Barnabas 36
  Bartholomew 16
  David 50
  George 36

James 88
John 93
Malikiah 36
Richard L. 55
Bowey, John F. 80
Bowie, Neil 20
Nelson 68
Bowing, Obadiah 15
Bowleyjack, James 97
Bowls, John 89
Jordan 89
Bowman, Andrew 97
George 110
Henry 32
Sperlin 116
Boyakin, William 85
Boyce, John 61
Moses 64
Boyd, Adam 95
Alex 92
Edward 44
James 7
Jesse 8
John 65, 95
Joseph 74
Thomas 105
William 74
Boyet, Nathaniel 21
Boyett, Arthur 5
Boykin, Britain 54
Irvin 68
John 21
Solomon 21
Thomas 21
Boylan, Abraham H. 29
Boyt, Henry 80
Bozeman, Josiah 24
Bozman, William R. W. 65
Brabble, James 62
Johm, Jr. 62
John 62
Tatum 62
Brabin, John 97
Bracker, Laban 39
Brackett, William 113
Bradberry, Bryan 76
Braddy, Benjamin 70
Elisha 74
George 39
James A. 106
Jesse 112
William 74
William, Jr. 87
Braden, James 112
Bradey, John 111
Bradford, Henry 14
John 14, 67
Matthew 76
Thomas 14, 25
Bradie, William J. 15
Bradley, James 99
Major 86
Nimrod 41
Richard 12
Spear 16
Spier 76
Summons 46
Terry 46
Bradshaw, James 89
John 89, 107

Vincent 90
William 26
Brady, Robert 83
Brag, Solomon 71
Brake, David 17
Jacob 17
Braker, William 86
Braley, James 46
Branch, James 31, 48
John 63
John W. 14
William 14
Brand, John 10
Brandle, Daniel 98
Brandon, John 51, 103
John H. 102
Braner, Michael 101
Branner, Alfred 32
Brannock, Samuel 103
Branock, Edmund 92
Branson, Wm. 97(2)
Brantley, Allen 68
Edward 5
Henry 65
Robert 5
William 29
Brantly, Benjamin 85
Edwin 18
Henry 5
James 14
John 55(2)
Joshua P. 55
Wilson 14
Braskett, Thomas 111
Brassie, James 81
Braswell, Aaron 81
Burwell 105
Marmaduke 67
Whitmell 67
William 68
Braughton, James 4
Braves, John 41
Brawley, Daniel 108
Robert 108
Brawlie, Neil, Jr. 39
Bray, Daniel 63
George 12
Jesse 3, 92
Joel 98
John 28
Joseph 3
Thomas 27, 42, 62
William 61
William, Jr. 1
Brayfield, Walter 31
Brazil, Shadrick 84
Brazwell, Parabo 31
Breadlove, William 18
Breedfore, William 68
Breedlove, George 96
Bremon, Nathan 76
Brevard, Hamden 39
James 114
Jesse 48
Brewer, Benj. 98
Elijah 66
Frederick 57
John 80, 100
Julius 57
Micajah 100

Perry 17
Samuel 93
Turner 67
William, Jr. 83
Wm. 91
Briars, David 46
Brickell, John 55
William 55
Brickhead, Kindrick 83
Brickhouse, Benjamin 6
Henry 103
John 61
Major 69
Matthew 69
Richard 69
Uzzell 6
William 6
Brickle, William 14
Bridger, James 76
Bridgers, David 86
Henry 17
Bridges, Aron 46
Barnes 16
Benj. 91
Benjamin 11, 26
Braswell 11
George 112
James 19, 111
John 54
Newit 11
Newsome 19
Richard 46, 112
Samuel 47, 58
Warren 16
Bridgmore, Pleasant 35
Brigat, John 92
Briggs, Benj. 97
Drucis 93
Edward 64
Henry 34
Jethro 5
John 102
Kader 64
Bright, Francis 9
Henry 62
Jabez 63
John 57
William 114
Brigs, James 102
Briles, Jacob 27
Briley, James 24
Jonathan 74
William 73
Brim, John 45
Brindle, Abraham 37
Brindon, Gideon 73
Brine, Benjamin 69
Brinegar, Jacob 100
Bringle, Jacob 36
Bringman, William 24
Brinigan, Joshua 58
Brinkhart, John 36
Brinkle, Robert H. 33
Brinkley, Jethro 64
Robert 15
William 51, 66, 67
Brinkly, Griffin 4
Brinsfield, Thos. 93
Brinson, Jos. S. 71
William S. 71

Brintle, Oliver 31
Britt, Burwell 81
Culiver 83
David 24
Drury 16
Gideon 11
Henry 76
James 76
John 10
Johnson 86
Shade 55
Thomas 81
William 25, 73, 83
Brittain, Benjamin 13
William 113
Brittan, Samuel 49
Brittle, Brittain 66
Britton, Benjamin 9
Robert 115
Samuel 64
Thoms [Thomas ?] 5
Brnat [Brant?], John 11
Brnkley [Brinkley], Henry 5
Broach, Richard 89
Broadstreet, Robert 75
Broadway, Jesse 8
Broadwell, Freeman 54
Brock, Caleb 37
David 80
George 115
Jesse 80
Moses 3
Thomas 80
Brocket, Hiram 14
Brockett, John A. 62
Brogden, Pearce 76
Timothy 17
Brogdon, Alfred 37
Benjamin 55
John 10
Ransom 87
William 37, 56
Wm. 88
Brook, Richard 68
Brooks, Constant 112
David 12
Frederick 7
George 31
George, Jr. 94
Isaac 46
James 24
Jesse A. 15
John 43, 90
John Jas. 90
Jonson 94
Joseph 80
Joseph, Sr. 80
Josh 28
William 74
Williams [sic] 72
Brookshire, William 43, 104
Broom, Allen 40
Gilford 74
Brothers, Benjamin 3
Caleb 63
Jos. 63
Joseph 63
Miles 63
Brower, John 100
Brown, Aben 22

Abner 37
Absalom 50
Alexander 24, 43
Allen 57
Anthony 5
Archibald 99
Asa 90
Bannet 105
Barnabas 20
Barnaby 74
Benjamin 38, 64
Bennet 85
Berry 75
Burwell 86
Claton 113
Daniel 35, 58, 92
David 64
Dempsey 88
Eldah 86
Eli 43, 99
Elisha 20, 99
Ezekiel 99
Fountain 12
Francis 9
Fredrick 27
George 43, 44
Gills 54
Harbert 95
Henry 53
Isaac 69
Israel 32
James 7, 12, 24, 43, 87, 94
Jesse 35, 65, 97
John 23, 28, 31, 40, 43, 64,
 70, 77, 87, 92, 97, 99,
 106, 114
John S. 71
John, Jr. 98
Joseph 68, 99
Joshua 99, 101
Josiah 10
Judson 101
Peter 33, 99, 102
Redding 74
Richard 89
Samuel 39, 99
Stephen 11
Sylvester 9
Thomas 5, 9, 18, 19
W. Elam 51
Whitfield 99
Wiley 5
William 5, 15, 25, 27, 29, 43,
 49, 51, 64
William G. 29
William W. 33
William, Jr. 34
Wm. 83
Zachariah 5
Browney, Zachariah 74
Browning, Edward 8
 James 26, 90
 John 90(2)
 William 8, 87
Broy, Edward 21
Broyhill, John N. 43
 William 43
Bruce, James 31
 Joel 39
 John 99

Jordan 75
Robert 31
Brumblow, David 85
Brumbough, William 63
Brumsey, William 62
Brunt, Peter 67
Bruton, Moses 79
 Simon 7, 60
Bryan, Armilain 79
 Aron, Jr. 28
 Bartholomew 16
 David 86
 Edmund 43
 Edward 13
 Elias 17
 Elijah C. 55
 Harry 86
 John 15, 20, 28, 71, 79, 103
 Joseph 40, 71, 87
 Joseph H. 55
 Nathan 11
 Samuel 15
 Sears 72
 Thomas 17
 William 79
Bryant, Charles 42
 Edward 88
 James 74, 88
 John 14
 Simon A. 65
 Thomas 18, 113
 William T. 67
Bryer, Samuel M. 47
Bryson, Andrew 116
 Cornelius 2
 John, Jr. 49
Buch, James 74
Buchan, Daniel 83
Buchannon, David 33
 Walter 31
 William 31
Buchannor, John 32
Buchanon, James 107
Bucher, Daniel 78
Buck, Henry 38
 John 37, 83
Buckanan, John 90
 Wm. 90
Buckannan, Alfred 92
Buckman, Samuel 72
Buckner, Edward 28
 Edward, Jr. 37
 Nimrod 115
Buckum, Simon 91
Bue, Archibald 23
Buffalo, Wm. 85
Buford, John 10
Buie, Allen 25
 Daniel 82, 83
 Nell 57
Buie, Duncan 24
Bukerdite, Ezra 27
Bulbee, Absalom 51
Bull, Jesse 31
 Samuel 90
Bullard, Elias 81
 Henry 79
 Richard 81
Bullock, Henry 81
 John 74

Leonard 88
Obediah 74
Stephen 55
Whitmel C. 75
Bultry, William 17
Bumgarner, John 110
Bumpass, Wm. 89
Bunch, Cader 55
 Edmond 61
 John 63
 Julius 4
 Nathaniel 4
 Nehemiah 65
 Salter 4
 Samuel 101
Bundy, Caleb 3, 63
 Enoch 6
 Jesse 3
 Nathan 3
 Williams 76
Bungardner, Absalom 45
Bungarner, Moses 45
Bunham, Joseph 97
Bunker, Zenas 33
Bunn, Alfred 17
 Barnaba 16
 Benjamin 7
 Budd 85
 Cader 54
 Henry 68
 Lewis 85
 William 7, 68
Bunnell, James 62
 John 61
 William 1
Bunton, Jeremiah 76
Bunyard, Larkin 58
Burch, Jesse 98
Burdeaux, Israel C. 14
Buress, William 105
Burfield, Littleberry 16
 Zachariah F. 14
Burge, Larkin 35, 96
Burgen, James 114
Burges, Anda 86
 Isaac 62
 John 29
Burgess, Dempsey J. 3
 Edward 58
 John 21, 27
Burgin, Merritt 42
Burk, Joseph 44
 Milliner 28
 William W. 33
Burke, Hugh 21
 Samuel 89
Burkett, Burges 66
 Lemuel 66
Burkly, Donald C. 12
Burn, Levi 46
Burnet, James 92
Burnett, Abram 13
 Ferrington 51
 Iredell 8
 Robert 16
Burney, Abel 19
 David 94
 Lewis 8
 Robert 94
Burnham, Joel 80

Thomas 63
William 4
Burns, Benjamin 112
 Hezekiah 49
 Hiram 93
 Jacob 45
 James 49
 James, Jr. 28, 93
 Jonathan 38
 Riddick 28
 Uriah 49
 Wenright 51
Burrage, James 27
Burrough, Joseph 31
Burroughs, Joseph 94
Burrow, Ephraim 95
 Solomon 95
Burrs, Hansford 55
Burrus, Zachariah 2
Burt, Abraham 94
 John 82
Burton, Absalom 93
 Bartlett 1
 Basel 104
 Emsley 104
 Francis H. 93
 Henry 27
 Hutchens 30
 Noel 31, 93
 Stephen 31
 Thomas Halley 31
 William 52
Burwell, Walter 115
Busbee, Jonathan 29
Busby, Alsey 87
 James 78
Bushbey, Will 39
Bushnell, Mathew 24
Bushup, Benjamin 22
 John 22
Busick, Caleb 92
 James 92
Bussill, Presly 99
Butler, Charles 22
 Curry 65
 John P. 65
 Jordan 71
 Joshua 31
 Samuel 20
 Silas 65
 William 8
 Zachariah 20
Butner, David 58
Butter, John 85
 Willis 63
Button, Daniel 106
Butts, James 10
Byers, David 29
 Francis 48
 George 29
 Robert 49
Bynum, Hampton 97
 John 109(2)
 John Wesley 93
 Kinchen 29
Byrd, John 9
 Samuel 116
 William 116
Byrns, Matthew 103
Byrum, Ransom 93

Bysam, John 4

C

Cable, John 27
  Joseph 26
Cade, Richard 20
  Waddel 20
Caffee, Jacob 7
Caffer, Hooper 95
Cagle, Leonard 105
Cahoon, James 69
  John 69(3)
Cain, Andrew 33
  Samuel 78
Caisar, Richard 87
Calaher, Mathew 108
Calbroth, Daniel 57
Caldwell, Allen 34
  Andrew 39
  John 39, 45
  William 45
Calhoon, Abel 69
Calicoat, George 104
  John 105
Call, Elijah 45
  Henry 103
  Jacob 58
  William 103
Callahan, Robert 58
Callaway, Hatter 65
  Jonathan 74
Callihorn, Joseph 116
Calliway, William 116
Calloway, David 65
  Jonathan 17
Callum, Augt. 56
  Sion 79
Calum, Robert 29
Calvet, Stephen 77
  William 77
Calway, Haller 55
Cam, James M. 12
Camade, John 48
Cambel, Richard 92
Cambell, Samuel 3
Cameron, Hugh 22
  James 82
  John A. 19
Camerson, William 39
Camp, Abner 45
  Francis 62
  Henry 111
Campbell, - -ies [?] 117
  Adam 109
  Alexander 56, 114
  Allen 20
  Anguish 52
  Charles 25
  Cyrus 40
  Dahald 83
  David 101
  Edley 94
  Enos 58
  Frederick 50
  James 19, 34, 60, 79, 82
  John 19, 57, 59, 79, 97
  Montesquien W. 77
  Murdock 20
  Neil 22
  Norman 83

Roderick 24
Samuel 7, 46
Shadrick 9
Thomas 39
Will 91
William 9, 59, 66
Campble, James 116
Camper, David 71
Camplain, Henry 95
Canada, Joel 98
Canaday, Elijah 56
  Kinchen 71
Canady, Right 10
Candy, Feliz 12
Cane, Daniel 37
Canik, Levin 33
Canley, Charles 26
Cannon, Daniel 80
  Dennis 8
  Henry 8, 74, 76
  John 8
  Palmer 8
  Sion 49
  William 35
  Wm. 96
Cantrall, Benjamin 31
  John 34
Cantrel, Jacob 47
Cantrill, Elijah 34
  George 34
  Robert 34
Canwadd, Wm. 85
Capehatt, Trustum 65
Capel, James 24
Capell, Gooden 84
Caperham, David 43
Capps, Henry 87
  Jasper 18
Caps, Cornelius 48
  Jeptha 68
  John 62
  Mark 94
  Wm. 91
Capts, Dennis 1
Car, Wm. 98
Caraway, James 17
  William 8
Carber, Evergain 63
  Jacob 115
Card, Sam'l 82
Carden, John 90
Cardwell, Joel 95
  Leonard 50
  Noah 96
  Thomas F. 26
Carey, Richard 76
Carig, David 51
Cariker, Adam 108
Carlbin, George 22
Carleton, Ambrose 99
Carley, James 56
Carlilsle [sic], Joel 67
Carlisle, Littleberry 74
  Richard 18
  Robert 23
Carlton, Lewis 43
  Thomas 43
Carman, Joshua 20
Carmichael, John 83
Carmichall, Abner 98

Carmichel, Daniel 24
Carmickdet, Hugh 82
Carmon, Stephen 12
Carn, William 115
Carnel, Reuben 69
Carnest, John 43
Carney, James, Sr. 8
  John 29
  Leonard 95
  Robert 9
Carothers, James 105
Carpenter, Benjamin 50, 87
  Christopher 110
  David 100
  John 86, 110
  Joseph 45
  Nicholas 110
  William 49, 110
  Wylie 29
Carr, Balis 23
  David 12
  Jesse 81
  Wm. 96
Carraway, Thomas 71
  William 77
Carrell, Charles 53
  John 41
Carrigan, Robert, Jr. 41
  Robert, Sr. 41
Carriher, Andrew 41
Carrington, Archibald 90
  Ephraim 90
  Murwin 21
  Wm. 90
Carrol, Lemuel 90
  William 45
Carrold, Jonathan 81
Carroll, Edward 109
Carrow, Henry 8
  Jordan 7
Carruth, Ephraim 112
  Leander P. 112
Carson, Alexander 19
  Henry 38
  James 49
  Jason 114
  John W. 114
  Richard 74
  Samuel 44
  Wesley 91
  William 38, 46, 105, 116
Carter, Barney 43
  Benjamin 3
  Daniel 34
  Isaac 22
  James 12
  Jesse 5
  Jiles 18, 68
  John 22, 96, 108
  Joseph 98
  Laban 59
  Lewis 5
  Miat 32
  Phillips 36
  Robert 89
  Samuel 15
  Thos. 96
  William 3, 9
  William O. 55
  Wilson W. 15

Wm. 92
Zachariah 12
Carteret, John 23
  Thomas 57
Carthodge, Elijah 85
Carthy, John 110
Carton, John 28, 31
Cartwright, Abraham 62
  Asa 62
  Christopher 3
  James 63
  John 3
  Joseph 42
  Joshua 3
  Robert 63
  Thomas 3, 63
  William 3, 63
Caruthers, Elias 52
  William 71
Carver, Isham 57
  John 20
  Joseph 115
  Richard 46
  Robert 57
Cary, Henry 48
  Miles 19
  Robert 88
  Thomas 17
Casa, John 3
Case, Charles 33
  James 48
  Jesse 114
  Jonas 33
  William 115
Casey, Henry 35
  John 10
  William 63
Cash, Boggan 23
  John 38
  Lewis 43
Casher, Thomas 112
Cashin, Pleasant 114
Cason, Burnel 56
  George 62
Casons, William 7
Casson, Witham 8
Cast, Archibald 109
  Daniel 100
Castellow, William 65
Casten, Whitlift 77
Castephens, John 98
Castill, Jacob 78
Castillow, John D. 61
Castle, Ebenezer 43
Caston, Jacob 14
  James 77
  Oliver 14
  Robert 77
Castor, Henry 102
Cate, Richard 91
  Thomas 26, 90
  Thos. 91
  Timothy 90
Cates, Richard 92
  Wm. 89
Cathberton, John 40
Cathey, Jethro 116
  Joseph 116
  William 61
Cathy, Archibald 44

Caton, Moses 71
Cauble, Adam 36
   Fredrick 35
   Jacob 52
Caudill, Jeremiah 99
Caudle, Edward 92
Caulans, Henry 36
Cauley, Bartholamy [sic] 73
Caulk, Daniel 94
Causby, Jesse 115
Cave, Miley 58
Caven, Wm. 91
Caveness, Richard 101
Cawil, Edmond 37
Cazart, Wiat 29
   Wyat 30
Cecil, Philip 104
   Samuel 37
   Thomas 104
Cecill, John 37
   William 37
Ceicel, Thomas 36
Center, Jacob 45
   Solomon 98
Cerlin, Edward 62
Chace, Levi 14
Chadwell, David 33
Chadwick, James 72
   Martin 72
Chaffin, Thomas 103
Chainey, Peter 107
Chamberlain, Enoch 37
Chambers, Benjamin 44, 60
   Henry 30
   James 26, 116
   Joseph 116
   Maxwell 108
   Samuel 39, 80
   William 116
   William W. 30
Chamblee, James 54
   Jerrod 85
Chamblers, Jos., Sr. 101
Chambles, Henry 29
Chance, Allen 8
   Cannon 8
   John 32
   William 8
Chandler, Joel 53
   Joseph 98
   Martin 27
   Matthew 89
Chaney, Stephen 3
Channels, Michael 106
Chaplain, John 27
Chaple, Jesse 41
Chapman, Enoch 43
   James 110
   John 58
   Stephen 71
   Valentine 68
   William 37, 103
Chappel, Caleb 63
   Edward 88
Chapter, Jonathan 2
Charles, Harry 6
   John 32, 104
Charlton, Samuel 61
Chase, John 24
Chauncey, Isaac 70

Chavers, Gorden 43
Chaves, Banston 28
Chavis, John 30
Cheaves, Abner 50
   James 50
   John 50
Cheek, Joab 22
   Randolph 40
Cheery, William 106
Cherehall, William 26
Cherr, John 56
Cherry, Benjamin 7
   Darling 17, 50
   Humphrey 7
   James, Jr. 65
   Jesse 74
   Samuel 12
Cheshen, Teneson 37
Cheshire, Philip 78
   Turpin 19
   William 61
Chesnut, Bailey 81
   Hardy 57
   James 81
   Joseph 81
   Joshua 57
   Phelix 21
   William 81
Chester, Stephen 10
Cheves, James 7
Chewning, John 24
Childers, Bedford 109
   Robert 48
   Solomon 110
Childress, Jesse 35
   Wm. 97
Chilton, Lemuel 31
Chinn, Jesse 43
Chipperd, Henry 45
Chisholm, Anguish 104
Chisolm, John 104
Chiton, Jonas 65
Chitty, Charles 34
Chitwood, Charles 46
   Jesse 47, 58
Chizenhall, Delamy 90
   Laney 90
Chopard, Cyprian 63
Chrisenburg, Aron 31
Chrisholm, Alexander 25
   Daniel 25
Christian, James 82
   Michael 30
Christie, Jesse 15
Christon, Michael 29
Christoon, William 105
Christopher, Ephraim 111
Chriswell, Daniel 37
Chube, Charles 97
Church, Isaac 97
   Wm. 99
Chustley, John 43
Cilgrow, William 62
Cinard, Jonathan 49
Cincard, William 115
Cisk, Jeremiah 96
Civins, Joseph 114
Claggett, John 108
Clampit, Richard, Jr. 97
Clandler, Zachariah 98

Clapp, Wm. 95
Clardy, Anderson 66
   Thomas 19
Claridge, John 96
Clark, Andrew 16
   Augus 78
   Benjamin 49
   David C. 7
   Duncan, Jr. 78
   Francis 29
   Henry 69, 95
   Hosiah 77
   James 45, 94, 115
   James K. 89
   James W. 60
   Jesse 90
   John 15, 32, 93
   Joseph 102
   Joshua 39
   Kenneth 65
   Malcom 82
   Nathaniel 71
   Neil, Jr. 78
   Reuben 6, 8
   Richard 3, 116
   Robert 37
   Thomas 5
   Thos. 92, 101
   Tilmon 94
   William 85
Clarke, Arther [sic] 112
Claton, Wm. 94
Clauds, Thomas W. 51
Clay, Charles 3
   John 107
Claybrook, George 37
Clayton, Benjamin 6, 69
   John 115
   Richard 3, 63
   Thomas 6, 69
Claywell, Solomon 38
Clegg, John 92
Clement, Samuel 30
Clements, Hardy 56, 65
   Simon 89
Clemer, Charles 32
Clemmons, Cornelius 112
   John 104
Clemons, John 56
   Samuel 29
   William 26
Clendenning, Fisher 26
Clendinen, Wm. 91
Clerk, Anthony 110
Clerland [Cleland?], John M. 38
Cleton, John 39
Click, Daniel 103
Clifton, Reuben 6
Clifwood, James 112
Clinard, Andrew 38
   David 104
Cline, Christian 32
   Daniel 45
   David 44
   Henry 36
   Jacob 107
   Phillip 36
   Solomon 45
   William 110
Clinton, Richard 57

   Robert 90
   William 113
Clisk, John 41
Clodfelter, David 108
Clominger, Adam, Jr. 44
Cloninger, Jacob 109
Clontz, Henry 40
Clotfelter, Joseph 101
Cloud, Jeremiah 96
Club, George, Jr. 44
   John 44
Clutz, John 36
   Martin 102
Coaley, Washington 105
Coaths, James 103
Coats, Jordan 81
   Rob't H. 96
   Wilson 62
Cobb, Ambrose 109
   Archibald 110
   Chales 16
   Daniel 32
   Hardie 74
   Hugh 51
   James 17, 55, 75
   John 65
   John B. 55
   Moses 53
   Richmon 55, 74
   Robert 53
   Thomas 68
Cobble, Isaac 102
Coble, Jacob 95
Cobman, Shelsby 83
Cobs, John 89
Coburn, Newton 17
Cochran, Abraham 41
   Robert 30, 107
   Robert M. 40
   Samuel H. 108
   Thomas 67
   Thomas S. 107
Cockburn, William 50
Cocke, John 92, 93
Cockeleress, Jacob 92
Cockeran, Henry 47
   James 47
   Squire 46
Cockerham, John 43
Cockhorn, Samuel 114
Cockram, Jacob 41
   James 98
Cockran, John 84
Cockrett, Futrill 86
Cockrill, Wm. 87
Cockrun, Robert 113
Cody, John 96, 115
Coe, Avery 91
   Giles 99
   John 91
Coffer, George 34
Coffey, Elijah 99
   John 99
   Reuben 114
   William 114
Coffield, Ira 67
Coffin, Elisha 94
Cofield, Cornelins [Cornelius?] 20
Cogdell, Daniel 57
   Ross 78

Crecy, Levi 5
Credworth, John 2
Creed, Solomon 6
Creff, Isaac 103
Crery, James 4
Cress, Daniel 36
Cretcher, John 89
Crews, James 35
Cribb, Anthony 23
    Jonathan 57
    Thomas 23
Crickmore, Robert 68
Crider, Benjamin 31
    George 44
Cripson, Thomas 48
Criscow, Daniel 27
Crisp, Reading 75
    Solomon 114
Criswell, Alex 91
Crites, Peter 44
Crocker, Francis 26
    John 86
    Josiah 17
Cromattee [?], Peter 78
Cronch, Jesse 43
Croner, Jacob 107
Cronfell, Jonothan [sic] 103
Croom, Peter 51
Croon, Simon 34
Cross, Benjamin 5
    Jacob 102
    Miles 14
    Whitfield 16
Crotzer, John 102
Crouse, George 99
Crow, James 92
    John 111
    John H. 46
    Stephen 44
Crowel, John 107
Crowell, Charles 40
    Edward 18
    James B. 18
    William 14
Crown, Henry 114
Crowson, Elisha 24
Cruchfield, Benj. 91
    Stephen 92
Cruid, Abraham 98
    Coleby, Jr. 98
Cruise, Jacob 59
Crump, Edward 5
    John B. 36
    John, Jr. 41
    Rolen 41
    Stephen 105
Crumpler, Owen 22
Crumpton, Thomas 43
Cruse, Peter 102
Cruthes, James 101
Cryder, Martin 108
Cude, James 27
    Timothy 101
Culberson, David 94
    Josiah 57
    Nathaniel 53
Culeper [sic], Nathaniel 55
Cullan, Willie 64
Cullipher, Benjamin 6
    Isaac 6

Culpepper, Charles 105
    Henry 85
Cumboe, Stephen 81
Cummin, Benjamin 42
Cumming, James C. 19
Cummings, Aaron 22
    George 80
Cummins, Isaac 58
    John 90
Cuningam, Josiah 36
Cunnigan, Alexander 27
Cunnigham [sic], Jacob I. 39
Cunninggem [sic], Jesse 73
Cunningham, Alex 83, 84
    Duncan 84
    Hugh 103
    Lancaster 53
    Thomas 102
Cunninghan [sic], Sharp 40
Cupples, Charles 59
Cupton, Turner 88
Curbee, Obadiah 84
Curby, William 43
Curfuse, Caleb 101
Curis, Thomas 2
Curl, Benjamin 28
    Isham 16
    John 5
    Richard P. 5
Curliles, William 66
Curlin, Edward 2
Curling, Jesse 67
    John 15
Currant, Hugh 38
Currell, David 39
Curren, Larkin 89
Curreteh, Leroy 58
Currie, John 82
Curruth, Leroy 47
Curry, Alex 83
    Archibald 57
    Hugh 57
    James 83
    John B. 96
    Malcom 57
    Neil 57
Curry [McCurry?], Cazor W. 58
Curthington, John 26
Curtis, Ben. 114
    David 114
    Henry 27
    Larkin 27
Cushing, Isaac T. 21
    Noah 16
Cutler, Nathan 70
Cuzine, Durum 108
    John 108

D

D'Holland, Marcus 59
Dabbs, William 24
Dade, Horatio 8
Daffin, James 13
Dafter, Obed 40
Dage, Isaac 79
Daggett, Charles Y. 47
    William 47, 58
Daggins, William 35
Daily, Frederick 62
Dain, Hardy 11

Dairymple, William 23
Dalby, Dick H. 88
Dale, Wiley 10
Dally, Micajah 88
Dalton, David 35
    James 46
    John 112
    Samuel 95
    William 34
    William L. 49
Damel, Joshua 11
Dameron, Christopher 94
    Gideon 15
    Thos 93
Damon, John 110
Damsell, Williams 85
Danals, John 71
Danaway, William 104
Dancey, Thomas 31
Dancy, David 16
Dandalow, Charnley C. 65
Danfont, Sion 21
Daniel, Asa 82
    Avra 2
    Baley 2
    Chisolm 47
    Christholm 46
    Curtis 10
    David 2, 17
    Elijah 52
    Goodwin 66
    Green O. 91
    Isaac 55
    James 55
    James W. 68
    John 2, 51
    Mathew 10
    Perian 113
    Robert 17
    Robert B. 50
    Samuel 89
    Thomas 2, 30
    William 20, 30
    William R. 15
    Willie 74
Daniels, Clement 7, 70
    James 7, 71
    John 30
    Jos. 101
    Morris 70
    Shadrick 7
    Thomas 7, 70
Darby, James 93
Darden, Henry G. 64
Dardin, David C. 66
    Robert 81
Dark, Joseph 83
Darlett, William M. 65
Darnald, George 114
Darnall, Wm. 99
Darnel, David 39
    William 39
Darnell, John 39
    John L. 39
Darnold, Raleigh 35
Darr, David 38
Darrlson, B. W. 52
Dary, Ambrose 89
Dasson, Early 49
Daugherty, Thos. 94

Daughety, Daniel 71
Daughtie, Edward 64
Daughtrey, Drew 81
Daughtry, Hardy 81
Davenport, Barrage 102
    Chancey 17
    David 59
    Enoch 7
    James 6
    Samuel 69
    Talket 69
Davey, Gabriel 30
David, Henry 73
    Thomas 18
Davidson, Andrew W. 108
    Ephraim 25
    George L. 39
    George W. 105
    Hiram 36
    Josiah 65
    Samuel 42
    Thomas 38
Davied, William 49
Davies, James 48
Davin, Daniel 49
Davis, Amos 62
    Andrew 108
    Anthony 56
    Archibald 34
    Benjamin 18, 86
    Blake 67
    Charles 98
    Daniel 106
    David 19, 63
    Davis 26
    Durham 17
    Edward 102
    Edward H. 67
    Elisha 11
    Epraim [sic] 45
    Frederick 3
    George D. 49, 115
    Gideon 88
    Hardaway 67
    Hardeway 18
    Hardy 6
    Hezekiah 107
    Isaiah 90
    James 3, 9, 43, 91, 97, 102
    James W. 16
    Jesse 28
    John 28, 29, 47, 79, 82, 84,
        107
    John S. 72
    John W. 59
    John, Jr. 102
    Johnston 63
    Jonathan 36
    Jones 11
    Joshua 12, 18
    Josiah 29
    Jourdan 92
    Lewis 66
    Malachi 63
    Martin 70
    Matthew 98, 100
    Matthias 2
    Maxy 6
    Micajah 112
    Moses 5

Nathaniel 24
Noah 17
Reading K. 73
Richard 18, 68
Robert C. 59
Sampson 19
Samuel 13, 18, 67
Solomon 77
Stephen 19
Thomas 1, 17, 19, 36, 46, 68,
    79, 80, 105
Westly 13
William 25, 29, 84
William F. 73
William, Jr. 19
William, Sr. 19
Willie O. 19
Winfield 7
Davison, Silas 27
Dawkins, George 84
   Micajah 84
Dawnson, Aaron 111
Dawson, General 67
   James 24
   John 67
   Joseph 90
   Lewis 72
Day, Ambrose 89
   Archibald 89
   James 66
   Phillip 30
   Samuel 51
Dayton, William 116
Deal, Abraham 113
   Adam 3
   Alexander 113
   Henry 80, 113
   John 48
   Peter 36
   William 76, 113
Deale, Julius 61
Dean, Hardy, Jr. 54
   James 82
   John 10
Dearing, Pleasant 95
   Willie 96
Dease, Smith 25
Deaton, Claiborn 92
   John 101
   Jonathan 116
   Thomas 104
Debnam, John B. 87
   William 19
Deboard, Gideon 108
Debode, George 98
Deck, Leonard 111
Decker, Richard 1
Dedman, James 103
   William 112
Dees, Levy 57
   Stephen 57
Dekison, Zekial 101
Delamar, James 8
   Seldon 8
Delinger, Martin 45
Dellbuck, David 47
Deloach, Brittain 85
   Jesse 66
   Thomas 66
Delow, Henry 70

Jacob 101
John 36
Meihall 36
Demdtund, John 2
Demill, Peter 70
Denby, Thomas 3
Denmark, John 12
Dennie, Charles 107
Dennis, Andrew 105
   Thomas 86
   Wm. 94
Denny, Ezekiel 98
   Spears 73
   Stephen 98
   Theophillus 20
   William 43
Dent, William T. 19
Denton, Basel 104
   Drury 19
   Jacob 97
   James 20
   John 5
   Jonas 116
   Levi 76
   Peter 87
   William 87
Derden, Joseph 64
Derryburry, John 113
Desern, Ezekiel 42
   May 90
Detheridge, Charles 103
Devane, Francis 78
Devenporte, Abner 114
   Thomas 114
Dever, Elijah 116
   John 116
Devoun, Elisha 76
Devout, William 2
Deweese, Garrat 116
Dial, Jonathan 79
   Samuel 37
Dick, David 110
   Reuben 95
   Samuel 95
Dickee, Rob't 91
Dickenson, Joel 70
Dickerson, Daniel 72
   Joseph F. 60
Dickey, William 38
   Wm. 92
Dickinson, John 65
   Wilie 43
Dickns [sic], James 112
Dickson, Booky 24
   Bork 76
   David 110
   Ephraim 8
   Gibbin 7
   Henry 78
   John 88, 95
   Joseph 12
   Patrick 10
   Seth 100
   Thomas 109
   William 36, 114
Dillahunta, Samuel 73
Dillard, James 115
   John 96
Dillbark, John, Jr. 113
Dillenger, Michael 110

Dilliard, John 109
Dillin, Nicholas 44
Dillord, John 116
Dills, Thomas, Sr. 113
Dilport, William 84
Dinkey, William 32
Dinkins, Asa 42
   James 105
Dishman, James 109
Dismaks, John W. 51
Dixon, Cornelius 72
   Franklin 70
   Hugh 107
   Ire B. 40
   James 28, 56
   Jebediah 9
   Jeremiah 89
   John 70
   John, Jr. 57
   Nehemiah 8
   Robert 107
   Rollin 71
   Thomas 75
   William 71, 75
Dixson, Edmond 30
Doak, William 51
Dobson, John 58
Docherty, Scearly 26
Dockery, Alexander 27
Dockins, William 103
Dockry, Elisha 53
Dodd, Hardy 85
   John 29
   Willie 57
Dodson, John 89
   Lambert 35, 96
   Lewis 34
Dogget, Charles Y. 59
Doggett, Henry 67
   Richard 67
Dolby, William 29
Doles, Britain 66
Dollar, Isaac D. 26
   James 26
Dollerhide, James 89
Dollihit, John 82
Dolten, Elijah 112
Donaldson, Joseph 38
Donally, William 43
Donalson, Hugh 116
Donaway, John 37
Donbe, Henry 34
Done, Nehemiah 78
Donell, Oliver 10
Donnel, James 94
Donner, George 95
Door, Frederick 23
Dorch, John 89
Dork, John 33
Dorman, Duncan 82
Dorsett, Moses 90
   Thomas 114
Dorson, Edmond 43
Doss, Thomas 96
Dossey, Demmon, Jr. 113
Doub, Henry 97
Douge, Benjamin 62
   Dempsey 62
   Jess 62
   John 103

Doughty, William 10
Douglas, John 74, 88
Douglass, Adam 26
   David 14
   Dempsey 62
   Joseph 39
Douthet, John 37
Douthit, Jacob 37
Dove, George 41
Dowd, Wm. 82
Dowdin, John 75
Dowdy, Benjamin, Sr. 28
   Isaac 2
   Jesse 2
   John 8
   William 2
Dowell, John 49
Dowers, Noah 7
Dowet, Walker 33
Dowlin, Samuel 18
Down, Jesse 5
Downer, Francis 24
Downey, John 30
   Thomas 30, 112
Downing, William 64
Downs, Aaron 108
   Kinyan 8
   Shadric 70
   William 47, 59, 74
   Wm. 107
Downy, Samuel 47, 59
   Thomas 47, 59
   William 39
Dowtey, William 62
Dowthard, Stephen 104
Dowton, Samuel 68
Dowty, John 71
Doxey, Dempsey 62
   Henry 1
Dozier, James 87
   Jasper 61
   Jordan 61
   Phillip 61
   Samuel 3
   Tully 61
   William 61
Drake, Francis 17
   George 92
   John 25, 48
   Jordan 84
Dramond, Stewart 33
Draper, William 66
Drew, Cordy 67
   Thomas 67
Drinkwater, John 25
Driver, Boan 65
   Thomas 88
Drye, Daniel 107
   John 107
Dubar, Archibald 27
Dubbins, Jacob 98
Ducary, Balum 48
Duchworth, Robert 39
Duck, James 68
   Thaddeus 11
Duckworth, George 48, 106
   Jonathan 48
   Thomas 52
Dudley, Allen 21
   David 81

Edward B. 60
Ervan 74
Jacob 71
John 72
Levan 1
Malachi 1
Pelasky 16
Due, Benjamin 78
Duff, Dennis 112
Richard 115
Duffy, William 37
Dugger, David 100
Joel 100
Duglas, James 65
Duke, Berry 91
Dabney M. 19
Elisha 64
William 87
Dulberson, Wm. 94
Dulin, William 103
Duncan, Charles 30
Hardy 23
James 100
John 89
Moses 23
Stephen 12
William 52, 114
Wilson 3
Wm. 96
Dunken, David 2
Dunket, Jacob 49
Dunkin, Demsey 62
Hiram 46
John 99
Zebulin 3
Dunlap, Jesse 97
Dunlop, John 83
Dunn, Batholomew 83
Elijah 71
George 101
James 85
Joseph 116
Levin 71
Newman 8
Noah 73
Robert, Jr. 105
Thomas 83
William 77, 105
Dunning, Thomas 33
William 32, 33
Dunsill, Jacob 45
Duporster, Joseph 38
Dupree, Sterling 16
Duran, George 85
Durden, Cornelius 76
Durgan, John 41
Durham, Charles 46
Mathew 26
Newman 93
Thos. 91(2)
Durning, Lewis 26
Durset, Duty 28
Duskins, Michel, Jr. 54
Dutcherow, Jacob 44
Duty, Wm. 92
Duval, Prosper Forma 23
Duvol, Daniel 74
John 74
Dvidson [Davidson], John 52
Dyal, Thomas 42

Dye, Martin 83
Dyer, Elijah 43
Joel 43
John 47, 58
William 51

E

Eads, William 35
Eaflin, John 112
Eagle, Martin 83
Micajah 37
Eaker, Peter 110
Ealey, Jacob 64
Eaperson, Wm. 98
Earley, Asa 98
Early, Isaac 65
James 5, 47, 65
Thomas 65
William 46
Earncy, John 111
Earnest, Daniel 103
Earwood, Thomas 110
Easley, Allen 15
Rhoderick 15
Eason, Abner 16
George 73
Ithiel [sic] 55
John 74
Obed 77
Solomon 64
East, Moses 43
Eastbridge, John 28
Easter, Michael 104
Solomon 70
William, Jr. 70
William, Sr. 70
Eastis, James 28
Eastwood, Abraham 89
James 73
Eatman, Irwin 68
John 87
Eaton, Abraham 116
James 35
Lazarus 116
Eavins, John 113
Ebert, Christian 97
Eborn, James 7
William 70
Echard, William 111
Eddins, Needham 84
Wm. 93
Eddleman, Adam 101
Eddlemon, Henry 44
Eddman, Jacob 44
Eddons, David 78
Edens, John 77
Eders, John 45
Edgar, William 9
Edgarton, Ransom 111
Edge, Duke 79
Jonathan 21
William 81
Willis 15
Edgin, Samuel 44
Edis, Ezekiel 109
Edlinian, Philip 102
Edmeston, Ninnion 115
Edmison, George 114
Edmiston, Archibald 115
Edmonds, Benjamin 50

Edmondson, John 77
Thomas 16
Edmonson, James 73
Edoll, Joseph 33
Edson, Joseph 38
Edward, Joshua 21
Peter 105
William 25
Edwards, Bartlet 96
Benjamin 16, 45
Charles 109, 112
Colin 43
David 95(2)
Edmond 116
Edom 28
James 28, 49, 67, 71, 116
Joel 92
John 49, 66, 79, 86, 97, 116
Littlebury 75
Newit 18
Nickolas 94
Pink 66
Robert 54
Thomas 10, 86
William 69, 87, 103
William E. 70
William N. 70
Williamson 66
Wm. S. 100
Young 100
Efland, Jacob 26
Egerton, Wilmot E. 18
Wilnet 67
Ehnore [Elmore?], John 31
Eights, William 41
Elder, David 116
Elders, David 49
Elenor, Thomas 33
Elerion, Thomas 64
Elerod, Peter 99
Eley, John 82
Eliot, Andrew H. 111
John 107
Elixor, Alexander 30
Elkins, Robert 32
Samuel 92
Thomas 32
Eller, George 102
Henry 58
Ellington, Bird 67
Daniel, Jr. 34
Grieff 34
Jesse 87
Joel 18, 68
Pleasant 18
Elliot, James 102
Joseph 28
Miles 4
Peter 12
Wm. 89
Elliott, Abram 27
Benjamin 25
Charles 63
Elisha 4
Foster 63
Hugh 39
Isaac 100
James 110
Jesse 63
John B. 39

John C. 47, 58
Joseph 63
Moses 94
Ricks 66
Robert 108
Saphem [sic] 4
Thomas 72, 106, 108
William 51, 106
Ellis, Absalom 112
Bartholomew 31
Daniel 11
Elkshel [sic] 30
Enoch 103
James 56
James A. 116
Joel 76
John 77
Josiah 5
Levin 26
Lewis 68
Michael 74
Miles 18, 68
Obadiah 18, 68
Ransom 37
Simes 18
Solomon 48, 58
Thomas 43, 66
Ellison, James B. 70
Jonathan 113
Nicholas 62
William 44
Zachariah 65
Elliston, Robert 30
Elmore, James 11
Elms, Edward 46
Elventon, John 76
Ely, Samuel 64
Elydon, Nicholas 1
Emery, William 74
Emmerson, Benjamin 28
Emmett, John 48
Endsley, Archibald 110
James 110
England, Andrew 113
Enoch 48
Ezekal 113
Joseph, M.[?] 113
William, Jr. 113
English, Mathew 69
Engram, Samuel 11
Enloe, Benjamin 116
Jesse 116
Ennes, Levie 82
Ennett, Thomas 13
Whitehurst 13
William 13
Enoch, Jones 37
Ensley, Daniel 69
Epes, Kinchen P. 10
Ephland, George 91
Epley, Peter 48
Eppes, Peter 10
Equals, Talbing 7
Ernell, Allen 9
Radford 9
Ernest, John 114
Errowood, Red 109
Ervin, Robert 95
Erwin, Christopher 37
Francis 39

George 108, 115
James 49, 114
James M. 47
James Miller 113
John, Sr. 108
Obadiah H. 53
William 15, 52
Escridge, Birditt 93
Eskins, William 50
Eskrige, John R. 30
Essleman, Archibald 39
Estes, James 86
Etchison, John, Jr. 103
Etheridge, Caleb 1
Josiah 61
Levi 61
Stephen 62
Thomas 1, 62
William 61, 62
Etherige [sic], Elijah 69
Silas 69
Eubank, Philip 93
Stephen 66
Eubanks, Aaron 72
Elijah, Jr. 77
Ezekiel 77
John 77
Eur, Burrell 64
Eure, Benjamin 64
Cypron 5
Henry 6
James 64
Stephen 5
Euse, Elisha 67
Eustia, James B. 88
Evans, Aaron 92
Arthur 14
Charles 28
Colin 84
David 20, 73
Dred 56
Edmond 74
Ephraim 48
George 18
Goodwin 31
Henry 16, 61
James 12, 78, 104
John 18, 20, 28, 61, 73, 82, 87
Jonathan 20
Nathan 18
Noah 5
Peter 44
Richard 28
Thomas 21, 30, 97
Thos. 93
Wight 74
William 30, 56
Wm., Jr. 86
Evenes, Charles 116
Evens, Brient 75
John 64
Eventon, Aaron 71
Everington, John 9
Everitt, Abraham 38
Daniel 21
James 75
John 5, 21
John B. 55
Richard 21

Robert 69
William 17
Eversale, John 43
Eves, William 86
Evett, Jesse 7
Moses 7
Evins, David 115
John 75
Leckariah [sic] 77
Evitt, John 71
Lott 71
Ewell, David 36
Ewin, Ephraim 39
Exum, William 76
Ezell, Benjamin 6
Patrick 80
Ezzel, Jesse 21

F

Faddis, James 91
Fadgett, John 86
Fagan, Aaron 69
Fagg, Joel 96
Fains, David 115
Fairbanks, David 33
Fairchilds, Lewis 100
Faircloth, Isom 81
Jacob 21
James 81
John 81
Kinchen 11
Noah 22
Raphial 81
Thomas 65
Faireloth [Faircloth?], Raiford 21
Fairfax, Needham 79
Faison, Sterling 66
Falconer, James 89
Falkim, Richard 10
Falkner, Lewis 9
Falls, John 52(2)
Theophilus 39
William 44
Fancher, Hillary 61
Fannet, Gideon 8
Fanney, John 5
Farabe, Jesse 104
Farabee, John 104
Joseph 38
Farker, Solomon 115
Farland, Laban 93
Farlass, Richard 64
Farles, Elisha 3
Farley, David 94
John 93
John B. 31
Stewart 31
Farmer, Ashael 55
Elisha 109
John 55, 88
Joseph 11, 75
Kedar 11
Solomon 100
William 48, 73
Farnel, Dexter 77
Farr, Christian 51
Henry 39
Robert 59
Farra, John 105
Farrand, Henry 14

Farrar, Richard 89
Farrell, John 82
Farrer, Miles 44
Farrier, David 80
John 80
William 80
Farrington, John 37
Farrow, Joseph 78
Wm. 87
Fasene, Asa 12
Fash, Christian 38
Fason, Jesse 85
Fassel, Arthur 87
Fat, John 39
Fatam, James 44
Faucestt, Anderson 91
Bobert 91
Eli 91
Fauckner, Rowland 20
Faulk, Hinnant 79
Sherwood 13
Thomas 79
William 79
Faulks, John 80
Fausett, Robert 92
Faw, John 100
Fayles, Josiah 77
Fealds, Counsel 72
Feamster, Abner 108
Feese, Peter 100
Felbet, Jesse 42
Felker, Samuel 36
Fell, Cason 71
Fellon, Elisha 55
Fellows, Bennet 14
Felton, John 5
Felts, Elisha 99
Fennell, James 14
Fennington, Edward F. 46
Fenny, Joshua 98
Fenster, John 39
Fentress, Frederick 27
Lot 3
Richard 32
Fentus, James 1, 62
Ferebee, Lemuel 61
Peter 61
William 61
Fereland, John 41
Ferguson, George 44
James 82
John 27, 99
Neil 57
Richard 54
Smith 43
William 43, 110
Ferrand, Bogle 20
Ferrel, Gabriel 106
John 106
William 106
Ferrell, Burton 18
Hutchins 18
James 18
Loody 18
Zachariah 7
Ferret, John, Sr. 40
Ferril, Cage 104
Ferrill, Bryan 85
Fetterton, William 70
Feveash, Thomas 63

Fewee, Zack 95
Fewel, James 95
Fidler, Henry 97
John 97
Field, Benjamin 32
Christopher 51
Isaac 28
Robert 95
Fielder, Thomas 31
Fielding, William 24
Fields, Brice 77
Curtis 79
Henry 93
John 92
Major 73
Robert 32
Fifer, Martin 95
Wm. 95
Figg, Willis 5
File, Jacob 107
Filgo, David 11
John 11
Filmor, Alexander 27
Filnlond [sic], John 31
Filyaw, John 14
Finaly, George 94
Fincannon, John 114
William 47
Finch, Caswell 88
John 89
John W. 88
Richardson 50
Fingo, Jacob 45
Fink, David 108
Phillip 41
Son 41
Finley, James 109
John 53
Finn, Gabriel 26
Finnen, Thomas 91
Finnie, Sterling 66
Finsher, Joshua 106
Finters, Hillary 61
Fiscus, Jacob 97
Fisher, George 1, 35, 45
Harman 52
Henry 59
James 111
Michael 71
Sander 22
William 106
Fitch, John 94
Fite, Jacob 110
Fitt, Samuel 4
Fitts, Morgan 89
Fitzgerald, James 98
Fitzgerril, John 108
Flake, Mansel 74
Flanigan, Samuel E. 40
Flanigen, Thomas 74
Flannigan, James 12
Flecher, Hiram 38
Fleetwood, David 56
Edmond, Jr. 55
Hatton 65
Fleming, Bailey 116
Beniah 94
Edmund 98
John 108
John M. 98

Mordecai 98
Flemming, George 41
  Isaac 45
  James 52
  John 33
  Joseph B. 19
  Robert 94
  Thomas 53
  Willis 74
Flenigan, Elias 40
  Michael 40
  Robert 40
  William 40
Fletcher, Abner 88
  James 114
  Joshua 76
  Nathan 48, 114
Flinn, Enoch, Jr. 7
  William 79
Floan [Sloan?], David 80
Floid, Aron 23
  Jesse 10
  Westley 17
Flood, Allen 15
  Enoch 68
Florence, James 93
Floro, Aaron 62
  John 61
Flow, John 40
Flowers, Bennet 79
  Bryant 21
  George 109
  Henry 106
  John 76
  Josiah 1
  Lowamy 80
  Philip 81
  Samuel 10
  Thos. 79
Floyd, James 105
  John 88
  Stacy 61
  Thomas 70
Fluman, George 46
  William 46
Flury, William 4
Fly, Aaron 16
Flynt, Richard 35, 97
Fobes, John 40
Foddree, Hugh 7
Fodz, Adolph 45
Fogleman, George 107
  John 95
Folk, David 56
  Richard 23
Folks, John 23
  William 41
Foller, Elisha 116
Folsome, Ebenezer 20
  Thomas 11
Folson, Frederick 71
Folsum, Malcolm 22
Fonstren, John 112
  Samuel 112
Fonts, Andrew 100
Fonville, Edward 13
Fooshee, Jephthy 92
Forbers, Levi 94
Forbes, Arthur, Sr. 32
  Caleb 62

Dempsey 62
James 2
Jesse 95
John 62
Silas 62
Forbis, Ralph 51
Forcum, Joseph 103
Ford, Austin 109
  Daniel 105
  John 37, 52
  Wyatt 90
  Zeblone 52
Forehand, Lewis 76
Foreman, James 76
Forest, James 51
Forguson, Andrew 44
Forkner, Lewis 98
  Martin 42
Forlan, William 6
Forlaw, James 69
  John 71
Fornberton, John 23
Forns, John 9
Forrest, Samuel 73
Forrester, John 97
  Thomas 114
Forster, Alanson 32
  Daniel 34
  John 47
  William 32
Forsythe, John 106
  Samuel 88
  Thomas 88
Fort, Austin 23
  Josiah 67
Forte, Elias 51
Forterner, Thomas 108
Fortiscue, John 7
  John Russell 7
Fortisqua, William 70
Fortunberry, Jacob 115
Fortune, Jaran 108
  Lindsey 111
  Livender 114
  Richard 46
  William 46
Foskey, William 72
Foss, John 58
Foster, Benj. 99
  Bennet 89
  Daniel 47
  Francis M. 64
  Henry 77
  Isaac 6
  James 95
  Joel 43
  John F. 50
  Richard 38
  Shelton 96
  Shipperd 2
  Skiles 36
  Thomas 47, 103
  William 103
Fountain, James 35
  Tobias 80
  William 80
Foust, John 27
Fowler, Burwell 85
  Daniel 23
  Elijah 97

John 91
Jones 54
Richard 23
Thomas 10
Fox, Aaron 13
  Aron 43
  Barnell 28
  David 38
  David, Jr. 28
  Francis 43
  Nickolas, Sr. 93
Frady, John 98
  William 42
Frail, Thomas 87
Francis, Sterling 65
  Thomas 58
Frank, Peter 102
Franklin, Alexander 87
  Barnard 98
  Bernard 42, 58
  James 58
  Jonas 64
  Thomas 35
  Thos. 98
Frasure, Thomas 59
Frazer, Enos 95
  James 72
  Malachiah 88
Frazier, Ephraim 89
  James 12, 22
  Thomas 22
  William 89
  Wm. 97
Frederick, William 12
Freeland, James 39
  John 108
  Samuel 39
  William 38
Freeling, John H. 60
Freeman, David 97
  Eaton 19
  Gideon 106
  Hamilton 111
  Hamlin 41
  Joshua 7
  Mathew 21
  Mertin 30
  Miston 30
  Moses 56
  Palmer 27
  Thomas 4
  Wiley 54
  William 46
  William H. 50
Freet, George 45
Freeze, Adam 41
Freling, Luke 5
Frew, David 63
Frey, Peter 111
Friday, John 44
Friear, William 16
Frisby, John 49
Frishy, John 115
Frits, Adam 38
  John 104
Fritt, John 114
Frost, John 37
  Nicholas 35
  Samuel 11, 37
Fry, Benj. 96

Benjamin 35
Bryant 36
George 52, 83, 113
Henry 34
Philip 45
Fryer, Jesse 77
  Thomas 77
  Wm. 95
Fulford, Charles 1
  Clifton 56
  Joseph 1
  Joseph, Jr. 56
Fulgem, John 66
Fulghum, Joseph 10
Fulk, Frederic 97
Fullbright, Daniel 110
  Jacob 111
  William 44
Fuller, Arthur 29, 30
  Benj. 100
  Bradshaw 89
  Edward 7
  Hosea 30
  John 31, 88, 107
  John N. 93
  Jonathan 11
  Walter 31
Fullerton, Welch 4
Fullington, William 31
  Wm. 94
Fulp, Solomon 35
Fulps, Solomon 97
Fulshire, Joseph 9
Fults, Henry 97
Fulwider, Jacob 102
Fune, Daniel 108
  Jacob 108
Furguson, James, Jr. 82
Furlly, John 47
Fussee, Daniel 51
Futcret, James 76
Futral, Nathan 77
Futrell, Benjamin 17
  Daniel 16
  Enos 66
  William 66
  Winborne 66
Futtrell, Calson 16
  Micajah 16

G

Gabard, John 103
Gabriel, David 72
Gage, Jacob 47, 58
Gaider, John 109
Gaither, Enock 109
  Gassaway 52
  Johnsey 103
  Lebishes 108
Gakey, Benjamin M. 46
Galbreath, William 51
Galden, Jacob 13
Gall, Thomas 67
Gallihan, Brantly H. 41
Gallimore, James 36
  Jesse 59
  Richard 100
Gallin, Levi 71
Gallispie, Macoy 38
Gallop, Isaac 3

Galloway, John 115
    Thomas 38
Gallup, John 2
    Joshua 2
Galoway, Thomas 33
Gamble, Andrew 95
    Benjamin 43
    Henry 43
    James 37
    William F. 53
Gammon, Richard 74
    William 63
Ganday, Griffin 18
Gandy, Alston 18
    John 18
Gangus, Jacob 41
Gannon, William 51
Ganny, John 44
Gantlia, Edward 24
Gapp, Allison 38
Gardener, Isaac 74
    Reuben 74
    Samuel 72
Gardenor, John 102
Gardner, Dempsey 75
    Elijah 56
    Francis 56
    Guilford 28
    J. 70
    John 73
    Obed 95
    William 55
Gardnor, Wm. 101
Gardon, Garret 49
Garenger, Andrew 95
Gargamy, Niehodemus
        [Nichodemus] 13
Gargely, John 48
Gargle, Jacob 22
Garland, Samuel 47, 59
    Winston 10
Garlick, Reubin 33
Garling, James S. 2
Garlington, Jabez 2
    James S. 62
Garman, John 107
    William 72
Garner, Bailey 22
    Barzilla 105
    David 102
    Guilford 93
    James 22
    John 22
    Lewis 27
    Thomas 93
Garnet, Caleb 4
Garnto, Thomas 13
Garoll, Valentine 33
Garrard, Carter 90
    John 90
Garras, Nehemiah 73
Garratson, Garrat 113
Garret, Henry 6
    James 2
Garretson, Arthur 40
    John 40
Garrett, David 55
    Everard 5
    Henry 3
    Jesse 56

John 16, 77, 116
Jonathan 3
Joshua 42
Mathew 47
William 1, 62
Garrigan, Sample 51
Garringer, Bartin 32
Garriot, Daniel 104
Garris, George 15
Garrison, John C. 105
Garrock, John 76
Garron, Adam 115
    Andrew 48, 115
Garrot, Jeremiah 70
Garrott, James 17
    Thomas 85
Garvay, John 102
Gary, Rhodes 16
Gaskett, Fama [sic] 72
Gaskill, William 56
Gaskins, Christopher 69
    James 14
Gaskitt, David 72
Gates, Philip 95
    Richard 93
    Samuel 47, 58
Gathings, Charles 84
    Philip 84
Gatlin, Abner 71
    Alfred M. 61
    Edward 66
Gattis, Thomas 90
Gatton, Hamilton 103
Gaugh, James 33
Gaullney, Ambroze [sic] 109
Gaun-- [sic], Mark 51
Gause, Benjamin 13
    Bryan 79
Gaust, William 79
Gavin, Samuel 21(2)
Gawood, Isaac 37
    Jacob 37
Gay, Abel 16
    Andrew 26
    Elias 29
    John 39, 95
    Joshua 51
    Thomas 87
    William 28, 55, 66, 108
Gaylard, John 70
Gayler, Theophilus 41
Gaylor, James 12
Gear, John 28
Gearron, John 115
Gears, Thomas 37
Gedsey, Wm. 96
Gee, John M. 28
Geer, David 54
    John 86
Geesling, John 96
Gelispee, James 35
Gennet, Matthew 76
Gennings, Goshen 101
Gent, Jasper 95
Gentle, Stephen 43
    Thomas 37
George, Daniel 29, 78
    Fredrick 14
    Isaac 97
    John 29

William 78
Gerald, Thomas 11
Gerganion [sic], Fredric 78
Gerganious, Samuel 78
    William 78
Geringer, Daniel 95
German, John 23, 45
    John H. 84
    William 23
Gerrell, Elijah 35
Gerwin, David 42
Gettig, John 8
Gibbans, Solomon 52
Gibble, George 56
    James E. 72
Gibbs, Archibald 113
    Bartee 70
    Charles 12
    David 70
    Jesse 29
    John 46
    Samuel, Sr. 70
    Stephen 70
    Washington 70
Gibony, David 39
Gibson, David B. 71
    Elisha 57
    Jasper 2
    John 48, 83, 100
    John, Jr. 77
    Moses 95
    Pleasant 96
    Reuben 62
    Robert 96
    Samuel 48
    Stephen 96
    William, Jr. 77
    Wm. 96
Giddens, Henzy [Henry?] 38
Giddins, John 10
    Jonathan 7
Gilan, William 25
Gilbert, Benjamin 3
    Isaac 13
    James 114
    John 72, 77
    Thomas 6
    William 56
Gilbreath, George 99
    Gideon 99
    Helen H. 99
    Hiram 99
    James 51
Giles, Daniel 49
    Jeremiah 69
    Jesse 116
    William 12, 113
Gill, Edward 55
    Gideon 88
    James 29
    John 88
    Robert 50
    Thomas 20, 89
    William 30
Gillan, William 41
Gillaspie, Gavid [sic] 53
    Giddal 93
    John 51
    Robert 51
    William 53

Gilleband, James 111
Gillespie, Abdi 51
    David 19
    James 51
Gilley, James 108
Gilliam, Charles 85
    Henry 16
    John 99
    Lestly 30
    Miles 65
    Nathaniel 66
    William 30
Gillikan, George 72
    Uriah 72
Gilliland, John 96
Gillis, Hugh 57
    John 57
    Malcom 104
Gillmore, Jacob 12
    William 22
Gills, Malcom 57
Gilman, John 93
Gilmore, Josiah 41
Gilreath, Thomas 51
Gilston, Samuel 91
Gingles, Edwin S. 44
Gipson, James 64
    John 48
Girkin, Harmon 17
Givens, Robert 59
    Samuel 40
Gladdon, Samuel 45
Gladson, Daniel 32
Glare, Edward 31
Glascock, Scarlet 52
Glasgow, John C. 61
    Samuel 61
Glass, Alexander 48
    David 32
    John 92
    Jos. 92
    Stephen 91
    Thomas 48
Glasscock, William 58
Glawson, Jasper 91
Gleen, James 36
Glenn, Benj. 98
    Elisha 26
    John 30
    Mark 89
    Robert 86
    Sampson 30
    Wiley 90
Glifford, Joseph 14
Glissen, Bryan 12
Glisson, Abraham 80
    John 12
    Stephen H. 80
Glotfelder, Daniel 110
    Elias 110
    George 110
    John 111
    Rudolph 110
Glover, Damel [sic] 67
    John 14, 110
    Jones 16
Gloveyer, Benjamin 18
Gobbel, John 104
Goddin, Nathan 101
Godfrew [Godfrey], Samuel 62

Godfrey, Francis 63
  Hiram 62
  James 2, 62
  John 62
  Thomas 84
  William 2
Godley, Jesse 70
Godsey, Edward 34
  Thomas 33
Godwin, Allen 82
  Lewis 11
Goff, James 14
  John 73
  Samuel 42
Goforth, George 106, 110
  Isaac 112
  Preston 110
  William 43
Goger, John 107
Going, John 112
Goings, Edwaard 22
  William 22
Goints, Amos 77
  John 77
Golden, Wm. 98
Golding, George 56
  Wm. 97
Goldsberry, Ignatius 19
Gonlan, Thomas 31
Gooch, John 115
  Pumphrett 89
Good, John 113
  Robert 113
  Solomon, Jr. 113
Goodbread, Joab 114
  John 46
Goode, William 35
Gooden, Daniel 19
Goodin, William 49
Gooding, Barge 12
Goodman, Henry 59
  Jacob 107
  John 9, 41
  Lemuel 4
  Tobias 107
  William 78, 103
Goodnight, George 107
  John 41
Goodson, Solomon B. 66
Goodwin, Abner 4
  Allen 92
  Cornelius H. 5
  Edmond 21
  George 14
  Granbury 21
  Isham 86
  John 23
  Matthews 86
  Silas 12
  Tobias 11
  William 81, 116
Gorden, Arthur 3
  James 70, 83
  Jeremiah 2
  John W. 53
  Nathaniel 53
  Thomas A. 53
  Wiley G. 53
Gordon, Alexander 84
  Archibald, Jr. 89

Jacob N. 69
James 93
John 20, 64
Richmond 43
Robert 30
William 30, 31, 38
Gore, Isaac 80
  John 23, 79
  Joseph 79
Gorman, Pleasant 96
Gorran, Andrew 115
Goss, John 102
  Joseph, Jr. 102
Gould, David 72
Goulde, Malach 23
Gower, Reuben 12
  Zadock 87
Gowin, John 84
Grace, Matthew 76
Grady, Andrew M. 40
  John T. 80
  Reuben, Jr. 34
  Robert 34
Graham, Archibald 82
  Archibald, Jr. 83
  Burrel 83
  Griffith 52
  James 88, 109
  John 22, 37, 57
  Joseph 58
  Richard 38
  Samuel 39, 101
Grahams, James 91
Grant, Bazzel 13
  Ephraim 76
  Jeremiah 91
  John 13
  Milton 96
  Shadrack 16
  Thomas 76
  William 13
Granthen, Benjamin 75
Granthon, Sion 77
Grantum, Needham 10
Graves, Boston 27
  Georges [sic] 58
  James 42
  John 3
  John W. 30
  Peter 42
  William B. 31
Gray, Abud [sic] 67
  Alexander 51, 77
  Benjamin D. 72
  Beverly 107
  Etheldred 16
  Hirom 116
  Jacob 106
  James 107
  Jesse 63
  John 1, 9
  Jordan 3
  Nelson 106
  Peter 18
  Peter M. 2
  Robert 100
  Samuel 103
  William 2, 9, 59
  Wm. 99
  Zachariah 73

Graybeal, David 100
  Henry 100
Grayson, Benjamin 111
  William 111
Greason, Henry 32
  Jacob 95
Green, Aaron 4
  Abner 5, 46, 86
  Abraham 4
  Allen 90
  Archibald 56
  Asa 29, 30
  Benjamin 15
  David 105
  Durant 73
  Jacob 26
  James 36
  Jesse 84
  John 43, 58, 86, 107, 112, 116
  John C. 60
  John N. 58
  Jonathan 92
  Joseph 18, 44, 48
  Malacha 56
  Mashack 102
  Nicholas 30
  Reddin 11
  Robert 104
  Samuel 64
  Thomas 8, 15, 22, 38, 48
  Thomas H. 15
  William 5, 11, 43, 52, 104
  William H. 55
  Wilson 15
  Zacheus 56
Greene, Richard 105
Greenlee, James, Jr. 49
  William 53
Greenwood, John 116
Greer, Freeman 96
  John 12
Gregan, Bartlet 33
Greggs, Hugh 39
Gregor, John 102
Gregory, Asa 55, 65
  Dempsey 61
  Edmond 63
  Edmond, Sr. 2
  Edmund, Jr. 2
  Frederick 2, 62
  Henry 2
  Herrin 21
  James 1, 109
  Jess 13
  Job 62
  John 1, 46, 61
  Jonathan 2, 62
  Joseph 99
  Lemuel 2
  Mitchel 1
  Nathan 2, 62
  Peter 61
  Samuel 2, 61, 62
  Thomas 2, 3
  William 35, 63
Gregson, George 102
Greves, Edward 3
  William 2
Grey, Hezekiah 39

Gribble, John 48
Gribils, Thomas 114
Grice, Reuben 109
Grier, Samuel 80
Griffen, Greenbury 112
  Joseph 68
  Lewis 71
Griffin, Abraham 84
  Allen 29
  Benjamin 16
  Claiborne 66
  David 3, 73
  Edward 74
  Elisha 23
  Enock 84
  Gilbert 16
  Horatio 20
  Isaac 88
  James 16, 35
  Jesse 71, 74
  John 2, 34, 71
  Joseph 66, 74
  Joshua 74
  Kitchen 86
  Levi 71
  Oliver 37
  Reuben 17
  Stephen 32
  Will 71
  William 18, 30, 50, 54, 65
  William H. 8
Griffis, James 75
Griffith, D. W. 13
  Daniel 98
  James 72
  John 42, 49, 109
  Samuel 100
  Solomon 42
  William 33
Griffy, James 46
Grigs, Henry 112
  Jesse 112
Grimes, Bryant 74
  George 104
  James 12, 27, 91
  Jesse 80
  John 12
  Mercer 19
  Stephen 12
Grimmer, Cullen 14, 65
  Moses 14
Grimsted, Thomas Y. 15
Grisham, Elijah 42
Grissel, Bannister 11
Grissom, Benjamin 30
  James 95
  Laban 89
  Moses 109
  Thomas 89
  Willie 30
Grisson, Neal 13
Grist, Allen 70
  Isaac 36
  James 52, 74
  John 8
  Rayford 22
  Sutton 22
  Will 7
Grizzard, Abraham 73
  Armstead 66

Joel 65
Grizzle, John 47
Grogan, John 94
    William 34
Grove, Jesse W. 111
Groves, Thomas 109
Grub, David 102
    George 103
    Jacob 38
    John 38
Gruson, Martin 44
Guant, Avery 111
Gudger, Joseph 115
    William 115
Gudyer, Joseph 49
Guffey, Archy Reed 111
    James S. 111
    John 111
Guffy, John 46
Guilford, William 61
Guiltney, Nathan 109
    Robert 109
    William 109
Gullet, Christopher 99
    Daniel 99
    William 43
Gullidge, Henry 84
    Jeremiah 24
Gunn, Allen 31
    John 93
Gunter, Asa 92
Guntlesey, William 110
Gupton, Jacob 88
    Robert 50
Gurganus, Aaron 70
    Thomas 70
    Willie 74
Gurgarmus, Swinson 14
Gurley, Needham 23
    William 23
Gurly, Anson 76
    Isom 116
    William 15, 84
Guthree, Samuel 72
Guthrie, Benjamin 56
    Elijah 56
Guthry, Shadrack 116
Guttis, James 90
Guy, Henry 11
    John C. 11
    Lemuel 80
    William 103, 114
Gwin, Ashman 109
Gwyn, Payten 53
Gyton, William 57

H

Hacket, William 32
Hackney, Jinnes 18
Hadder, Nehemiah 83
Hadley, James 107
Hadnok, Seth 13
Hadok, Michael 7
Hadrick, John 111
Haffler, William 5
Hagan, John 109
Hager, George 44
    Jacob 95
    John 44
Haggard, Elisha 65

Haggins, Isaac 13
Haglas, Hugh 26
Hagler, John 23
    Philip 84
    Wm. 99
Hague, Jacob 104
    John 104
Hailey, Henry 66
    Henry Booker 31
Hain, Phillip 44
Haines, Overton 30
Hainline, William 103
Hains, Francis 96
    Jonathan 116
Hair, John 79
Haire, Greenbury 38
Haireld, Joseph 63
Hairis [sic], Harvey 63
Haislip, Branson 74
    John 74
Hait, John 39
Hakee, Beliher [sic] 56
Haket, Thomas 63
Hakins, Enock 77
Hale, Hardy 16
    Joshua 65
    Owen 12
Hales, Kader 16
    Nathaniel 84
Haley, Henry 86
    John 88
Hall, Abram 14
    Alexander 108
    Charles 63
    Daniel 21
    Darham 54
    Dempsey 64
    Egbird 57
    Henry 22, 81
    James 41, 46, 81
    Jeremiah 7, 70
    John 43, 107
    Jonathan 86
    Joseph 72, 107
    Lewis 14, 31
    Martin 11
    Mathew 22
    Pleasant 89
    Richer 50
    Robert 10, 33, 54, 96
    Robert C. 50
    Solomon 102
    Thomas 49, 71
    William 71
    Willie 76, 87
Hallsey, Benjamin F. 75
Hallstead, John 63
Hallswell, Reddick 4
Halsey, Miles 4
Halstead, Ivy 1
    William 1
Haltom, Joseph 41
Ham, Beriman 88
    Giles 10
    Henry 76
    James 34
    William 76
Hamblet, Jesse 15
Hambleton, Edley 113
    James 106

Hamby, Eli 99
    Reuben 99
Hamilton, Alexander 72
    David 72
    Joseph 41
    Thomas 72
    William 110
Hamm, Benjamin 88
    Haywood 11
    Seth 97
    William 11
Hamman, Solah 70
Hammock, Bartlet 58
Hammonds, Absalom 20
    William 58
Hammons, Dothan 79
    Elijah 25
    John 81
    Roland 84
    Willis 68
    Wilson 18
Hammuns, John 40
Hamn, Joel 84
Hamnor, Washington 13
Hampton, Adam 111
    David 37
    Jesse 71
    Jonathan 111
    Noah 112
    Thomas 98
Hamrick, Elijah 112
Hamsick, James 46
    Samuel 46
Hancock, Eli 96
    Elisha 95
    Felic [Felix?] 80
    Isaiah 96
    Isham 101
    John 34, 42, 83
Hancy, Thomas 114
Hand, William 14
Handcock, Thomas 24
Hanes, Eli 111
Haney, Robert 46
    William S. 34
Haning, John 97
Hankens, William 56
Hankin, John 12
Hanks, John 89, 110
    Willis 89
Hanley, Benjamin 24
Hannah, Abner 51
    Eli 51
    Isaac 100
    John 51, 100
    Solomon 100
Hanner, Alexander 51
Hanners, William 61
Hannon, John 47
    Thomas 45
    William 52
Hanny, Timothy 52
Hanrahan, Michael 70
Hansen, William 42
Hansley, Edmond 78
    Owen 14
Hanson, Abijah 14
    Stephen 106
Hapler, Philip 103
Happner, Mertin 36

Harald, John 35
Harbeson, Hiram 52
    James 106
Harbin, Miley 15
Harbison, John 53
Harchie, John 108
Harching, Israel 70
Hardee, John 8
Harden, Aquilla 65
    Charles 51
    James 21
    John 51
Harder, Jonathan 47, 59
    Mark 46
    William 46
Hardeson, Elijah 13
    James 17
    Jesse 17
    Joshua 17
Hardin, James 109
    Stewart 32
Harding, Henry 8
Hardison, Edward 75
    Jesse 77
    William 80
Hardle, John 4
Hardle [Hurdle?], Henry 27
Hardwick, Younger 31
Hardy, Arthur 57
    Benjamin 73
    John 76
    Lemuel 73
    Whitmell 16
Hare, Aaron 64
    Arthur 21
    Henry 76
    Jacob 5
    John 5, 81, 103
    John P. 65
    Jonathan 21
    Luke 64
    Martin 81
Harget, Alfred 72
    Peter 73
    William 73
Hargett, Henry 107
    William 107
Hargis, Thomas 51
Hargrove, James 34
    William 30
Haris [sic], Willis 104
Harkey, David 107
    John 107
Harlow, Jesse 15, 66
Harlson, William 45
Harman, George 92
    Jacob 110
    James 75
    John 58
    Peter 45
    William 110
Harmon, Joseph 46
    Solomon 45
Harner, Jacob 110
Harp, Willie 98
Harper, Absalom 27
    Cornelius 9
    Gradathan [sic] 32
    Jesse 10
    John 10

Joshua 18, 68
Stephen 16
William 71, 73
Harralson, Archibald 89
John 89
Solomon 112
Harrass, John 76
Harrel, Gilbert 112
Jesse 75
John 10
Joseph 73
Samuel 73
Harreld, Elisha 3
Harrell, Aaron 5
Bray 13
Dancy 65
David 55
Eli 64
Elias 10
Elijah 97
Francis 11
Henry 65
Isham 85
Jacob 12
Joel 10
Joseph 3, 10, 56, 64
Joshua 65
Meredith 65
Powell 65
Simeon 56
Thomas 65
Harress, Caleb 2
Harrill, Hardy 75
Harrington, Isaac 92
John 84
Harris, Alexander 48
Alexander W. 107
Allen 41
Charles B. 32
Clifford [sic] 50
Cyrus 59
Daniel 4
David 103
Edwin 68
Eli 41
Elisha 70, 93
George 70
Green 41
Henry 28, 67, 92
Hiram 110
Houston 40
Howel 95
Hugh 39
Isaac 40, 47
Isham 27
James 27, 42, 70
Jeptha 104
Jessee, Jr. 102
Joel 104
John 3, 49, 68
John B. 110
Jonathan 104
Joseph C. 19
Josiah 70, 72
Mark 2
Micajah 88
Milton 59
Noah 74
Orren 66
Ransom 30

Reuben 88
Richard 56, 58, 88
Richard, Sr. 90
Rinchen 15
Robert 70
Robinson 109
Sam'l H. 40
Samuel 28, 56
Seke [?] 38
Silvenus 74
Simpson 91
Timothy 55
West, Jr. 41
Wiley 41, 45
William 24, 26, 35, 42, 86, 111
William G. 107
Willie 105
Zedekiah 111
Zemeriah 72
Harrison, Abner 73
Adam 39
George 17, 69
Henry W. 2
Isaac 62
James 18, 98
James C. 15
Jesse 64
John W. 2
Nathan 62
Owen W. 2
Reding 71
Richard 16
Rob't 107
Robert 29, 63
William 29
Willie 86
Harriss, Byrum 15
David 15
Elias 66
Gideon 66
Henry 88
John 74, 88, 114
Maxamillan 116
Solomon 74
William 66
Harshaw, Joshua 114
Hart, Alfred 10
Charles 40
Edward 44
Elijah 26
Graves 89
Green 66
Hempley 98
Henry 22, 66
James 44
John 26
Joseph 28
Peter 100
Samuel 38
Hartam, Elijah 41
Hartfield, Solomon 54
Harthy, Clinton 47
Hartie, Thomas 104
Hartley, John 113
Reuben 100
Richard 106
William 113
Hartman, Charles 107
John 102

Harton, Hardy 84
Thomas 18, 68
Hartsell, Jacab [sic] 105
Leonard 105
Hartsfield, David 73
John B. 9
Hartzog, David 100
Harvener, John 45
Harvey, Absalom 91
Duncan 27
James 77, 100
John 97
Nathan 70
Harvil, Mills 75
Harwell, Alfred 66
Mason 44
Robert 20
Samuel 44
William 31
Harwood, Britain 93
William 28, 29
Hasby, Jacob 103
Hashford, Wm. 91
Hasket, John 63
Haskett, Jesse 72
Haskey, John 107
Haskin, Robert 27
Haskins, Purnal 77
Haskitt, John 100
Hasley, John 59
Hass, Christian 114
Hassel, William 74
Zadock 69
Hassell, Benjamin 6
Zadoch 6
Hastey, Williby 15
Haswell, Benjamin 90
Reddick 19
Thomas 19
Hatch, Anthony 12
Samuel 13
Hatcher, William 85
Hately, Henry 100
Hatfield, Benjamin 116
William 4
Hath, John 38
Hathcock, Hansel 15
Hatheway, Hugh 66
Hathway, David 74
Hatley, Britain 93
Hattaman, Christopher 107
Hatton, Charles, Jr. 109
Haughton, Josiah 69
Thomas 17
Hauley, John 106
Hausar, John L. 97
Hauser, Daniel 97
Hauston, John 36
Hawes, John 15
Hawett, Richard 69
Hawey, Abraham 27
Hawkins, Achilles 70
Gabriel 15
John 13, 17, 43, 105, 115
Joshua 47, 58
Josiah 77
Littleton 70
Micajah T. 18
Otway 77
Reuben 30

Richard 43
Stephen 13, 71
Thomas 70, 77
William 44
Hawks, John 18, 68
Hawley, Charles 24
Hawn, David 111
Haworth, Jeremiah 37
Micajah 37
Hawser, Abner 83
Hawsley, William 14
Hawthorn, Nathaniel 25
Haxwood, Richard 37
Hay, George 12
Haswell 73
James 89
Joseph 12
Samuel 10
Thomas 12
Hayes, Absalom 86
Charles 49, 50
Daniel 99
Elias 101
Harmon 64
Hugh 19
James 5
Jesse 67
Mathew 20
Nathaniel 19
Peyton 30
Richard 91
Samuel 38
Solmon [sic] 29
Thomas 89
Willis 87
Haygood, Jesse 105
Hayly, Lewis 11
Hayner, Thomas 75
Haynes, Benjamin 35
Mathew 52
William 33
Hayness, Philip 110
Hays, Colbert 114
Harman 5
Joseph 115
Hayse, Elijah 113
John 113
Haysell, James 6
Haywell, Cullen 11
Haywood, George 91
James 59
Robert W. 118
Shadrack 29
Hayworth, William 104
Hazelett, Ezekiel 52
Hazlewood, George 18, 67
Head, James 29
Headen, Isaac 92
Headrick, Phillip 36
Heair, George 41
Heard, Stancel 76
Hearing, Benjamin 9
Nathaniel 9
Hearn, Ezekiel 41
George 105
Heartley, Abner 71
Heath, Alexander 80
Andrew 1
Arthur 61
Edmund 71

Frederick 71
John 76
Samuel 35
Solomon 59
Heathcock, Ned 27
Heckworth, James 68
Hector, Hiram 46
Hedgepath, Henry 68
Holliday 68
Hedgepeth, Jesse 55
Hedgepith, Thompson 30
Hedrick, Phillips 111
Hefley, Martin 116
Hefner, Daniel 115
Hegler, Philip 105
Hegles, Jacob 108
Heifer, Jacob 58
Heldebrand, Joseph 110
Heldebreand, Comrade 110
Helfer, Daniel 103
Hell, Swinefield 114
Hellen, Isaac 71
James 41
Walter 13
Helmer, Joel 107
Helmes, Charles 106
William 106
Helms, Isaac 59
Helsepeck, Jacob 97
Heltan, Joseph 88
Helton, Leps 114
Hemphill, John 95
Hena, Isaac 109
Henby, William 52
Henderson, Danile [Daniel?] 78
David 40
Duncan 78
Henry 13
Hillory 13
Hilory 77
Isaac 13
James 105, 113
John 44
Kilby 77
Morris 90
Samuel 38
Selden 7
William 33, 114
Hendesty, Bartoa 72
Hendley, Ezekiah 92
Henry 30
Hendrick, Adam 36
David 23
James 51
Michael 61
Hendricks, Jesse 103
Seth 63
Thomas 4
Hendrickson, Joshua 99
Hendrikson, Jeremiah 43
Hendrix, Henry 103
Thomas 103
Henil, Jesse 114
Henley, Thomas 40
Henlin, Wm. 101
Henry, Eli N. 49
Green 17
Jacob 56
John 52, 115
Rigdon 73

Thomas 44
Hensley, Charles 49
Henson, Joseph 9
Reuben 48
Hepler, Christopher 103
Henry 36
Hepley, Martin 49
Hepner, Michael 45
Heps, Willie 110
Herndon, Pleasant 26, 90
William 26
Wm. 90
Herney, Samuel 32
Heron, David 33
Davis 34
Moses 52
Herren, Robert 46
Herrin, Joseph 21
Lewis 114
Stephen 21
Herring, Ashael 9
Benjamin 80
Burwell 73
Giles 82
Jehabud 10
Joseph 76
Joshua 22
Moses 44
Stephen 12, 83
William 9
Herrington, John 72
Moses 74
Hertee, Benjamin 50
Herton, Harbert 111
Hervey, Stephen 27
Hester, Alfred 89
Benjamin 89
Jasper 19
Joseph 20
Ransom 30
Robert 89
Stephen 57
Heulin, Edward 36
Heures, Thomas 7
Heuser, John 110
Hewet, Randal 56
Hewit, Rigden 13
Hews, Malachiah 79
Reddick 11
Heynes, Armstead 28
Heyson, Loyd 116
Hez'ah, Bresom 38
Hickason, Little 53
Hickerson, David 43
Hickeson, John 53
Hickman, Joseph 42
Hicks, Abner 89
Aldridge 13
Alfred 88
Daniel 46, 89
Dempsey 55
Isaiah 36
James 54, 109
Jesse 92
Queen 46
Reuben 41
Robert 85
Stephen 11
West 27
Whitmell 68

William 66, 108, 111
Hickson, James 49
Hicky, William 48
Hid, Rea 111
Hiett, Moses 35
Hiffley, George 116
Higdon, Leonard 48
Higgs, Barnett 30
John 65, 77
Kinchen 29
Moore 66
William 56
High, Julias 19
Michel 23
Silas 50
Highaldn, Jesse 92
Highsmit [Highsmith], James 79
Highsmith, John 78
Hight, Willie 19
Hightower, Joshua 31
Hilemon, John 47
Hill, Aasa [sic] 46
Alfred 26
Aquila R. 13
Asaph 111
Benjamin 5, 64
Green 81, 86
Henry 38
Henry, Jr. 102
Isaac 76
James 39, 66, 73, 85, 111, 113
James J. 14
Jesse 47, 59
John 19, 44, 103, 104
John G. 70
Jonathan 46
Joseph H. 86
Julius 19
Martin 9
Micajah 36
Richard 9
Robert 34, 50, 97
Samuel 79
Shadrick 36
Sion 87
Smith 36
Thomas 85, 112
Thomas E. 50
Whitmill 64
William 48, 109
Willie 70
Wm. 90
Hillbourn, Henry 79
Hillbourne, Zadock 79
Hilley, Watson 64
Hillman, Dempsey P. 67
Hillmon, Caleb 94
Joshua 94
Samuel 94
Hilton, Joseph 47
Himpman, Henry 108
Hinchey, Bartlet 90
Hindcastle, John 112
Hindrix, Joshua 103
Hines, Alexander 10
Charles 87
John 17, 76, 80
Samuel 73
William 17

Hinkle, Anthony 109
William 44
Hinkley, George 77
Hinklin, Ensign 78
Hinnant, Hardy 11
Jonathan 11
Josiah 11
Hinshaw, Jonathan 98
Hinsley, James 61
Hinson, John, Jr. 84
Joseph 100
Robert 10
Hinston, Enock 33
Hinton, Elam 51
James 87
Mathew 11
Willis 11
Wm. 92
Hiott, Isaac 5
Hips, Jacob 48
Hirter, Isaac 50
Hise, Jacob 48
Hister, Joseph 88
Thos. 94
Histers, William 81
Hitchins, John 90
Hite, William 3
Hitlin, William 88
Hitner, Henry 34
Hixt, Jacob 34
Hoard, Willis 17
Hobbs, Amos 64
Barnabas 101
George 85
Henry 4, 70
Isaac 55
James 21
Michael 81
Miles 5
Noah 2
Reuben 4
Samuel 55
Simon 77
Thomas 23
Thos. 94
Hobby, Francis 20
Harbut 54
John 87
Hobson, George 98
Hocall, Benjamin 64
Hodge, David 111
George 36
John 93, 107
Joseph 25
Joshua 74
Phillip 27
Hodgers, John 37
Hodges, Gentry 42
John 20
Philemon S. 78
William 20, 42, 74
Wilson B. 70
Hoedridge, Nathan 100
Hoffman, Christopher 45
George 45
Hofler, William 64
Hogan, Isaiah 104
Matthew 28
Hogard, Thomas 56
Hoge, Jonathan 52

Hogg, Gaven 65
Hoggard, James 65
Hogler, Isaac 99
Hogwood, Josiah 22
Hohfield, Elijah 112
Hoke, Daniel 110
    Peter 110
Hoket, James 53
Holbert, Joseph 46
Holbrook, Joseph 34
    William, Jr. 34
    William, Sr. 34
Holbrooks, John 40
Holden, Daniel 90(2)
    Samuel 40
Holder, James 93
    William 42
Holderfield, Daniel 99
    Willis 29
Holdesnes, James 94
Holding, Isham 54
Holebrooks, Samuel 107
Holeyfield, William 47
Holifield, John 85
    Ralph 42
    Watson 42
Holifyeld, Wm. 98
Holland, Arnold 109
    Charles 70
    Enos 10
    Henry 44
    Kenrard 76
    Marcy D. 47
    Matthew, Jr. 44
    Richard 116
    Thomas 5
    William 28, 112
Holleman, David 108
Holley, John 71
Holliday, Joseph 93
Hollin, Daniel 22
Hollingsworth, Henry 80
    Wm. T. 88
Hollis, Edward 69
Holloman, Elisha 8
    Lemuel 5
    William 43, 56
Hollomon, George, Jr. 64
    Justin 64
Holloway, Abram 4
    John 86
    John, Jr. 54
    Luke 4
    Shad 71
    Taylor 94
Hollowday, Riinehen [sic] 10
Hollowell, Joseph 11
    Thomas 11
    William 71
Holly, John 56
Holmes, Edward 10
    George 21
    Hugh 40
    James 57
    John 14, 66
    Moses 36
    Robert 7
    Solomon 15
    William S. 70
Holomon, John 75

William 103
Holsclaw, Henry 44
Holshansen, Fred 102
Holshouse, Andrew, Jr. 36
Holshouser, John 36
    Windle 108
Holstead, Malachi 61
Holston, Averytt 86
Holswell, Edwin 11
Holt, Henry 64, 91
    Lemuel 114
    Richard 93
    William 11, 27
    Wm. 91
Holtfoot, Matthew 67
Holton, Jesse 95
    John 104
    William 41
Holtrooks, Isaac 42
Holyfield, William 58
Holznd [sic], William 54
Honecut, Brittain 12
Honeycut, Isham 105
    Reuben 105
    Sarquel 105
Honeycutt, Samuel 108
    Uriah 116
Honse, Green D. 19
Hood, Bold Robin 11
    James 47
    Jeremiah 52
    Joseph 48
    Junius 39
    Nathaniel 87
    Reuben 107
    William 73
Hoofman, Phillip 35
Hook, Hillary 76
    William 79
Hook [?], Jacob 110
Hooker, Hiram 7
    Hymerisk 10
    James 10
    John 40, 97
    Spence 69
    Stephen 63
    Thomas 10
Hooks, Hermant 76
    Phillip 10
    William 10, 23
Hooper, William 10
Hooten, William 70
Hoots, Henry 98
    Jacob 58
Hoover, Jacob 58
    John 97
Hop, William 12
Hope, Christopher 110
    Thomas 105
    Wm. 81
Hopgood, Theophilus 84
Hopkins, Farley 105
    John 84, 89
    Miles 6
    Robert 7, 70
    William 85
Hoppass, John 100
Hopper, Andrew 116
Hoppis, Adam 45
Horbet, Henry 46

Horn, Amden 68
    David 77
    Harrell 18
    Hausel 85
    Hillkiah 77
    Howell 37
    J. Jolly 76
    John 26
    Lee 68
    Michael 76
    Peter 33
    Silas 87
    Thomas 37
    William 21
Hornaday, John 27
Horne, Hansel 14
    Henry 17
    Isaac 17
    Jeremiah 75
    Martin B. 75
    Sion 20
Horner, John 26
Horniday, Ziah 26
Hornsby, John 88
Horoh, William H. 36
Horsliam, William 39
Horton, Canady 90
    Charles 85
    David 44, 100
    Elisha 5
    Jeremiah 66
    Joseph 98
    Joshua 90
    Josiah 73
    Nathan 42
    Phillip 20
    Phineas 100
    William 44
Hoskins, Edmond 61
    Ellis 94
    John 94
    Jos. 94
Host, James 48
Houp, John 39
House, George 109
    Isaac 50, 88
    Jacob 40
    John 21
    Joseph J. 10
    Thomas 30
    Turner 74
Houser, Henry 110
    Jacob 110
    John 102
Housten, Wm., Jr. 107
Houston, David 41
    Joel S. 107
    Mathew 52
    Richard F. 108
    William 107(2)
    William Hubbard 13
Hover, Henry 107
Hovis, Frederick 44
Howard, Benjamin 42
    Bewdie 30
    Calvin 13
    Edmund 13
    Elwin 37
    George 103
    Groves 50

Henry 77
Hugh 31
Isaac 57
James 7
Jesse 42
John 14
Joseph 43, 52
Lewis 40
Menas 57
Richard 26
Samuel 77
Thomas 30, 81
Titus 77
William 13
Howe, William 27
Howel, Christian 116
Howell, Caleb 76
    Isaac 107
    James 17
    John 10, 32, 84
    Joshua 110
    Osborn 87
    Richard 6
    Samuel 114
    Stephen 65
    William 84
    Woodard 10
Howie, Aaron 106
Howington, Edward 26
Howland, Thomas 56
    William 72
    Zephaniah 72
Howlet, Isaac 33
Howood, Robert 106
Howzer, Peter 45
Hoyle, Jackson S. 61
    John 47, 59
Hubbard, Aquilla 86
    George 35
    Mathew 24
    Matthew 31
Hubbart, William 34
Hubbs, Reuben 9
Huckaby, Benjamin 22
    James 82
Hudgins, Asa 30
Hudler, Amos 71
Hudlow, Kenon 73
    Michael 46
Hudnal, William 71
Hudson, Hall 14, 66
    James 33
    Joshua 85
    Laurence 103
    Robert 96
    Thomas 4
    William 53
    Willis 78
Hudspith, George 98
Hueston, Plesabo 109
Huet, Lewis 110
Huff, Daniel 35
    William 57
Huffins, Jacob 92
Huffman, Abram 48
    Adam 104
    Benjamin 29
    Frederick 48
    Lott 77
    Philip 97

Huffsteddler, Henry 110
John 110
Hufman, Jacob 13
Hugey, John 38
Huggins, John 108
Robert, Jr. 44
Hughes, James 102
Joseph 92
Nathaniel 2
Richman 101
Hughey, David 115
Joseph 49
Samuel 116
Hughs, James 52
John 52
John W. 62
Richmond 52
Robert M. 39
William 27, 102, 114
Huit, James 2
Hulett, John 14
Hulgan, Stephen 100
Hull, John 54
William 45
Humphis, Thomas 3
Humphrey, Burney 13
Daniel 9
Lewis 9
Malichi 11
William 13
Humphreys, Henry 95
John 95
Humphries, John H. 31
Samuel 46
William 64, 103
Wm. 95
Humphry, Cewen 99
Hunhill, James 48
Hunley, Cobelas 105
Hunn, Charles 98
Hunnings, Elijah 2
Hunt, Abraham 36
Charles 3
David 68
Elijah 90
Henry 18
Ishum 2
James 19
John 104, 109
Jonathan 52
Laban 31
Nathaniel 19
Noah 102
Oliver 36
Thomas 30, 33, 89
William 44, 111
Wm. 98
Hunter, Anderson 51
Cader 56
Henry 55
Henry, Jr. 106
Isaac K. 64
James 47, 58, 68
John 65, 111
Joseph 46
Joshua 110
Samuel 32, 53, 60, 117
Whitmill 28, 54
William 56
Huntington, Minor 71

Huntley, David 110
Huphines, Jacob 97
Hurdle, Elisha 4
Kader 5
Hurley, Daniel 41
William 41
Hurst, James 77
Hurstle, James 116
Hurt, John 26
Husford, William 33
Huskey, Isham 88
Jesse 46
Thomas 45
Husky, Ransom 110
Hussey, John E. 80
Husslatter, Adam 45
Huston, James 12
Levi 51
Thomas 36
Hutchers, James 96
Hutchins, David 85
John, Jr. 54
Lewis 90
Wallis 61
William 111
Hutchinson, Alexander 94
Charles 105
James 94
Hutchison, Benjamin 35
James 39
Samuel J. 39
Wm. 94
Hutson, Azariah 6
James 101
Littleton 28, 29
William 37
Hyatt, Alsey 23
John 85
Hyde, Henry 77
Hyer, John 34
Hyett, Jesse 64
Hyley, Philly 49
Hymon, Stephen 56
Hynes, James 17
Robert 66

I

Icehour, Martin 41
Idol, Barnabas 37
Joseph 97
Matthias 37
Ijams, John 103
Inge, John J. 89
Ingerham, Jacob 100
Ingle, John 95
Michael 110
Ingram, Ambrose 86
Hezekiah 24
Isham 24
James 93
John 23, 31, 84
Lemuel 23
Mathew 41
Moody 24
Nathaniel 66
William 66
Innman, Austin 80
Inscore, John 88
Ipock, Henry 71
John 71

Lazarous 71
Irby, Turner 94
Iredell, James 61
Ireland, David 56
John 26
Irrard, William F. 50
Irvey, Will U. 40
Irvine, Abram 46, 112
James 111
Irwin, Abijah 103
Alexander 44
Andrew 61, 117
Giles 106
John 40
Samuel 95
Isaac, Gabriel 111
Jacob 45
Isam, Brice W. 37
Isbell, Littleton 98
Pendleton B. 50
Ision, Philip 96
Isley, Christian 32
Israel, Henry 70
Ives, Duran 71
Elijah 71
Mason 71
William H. 8
Zadock 71
Ivey, Charles, Sr. 25
Hartwell 86, 87
Isham 25
James 25, 87
Jess 106
Lind-ton [sic] 54
Wm. 91
Ivy, John 26
Richard 76
Izzard, Elijah 19

J

Jaccour, John 40
Jack, William Boly 34
Jackson, Abner 26
Alex 93
Beverly 15
Daniel 27, 86
Edmund 15
Eleazer 7
Elijah 76
Elisha 28
Ephraim 112
Ervin 81
Francis 35
George 95
Hezekiah 63
Isaac 35
Isam 73
Jackariah [sic] 77
Jacob 9, 26
James 3, 47, 48, 57, 63, 92, 102
John 4, 10, 20
John, Jr. 63
Joseph 4
Joshua 3
Josiah 88
Law 10
Michel 27
Moses 48
Oram 88

Peavon 106
Robert H. 51
Sam'l 92
Samuel 35
Spencer 31
Thomas 32, 33
Thos. 63
Warren 21
William 22, 27, 32, 63
Wm. P. 93
Jacobs, James 31
Solomon 58
Thomas 21
William 26, 108
Jacocks, Jonathan H. 65
James, Benjamin 55
Conel 37
David 23
Henry 18, 23, 38, 67
Hosea 23
Isaac 37
Jacob 2
James F. 6
Jesse 36
John 16, 24, 37, 70, 78
Joseph 43
Lemmuel 75
Martin 24
Osborn 27
Thomas 80, 114
William 17, 23, 48, 104
Japs [Hays?], John 43
Jarold, Thomas 34
Jaron, Jacob 115
Jarral, John 86
Jarrall, John 45
Jarralls, Joshua 33
Jarrat, Isaac 99
William 102
Jarrels, John 47, 59
Jarvis, Caleb 2
Dennis 37
Merese 1
Richard 37
Samuel 63
Thomas B. 2
Zebediah 58
Jasey, Willis 15
Jasper, William 23, 56
Javette, Aaron 115
Javiette, Irea 115
Jeague, James 104
Jean, David 97
Jeffers, James 50
Jeffery, M---a [?] D. 50
Jeffreys, Marmaduke N. 19
Jeffries, Robert 26
Jelks, Jarrat M. 11
Jelton, Samuel 33
Jenkins, Benjamin 66
Charles 5
Henry D. 5
Irwin 5
Jenky 112
John 66
Lodowick 65
Reuben 109
Robert 30
Samuel R. 75
Simson 19

Solomon 18
Theophilus 75
Wiett 109
William 50
Willie 65
Jennett, Robert 7
Jennigan, David 10
Jennings, Frederick B. 6
    Geo. W. 95
    Levi 65
Jerald, Abram 33
Jermanny, Josiah 69
Jernigan, Buk [sic] 12
    Daniel 12
Jerrell, John 62
Jesop, Joshua 20
Jeter, Barnett 88
Jethro, John 69
Jetton, Benedict 109
Jewter, Jiles 16
Jimison, Arthur 39
Jinkens, Azra 115
    John 109
    Steward 110
    Thos. 97
Jinkins, Irvin 64
    Moses 77
    Samuel 115
    Thomas 35
    William 83
Jinks, Matt 28
Job, Moses 95
Johis, Electris 94
John, Ash 40
    Isham 112
    Samuel 112
    Will 40
    William 106
Johnson, Abram 97
    Alex 82
    Anderson 109
    Charles 69, 85
    David 115
    Elias 66
    Elisha 97
    Grady 115
    James 64
    Joel 99
    John 66, 97, 103, 107
    Joseph 43
    Levy 98
    Lewis 112
    Matthew 98
    Moses 87
    Reddin 87
    Robert 66
    Samuel 87
    Shadrack 20
    Talton 104
    Timothy 78
    Wiat 29
    William 84, 86, 103
    William W. 65
    Willis 67, 88
    Wm. 96
Johnston, Abram 36
    Andrew 100
    Angus 21
    Ashiey [Ashley?] 38
    Bailey 42

Baker 37
Benjamin 11, 41, 101
Brittain 12
Carter 111
Charles 92
Daniel 92
David 49
Edward 89
Greenberry H. 108
Henry 27, 46, 79
Hugh 115
Isaiah 73
James 10, 12, 31, 32, 56, 74,
        89, 93, 94, 102
Jeremiah 58
John 20-22, 28, 41, 53, 55,
        82, 93, 106
Joseph 52, 83
Joshua 50
Leonard 28
Lewis 21
Matthew 78
Mitchel 39
Moses 101
Nathaniel 11
Robert 51, 52, 111
Rufus 41
Sam'l 99
Samuel 93
Samuel, Jr. 105
Solomon 42
Stephen 10
Strangerman 42
Tapley 82
Wiley 105
Will 59
William 10, 30, 31, 41, 44,
        45, 55, 106
Willis 29, 67
Wm. 93
Joice, Ambrose 33
    Pleasant 33
Joiner, Abraham 81
    Charlton 84
Jolley, Gideon 16
    Henry 74
    William 109
Jolly, Thomas 67
Jonagon, Ryan 55
Jones, Alfred 29
    Allen 80, 81, 86, 89
    Anderson 89
    Ariel 72
    Bartlett 6
    Benjamin 67
    Bennett 18
    Bradford 86
    Charles 51, 101
    Churchwell 89
    Cornelius 1
    Daniel 80
    Darling 28, 54
    David 12, 13, 22, 30, 54
    Deray [?] 42
    Drury 103
    Edmund 13, 50
    Edward 31, 94
    Ehisha [Elisha] 75
    Elijah 80
    Evan 71

Felix 13
Francis 86
Fred 9
Frederick 50
Gardner 73
George 20
Hardy L. 8
Henry 30, 67
Hezekiah 88
Hugh 53
Isaac 42
Isaac James 13
Jacob 98
Jacob P. 5
James 21, 36, 38, 64, 71, 79,
        89, 92, 111, 114
James B. 6
James C. 88
Jeremiah 2, 62
Jesse 66, 79, 98
Joel 106
John 12, 15, 19, 23, 26, 34,
        46, 52, 53, 62, 64, 71,
        77, 84, 85, 96, 113
John, Sr. 7
Jonas 80
Jonathan 12, 51, 103
Joseph 78
Josha [Joshua?] 48
Josiah 111
Laban 86
Lavin 50
Lemuel 54
Lemuel B. 98
Martin 34
Maurice 7
Miles 26, 63
Nathan 80
Nathaniel 87, 92
Readin 10
Reddick 21
Richard 9, 31, 37, 89
Richard, Sr. 26
Ridley 86
Robert 10, 15, 89
Samuel 3, 6, 13, 86
Seth 85
Simeon 62
Simon 2, 73
Smith 8
Stephen 24
Thomas 4, 24, 76, 80, 84,
        114, 115
Timothy W. 86
Vinson H. 5
Westley 86
William 10, 14, 31, 78, 79,
        87, 114
William D. 19
Willie 88
Willis 81
Wm. 83, 92, 94
Joplin, Mordecai 86
Jordan, Alexander 115
    Cooper 96
    Dickson 85
    Francis 41
    George 91
    James 5, 11
    Jesse 3

John 15, 87, 90, 101
John, Sr. 66
Joseph 63
Matthew 3
Micajah 54
Osbourn 85
Richard 70
Ruton 109
Seth B. 69
William 28, 61
Jorden, Hana 4
Joy, Myrick 11
    Reeves 11
Joyce, John, Jr. 96
    Robert 96
Joyner, Abram 73
    Amos 74
    Andrew 14, 60
    Nelson 65
Judkins, Joseph 74
Juhuy [?], Charles 59
Julding, John 24
Julin, Jacob 105
Julke, William 24
Junderbusk, John 106
Junigan, Willie 87
Jush, George 104
    John 104
Justice, Eli 114
    Garrison 95
    John 114
    Joseph C. 67
    Laben 77
    Thomas 48
    William 114
Justin, George 114

K

Kagle, Leonard 111
Kallum, Shadrack 2
Kanady, Frederick 62
    William 62
Kances, John 97
Karney, John 97
Karr, Adam 106
Kart, John R. 29
Kary, William M. 39
Kasier, Ralph 36
Kastor, John 35
Katts, Henry 36
Kay, Jonathan 72
Kea, William 76
Kean, John 11
Keater, Jonathan 56
Keath, George 79
    James 79
Keaton, Henry 63
Keel, John 3
Keelin, Thomas 43
Keelough, Ebaneser 41
Keen, Gardner 21
    Isaac 87
Keeter, William 67
Keeth, Sion 35
Keeton, Clifton 43
Kegle, George 107
Keith, Henry 49, 115
    Reuben 115
    William 115
Kell, Thomas 43

Aven 73
George 71
Hardy 72
Jacob 35
Jesse 36
Joel H. 85
John 36
Lemuel 66
Thomas 32
Wm. 98
Lang, Joshua 64
Langdon, John 20
Langford, Champ 116
Langley, John 7
William 68
Langly, Matthias 58
Langon, James 87
Langston, Richard 76
Lanier, Alfred 7
Benjamin 19
Hosea 17
John 12
Lovett 75
Noah 80
Owen 12
Laniere, Benjamin A. 84
Lanin, David 33
Lanner, Joseph 114
Lanning, Amos 115
Lanoir, Walter R. 43
Lanon, Henry 58
Lanson, Henry 47
Lap, James 94
Lapland, James 64
Larder, Benjamin 75
Lare, Wiat 33
Lareson, David 31
Largant, James 113
Lark, Daniel 37
Larkabee, David 58
Larkins, Aaron 78
James 77
Joel E. 77
Robert 78
William 14
William Jones 14
Lash, Abram 97
Laslie, Daniel 83
Neill 83
Lasly, Alex 91
Lassater, Wm. 92
Lasser, James 79
John 79
Stephen 87
William 76
Lassiter, Alex 92
Brittain 16
George 21
Isham 73
Jacob 27
John 65, 84
Robert 21
Silas 73
Thomas 17
Latham, Alfred 7
Arnett 7
David 70
Lathem, William 20
Latta, James 25
Laughon, John 22

Launcan, John 84
Laurence, George 43
Nicholas 45
Samuel 42
Laving, Reuben 77
Law, Andrew 32
John 21
Lawler, John 28
Lawrann, Branson 100
Lawrence, Abram 29
Benjamin 66
Caleb 33
James 14
Malachai 99
Reuben 55
Lawrey, James 97
Laws, William 53
Lawson, Hiram 108
James 96
Jesse 72
Thomas 31, 116
Lawther, John 112
Layle, Robert 99
Layton, John 59
Lazenbury, Elias 38
Lazenby, Erasmus 58
Robert 108
Lea, Elam 80
James 46
John 31, 46
Larkin 46
Nathaniel 94
Reuben 90
Richard 112
Vincent 90
William 46, 112
Wm. 92
Leach, Elisha 103
Thomas 37
Lean, Aaron 10
Bird 26
George 28
Learcey, Asa 87
George 82
Samuel 87
William 85
Leary, Downing 69
Leath, Archibald 4
Thomas 8
Leay, Jesse 23
Ledbetter, Henry 112
Ledbury, Woodman S. 78
Ledford, Jesse 112
Lee, Anthony B. 5
Burwell 82
Edward, Sr. 11
Enoch 62
Gabriel B. 94
Henry 11, 21, 65
Isaac 33
James 62, 78
Jesse 13
John 11, 62
John W. 86(2)
John, Jr. 15
Jonathan 72
Josias 21
Lewis 64
Pharo 21
Richard H. 5

Thomas 12
William 21
Wright 84
Leech, Dugal 83
John 83
Leecham, Lemuel 109
Leek, Henry 66
Leeper, John 110
Lefever, James 46
Leffers, Samuel 56
Lefort, George 107
Leget, David 74
Legett, Harman 69
Jeremiah 65
Legget, Benjamin 70
Erick 82
Joseph 70
Legoe, John 84
Joshua 84
Leigh, Drury 90
Leight, John S. 35
Leimpoon, William 2
Lemay, Richard 89
Lemmond, George 32
Wm. L. 40
Lemon, Archivald [Archibald] 18
James 33
Lemons, James 46, 110
Lenhart, Joseph 110
Lenmon, William 33
Lenoir, - -mias [?] 117
Lenton, Luke 71
Lenville, George 97
Moses 97
Leod, William 57
Leonard, Isaac 32
James 3, 32
John 20
Linus 55
Obediah 32
Philip 104
Robert 85
Leopard, John 85
Lepford, William 17
Lesbury, James 59
Lester, John 63
Nathan 94
Lettimore, William 110
Levan, John 46
Levant, Benedict 111
Levity, Lewis 47, 58
Levy, Jacob 14
Lewin, Sterling 111
Lewing, Andrew, Jr. 105
John 105
Lewis, Briant 68
Bussee 89
Christopher 44
Daniel 108
David 9
George 71
Gideon 57, 100
Griffin 68
Guilford 19
Hardy 85
Henry 59
Isaac 100
James 8, 99
James, Jr. 54, 89
John 2, 20, 27, 56, 92

Joseph 37
Lewis 15
Martin 25
Nathaniel 71
Price Wm. 71
Robert 89
Samuel 89
Simon 22
Thomas 30
Thomas H. 83
Ully 10
Uriah 69
Wiben 10
William 13, 24, 34, 56, 57, 77, 79
Zacha 34
Libscomb, Thomas 51
Lickman, Henry 110
Henry, Jr. 110
Martin 110
Lieuter, George 29
Liggett, Martin 26
Light, John 41
Lile, Thomas 29
Liles, Edwyn 66
Harris 85
John 79
Martin B. 55
Lillard, Morgan 34
Lillington, John A. 7
Lilly, William 104
Limbory, James 92
Lincard, Jonathan 115
Linch, Edmond 90
John 56
Lincheum, Thomas 32
Lindley, Jonathan 92
Lindsay, James 45
Johnston 43
Reuben 95
Reubin 33
Lindsey, Asberry 68
George 115
James 26, 90
Linebarge, David 44
Linebarger, John 44
Lingle, Jacob 36
John 36
Lingo, William 26
Lingold, Elijah 32
Linguish, George 72
Link, Robert 59
Linker, David 108
George 41
Linn, Kisman 102
Linsey, James 90
Linton, Augustus 1
Burage 71
Linvill, David 34
Lippard, John 108
Lippart, Henry 35
Lipperd, William 108
Lippert, John 102
Lipps, Jacob 99
Lipscomb, Henry 89
Lirk, Robert 47
Liscomb, James 67
Lisk, Micajah 113
Lisley, John 79
Lissum, David 112

Litchworth, Frederick 8
Litten, John 114
Little, Archibald 92
    Bryant 75
    Enoch 84
    Erandal 74
    George 105
    Henry 104
    Isaac 24
    Jacob 81
    Jesse 84
    John 44, 57
    Joseph 48
    Josiah 56
    Matthias 115
    Robert 66
    Sherod 44
    Whitmil 92
    William 79, 109
Littleton, Benjamin 77
    Edmund 77
Litz, John 109
Livenger, Peter 36
Liverman, Daniel 4
    Isaac 6, 69
    Willis 69
Liversage, Thomas 65
Living, Barnard 36
Livingston, Martin 99
    Peter 57
Lloyd, James 77
    Thomas 18
Loafmand, Benjamin 32
Loar, James 94
Lochlan, Wm. 101
Lock, Aquilla 67
    Francis 51
    George 51
    Hezekiah 33
    Jonathan 79
    Robert 51
Lockart, Andrew 115
Locke, James 102
    John 51
Lockhart, Andrew 114
    John 84(2)
    Osborn 54
    Owen 73
Lockinbill, John 104
Locklear, Samuel 15
    Solomon 15
Locklier, Hugh 25
    Thomas 25
Lockrage, Samuel 113
Lofter, Bird 89
Loftin, Cornelius, Jr. 102
    John 59
    William J. 8
Logan, George 47
    John 42, 113
    Julius 46
Lolly, Jesse 17
Long, Adam 27
    Alexander 109
    Anthony 109
    David 59
    George 107
    Hardy 110
    Henry 38
    Ice 104

Jacob 79
John 27, 40, 107
John, Jr. 58
Jonathan J. 78
Joshua 69
Levi 55
Nickolas 93
Robert 55, 75
Thomas 44
William 83, 102
Longbottom, Joseph 43
Longmire, Robert 30
    Wm., Jr. 89
Lonona, John B. 36
Looper, William 38
Loops, Maulden 76
Loot, Stephen 92
Lopp, Jacob 104
Lorance, Peter 110
Lord, John 116
    Nicholas 17
Lore, Joseph 39
Lorraman, Joseph 81
Lorrik, George P. 9
Losset, John A. 15
Louis, Archibald 72
    Thomas 72
Love, Charles 15
    Christopher 105
    Daniel 22
    David 98
    Dell'd 49
    Harrison 11
    James 16, 107, 116
    John 48, 93
    Joseph 62
    Robert, Jr. 49
Loveing, William 11
Loveland, William 7
Loveleps, Edmond 98
Loveless, Asa 47
Lovell, Jacob 33
Lovelus, Thomas 38
Lovet, Benjamin 81
Lovick, James 9
Lovill, Edward 42
    Joseph 42
Loving, Briant 84
    Landerford 84
Lovit, Herod 73
Low, Exum 15
    George 63
    John 3
    Nixon 3
Lowden, Joel 95
Lowdor, Swinton 113
Lowe, James 36, 101
    Thomas 25, 67
    William 45
Lowry, Benjamin 3
    George 37
    Jethro 50
    John 3, 48
    Thomas 63
Loy, Henry 26
Loyd, David 95
    James 70
    Johnston 86
    Joseph 76
    Myerdoh 41

William 57
Wm. 88
Luallen, John 86
Lucanbill, Christian 36
Lucas, Allen 39
Lucaus [sic], Wilkins 32
Luced, Israel 83
    John 85
Luckey, Henry 37
    Richard 37
Lucky, Rob't 109
Luguire, Joseph 112
Luken, Jacob 105
Lumpkin, George 89
Lunding, William 5
Lunsford, Peyton 84
Luter, Thos. 90
Luther, Daniel 41
    Jos. 101
    Solomon 27
Lyerly, William 105
Lyhn, William 26
Lyman, Lawrence 17
Lymons, Asa 4
Lynch, Daniel 38
    Nicholas 11
    Thomas 26
Lynn, John 29
Lyod, John 29
Lyon, Elkanah 89
    Jas. G. 96
    Peter 96
    Robert 42
    Wm. V. 99
    Zackariah 88
Lyons, Elijah 64
Lysle, Joseph 88
Lytiker, Phillip 36

M

Ma-l-r [?], Oram 54
Mabane, George 91
    Gray 65
    Wm. 91
Macban, Jason 10
MacBeth, John 83
MacDonald, Eli 84
    John 83(2)
MacDuffie, Dugal 83
MacFarland, Malcom 83
Macgee, Archibald 83
MacInnis, John 84
MacIver, John 92
    John, Jr. 83
Mackey, James 34
    Josiah 3
MacKinnon, John 83
Macklewain, Richard F. 8
Mackney, Thomas 72
MacLane, Alexander 83
MacMasters, Rufus 93
Macner, William 80
Macon, Gideon H. 88
    Wm. 100
MacRae, Daniel 84
    Huncan [Duncan?] 84
Macray, John 103
Madaris, David 94
Madden, William 103
Maddux, Jesse 63

Made, Samuel 112
Mades, Jones 72
Madison, Payten 30
    Payton 30
Madre, John 63
Madrew, Richard 63
    Thomas, Jr. 63
Mafee, Samuel 115
Maga, Henry 32
    Thomas 33
Mage, Calvin 10
Maglanchlin, John 107
Maglehan, Arthur 74
Mahaly, Garret 43
Mahew, John 109
Mahoon, Henry 93
Mahow, James M. 7
Maiden, John 109
Mailer, Jacob 104
Main, Charles 43
Mainard, George 12
Mair, George 108
Mairs, Absalom 79
Makins, Stephen 11
Malcomb, Nathan 26
Malfrass, James 78
Mallard, Daniel 72
    Elijah 12
    George 80
    Jacob 80
    Shadick 72
Mallery, William 50
Malloy, Edward 82
Malone, Carter 31
    John 27
    Robert 93
Man, Edward 69
    Joseph 6
Manchy, Moses 12
Maner, Stephen 21
Manes, Richard 23
Mangam, Pleasant 30
Mangham, Wm. 96
Mangrum, Samuel 89
Manly, Arthur 15
    Frinifold 10
Mann, Calibourn 68
    Clalon 18
    German 68
    Haman 55
    James 31
    John 15, 30, 92, 116
    Martin 86
    Robert 31
    William 88
    Wm. 90
Mannels, Jacob 21
Manner, Isaac 21
    Jesse 21
Manney, Isaac 110
    Peter 110
Manning, James 68
    John 5, 17
    Joseph 61
    Joshua 67
    Marcum 75
    Willoughby 17
Manor, John 12, 22
Mansfield, Dachim 4
    John 94

George 92
McCullin, Council 20
  James 76
  Pitkin 20
McCulloch, Hunter 91
McCullock, Alex'r 109
  Alfred 103
  John 51, 106
  Jos. 90
  Robert 44
  Thomas 51
McCullok, James 13
McCullough, Hugh 70
McCullum, Angus 25
McCurdy, Samuel 59
  William 77
McCurry, Cazor 47
  Jacob 47, 58
  William 46
McCurston, Jesser 94
  John 94
McDade, Edward 90
McDaniel, Alex. 91
  Alfred 73, 90
  Aron 43
  Daniel 99
  David 10
  George 28
  Hugh 22
  James 12, 20
  John 73
  Kesdon 72
  Marshall 99
  Patrick 14
  Risdon 73
  Zeckeiah 112
McDate, John 108
McDavid, William 26
McDill, Isaac 95
McDonald, Alexander 24, 57
  Archibald 24
  Bartlett 66
  Donald 24
  Duncan 60
  James 24, 98
  John 22, 24, 43, 47, 58, 79,
    81
  Jonathan 105
  Joshua 13
  William 70, 84
McDongald, Duncan 82
McDonnell, Ignatius 103
McDougal, John 20
McDowel, Hugh 106
McDowell, Athan 48
  Benjamin 48
  Charles 53
  Freeman 8
  James 113
  John 48
  Mechat 53
  Nathan A. 61
McDuffee, Duncan 83
McDuffy, Daugle 41
  Dugald 57
  John 57
  Malcolm 22
McEachern, Duncan 81
  Malcom 81
McEacheron, Peter 82

McEachin, Gilbert 24
McEathan, Daniel 57
McEniston, Rob't 94
McEntire, William 112
McEntosh, George 45
McEwen, Daniel 79
  John 24
  William 79
McFallen, John 20
McFalls, Daniel 48
  James 113
McFarland, James 57, 116
  John 14, 47, 59
  Robert 108
  Samuel 108
  Thornton 90
  Wm. 88
McFarlin, Thornton 26
McFerson, Stephen 97
McGee, Blewford 53
  Isham 85
  Jesse 90
  John 100
  Ralph 53
  Tobias 81
McGehe, Gilliam 88
McGilvery, Malcolm 22
McGinley, John 107
McGinnis, James 44
McGire, Samuel 37
McGlanklin, David 88
McGlaughlin, John 4
McGlaulum, Luke 5
McGlawhon, Turner 55
McGraw, James 41
McGregar, Duncan 57
McGregor, Archibald 82
McGridor, Alexander 16
McGrmusey [sic], - - - [?] 117
McGruder, William 55
McGuffe, Hardy 85
McGuffee, Abraham 114
McGuin, Edward 112
McGuire, Hugh 20
  John 99
  Robert 108
McHague, Alexander 109
McHan, John 111
McHarney, James 62
McHenry, Enos 49
  John 49
McHock, Sammuel [sic] 24
McIlie, Thomas 40
McIlwines, Reyney 21
McInnis, Kenneth 24
McInnish, Duncan 83
McIntire, Samuel 112
McIntyre, Archibald 81
  Dugald 21
McInvail, Turner 54
McIver, Alexander 19
  Robert 83
McKackie, Allen 41
McKay, Alex 97
  Alexander 25, 57
  Cornelius 80
  Daniel 84
  Hugh 82
  James 25
  John 25, 82

Neal, Jr. 108
Neal, Sr. 108
  William 19
McKee, John 108
  Robert 19
McKeithan, Gilbert 79
McKellar, John 20, 25
McKellerand, Joseph 106
McKelro, Thomas 72
McKelvia, William 105
McKennon, Angus 83
  Neel 82
McKennoy, William 47
McKenny, John 12
McKenzie, Andrew 108
  Hugh 82
McKey, Joel 49
  Thomas 63
McKinly, Andrew 114
McKinney, Benjamin 72
  George 113
  Jacob 112
  James 69
McKinnon, Lauchlan 22
McKinsey, Hennith 41
  Kenneth 48
McKinsie, Hector 41
  Kenneth 24
  William 20
McKinzie, Anguish 52
  John 20
McKitchen, Dugald 20
McKnight, Hugh 35
  James 108
  Robert 106
McKoy, Elias 2
  Lewis 9
  Samuel 38
McLain, Charles 114
  John 107
McLanchlin, Duncan 83
McLane, John 83
McLauchin, Lauchlin 81
McLaughlan, Douglass 20
McLaughlen, James 38
McLaughlin, James, Sr. 102
  Samuel 102
Mclean, Donald 22
McLean, Duncan 19, 22, 82
  Hugh 82
McLelland, James 19
  John 20, 108
McLemore, Sugar 88
McLennan, Lechlin 24
McLeod, Alexander, Sr. 24
  Allen 83
  Archibald 24
  Daniel 82, 83
  Donald R. 78
  John 22, 24
  Murcock [Murdock?] 21
  Murdock 82
McLeon, Hector 25
  Neil 22
McLeran, Daniel 24
  Neil 24
McLewinnen, John 81
McLindon, Jesse 84
McListro, Younger 51
McLiven, Braxton 53

McLon, Andrew 116
McLoud, Angus 24
  Malcom 82
McLoyd, Daniel 40
McLure, John 39
McMahan, James 116
McMahew, James 107
McMasters, Aaron 92
  James 27
  Rufus 92
McMath, James, Jr. 28
McMillam, Anguish 19
McMillan, Archibald 57
  Duncan 25, 57
  Ever 78
  James 44, 82
  John 25, 82
  Neil 19, 81, 83
  Samuel 39
  Wm. 85
McMillian, Ever 79
  John 24
McMillion, William 51
McMin, Samuel 52
McMooney, Thomas 1
McMullen, Benjamin 116
McMurray, Thomas 20
McNabb, Alex 57
McNair, Daniel 24
McNealey, Timothy 102
McNeel, Archibald 82
McNeil, Archibald 57, 60
  Hector 20
  John 25, 81
  Malcolm 22
  Neil 20, 57
  Norman 20
  William 57
McNeill, Alex 82(2)
  Angus 83
  Daniel 82
  Neil 82
McOnnel, William 58
McPhallair, Daniel 25
McPhattair, John 81
McPhaul, John 81
McPherson, Alexander 24
  Hugh 82
  James 92
  John 35
McQuain, John 83
McQueen, Angus 25
  Hugh 81
McQuillar, Thomas 72
McRae, Alexander 24
  Christopher 24
  Daniel 25
  John 24, 41
  Jurguhard [sic] 24
  Murdoc 20
  Phillip 20
  Thomas 39
McRainey, Malcom 82
McRannolds, Hugh 112
McRee, David 107, 108
  James 81, 108
McReel, Meshart 7
McReely, Thomas 47, 59
McReley, Roderick 40
McRoy, Angus 108

McSween, Donald 24
  Fenly 24
  John 24
McTuller, Leven 65
Meador, Joel 85
Meadors, Elias 56
Meadows, Daniel 89
  Riley 89
  Samuel 109
  Thomas 72
Means, James 105
Mears, Joel 73
  John 108
  Richard 38
Measles, William 10
Meats, William 32
Meazel, Aaron 17
  Jesse 17
  Seth 17
Mebane, Alexander 51
  Allen 91
  George 25
  John 51
  William 26
Medcalf, Absolom 116
  David 84
Medders, James 29
Meddows, James 30
Medford, Daniel 17
  Ith [?] 75
Medlin, Alexander 22
  James 88
  John 22
  Kinchen 54
Medlock, Charles 48
Medor, Levi 84
Meed, William 32
Meek, James 106
Meekins, William 69
Meeks, Simpson 74
Meggs, John 84
Meginess, John 109
  William 109
Meguire, John 4
Mekellan [McKellan?], Alexander
  20
Mekins, Nathaniel 41
Melone, Abraham 114
Meloney, Kenon 73
Melton, Beuben [sic] 111
  John 111
  Reuben 77
  William 111
Melvan, James 92
Melvin, Daniel 79
Menice, James 113
Menos, Fred 102
Mentith, James 106
Mercer, Cornelius 61
  Jeremiah, Jr. 61
  Miles 62
  Reding 2
  Thomas 2
  William 62
Meredith, Green 4
Merick, John 38
Merner, John 110
Merrell, Eli 48
  Nimrod 48
  Samuel 8

Merrett, George 28
  John 41
Merril, Laza 100
Merrill, Eli 115
  Nimrod 115
Merrit, Benjamin 105
  James 14, 97
  John 88
  Thomas 67
  Wiley 81
Merritt, Felix 80
Merys, Gardner 44
Messenger, William 61
Messer, Burwell 84
  Ephraim 85
  Jeremiah 84
Messick, John 14
  Lean 14
Mesthinghams, Tobias 107
Mewbern, George 61
Mhoon [sic], John 65
Michael, David 104
Michaels, Thomas 113
Michel, John 58
Micks, Hardy 14
Middleton, George 33
  John 4, 116
  Robert 94
Midgett, Sparrow 69
Midgitt, Spencer 6
Midlin, Thomas 73
Mifee, William 48
Migett, Ricyhard [sic] 7
Migginson, John 24
Mikel, Jacob 100
Milcan, Lemuel 47
Miles, Augustus 106
  James 91
  Jonathan 92
Milken, Christopher 107
Millar, Anth'y N. 96
  David 115
  Fredrick 97
  Godfrey 97
  Harman 97
  Henry 98, 100
  John 100
  Joseph 70
  Joshua 72
  Randolph M. 79
  Richard 78
Millard, Bennet 80
Miller, Abraham 100
  Benjamin 12
  Charles 4, 65
  Frederick 34, 55
  Fulty 58(2)
  George 58, 102, 107
  Henry 34, 40, 73
  Isaac 27
  Isaiah 58
  Jacob 38, 45
  Jacob, Sr. 34
  James 24
  James B. 9
  John 45, 101, 104
  John, Jr. 80
  Jonathan 101
  Josiah 55
  Lewis 65

Mertin 36
  Nathaniel 61
  Reuben 64
  Silas 8
  Solomon 36
  Thomas 40
  Tobias 108
  William 9, 22, 34
  William K. 65
Milliken, Gilbert 110
  Samuel 101
Millington, Thos. 91
Mills, Britain 86
  Edward 52
  Ezekiel 27
  Fred, Jr. 8
  Frederick 8, 77
  James 77, 104
  John 100, 101, 105
  Naisby 74
  William 71, 74
Millsaps, Joseph 115
  William 38
Milsaps, John 59
  Joseph 109
Milson, Edmund 77
  John 13
Miltoe, Samuel 46
Milton, Henry 77
  Jeptha 41
  Jesse 46
  John 57
  Joseph 105
  Sterling 15
  William 46
  Wm. 83
Mims, Joseph 93
Minis, Elisha 6
Mink, Wm. 100
Minnis, James 91
Minor, John 55
  Lazarus 29
Minshew, John 10
Minster, John 101
Minter, Abner 92
Minton, Jason 65
  Valentine 67
Mires, Conrad 103
  Ezekiel 109
  Henry 104
  Thomas 61
Mirow [sic], Zedekiah 71
Miskingham, David 108
  Matthias 108
Mitch, Rheuben [sic] 77
Mitche, Silas 55
Mitchel, Cader 55
  Daniel 32
  Edmond 31
  George 10
  James G. 29
  Jesse 61
  John 13
  King 65
  Lemuel 18
  Samuel 38, 51
  Thomas 1
  William 13
  Zachariah 30
Mitchell, Archibald 88

  Cullen 15
  Daniel 13
  David 94
  Gilliam 89
  John 2, 30, 31, 76, 107
  Joshua 72
  Lemuel 68
  Reuben 85
  Robert 9
  Watson 93
  William 77, 108
Mitchiner, Samuel 87
Mizell, James 65
Mizells, George 65
  Lawrence 65
  Timothy 65
Mobley, Lurrel 81
Mobly, William, Jr. 34
Mock, Peter 103
  Phillip 104
Mofet, Jonathan 100
Moffet, Aaron 101
  Henry 101
Molenby, Lelin 34
Molesby, John 34
Molton, James 24
Monet, Peter 51
Monford, James, Jr. 73
  James, Sr. 72
Mongar, Wilson 66
Mongus, William J. 34
Monno [?], John 67
Monroe, Colin 78
  Hugh 84
  Mark 54
  Peter 81
Monser, John 110
Montague, John 30
  Young 89
Monteath, Thomas 48
Montford, William 15
Montgomery, Abraham 94
  George 32
  John 94
  John C. 6
  Robert 65, 106
  Samuel 32
Montgory [sic], William 116
Moody, Alexander 34
  Benjamin 38
  John 38
  Thomas 113
  Thomas L. 32
  William 38
Moon, John 75
  Joseph 38
Mooney, Arthur 79
  Christy 46
  Elias 70
  William 79(2)
Moor, William 41
Moore, Aaron 110
  Abijah 28
  Alexander 28, 39, 44, 47
  Alfred 15, 45, 63, 92, 112
  Alfred [?] 112
  Allen 64, 74
  Anthony 88
  Archibald 46
  Aron 45

Asin 51
Augustin 73
Barnwill 55
Benjamin 20, 78
David 39, 106
Ebenezer 102
Edw. 94
Edward 22
Elazard 54
Eleon G. 42
Geoge 90
George 45, 75, 78
Gideon 57
Gregory 67
Henry 74, 80, 86
Icabod 74
Jacob 74
James 39, 55, 88, 111
Jesse 15
John 20, 24, 31, 32, 78, 83,
    86, 111
John, Jr. 15
Jordan 13
Josephus 75
Joshua 71
Lain 29
Levi 39
Lewis 20
Mari 111
Matthew 96
Maurice 60
May 55
Moses 14, 55, 75
Needham 20
Presley 93
Radner 73
Robinson 109
Samuel 74
Samuel, Jr. 14
Thomas 26, 48, 55, 70
Thos. 91
Travner 115
Walker 73
William 14, 15, 26, 73
Williamson 93
Moorey, John 92
Mooring, William 8
Mooss [sic], Daniel 107
Morce, Isaac 84
Morefield, Wm. 100
Morel, John 84
Moreland, Francis 42, 99
    William M. 7
Morgain, Benjamin 5
Morgan, Andrew 71
    Benjamin 35
    Daniel 31
    Elias 95
    Ezekiel 108
    Hardy 41, 61
    Henry 18
    Hugh 63
    James 22, 99, 102
    Jesse 66, 111
    Joseph 41
    Joshua 43, 66
    Keder 63
    Laban 21
    Nathan 101
    Newit 16

Robert 95
Seth 65
Thomas 65
Valentine 33
William 17, 41, 43, 85
Willis 63
Winkfield 88
Wm. 99
Moring, Henry 73
Morissett, Phillip 2
Morris, Benjamin 22
    David 17
    Eaton 67
    Elias 42
    Harvey 71
    Henry 4, 29, 67, 111
    Isaac 26
    James 23, 29, 80
    Jessy 75
    John 13, 83, 107, 114
    Lawrence 98
    Leonard 31
    Nathan 17, 87
    Solomon 40
    Thomas 7, 70, 75, 89
    Thomas, Jr. 41
    William 63
    Wm. 100
Morrison, Andrew 37-39
    Archibald 25
    Argus 22
    Benjamin 20
    Daniel 44
    Henry 108
    Isaac, Jr. 106
    James 107
    Jno. 40
    John 39, 82, 83, 106
    Malcom 83
    Malcomb 33
    Neel 107
    Neil 22
    Robert C. 40
    Thomas 39(2)
    William 108
Morriss, Everret [sic] 68
    James 16
Morrissett, Tully 2
Morrow, Daniel 114
    John 51
    Joseph 49
Morse, Charles 6
    James 61
Morsham, James 24
Morten, James 108
Morton, John 77
    Joseph 72
    Stephen 41
    William 41, 72
Mosely, Joshua 9
    William 9, 73
Moser, Frederick 91
    Henry 40
    Tobias 51
Moses, Peter 34
Mosley, Joshua 73
Moss, James 36
    John 4, 103
    Thomas 85
    Tully 4

William 105
Mossman, Frederick 105
Mosteller, George 45
Motholand, John 18
Motsingen, Daniel 104
Mott, Benjamin 78
    Richbell 37
Motton, John 10
Mount, John, Jr. 34
    Matthias, Jr. 34
    Pleasant 34
Mourey, Peter 58
Moxley, Samuel 96
Moye, Franklin 74
    John 74
Mulder, George 23
    William 23
Mulford, John 79
Mulhollan, Henry 91
Mulholland, David 39
Mull, Peter 113
Mullen, Benjamin 49
    John 107
    Nathaniel 67
    William 9
Mullens, Jonathan 111
Mullinax, Isaac 110
Mullins, Thomas 28
Mullis, Francis 23
Mumford, Joseph 78
    Thomas 103
    William 8
Mumis, Allen 50
Munbollen, Hugh 25
Muncas, Elijah 42
    Joseph 42
Mund, Edward 104
Munden, Benjamin 4
    Elijah 3
    James 63
    William 3, 63
Munhollon, John 25
Munro, Neel 20
    Peter 20
Munroe, Daniel 83
Munteeth, William 40
Murchinson, William 23
Murchison, Angus 84
Murder, Samuel 67
Murdock, David 8
    John 39
Murdough, John 65
Murdy, William 58
Murett, Joshua 12
Murphray, Martin 19
Murphree, William 88
Murphrey, Parker 50
Murphy, Alexander 60
    Cornelius 14
    Daniel 84, 101
    Duncan 81
    James 19
    John 45, 95
    Joseph 113
    Patrick 19
    Wm. 99
Murrah, John 73
Murray, Andrew 91
    Bethue 6
    Joseph 27

Nathan 80
Robert 9
Walter 91
William 115
Murrel, John 77
Murrell, Isaac 109
    Kinchen 15
Murrey, William H. 115
Murry, Coleman 49
    James H. 88
    Samuel J. 48
    Thomas 115
    William 48, 49, 116
    Wm. 93
Muse, Joshua 7
    Lewis S. 29
    Richard 3
    Sampson 22
    Thomas 83
    William 72
Musgrove, John 10
Musick, George 113
Muskram, Arthur 97
Musslewhite, Jesse 25
    Reuben 81
Musuck, Austen 112
Myatt, Acril 85
Mydgett, Benjamin 69
    John 7
    Lewis 69
Myers, George 36, 38
    Jacob 59, 104
    John 97
    John, Sr. 36
    Michel 36
    Thomas 3
Myre, Daniel 103
    Michael 103
    Philip 103
Myres, Ashur 84
Myrick, Azel 28
    Cornelius 28
    James 28
    James C. 57
    John 22
    Moses 83
    Owen F. 18, 67

N

Nail, Alexander 52
Nailing, Wm. 88
Nailor, Abram 21
Nance, Egreppy [sic ?] 30
    Egrippy 88
    James, Jr. 54
    William 109
    William, Jr. 109
    Wyatt 85
Nancy, James 111
    Nicholas 47, 58
Napper, Hughs 99
Nar, Edward 6
Nardlike, Jonathan 44
Naresworthy, William 66
Narris, Samuel 86
Nash, George 85
    Josiah 3
    Stephen 24
    Wilson 61
    Wilson W. 3

Nawl, John 87
NayBo, Alex. 91
NayUts, Alex. 91
Neagle, John 44
Neal, Cudberth 67
  Cudburth 18
  John 97
  Thomas 85
Neale, Abner 8
  Reuben 87
  Samuel 97
  Thomas 5
Neathery, Samuel 99
Neblock, Johnsten 101
Needham, James 64
  Lot 63
  Samuel 62
Neel, Clayton 114
  Jacob 97
  Samuel 107
Neele, Andrew 41
  George 96
  James 41
  Robert 96
  Samuel 107
Neeley, Samuel 106
Neil, Andrew 108
  Samuel 35
Neill, William 48
Neilsmall, Reddick 19
Nellum, David 31
Nelms, James 19, 88
  John 87
  Willis 29
  Wm. 93
Nelson, Abisha 72
  Abram 38
  Alexander 13
  Benj. B. 93
  Caleb 74
  Charles 9
  Elijah 96
  Elisha 35
  Frost 103
  Jacob 96
  James 33
  Jesse 93
  John 116
  Jordan 74
  Naboth 74
  Samuel 51
  Thomas 27, 72
  William 27, 35, 103
Nelums, William 30
Nesbet, Ross 52
Nesbitt, Alexander 53
Never, Eli 68
Nevill, Elijah 67
Nevin, Daniel 28
New, Gilbert 78
  John 79
  William 14
Newby, Exum 4
  Mexum [sic] 63
Newcomb, Thomas 58
Neweam, Richard 111
Newel, Francis 59
Newell, Eli 59
  Hardy 50
  Jesse 50

Thomas 50
Newit, William 41
Newman, Benjamin 111
  Thomas 18
  William 112
  Willis 50
Newsman, Thomas 68
Newsom, Benjamin 16
  Riggan 16
  Samuel 99
  Willis 73
Newson, Cordal 16
  Elijah 10
  Jacob 10
  John 16
  Joseph 10
  Seamore 16
Newsum, Randolph 15
Newton, Hardy 13
  Henry 26
  Jacob 37
  James 47, 59
  William 112
Nibleek, Wilson 102
Nichilson, Abel 43
  Ephraim 43
  Nathan 4
  Thomas 15
  William 3
Nicholas, Neal 56
  Samuel 77
Nichols, Alsey 54
  Amos 26
  David 3
  Eli 23
  Isaac 23
  Jeremiah 34
  John 26
  Joseph 47, 58
  Kinchen 14
  Moses 9
  William 74
  Willie 54
Nicholson, Guilford 15
  James 1, 107
  John 19
  Samuel 61
  Wallis 14
Nickolas, Amos 90
  George 90
Nickolls, William 61
Nickols, Elisha 79
  Jeremiah 78
  Robert 78
  William S. 78
Nickolson, James 115
  John 83, 94
  Nathaniel 87
  Peter 81
Nicolson, Jos. 100
Niehilson [sic], Daniel 25
Night, Elijah 35
  William 31
Nighton, James 94
  John 31
  Turner 31
Nillens, Curtis 81
Nilman, Wekins [sic] 46
Nipper, Samuel 30
  William 31

Nisler, David 107
Nixon, Delight 4
  James 77
  Richard 60
  William 78
Noals, William 87
Nobles, Eli 79
Noblet, John 28
Noles, David 12
  Stephen 80
None, John 40
Nooton [sic], Aaron 98
Norman, Aquilla 69
  Daniel 99
  Eliakim [sic] 6
  George 99
  Henry 69
  Isaac 98
  James 96
  John 45
  Thomas 16
  William S. 106
  Wm. 101
Normand, Isham 31
  Westly 31
Norris, James 20
  John 94, 99
  Noel 28, 54
  Peyton 86
Norriss, James 80
  William 74
Norten, Berry 24
North, Danut 33
Northam, Eli 25
  James 1
Northcut, James 67
  William, Jr. 80
Northern, Elijah 36
  Frederick 61
  James 61
  Walter 36, 102
Northington, Allen 20
  Jesse 20
Norton, Silas 83
Norvil, James 75
Norwood, Burwell 66
  John 30, 51, 93
  Samuel 66
Norworthy, John 15
  Thomas 16
Notton, Septhen 77
Nowell, John 16
Nowells, Luke 75
Noxon, Martin 61
Nuby, Exum 3
Nunby, Reuben 37
Nunn, Hie [sic] 29
Nunnery, William 20
Nunon, Edward 34
Nusman, John 107
Nutt, Cader 29
  Elhannon 54
  Robert 54

O

O'Brian, John 50
O'Briant, Elijah 89
O'Bryan, Lewis 73
O'Conner, Dennis 16
O'Kelly, Zenas 85

O'Neal, Asa 69
  James 103
  John 26
  Spencer 62
O'Neale, Levi 7
O'Neill, John F. 113
Oakley, Mark 90
  McFarland 90
  William 30
Oaks, Barnard 48
  John 38, 48
  Lemmuel 94
Oats, Jesse 57
  John 82, 110
  Robert 44
Ochiltree, Murdoch 82
Odium, Thdolifus [sic] 72
Oens, John 97
Ogborn, Nicholas 32
Oglesby, Archibald 113
  Thomas 58
  William 58, 113
Oldham, Ephraim 92
Olery, Robert 20
Olington, James W. 34
Oliphant, George 79
Olive, James 29
  John 29
Oliver, Alexander 83
  Andrew 5
  Charles 78
  Everet 66
  Francis 89
  Frederick 69
  George 44
  Isham 86
  James 73
  John 111, 116
  Josiah 89
  Lewis 13, 77
  Thomas 42, 93
  William 18, 22, 35, 44, 68
Oman, James 77
Oneal, Frederick 11
  Henry M. 113
  John 80
  Micajah 87
  Stephen 87
Oniel, William 23
Onions, William 15, 67
Orchillred, Murdock 20
Orion, John 22
Ormand, Adam 40
  Jacob 83
  Samuel 40
Orme, William 77
Orneal, Michael 2
Orr, Luten 78
  Nathan 52
  Robert 115
Orsburn, Robert A. 106
Orton, James 37
Osborn, Jeremiah 115
  John 115
Osbourn, Thomas 42
Osburn, Christopher 107
  John 32
  Joseph 12
Osby, Meady 79
Ostian, Caleb 80

Otary, Starling 21
Outland, Thomas 76
Outlaw, David 56
  Jesse 12
  John 5
  Levi 55
  Noah 65
  Ralph 65
Overcast, Jacob 107
Overman, Reuben 3
  Samuel 3
Overstreet, James 14
  Moses 83
Overton, Elisha 64
  Jacob 64
  John 72
  John C. 96
Owen, Abraham 102
  Bleasant [sic] 38
  Elijah 94
  Ezekiah 102
  James 22, 36
  Martin 102
  Thomas 103
Owenby, Arthur 47
Owens, Aaron 100
  Alfred 36
  Dempsey 75
  Ezekiel 81
  James 7, 37, 62
  John 47
  Joseph 83, 114
  Joshua 48
  Levi 90
  Raleigh 47
  Reuben 91
  Stephen 69
  Thomas 81, 103
  William 47, 88
Owerly, Arthur 59
Ownby, William 113
Ownley, John 46
Ownsby, John 112
  Sims 112
Owrey, Michel 41
Oxendine, Charles 25

P

Pack, Austin 114
Padge, Silas 96
Padgett, Abraham 112
  Nehemiah 112
Page, Absalom 74
  Amos 94
  Balentine 17
  Benj. 101
  Burwell 75
  Joseph, Jr. 75
  Lawrence 75
  Owen 81
  Samuel 96
  William 22
Paget, David 78
  Lemuel 48
Paim, John 101
Pain, Benjamin 37
  John 104
  Joseph 4
  Solomon 30
  Thos. 100

  William 38
Paine, David 69
  Micajah 47
  Mitchel 6
  Robert 50
  Thomas 20
Painter, Leonard 46
  Wyatt 89
Paisley, Hezekiah 99
Palin, Thomas 63
Pall, Colin 41
Pallen, John 87
Palmer, George 105
  John 49, 115
Paquanett, Jacob 72
  John 72
Parham, Mathew 105
  Mitchel 114
  Thomas 54
Parish, Absalom 88
  Alexander 61
  Andrew M. 105
  Edward 6
  Frederick 68
  Hillsman 86
  James 90
  Joel 26, 88
  John 42, 96
  Jones 61
  Joseph 84
  Jyre [sic] 28
  Nicholas 39
  Noel 32
  Reuben 30, 33
  Tyrel 54
  Wm. G. 97
Park, James 37
Parke, George 106
Parker, Abram 5
  Allen 21, 86, 93
  Daniel 80
  Darus 66
  Elisha 4
  Francis 16
  Gabriel 9
  George 89
  Hardy 82
  Harrison 26, 90
  Henry 9
  James 2, 6, 39, 64
  Jesse 64
  John 9, 14, 16, 39, 75, 78, 84, 93, 106
  Jonathan 73
  Kindred 64
  Lea 82
  Luke 5, 22
  Michel 17
  Miles 5
  Mills 67
  Morris 16
  Moses 57
  Payton R. 80
  Robert 5, 64
  Samuel 16, 64
  Theophilus 16
  Thomas 2, 95
  Thomas B. 14
  William 65, 77
  Willis 29

  Zachariah 80
  Zepheniah 80
Parkes, John, Sr. 105
  William 8
Parkey, Jesse 55
Parks, Allen 29
  Benjamin 47
  David 91
  Hiram 31
  James 47, 58
  James M. 53
  Jepthah 31
  John 9, 42, 98
  Jonathan 61
  Joseph 108
  Joshua 99
  Noah, Jr. 101
  Reuben 48
  Samuel 53, 105
  William 29
Parmarle, Timothy 70
Parmer, John 110
  William 14, 33
Parnell, John 82
Parr, James 61
  Jesse 1
  Peter 61
Parram, Littleton 46
Parris, Peter 71
Parrish, James 58
Parrot, Charles 51
  John 89
Parson, James 104
Parsons, Richard 71
  Robert 32
  Thomas 104
Partin, Benjamin 67
  John 104
Parvis, William 25
Paskill, John 29
Pass, James H. 94
Passenger, Methias [sic] 107
Passmore, Enock 100
Pate, Bryan 73
  Charles 81
  Daniel 25
  Elias 24
  John 83
  Zachariah 9, 81
Patillo, Edward 67
Patrick, Isaac 71
  Shelby 6
Patridge, Jesse 28
Patten, Alex 91
  Alexander 26
Patterson, Archibald 82
  Berry 98
  David 51, 97
  Edward 22
  Isaac 31, 94
  James 45, 110
  Joel 42
  John 22, 36, 84
  John S. 109
  John, Jr. 87
  Julius 97
  Malcomb 21
  Mathew 49
  Nathan 87
  Peter 24

  Robert 49, 95
  Samuel 66
  Thomas 26
  William 27
  Wilson 32
Pattin, Bennet 90
  Lewis 90
Pattison, Archibald 19
  Malcom 20
Patton, George 53
  John 115
  John M. 49, 115
  M. Haustin 115
Paul, Benjamin 67
  Irra [sic] 70
  Wm. 98
Pawnly, Luke 14
Paxton, John 53
  Richard 61
Payner, Samuel 62
Peace, Henry 98
  Isaac 5
  James 54
  John T. 30
Peacock, Abraham 73
  Asa 27
  Isaac 70
  Jacob 87
  Jesse 11, 77
  John 11(2)
  Noah 11, 76
  Simon 76
  Wiley 76
  William 102
Peal, Jesse 17, 98
Peale, John 12
  Willis 87
Pealer, Jesse 102
Pealor, Anthony 102
Peane, Hardy 85
Pearce, Arthur 76, 87
  Asa 84
  Ason 23
  Benjamin 14, 80
  Durham 33
  Ezekiel 58
  Isham 6
  Jehu 17
  Jesse 50
  Loverd 11
  Meredith 37
  Moses 23, 84
  Pleasant 50
  Sion 41
  Thos. 100
  William 23, 64
  William A. 77
  Wm. 100
Pearcy, Bryant 33
Pearson, Asey 82
  Edward 13
  Henry 18
  Jesse A. 35, 60
  Joon [John?] 99
  Jos. 92
  Preston 29
  Samuel 29
  Stephen 86
  William 73
Peartree, John 7

Peaster, William 64
Peck, Ezra 14
   John 103
   Louis F. 57
Peckham, Mouncen 70
Peddy, John 86
Peden, Amos 11
   John 11
Peebels, John 67
Peebles, Anderson 18
Peed, Cyrus 45
Peel, Elisha 5
   Reddick 5
Peele, Joel 66
   John 55
   Lewis 75
Peettigrew [sic], Ebenezer 69
Pegford, William 14
Pegg, Jesse 33
   Joab 33
   John 33
   Martin 33
Pegram, John 95
Pelet, Amos 74
Pelon, Asa 64
Pelt, Jonathan 74
   Simon V. 106
   William 107
Pemberton, Edward 19
   Thomas 52
Pender, David 75
   James 55
   John 11
   William 11
Pendleton, Henry 63
Pendry, Jonathan 42
Penix, Thos. 94
Penland, Abraham 115
   George 116
   James 48
   Robert 116
Penly, Jonathan 114
Penney, John 76
Pennington, James 80
   Joshua 100
   Wm. 93
Penny, Francis 51
Pennywell, William 75
Peoples, Richard 106
Peppin, Banister 88
Perdue, Daniel A. 18, 67
   Isham 67
   John 94
   Philemon 68
   Phlemon 18
   Robert 99
   Rowland 30
Perkins, Alexander 53
   Charles 62
   George 62
   James 23, 96
   Job 4
   John 48
   Jonathan 8
   Levi 44
   Linkfield 71
   William 1
Perkinson, Valentine 68
Pernerter, James 55
Perry, Albert 19

   Barnabas 91
   Bennett 19
   Bennt 85
   David 78
   Francis 105
   Jacob 4
   James 13, 28, 64
   John 68, 85
   John G. 19
   Kader 63
   Micajah 17
   Noah 3
   Reuben 11
   Richard 100
   Simon 75
   Solomon 87
   William C. 19
   Wm. 92
Persithe, Samuel 30
Person, Henry 67
   Nathaniel 49
   Wiles 18
   Willis 68
Persons, Levi 4
Persyth, Samuel 30
Pertilla, Edward 18
   William 18
Peters, Redding 8
Peterson, Aron 22
   Daniel 45
   Duncan 81
   Gabriel 81
   Jacob L. 58
   James 116
   Samuel 111
Petery, Henry 107
Petman, James 76
Pettes, John D. O. K. 52
Pettiford, Lervey 30
   Moses 30
Pettiger, Abraham 4
Petty, John 75
   Wm. 98
Pew, Nathaniel 110
   Samuel 109
Pharis, Daniel 57
   Duncan 21
Phelps, Charles 69
   Darius 69
   Evin 69
   Hezekiah 69
   Killion 52
   Lovet 38
   Thomas 104
   William 88
   Willibough 69
Phifer, Matthias 102
Philips, Bennet 98
   Dixon 87
   Enock 102
   Frederick 93
   Henry 83
   Isaac 96
   James 101
   John 81, 103, 106
   Wm. 85
   Zacheriah 92
Phillippie, Leonard 95
Phillips, Aswell 115
   Benj. 92

   Charles 7
   Curtis 9
   Edmund 99
   Frederick 28
   Henry 10
   Isaac 92
   Jacob 23
   Jeremiah 7
   Jesse 66
   John 22, 39, 48, 73
   Joseph 5
   Kinchin 5
   Michel 3
   Peter 9
   Phillip 38
   Ralford 22
   Ransom 5
   Robert 71
   Spencer 9
   William 13
Philpot, Samuel 8
Phinney, Joseph 42
Phips, Isaac 12
Picket, Joseph 14
Pickett, Jacob 78
   Walker 91
Pickhart, Elisha 91
   Jesse 91
Pickle, Henry 9
   Richard 9
Pickler, James 103
Pickolson, Mathew 75
Pierce, James 66
   John 27, 103
   Peleg 14
   Whitel 17
Piercy, Ephraim 49
Pigett, William 72
Pigg, William 42
Pike, Joseph 4
Pilano, Richard 16
Pilcher, James 43
   John 99
Pilear, Jacob 58
Pilkinton, Anthony 28, 54
Pilley, John 70
Pindar, James 91
   Thomas 10
Piner, Josiah 14
Pinkard, Thomas 117
Pinkham, Nathaniel 72
Pinkston, Morris 36
Pinner, Arthur 56
   James 14
Pinney, Isaac 87
Pipes, Hiram 99
Pipkin, Bryan 76
   Joseph 10
   Need 10
   William 10
Pippen, Breedlove 19
Pippin, Etheldred 50
   Lalathel [?] 81
Pirant, William 40
Piror, Samuel 52
Pitell, Benj. 98
Pitle, Isaac 34
Pitman, Brittain 17
   Dempsey 24
   Jacob 25

   John 12
   Reuben 17
Pitt, Edmond R. 29
   Isaac V. 39
Pittard, Thos. 93
Pittcord, Kelan 35
Pittman, Dempsey 67
   Elijah 82
   Elijah V. 72
   Jesse 81
   John 71
   Joseph 75
   Michael 101
   Thomas 72
Pitts, Hardy 13, 77
   John 67
   Philip 113
Piver, James 72
   Samuel 72
Pleasants, Joseph 88
Pledger, Joseph 69
   William 66
Pledget, George W. 66
Plemmons, Andrew 49
   John 49(2)
   John, Jr. 49
Plot, Elias 45
Plumber, Samuel 19
Plummer, Aaron 78
   Edward 79
   James 52
Plunkett, Richard D. 107
Pobete, Elrod 113
Poe, Hasten 92
Poindexter, Archer 42
   Francis A. 99
   Wm. 96
Pollard, Equilla 8
   Hansford 96
   John 96
   Willie 85
Pollock, John 80
Polson, John 64
Polyard, Joseph 9
Ponder, Joseph 115
Pool, Elijah 111
   Farniford 73
   Hardy 86
   Howard 54
   James 87
   John 51
   Joshua 63
   Moses 73
   Patrick 51
   Phillip P. 30
   Samuel 79
   Theophilus 87
   William 40
Poole, Jacob 102
Pope, Archibald 76
   Barnathy 66
   Benjamin 22
   David 112
   Hardy 25
   Henry 21
   Jacob 84
   James 104
   Jesse 10
   John 22
   Juni [?] 81

Thomas Gaines 115
Warren 103
Wiley 29
William 114
Willis 3, 90
Robertson, And. 96
Buck 18
Calvin 42
Clisby 35
David 43
Doc't M. 18
Edward 115
Elisha 5
Enoch 55
Eps 36
George 116
George W. 38
Hugh 37, 104
Isaac 8
James 4, 40, 106
John 18, 49, 57, 96
Joshua 8
Newmon 29
Robert 87
Thomas 48
Thos. 96
Timothy 5
Will 40
William 56, 104
Wm. 99
Robeson, Amos 109
Archibald 79
David 17
Elias 58
Henry 17
Jesse 2, 8
John 78, 112
Joseph 52, 83
Nathaniel 27
Noah 17
Samuel 17, 21, 116
William 24, 78, 79, 83
Robinet, James 58
Robinett, Allen 99
Robins, Alexander 27
Daniel 101
Enoch 70
Joel 56
Joseph 47
Thomas 47
Robinson, Allen 72
Edward 67
George, Jr. 81
Israel 97
Jesse 61
Jonathan 111
Joshua, Jr. 75
Robert 59
William, Jr. 44, 81
Robison, John 52
Robling, Lewis 103
Robson, Niel 14
Rockell, Benjamin 78
Rockett, Alsey 54
Rockford, William 109
Roddick, Timothy 73
Roden, Upton 39
Rodes, Wilson 104
Rodford, Miles 76
Rodgers, George 92

William 65
Roe, James 78
Robert 66
Roebuck, William 75
Rogers, Benjamin 54, 56
Chewry 11
David 49, 115
Edmond 17
Elisha 22
Giles 30
James 73, 107, 115
John 6, 51
Joseph 30, 39
Joseph, Jr. 108
Micajah 41
Nicholas 80
Ozni 107
Samuel 54
Stephen 49
Thomas 115
William 17, 116
Wm. 101
Rogerson, Abel 3
David 17
John 17
John, Jr. 63
Josiah 75
Rolan, Abel 41
Isaac 32
Rolins, John 105
Roll, John 71
William 56
Rollins, Miles 56
Richard 11
Rone, James 106
Rooker, John 112
Rooks, Job 10
Joseph 78
Timothy 78
Rorden, James 98
Jeremiah 98
Rose, Benjamin 43
Duncan 31
Edward 69
Fracis [sic] 97
Joel 100
Philip 92
Sterling 43
William, Jr. 10
Wm. 101
Rosea, Jonathan 43
Roser, Arris 23
Ross, Alexander 52
Dennis 114
George 111
James 35, 40, 95, 107
John 24, 114
John, Sr. 36
Leaven 51
Levy 32
Thomas 17, 32
Rosser, Horantio 84
Rosson, Bennona 92
Ira 92
Rothwell, Jonathan 56
Rough, Philip 114
Roughton, Ozias 6
Roulhac, John M. 69
Roundtree, Obed 8
Rouse, David 12

John 83
Lewis 80
Row, Jacob 18
Rowbuck, John 17
Raleigh 17
Rowe, Henry 41
Rowell, Hermon 16
Rowland, Alfred 19
Joel 105
Mitchel 57
Rowling, Gardener 83
Rows, Thomas 73
Rowse, Burwell 10
Roy, John 8
Royal, Isom 81
John 81
Willis 21
Royall, Hardy 22
Royals, John 81
Owin 81
Royer, Samuel 101
Royster, John 89
Wm. 90
Rozwell, James 94
Rudaice, John 45
Rudasil, Henry 44
Rudd, Pleasant 31
Ricardo 6
Rudisil, John 36
Rudsil, Jonas 110
Rue, Hardy, Jr. 71
John 13
Ruffin, John 55
Joseph 75
Thomas 65, 90
Whitmell 65
Rulland, Whitmel 15
Rumage, Mathew 23
Rumbley, Thos. 92
Rumfelt, Ebner 110
Rumple, Philip 101
Rundles, Elsy 115
Runnels, Coleman 56
Runnion, James 49
Runnols, James 84
Runyan, Jeremiah 52
Rupard, Peter 52
Rush, James 20
Reuben 100
Zebidee 100
Rushing, Asa 23
John 23
Stephen 84
Rusley, Richard 12
Russ, David 79
George 79
William 6
Russand, James 51
Russel, Elijah 13
Ezra 82
John 89
Jordan 105
Joseph 104
Levi 104
Martin 104
Robert 95
William 105
William, Sr. 104
Russell, Aaron 104
David 9

Isaick 102
Jarrett 104
John F. 84
Louis 57
Major 41
Nevil 56
Samuel 101
Russon, John 24
Ruston, John 101
Ruth, James 112
James B. 29
Rutherford, John 49, 100
Robert 29
Ruthoen, Daniel 82
Rutland, Johnston 56
Redden 56
Rutledge, John 98
Ryal, Parks 71
Ryan, Hyram 43
John 42
Peter 21
Ryer, Charles 36
Ryke, Michel 27
Ryman, James 56
Rynalds, Nicholas 104
Ryne, John 44
Ryno, Elisha 16
Ryold, David 21
Owen 21
Ryolds, Whiting 21
Ryon, William 21

S

S-lah [?], Jesse 49
Sadler, Henry 109
John 105
Richard 70
Thomas 109
Sailer, Mickael 97
Sale, John 43
Salenger, Rebuen [sic] 75
Sales, Clemm 81
Saller, Joseph 56
Salmon, Samuel 20
Salmons, John D. 97
Salter, Edward T. 8
James 20
Walace [sic] 56
Sammons, James 101
Thomas 15
Sammons [sic], William 77
Sampson, Benjamin 90
Sams, John 49
Samuel, Archibald 93
Harbert 93
Lewis 94
Rowzee 94
Sand, Robert 12
Sandeford, Elisha 88
Sandefur, John, Jr. 15
Sandelin, Ezekiel 115
Sander, John 89
Sanderford, Noah 84
Sanderlin, Abner 2
Forebee 62
Josiah 62
Sanders, Benj. 100
Britton 28
Edward 52
John 56

Joseph 8
Larkin 91
Lemuel 65
Luke 94
Samuel 72
Seth 69
Sherrod 87
William 48, 71, 88
Sanderson, Amos 72
Joseph 2
Joy 7
Thomas 70
Sandifurd, Charles 54
Sanding, Ebrey 13
Sandler, Trininger 2
William 80
Sandline, James 13
Sandy, Uriah 71
Saner, George 37
Sanford, Linas 44
Sankard, Andrew 109
Saoars, Charles 61
Sap, Brummel 37
Sargent, Dempsey 93
James 46
Sarsnot, John 76
Sasser, Frederick 23
John 10
Sattenfield, Michael 111
Satterswhite, Solomon 30
Satterwhite, Anderson 89
Saulter, Henry 72
Saunders, Benjamin 15
Edward 4
Elisha 110
Hardy 12
James 13
Jesse 14
John 5
John, Jr. 12
Richard 77
Robert 14
Solomon 99
Savage, Charles 36
Hezekiah 63
James 27
John 20
William 16, 75
Sawers, Henry 104
Sawyer, Archibald 3, 40, 62
Charles 1, 61
Enoch 3
Freeman 62
Hollowell 1
Isaac 63
James 2, 62, 63
Joseph 1, 61
Maxsey 62
Miles 69
Robert 63
Thomas 6
Willis 69
Wilson 70
Zephaniah 7, 62
Sax, Joseph 6
Scaboro, Edward 52
Scales, Alfred 95
John 95
Scarborough, Isaac 75
James 80

Jesse 78
Samuel 105
Thomas 2
Willie 104
Scarbrough, Benjamin 10
Miles 54
Scarlet, Lewis 27
Scarlott, John 90
Scentill, Richard 115
Scoggin, Charles 46
John 89
Samuel 46
William 45
Scott, Benjamin 13, 83
Charles 77
Cornelius 3
David 13
Edward 3
Herbert 16
Hillery 46
Isaac 13
Isham 84
James 31
John 5, 14, 15, 28, 29, 39
Larkin 38
Patrick 47
Reuben 16
Samuel 49
Stephen 3
Will 40
William 24, 83, 107
William A. 105
Wyett 41
Scotte, Daniel 35
Scruggs, - - [?] 112
P - - [?] 112
Scull, John 5
Seabold, Ludwith 32
Seabrook, Daniel 69
Seagraves, William 104
Seagroves, Stephen 86
Seales, James H. 34
Seall, John 65
Seamon, Joseph 62
Searcy, Aron 20
Lemi 82
Seares, William 30
Searsey, Samuel 20
Seaton, William W. 29
Seaward, John 70
Seawell, German 21
Jacob 21
Sebastian, Hezekiah 99
Sedberry, David 105
Sedford, William 53
Segimore, John 35
Selby, Burrige 7
Samuel 69
Sell, Jonathan 97
Sellars, Daniel 79
Duncan 78
John 78
Seller, George 110
Sellers, Abram 22
Benjamin 11, 56
Elisha 79
John 11
Richard 12
William 12, 79
Semple, Samuel 53

Senter, Joseph 44
Sergant, Noah 111
Serjiner, Thomas 83
Serkin, John 34
Sessions, Isaiah 23
Sessoms, William 64
Sessums, Joseph 76
Settle, Josiah 95
Setton, Edward 30
Samuel 111
Sewell, Jacob 5
James 9
Jethro 5
William 64
Sewit, James 29
Sexton, Miller 28, 54
Seth 86
Seymore, Peter 2
Shackleford, John 31
Shafer, John 110
Shamel, Jacob 97
Shamell, Peter 97
Shank, Martin 41
Shanklin, Robert 91
Shanks, Charles 27
Shannon, James 110
John 2
Nathan 2
Robert 40
Sharp, Benjamin 55
Eli 31
Fans 58
John 96
William 33, 40
Sharpe, Amos 60
John 75
Sharpless, Thomas 14
Sharply, William 39
Shavener, John 70
Shaver, Jacob 40
Shaw, Alexander 24
Colin 19
Daniel 20
Findley 51
Henry 32
James 67, 107
Jepeth 44
Jesse 95
John 20(2)
John, Jr. 82
Jos. 95
Joseph 86
Joseph B. 51
Malcom 24
Robert 20
Simon 99
Simpson 25
Thomas 27
William 70
Shearer, Andrew 100
John 100
Shearod, John 64
Sheaver, Frederick 32
Sheets, David 103
Sheffield, Everitt 22
Nicholas 29
Shehorn, Morris 106
Shelby, Joseph 109
William 84, 95, 106
Shelfer, John 72

Shellers, Moses 78
Shelly, William 33
Shelton, Freeman 109
Lodiman 67
Menucan 45
Willis 14
Shelvey, William 105
Shemeel, Henry 102
Shepard, Isham 83
James 90
John 77
Joseph 115
Thomas 83
Sheperd, Peter 115
Shepherd, Andrew 53
Egbert 91
Henry 13, 26
Joseph 49
Josiah 24
Thomas 39
Woodman 14
Sheppard, Larkin [?] 99
Shepperd, John 32
Joshua 13
Wader 24
Sherod, Edward 55
Elisha 18
Gabriel 11
John M. 19
Selathiel 17
Sherrell, Colbert 45
Sherren, Elish [sic] 67
Lewis 68
William 68
Sherril, Alfred 111
John 29
Sherrin, Lewis 18
William 18
Sherwood, Edwin 75
Neil 4
Shewcraft, Silas 64
Shields, John 14
Shillington, John 52
Shine, Elias 111
Shiner, Aaron 54
Shines, William 8
Shinner, Benjamin 4
Ship, John 1
Peter 15
Robert 98
Shipman, Edward 48
Shipp, Bartlet 96
John 42, 58, 71
Reading 8
Wm. 96
Shipton, John 102
Shipwash, William 81
Shirley, David 73
Kelly 97
Shiver, Edward W. 77
Shivers, John 34
Shoaf, John 102
Shoemaker, John 43
Tarlton 52
Shook, George 111
Shoolders [?], Cullen 65
Shoots, Bryant 55
Shore, Henry 99
Ramsome 99
Short, James 84, 102

Smithall, George 102
Smitherman, John 27
Smithson, William 63
Smithwick, Joel 75
    John 17
Smithwitk [sic], Luke 65
Smitteds, Conrad 35
Smoot, Hiram 99
    Thomas 103
Smothers, William 33
Smoyer, Jacob 52
Smyth, James 98
Snead, Hanly 24
Sneed, Benjamin 51
    Edward 45
    Reuben 41
Snell, Hiram 6
    Roger 6, 69
Snider, George, Jr. 37
    Henry 101
    Jacob 104
    John 107
    William 1
Snipes, Robert 66
    Wm. 87
Snow, Hail 98
    John 58, 97
    Levi 58
    Thos. 97, 98
    William 35
Snowden, Isaac 62
    James 62
    Thaddeus 3
Snyder, John 111
    Joseph 6
Sohlar, Archibald 113
Sollace, Joseph 80
Solomon, Bennet 105
    Drury 40
    Jeremiah 87
Solon, John 39
Somers, James 31
Sommerlin, Frederick 74
    Henry 80
Sorrals, William 113
Sorrat, William, Jr. 102
Sorrel, Jacob 86
    James 20
Sorrell, Thomas 56
Sorsby, Samuel 17
Sossiman, John 107
South, Nathan 12
Southam, Joshua 35
Southan, John 98
Southerlin, John L. 16
Southward, Wm. 90
Sowell, Isom 22
    Jethro 64
Sowens, Jacob 38
Spafford, Samuel 102
Spain, Littleton 88
    Taswell 88
Spaind, Frederick 54
Spainhower, David 97
    Henry 97
Spanehour, Solomon 35
Sparger, Henry 42
Sparks, Elijah 111
    George 99(2)
    James 33

    Joel 98
    John 99, 103
    John, Jr. 58
    Jonathan 99
    Richard 38
    Solomon 58
    William 42
    Wm. 98
Sparrow, John 71
    Patrick 73
Speak, John 37
    Samuel 98
Spear, Abner 15
    Arthur 15
    Jehu 29
    Noah 70
Spears, Willie M. 29
Speer, George 42
    Samuel 42
Speight, Adam 45
    Christy 45
    Lemuel 10
    Noah 64
Spell, Lavis 21
Spelman, Davis 3
    Samuel 3
    William 42
Spence, Arthur 1, 61
    Daniel 63
    Henry 1
    Robert 3
    William 3, 61
Spencer, Abraham 13
    Christopher 94
    Elijah 82
    Frisby 70
    John 47, 56
    Selby 7, 70
    William 104
    William B. 69
Spengler, Jacob 45
Spiar, Thomas 86
Spicer, James 83
    John 22
Spier, Christopher 86
    Miles 74
    Samuel 100
Spikes, William 71
Spillman, John 99
Spinks, Enock 100
    Garrat 27
    Raley 27
Spinner, Carney 69
Spires, James 5
    Joseph G. 107
Spivert, Robert 94
Spivey, Elisha 115
    James 8
    John 51
    Matthew 66
    Moses 5
    Richard 88
    Timothy 64
    William 28, 49, 64, 115
Spivy, Caleb 10
Spolson, Thomas 115
Sponse, Christopher 35
Spont [Spout?], Aron 28
Spoon, David 27
    George 91

    John, Jr. 32
    William 32
Sprat, William 111
Spravey, Benjamin 106
Spright, James 5
    John 5
    William 5
Springle, William 71
Sprinkle, John 97
    Peter 99
Sprouts, Aron 32
Spruel, Samuel 75
Spruell, Uzziah 69
Spruill, Andrew 6
    Emri 6
    Joseph 6
    Uriah 6
Spry, William 2
Spurgia, Samuel 38
Spurlin, Hugh 110
Spyva, John 76
Squiers [sic], Dempsey 62
St. George, John 14
Stableford, William 9
Stadler, John 31
    Robert 31
Stafford, Adam 63, 93
    Eli 93
    George 92
    Markum 3
Stagg, James 90
Staley, Frederick 100
Stalling, Lott 17
Stallings, John 55
    Richard 18
    Simon 4
    Uriah 75
Stallions, Joseph 76
Stallons, Bryant 75
Stalls, James 17
Stamper, Jacob 44
    Robert 30
Stamy, John 111
Stanala [Stanaland?], Henry 79
Stanaland, Peter 79
Stanback, John B. 66
Stancel, Nathan 11
Standen, William 3
Standford, William 48
Standing, John 4
Standley, Etheridge 2
    Nash 86
Standly, Samuel 21
Stanfield, Jeremiah 30
    John 31
    Joseph M. 90
    Josiah 31
    Major 93
Stanford, Jonathan 107
    Moses 40
Stanley, Daniel 73
    Elisha 87
Stanly, Jacob 21
    James 14
    John 12
    Wm. 96
Stansberry, Moses 99
Stansill, Godfrey 86
    John, Jr. 87
    Nathan 12

Stanton, George 49, 116
    James 4
    John 64, 116
Stanul, Allen 73
Staples, Abner 48
    Elijah 62
    John 48
Star, William H. 69
Starkhouse, Thomas 18
Starks, Asa 8
    John, Jr. 32
Starns, Daniel 58
    Frederic 106
    Jacob 40
    Nathaniel 106
Starnt, John 94
State, Abner 116
Staton, Bythel 16
    Frederick 23
Stator, Elisha 34
Stawls, Bond 75
Steatman, William 6
Stedman, Charles, Jr. 98
    William 28
Steed, Frederick 27
    Isham 27
    John 27
    Thomas 99
Steedman, Thomas 113
Steel, John 106, 108
    Moses 105
    Ninia 108
    Ninian, Sr. 39
    Simon 111
    Thomas 26
Steele, James 106
    John 20, 83
    Robert G. 41
Steely, Enoch 6
Stegall, Absalom 23
Stenkman, Lewis 13
Step, Reuben 48
Stephen, Jones 82
    Lorick 24
Stephens, Arthur 90
    Benjamin 87
    Caleb 23, 79
    Calloway 25
    Erwin 22
    George 95
    Hardy 21
    Izekiah 19
    James 20, 41
    Joel 81
    Joseph 22, 71
    Levi 79
    Miles 27
    Moses H. 71
    Reuben 79
    Simon 85
    Thomas 21
    William A. 33
    Wm. 81
Stephenson, Benjamin 87
    Brittain 29
    John 13, 29, 30, 64, 88
    Mosey 39
    William 44, 87
Sterling, William 22
Sterns, Benjamin 39

Stevens, Bartley 12
    Edward 87
    James 21
    Joseph 19
Stevenson, Hugh 40
    James 12
Steward, Hugh 104
    John 104
    Joseph 104
Stewart, Alexander 106
    Allen 40
    Andrew 40
    Archibald 25
    Benjamin 19
    Charles 4, 67, 85
    Daniel 25, 82
    David 51
    Dugald 57
    George 34
    James 25, 82
    Jesse 34
    John 51, 84
    John, Jr. 55
    Neil 81
    Ralph 108
    Robert S. 34
    William 81
    Wm. 91
Still, John 35, 41
Stillar, Henry 102
Stillwell, Daniel 48
    Tilman 48
Stilwell, Elias 107
Stipe, Henry 34
Stipp, Achillis 43
Stirran, Wallis 2
Stirum, Elisha 6
Stirwatt, Jacob 107
Stockard, John 26
Stocks, Cannon 8
    John 74
    Levi 8
Stockton, Thomas 111
Stoddard, Charles 18
Stofel, John 34
Stogner, John 25
Stokely, Buckner 78
    Harvey 63
Stoker, Richard 105
Stokes, Montfort 60
    Moses 104
Stone, Asa 92
    Conway 42
    Enock 97
    Ephraim 42
    Joseph 104
    MacKollach 87
    Tilmore 31
    William 35
Stoner, Jacob 36
Storm, Charles 25
Story, David 32
    David W. 107
    Elias 112
    George 48
    James, Sr. 107
    John 49
Stough, Jacob 59
Stout, William 102
    Zachariah 104

Stoutenberg, John 36
Stover, Isaac 58
Stow, Benjamin 2
    Daniel 2
Strahorn, Samuel 26
Strain, David 90
Strange, James 77
    Julius 36
Stranghan, Samuel 78
Strape, John 97
Straughan, Green 93
Straughn, Larkin 28
Strawn, Marmon 94
Strayhorn, Samuel 90
Streaker, Isaac 25
Stredy, James 20
Street, William 111
Streets, William 80
Strickland, Alfred 68
    David 81
    Edward 68
    Elbert 81
    Gadi [sic] 82
    Jesse 22
    John 32
    Martin 81
    Nathan 81
    Reuben 68
    Silas 25
    Thomas 76
Stricklin, Micajah 54
Strickling, Benjamin 66
Strilling, James 10
Strong, Hardiman 96
    Zack 95
Strother, Charles 23
    William H. 50
Stroud, David 48
    George 50
    Peter, Jr. 48
    Ransom 18
Struter [Streater?], Willis 84
Stuart, James 80
    John 82, 94
    Samuel 26
    Stephen 94
Stubbs, George 79
    William 79
Stublefield, Peter P. 93
Stud, Mark 100
Studard, Richard 98
Studer, Henry 115
Studivant, Joseph 15
    Whiles 15
Studman, Joseph 113
Sturdivant, Daniel L. 67
    Joseph A. 67
    Thos. M. 93
Stuts, Henry 83
Styers, John 97
Styson, James 72
Suart [sic], Joseph 46
Sudler, Henry 36
Suduth, James 95
Sugg, Raging 16
    Samuel 85
Suggs, Allegood 56
    Harbert 105
    Lewis 79
    Marrel 41

    Uriah 72
Suirasy, Elijah 46
Suit, Riley 89
Suite, James 88
Suits, Wm. 95
Sullivan, Dickson 80
    Felix 80
    George 51, 95
    Isaac 25
    James 12
    John 56
    Levin 32
    Samuel 110
    Thomas 103
    Whittenton 95
    William 40
    Zachariah 15
Sullivant, Neil 83
Sumerlin, Benjamin 55
Summerlin, Stuart 73
Summers, Charles 108
    George 58
    Jacob 52
    Thos. 99
    William 38, 108
    Zera 33
Summey, Frederick 45
Summitt, Daniel 110
    Francis 110
Summon, Thomas 61
Summons, Dixon 55
    Mitchell 62
Sumner, Asa 13
    James 66
    Samuel 12
    William 5
Sumners, Solomon 108
Sumpter, John 114
Surls, John 86
    Rayman 9
Surry, Thomas 62
Suthard, Argis 33
Sutherland, Jeremiah 14
    Roderick 25
Sutliff, John 43
Suttle, Benjamin 52
    Robert 47
Sutton, Campbell 35
    Coleby 46
    Edward 88
    John 114
    John, Jr. 113
    Joseph 3
    Nathaniel 78
    Thomas 80
    Whitfield 80
    William 73, 109
    William R. 63
    William, Jr. 113
    Zachariah 6
Swafford, Enock 101
    Nathan 101
    Wm. 100
Swain, Elixim 69
    James 75
    Joseph 69
    Joshua 6, 69
    Levi 56
    Michael 95
    Michel 43

    Nathan I. 6
    Simeon 6
    Stephen 69
    William 6, 75
    Wm. 95
Swan, James 4
    Jesse 103
Swann, Abraham 98
    James 93
    Jos. 94
    Jos. Jr. 94
    Thomas 94
Swean, Marmaduke 27
    Michael 101
Sweaney, Wilie [sic] 90
Sweany, James 27
Sweat, Virtue 37
Sweedy, Thomas 69
Sweeney, William 104
Swenny, Edmond 42
Sweter, Benjamin 66
    Henry 66
Swift, Haroway 31
    Richard 31
    Thomas 100
Swim, Jesse 35
    William 37
Swindell, John 69
    Zedekiah 70
Swing, Henry 32
Swink, Daniel 102
Swinson, Daniel 80
    John 80(2)
Swivit, Harris 38
Swonner, Jesse 70
Sworner, James 70
Sydes, George 105
Syke, Etheldred 20
Sykes, Isham 67
    Jacob 67
Sylvester, John 4

T

Taddis, Alexander 27
Tade, William 32
Tague, Michael 38
Tailor, William 63
Tallow, John 81
Tally, James 18
    Joel 18
    Thomas 18
Talton, Joshua 4
Tamon, Oram 54
Tansey, Eli 98
Tapley, Pleasant 35
    Robert 22
Tapp, Vinson 31
Tapping, Thomas 4
Tarckler, Lewis 44
Tarkinton, Enos 6
    Starkey 6
    Zebedee 6
Tarlington, Israel 22
Tarlton, Thomas 4
Tart, James 75
    John 81
Tate, David 91
    George 25
    James 88
    James G. 29, 30

Joel 27
William R. 26
Tatlock, James 64
Tatom, Edward 34
Tatum, Daniel 62
  Harbert 33
  Joseph 62
  Maxey 62
Taunt, Ervin 71
Taylar, Hiram 50
Taylor, Abraham 75
  Absalom 52
  Alexander 23
  Amos 25
  Anderson 81
  Archibald 23
  Arden 17
  Benjamin 1
  Cornelius 68
  David 104
  Edmond 39
  Edwin 9
  Elijah 77
  Elisha 74
  Fisher B. 32
  Flecher 29
  Georg [sic] 37
  Isaac 64, 78, 80, 100
  Jacob 80
  James 34, 75, 82, 104, 111
  Jesse 76
  John 20, 28, 45, 55, 71, 78,
    90, 92, 103
  John H. 34
  Jonathan 58
  Joseph 10, 111
  Joshua, Jr. 75
  Josiah 1, 72
  Kinchen 64
  Kinnon 9
  Mark 73
  Micajah 23
  Nathaniel M. 88
  Reuben 62, 76
  Richard 79
  Samuel 57, 70
  Saunders 84
  Sutton 95
  Thomas 11, 37, 115
  Valentine 111
  William 9, 20, 78, 79, 84,
    100, 116
  Wilson 107
Taylous, John S. 41
Teachey, David 80
Teag, Michael 97
Teague, John 110
  John 38
  Joseph 43
  Moses 104
  Moses, Sr. 104
Teal, Benjamin 24
  John, Jr. 74
  Micajah 74
Teaque, Isaac 83
Teasly, Daniel 42
Teat, James 17
Teats, Jacob 34
Teddar, Benj. 92
Tedder, David D. 83

Sion 20
Tedrick, John 86
Teler, Enos 10
Telfair, Hugh 74
Tellers, Eldred 56
Telley, John 116
Telliton, William 70
Temple, Britton 3
  Henry 63
  Jesse 62
Templeton, James 38, 39
  Joseph 39
  Samuel 38
Tenneyhill, Zachariah 37
Tennison, David 17
Terrell, William 31
  William C. 65
Terry, James 24
  John 85
  Thomas 89
  William 30
Tews, Blackman 22
Thach, James 63
  William 63
Thagard, John 20
Thalley, Caldwell 80
Tharington, Thomas 19
Tharp, Samuel 79
Theek, Daniel 91
Therue, Jacob 45
Thespin, John 75
Thigpen, Gray 16
  Howell 16
  James, Jr. 16
  Jonathan 16
  Reddin 55
Thigper, Lemuel 80
Thomas, Alderson 9
  Andrew 32
  Benj. 96
  Benjamin 24, 87
  Daniel 27
  David 55, 57
  Elias 25
  Elijah 33
  Elisha 17
  Even 36
  George B. 19
  Henry 19, 83
  Hillard 75
  Jacob 51, 102
  James 49, 68, 93
  James B. 108
  Jesse 34
  John 32, 54, 55, 74, 102
  John Wm. 84
  Jonathan 75
  Lewis 83
  Martin 83
  Moses 23
  Nehemiah 27
  Robert 8
  Samuel 50
  Soloman 18
  Solomon 25, 68
  Theophilus 17, 55
  Thomas 26
  William 74
  Wm. 92, 95
Thomason, Benjamin 50

  John 98
  Nelson 50
  William 71
Thomes, Robert 19
Thompson, Alexander 9
  Anderson 91
  Andrew 112
  Bartholomew 62
  Benjamin 39
  Bryan 76
  Charles 77
  David 10, 76
  Drury 67
  Duncan 83
  Edmund 16
  Elijah 98
  Everit 76
  Henderson 98
  Henry 106
  Isaac 102
  James 18, 40, 46, 59, 86, 90,
    94, 108, 111
  James, Jr. 91
  John 10, 25, 26, 66, 76, 91,
    94, 98
  Joseph 113
  Lemuel 25, 27
  Lewis 77
  Moses 38
  Nathan 13
  Neil 22
  Neill 82
  Newcomb 90
  Nickolas 94
  Patrick 41
  Robert 16, 26, 47
  Samuel 54, 112
  Theophilas 26
  William 2, 41, 51, 113
  Wm. 87, 92, 101
Thorn, James 29
  William 63
Thorne, Thomas 5
Thornton, John 103
  Solomon 7
  Thos. 99
Thorp, Jesse 68
Threadgill, Gideon 84
  Howell 24
  Thomas C. 23
Thrower, John 15
Tidder, James 28
Tiley, Boston 92
Tilley, Edmond 100
  John 96
  Reuben 96
Tillingast, William 20
Tilly, John 90
  Lewis 35
Tilman, David 42
  John 73
  Wm 92
Times, Thomas M. 37
Timpleton, Robert 108
  Samuel 108
Tindal, James 76
Tindall, Charles 73
  James 23
Tiner, Lewis 87
Tines, West 56

Tingle, James 8
  Major 8
Tinkle, John 35
Tinnon, Thomas 91
Tipps, George 98
Tirrel, Lewis 93
  Paul 93
Tirrell, John 93
  Wm. 93
Tisdal, Elisha 68
Tisdale, Eli 18
  Nathan 7, 60
Tison, Charles 74
  Stephen 73
Titman, Peter 109
Tobin, James 94
Tocke, Littleton 16
Tod, Pleasant 95
Todd, Elijah 54
  Henry 65
  Hugh 39
  James 59
  John 97
  Levi 55
  William 61, 85
Tolby, James 43
Toler, Charles 49
  Isaiah 57
  John 31
Toliver, Wm. 99, 100
Toller, John 116
Tolley, James 67
  Joel 68
  Thomas 68
Tolliver, William 44
Tolloch, Wm. 93
Tolson, David 56
Tomberlin, Freeman 48
  Moses 107
Tomerlin, David 84
Tomison, Joseph 28
Tomlinson, Enoch 33
  Humphrey 108
  Perry 108
  William 58, 105
Tonley, Sheldon 70
Tooley, Jeremiah 70
Tore, Hezekiah 35
Towd, John 106
Townsell, James 105
Townsend, Eli 105
  Jesse 57
  John 81, 104, 105
  Thos. 90
Tragall, Solomon 84
Train, James 106
Trawick, Henry 81
Traxler, Peter 101
Tray, Abraham 110
Traywick, John 85
Trebble, Abner 43
Treble, Benj. 99
Trees, Jacob 58
Trentman, Jacob 109
Tretman, Demsey 4
Trewblood, Joshua 63
Tribble, Abner 53
Triggler, Richard 18
Trill, Henry 26
Trip, Hardy 74

Triplett, George 48
   William 48
Tripp, Cullen 8
Trollenger, Adain 95
Trott, Murphy 72
Trout, John 45
Troxler, Barney 91
   John 91
   Nicholas 91
Troy, John B. 21
Trull, Charles 85
   Solomon 23, 84
   Thomas 84
   William 84
Trully, David 112
Trulman, Andrew 107
Trulove, Michena 61
Truss, Samuel 74
Trussel, Ezekiel 14
Trusty, Abram 41
   David 99
   Henry 43
   William 41
Trutman, George 107
Tucker, Aron 37
   Charles 98
   Daniel 34, 44, 89
   Elijah 12, 39
   Enock 100
   Frederick 114
   Ira 80
   Jacob 108
   James 99
   Joab 68
   John 44, 95, 96
   Joseph 18
   Lemuel 3
   Lewis 68
   Nathaniel 22
   Thomas 109
   William 109
   Wm. S. 96
   Woody 18
Tulcher, Joseph 72
Tull, Arthur 73
Tunmire, Isaac 113
Tunstall, Peyton 88
   Peyton R. 67
Turnage, William 73
Turner, Alfred 63
   Axum 84
   Benjamin 69
   Edward 55, 100
   George 110
   Harrison 3, 63
   Isaac 74
   James 27, 63, 67
   James, Jr. 3
   James, Sr. 3
   Jesse 24, 54, 76
   John 26, 45
   John W. 81
   John, Jr. 57, 87
   Miles 3
   Myles 4
   Nathan 18
   Samuel 45
   Silion 33(2)
   Thos. 94
   Urias 3

   Washington 14, 55
   William 3, 18, 21, 22, 114
Turrege, John 57
Turrell, Nathan 11
Turrentine, Robert 90
Tussell, Arthur 18
Tuter, George 107
Tutral, Matthew 91
Tutton, Person 10
Tweddy, William 3
Tweed, James 115
Tweedy, James 63
Twiddy, Isaac 4
   Stephen 4
Twidwell, Obadiah 37
Twitty, Burford 50
Two, Daniel 21
   Elias 21
   Joseph 21
   Landen 21
Twonay, William 37
Twoney, Isaac 103
Tyal, Tolson 9
Tyler, Absalom 10
   Lemuel 30
Tyner, Arthur 16
Tyrell, Jephthah 86
Tyser, Frederic 99
Tyson, Amos 23
   Hosea 70
   John 22
   Thomas 24

U

Umphlet, Elisha 64
Umphreys, John 15
Underwood, David 21
   Henry 27
   James 94, 96
   John 22
   Lemuel 28
   Major 95
   Moab 16
   Nathan 33
   Pendleton 49
   Thos. 96, 101
   William 43
   Wm. 92, 101
Upchurch, Beatess 29
   Berkely 88
   Burtess 28
   James 88
   Ruffin 93
   Stephen 28
Upright, Peter 36
Upsom, James 27
Urquhart, Henry 82
   Norman 82(2)
Urry, Richard 41
Ussery, James 104
   Samuel 89
   Welcome 104
Utley, Alvin 28, 54
   Jacob 54
   Little John 28, 29
Utly, Burrel 113
Utzman, George 36
   Jacob 36
   John 36
Uutly [?], Sion 86

Uzzell, James 9

V

Valentine, James 16
   Thomas 18, 68
Vance, David 115
   David, Jr. 49
Vancey, Charles 89
Vanderpool, Isaac 43
   John 100
Vandiford, Wm. 84
Vandigriff, Jacob 86
   John 85
Vaney, Joel 53
Vanhook, Isaac 30
Vann, Eli 17
Vannay, Joel 99
Vannoy, Andrew 99
   John 43
Vanover, Wm. 100
Vanpelt, John 8
Vanter, Bradford 35
Vanzant, Isaac 52
Vardell, Holowell 3
Varnel, Benjamin 55
Varner, William 52
   Wm. 100
Varnum, Francis F. 25
Vaughan, Benjamin 16
   Caswell 89
   Isaac 24
   James 15, 96
   John 14, 96
   Kinchen 32
   Lemuel 16
   Payton 45
Vaughn, Gideon 86
   Hilary 65
   John 65
   Vincen [sic] 76
Vause, William 73
Veark, John 58
Veazant, Jacob 111
Venable, John 109
Vendick, James, Jr. 72
Vendrich, Jesse 8
Venters, Francis 13
   Peter 77
   Samuel 8
Vermillon, Jesse 33
Vernon, Elisha 35
   Green 95
   John D. 96
   Josiah 96
   Richard 35
   Samuel 96
Verval, Henry 51
Vest, Charles 97
   Peter 99
   William 42
Vestal, David 28
   David, Sr. 93
   Isaac 98
   Wm. 101
Vick, Arthur 65
   Benjamin 67
   Joseph 68
   Moses 106
   Richard 67
   Samuel 68

Vickers, Charles 99
   John 45
   William 46
Vickery, Marmaduke 101
Vincent, Jacob 87
   James 19
   Oran 29
Vines, John 7
   Samuel 7
   Thomas 7, 56
Vins, Lat. 54
Vinson, Groves 106
   Isaac 27
   John 65
   Laban 67
   Nehemiah 16
   Reuben 23
   Warren 67
Vonn, William 114

W

Waddy, James 31
Wade, Caleb 56
   Downey 89
   Eliza 56
   Isaac 72
   Jahn [sic] 66
   James 13, 27, 80
   Seth 27
Wadkins, Alfred 78
   Isaiah 46
Wadsworth, Barney 8
Wafer, William 115
Waff, George 61
Waggerman, Christian 97
Waggoner, Jacob 33
   John 47
   Valentine 33
Wah, Samuel 39
Wailes, Isaac 109
Waite, Henry 112
   Valentine 2
Wakins (Watkins?], William 24
Walden, Drew 16
   Jesse 63
   John 23
Walder, Amos 12
Waldriss, Elis 114
   William 114
Waldrop, Ezekiel 46
Walford, James 9
Walk, Jonathan 37
Walkefield, John 48
Walker, Amos J. 80
   Andrew 39, 59, 106, 107
   Aron 32
   Bird 31
   Burk 91
   Daniel 90
   Edward 83
   Elijah 113
   Green B. 29, 88
   Jacob 11
   James 14, 32, 34, 35, 40, 83,
      86, 96
   James, Sr. 69
   John 33, 46, 77, 81, 105, 113
   John F. 66
   Jones 87
   Lewis 82

Martin 69
Mathew 19
Matthew 94
Owen 97
Reuben 113
Richard 98
Robert 33
Solomon 30
Tandy 29
Thomas 18, 68, 90
Thos. 97
William 33, 39, 45, 47, 68, 71
Zachariah 59
Wall, Abraham 66
Absalom 83, 95
David 18
James 95
John, Jr. 34
Micajah 85
Peter 33
Wm. 95
Zack 95
Wallace, Andrew 12
David 56
David A. 72
John 74
John E. 66
Jonathan 7
Levin 70
Matthew 39
Robert 13
William 84, 111
Waller, George 102
Henry 75
Joseph 80
Walles, Ruel 108
Wallis, John 27
Joseph 72, 106
Mathew, Jr. 105
Walls, Burges 88
Kinchen 108
Walsh, Jonathan 100
Wm. 99
Walston, Amburrus 1
Amos 75
Waltan, John 56
Walter, Charles 41
Henry 55
Paul 107
Peter 107
Walters, Alexander 88
Dawson 25
Isaac 9
John 25, 58
Joseph 25, 56
Lewis 99
Mills 6
Nathaniel 9
William 25
Walton, Hermon 102
John 28
Lewis 100
Thomas 51
Thomas J. 86
William 4, 5, 64
Wamble, James 28
Wamick, Peter 32
Wammot, Thomas 34
Wamock, David 111
Thomas 111

Wanley, Sampson 8
Ward, Amos 93
Barnabus 63
Benjamin 13, 30
Charles 30, 110
Charleston 61
Conrade 111
Elijah 32, 57
Fountain 73
George 56
Hardy 51
James 4, 17, 92, 111
Jasper 65
Jesse 4
John 4, 79, 86, 111
Joshua 91
Josiah 61, 77
Lewis 48
Micajah 4
Minos 101
Nathaniel 28, 29, 79
Richard 18
Robert 79
Robertson 54
Samuel 103
Solomon 32
Thomas 15, 23, 84, 91
Thomas A. 42
Thos. 90
William 6, 9, 35
Wardlow, James 34
William 34
Ware, Joseph 76
Rob't 94
Robert 31
Warford, Joseph 36
Warley, Elijah 23
Warlie, David 111
Warlow, James 48
Warner, Herbert 67
Jeremiah 7
Warr, Lemuel 66
Warrels, William 88
Warren, Daniel 71
James 37, 101
John 25
Joshua 16
Kalib 17
Lewis 71
Peter 89
Robert 16
Samuel 66
Timothy 93
Warrick, Hardy 81
Wartham, Benjamin H. 29
Warturs, Jesse 76
Warwick, George 21
John 15, 21, 87
Warwik, James 16
Wasden, James 73
Wasdon, David 9
John 76
Washam, Alexander 40
Washburn, John 47, 58
Washington, George 8
Jeremiah 8
Woodson 89
Wasnor, John 102
Waters, Charles 7
Fredrick 7

James 70
Jeremiah 73
John 47
Jonathan 7
Nias 81
Reason 33
Waterson, Benjamin 45
Watington, Armstead 31
Watkins, Benjamin 83
Edward 99
Isaac 17, 68
James 24
Moses 83
Needham 81
Reece 33
Watlen, John B. 16
Watman, Daniel 48
Watson, Alexander 31, 79
Allen 87
Daniel 24, 111
David 9
Frederick 71
Hugh 111
Isaac 23
James 40, 57, 81
John 4, 13, 28, 42, 54, 65
Michael 76
Richard 57, 81
Stott 16
Thomas 116
William 32, 46, 82, 87, 116
Willie 14
Wm. 95
Watters, Joel 99
Watterson, John 110
Wattington, Edward 94
Francis 31
Jonathan B. 31
William H. 31
Wattoman, Nath'l 56
Watts, Alexander 108
Andrew 39
Ewell 86
Robert 45
Waugh, David 53
William P. 53
Waworth, Daniel 37
Wayne, William 9
Weab, John 102
Weaks, Hewet 105
John 72
Weant, Jacob 102
Wear, Joseph 110
Weather, Isom 46
Weatherington, Jesse 71
Southey 9
Weatherly, Henry 95
Weathers, Edward 30
Weathley, John 17
Weaver, Cannor 24
Isaac 100
James 91
Jared 50
Jethro 55
John 6, 53, 101
John, Jr. 49
Mark 100
Moses 17
Timothy 92
Webb, Benjamin 116

Caleb 38
Dempsey 63
Floyd 96
George 4
Iasah [sic] 50
James 91
Jeremiah 111
John 23, 91
John, Jr. 83
Lewis 107
Moses 4
Reuben 48
Robert 111
Samuel 104
Thomas 4
William 75
Webbs, Darlin 112
Webster, Charles 91
James 96
John 96
Pleasant 96
Wilson 2
Wedenton, Cirus 107
Weed, Richard 29
Weeks, Archibald 46
Joseph W. 63
Perry 63
Samuel 4
Weer, David 104
John 104
Samuel 38
William 38
Wehunt, Michael 113
Weir, Howard 40
Welborn, Moses 103
Moses, Jr. 103
William 37
Wm. 100
Welch, David 4
David, Jr. 64
James 49, 107
John 98
Michel 28
Turner 38
William 35, 49
Wm. 97
Weldon, Samuel 67
Thomas 67
Well, Andrew 38
Miles K. 83
Wellbourn, Samuel 53
Wellington, John 34
Wellons, Jesse 11
Wells, Anderson 110
Henry 77
John 91
Joshua 113
Stephen 92
Welsh, James 116
John 116
Richard 83
Welton, Henry 43
Wenters, William 113
Wessen, Abner 46
West, Alexander 114
Benjamin 49
Charles 46
Isaac 6, 31
John 6, 56, 103
Jonathan 37, 44

Joseph 92
Mathew 106
Nimrod 4
Noel 87
Robert 39
Stephen 75
Thomas I. 65
William 12, 24, 71
William M. 50
Westbrook, John 73
Thomas 35
Uriah 81
Westmoreland, Peterson 108
Rhoda 108
Robert 39
Thomas 34
Thos. 97
Weston, Isaac 12
Thomas 6
Wether, Shadrack 79
Wetherby, Peter 32
Wetherford, Hiram 31
Wetherly, Allen 52
Isaac 51
Isaiah 51
Wever, James 115
Weymire, Rhudolph 27
Whaer, Joseph 68
Whaley, Rigdon 77
Whally, Willoughby 62
Wharton, Evan 51
John 51, 56
Wheedleton, Elijah 71
Wheeler, Ezekiel 88
James 66
Jesse 45
Nathaniel 14
Samuel 89
Sion 66
Whelas, Elijah 68
Wheless, Archibald 17
Whidbee, George P. 3
Whidler, Benjamin 61
Whiley, Jeremiah 108
Joab 21
Whilly, Elias 21
Whirly, Pleasant 112
Whishenhunt, Henry 51
Whitaker, Isaac 98
James 14
Jesse 98
Nathaniel 54
Peter 102
Willis 54, 86
Wilson C. 14
Wm. 98
Whitamore, John 89
Whitbee, James 6
Whitby, Samuel 11
White, Alexander 62
Cader 56
Daniel 3, 18, 63, 67
David 19, 65, 107
Edward 18
Elisha 47
Frederick 1
George 3, 65
Hardy 56
Isaac 65, 71, 94
James 9, 13, 23, 26, 62, 84,

93, 109
James I. 14
John 21-23, 63, 104, 106, 112
John, Jr. 1
Joshua 1
Marshal 75
Michel 39
Moses 111
Perry 75
Peter 65
Reuben 48, 84
Richard 42, 54
Shadrach 32
Stephen 76
Thomas 48, 68, 88
Thos. 100
Whitmall 65
William 6, 29, 30, 55, 64, 79, 80
William M. 85
Worley 74
Whitehall, Thomas 2
Whitehead, Abner 9
James 74
John 28, 97
Jos. 93
Joseph 17
Nathaniel 93
Whitehouse, Alexander 3
Whitehurst, Hilery 71
William 74
Whitenet, Daniel, Jr. 45
Whiteral, James, Jr. 1
Whiteside, Joseph 106
Whitesides, William 111
Whitfield, Arch G. 68
Guilford 17
Hatch 9
John 9
Needham 9
Wm. W. 64
Whitford, Will 71
Whithead, Anderson 90
James 90
Whithurst, Enoch 61
Samuel 61
Whitley, Eunuch 87
George 65, 105
John 70
Whitlock, Bowen 42
John 98
Whitly, Thomas 55
Whitney, David 22
Dempsey 32
Ebenezer 32
Whitsell, Jacob 91
Whittenburg, Daniel 114
Whittington, Nehemiah 95
Richard 12
Whitworth, Archibald 33
John 110
Wm. 96
Whorton, William 17
Wiat, John 40
Wiatt, Abraham 44
Aron 43
John T. C. 29
William 37
Wichel, Jacob 1
Wichidht [sic], John 19

Wicker, Benjamin 23
Mathew 22
Robert 92
Wier, David 45
Wiggins, Anthony 55
Edmund 67
Elijah 18
Harrel 88
Henry 5
Isaac 56
James 88
John 9, 88
Joseph 9
Robert 9
Thomas, Jr. 76
William 85
Wiggs, Abner 10
Raiford 70
Wilborn, John 37
Wilcox, Archibald 71
James 81
John 72
William 72
Wilcoxen, Elijah 58
Samuel 44
Squire 44
Wild, Henry 49
John 49
John J. 49
Wilder, Abram 56
Jesse 77
John 61
Malachi 13
Myles 61
Sampson 61
Samuel, Jr. 87
Wilds, Henry 113
Wiley, Charles 69
David 51
Hugh 39
Isaac 40
Josiah 51
Samuel 40
Wilker, Jacob 32
Wilkerson, John 25, 85, 90
Jonathan 105
Jos. 92
Wilkes, Henry 55
James 56
John 55
Rheuben 55
Wilkey, William 112
Wilkins, Alfred 86
George 35
James 112
John 25
Lemuel 15
Richard 91
Robert 81
Thomas 35
Wil 55
Wilkinson, Jacob 70
John 20, 52, 57, 108
Micahah 11
Neill 82
Oden 7
Osburn 106
Richard 20
Thomas 21
Willie 16

Zachariah 70
Wilks, Elijah 82
Kinchen 65
Willard, Allen 42
Willdnson [Williamson?], Joseph 26
Willey, Even S. 107
William 14
William, Henry 93
Peter 3
Williams, Aaron 95
Absalom 33
Alexander 10
Anson 64
Anthony 5
Benjamin 23, 59, 65
Benjamin B. 65
Bennet 24
Britain 116
Bryant 13
Burwell 92
Byrd 80
Caleb 113
Charles 81, 110
D. G. 18
Daniel 24, 65
David 65, 85
Edward 37
Elbert 93
Elijah 27, 55
Enoch 27
Enock 115
Ephraim 42
Frederick 64
Garrot 73
George 77, 85, 101
Green 90
Guilford 67
Hardy 64
Henry 14, 70, 101
Henry E. 109
Hill 13
Howard 111
Isaac 3, 45, 63, 85
Isom 59
Jacob 1, 38, 54
James 24, 32, 63, 64, 76, 85, 108, 116
Jess 24
Joel 84, 112, 114
John 18, 24, 31, 36, 46, 63, 68, 100, 113
John C. 17
John M. 15
Joseph 67, 73, 106
Laban 21
Lewis 80
Littleberry 29
Manassah 80
Mathias 50
Matthew 9
Matthias 44
Miles 62, 64
Nathan 81
Nathaniel 88
Newbern 23
Richard 95
Robert 12, 30, 45
Robert B. 85
Samuel 17, 36, 68, 74, 110

Simon 85
Stephen 12, 85, 103
Theophilus 13, 80
Thomas 16, 46, 55, 85, 105
Thos. 91, 93
Tully 4
William 5, 9, 13, 34, 50, 55,
    72, 116
William, Sr. 55
Willie 50
Willis 85
Wm. 98
Zachariah 21
Williamson, Anthony 78
    Henry 62
    James 12, 21
    Kinchen 18, 68
    Kindrick 83
    Louis 57
    Samuel 69
    Stephen 87
    Thomas 68
    Timothy 21
    Urban 12
    William 22
    Wm. 101
Williavy [?], Anderson 51
Willie, Andrew 98
Williford, James 65
    Jonas 75
    William 81
Willis, Augustin 67
    Benjamin 56
    Cason 56
    Elijah 93
    Elisha 27
    Hardy 8
    Henry 94
    Jacob 112
    James 2
    Joseph 47, 59, 72, 112
    Lewis 67
    Littleton 72
    Moab 82
    Phillip 37
    Reubin 72
    Royal 26
    Samuel 26
    Stephen 92
    Thomas 56, 102
    Washington 72
    William 110
    Wilson 93
    Zachariah 56
Willons, William 87
Willoughbee, Willie 64
Willoughby, John 74
Wills, Francis 4
    John 13
Willson, Joseph 113
Willy, John 33
Wilmath, Gabriel 112
Wilson, Abner 47, 59
    Amous 94
    Andrew 114
    Benjamin 48, 106
    Caleb 1
    Charles 47
    David B. 39
    Dempsey 2

Dennis 85
Densy 13
Edmond 66
Edward 33
George 27, 56, 103
Henry 93, 95, 112
Hugh 107
Isaac 4, 55, 80
James 25, 37, 74, 81, 91, 105,
    112
James, Jr. 65
John 25, 27, 32, 40, 45, 62,
    79, 91, 96, 102, 104,
    106, 108
John, Jr. 79, 106
Levi 99
Lodwick B. 33
Luke 47
Mathew 115
Maxwell 32
Meskick 79
Peaton 26
Philip 49
Richard 26
Robert 30, 31, 45, 64, 81, 95,
    114
Samon 32
Samuel 93, 112
Shadrick 79
Silas 45, 56
Stogdol 114
Thomas 82, 116
William 10, 22, 47, 48, 58,
    91, 113, 114
William J. 109
Willis 2
Wm. 90, 94
Wimberly, Abam 23
    Fred 55
    Lewis 65
Wimborne, Stephen 16
Winborne, Lemuel 66
Winburn, Benjamin 55
Winchester, William 33
Winctuster [Winchester?], John 23
Windley, Israel 70
    Moses 7, 70
    Wyriott 69
Winecof, David 107
Wines, William 41
Winfield, John 7
    Thomas 7
Winflet [Winslet?], Levi 76
Winfrey, Isaac 98
Wingate, Jesse 14
    John 63
    Needam 109
    William 4
Winkfield, Freeman 84
Winklar, Peter 103
Winkler, Henry 113
    Matthew 114
Winn, Miner 111
Winningham, Abel 27
    Adam 27
Winslow, Joseph 61
Winson, Elisha 111
    Nimrod 111
Winstead, Samuel 90
Winston, Jesse 87

Joseph, Jr. 60, 117
Moses 29
Wintosh, Alexander 39
    John 39
    William 39
Wiot [?], James 41
Wisdom, Bird 93
Wise, Benjamin 48
    Thomas 88
    William 12
Wiseman, James 36, 102
    Thismothy [sic] 103
    Wilson 36
Wishon, Leonard 108
Wisinghunt, Michael 113
    Peter 113
Witcher, Ephraim 58
Withellens, George 36
Witherell, Radford S. 25
Witherington, James 5
    Thomas 73
Witherly, James 32
Wodel, Richard 76
Woldrige, Joseph 34
Woldson, Luke 112
Wolf, Jacob 97
Wolfingtan, Isaac 95
Wollard, David 55
    John 70
    Nathaniel 17
    Silas 17
Wolles, William, Jr. 105
Womack, James 102
    Rora 93
    Wiley 54
Womak, Wiley 28
Womble, Jacob 93
    Neal 86
    Tyson 92
Womouth, Washington 88
Wood, Anthony 89
    Augustus 17
    Daniel, Jr. 104
    Green 19
    Hardy 13
    Henry 104
    Hugh 26
    Isaac 90
    James 8, 13, 26, 49, 67, 115
    Jaret 37
    John 26, 27, 36, 78
    John C. 66
    Jonathan 72
    Joseph 112
    Josiah 16
    Newton 85
    Reddick 4
    Robert 36, 40, 95
    Robert B. 41
    Samuel 16, 31
    Simeon 66
    Stephen 42
    Thos. 99
    Truth 101
    Vincent 111
    William 24, 46, 79
    Young 81
Woodall, Absalom 11
    Alexander 87
    John 87

William 106
Woodard, Caleb 2, 15, 61
    Christopher 29, 86
    Henry 7
    James 11
    Jethro 61
    John 108
    Joseph 29, 86
    Micajah 11
    Nathaniel 71
    William 86
    Willis 11
Woodburn, Robert 51
Wooders, Chesley 33
Woodle, Luke 24
Woodley, Eli 69
    John 63
    Thomas 3, 4
    William 6
Woodrige, Aurelua 35
Woodruff, John 15
Woods, Henry 81
    James 90
    John 72, 90, 94
    John I. 90
    Thomas 91
    William 26
    Wm. 90
    Zadock 9
Woody, John 91
Wooten, Abraham 42
    Benjamin 13
    Ephraim 55
    Henry 75
    John 9
    Peter 11
    Thomas B. 23
    William 112
Wooton, Ephraim 75
Word, Elisha 102
Worhine, William 24
Workman, Henry 47, 59, 102, 112
    Richard 91
    Thomas 36
    William 36
    Wm. 91
Worlaw, Michael 104
Wormington, John 100
Wornam, Joseph T. 66
Worrel, Jesey 76
    Richard 76
Worrell, Demsey 79
    James 65
    Ransome 68
Worsham, Henry 89
Worsley, Pitman 16
Wortham, Benjamin H. 30
Worthington, Jacob 27
Wortman, John 103
Wortrind, Westly 24
Wray, John 94
    Skipwith 34
Wren, Allen 18, 67
    Boen 68
    John 101
    Joseph 18
Wrier, James 47
Wright, Benj. 100
    Cader 62
    Charles 62

www.ingramcontent.com/pod-product-compliance
Lightning Source LLC
Chambersburg PA
CBHW080240270326
41926CB00020B/4322